The University of Ottawa Press is grateful for the support
of the Department of Canadian Heritage in the publication of this book.

Cover photograph and design: Kevin Matthews

Library and Archives Canada Cataloguing in Publication

Accounting for Culture: thinking through cultural citizenship / edited by Caroline Andrew,
    Monica Gattinger, M. Sharon Jeannotte, and Will Straw.

    Includes bibliographical references and index.
    ISBN 0-7766-0596-8

    1. Canada—Cultural policy.
    2. Canada—Intellectual life—21st century—Citizen participation.
    3. Canada—Civilization—21st century.
    I. Andrew, Caroline, 1942-

FC95.5.A32 2005   306'.0971   C2005-901624-8

Accounting for Culture:
Thinking Through Cultural Citizenship

edited by
Caroline Andrew
Monica Gattinger
M. Sharon Jeannotte
Will Straw

Contents

Introduction

PART I
The Evolution and Broadening of Cultural Policy Rationales

PART II
Voices

PART III
New Approaches in a Changing Cultural Environment

PART IV
Governance, Indicators, and Engagement in the Cultural Sector

Conclusion

Annex

Foreword

Accounting for Culture:
Examining the Building Blocks of Cultural Citizenship

The following are the opening remarks made by Judith A. LaRocque, Deputy Minister for the Department of Canadian Heritage, at a colloquium held in Ottawa in November 2003 celebrating the fifth anniversary of the Canadian Cultural Research Network and the tenth anniversary of the Department of Canadian Heritage.

On behalf of the Department of Canadian Heritage, I would like to welcome you all here tonight on an occasion that marks a number of important milestones.

First, it is the fifth anniversary of the Canadian Cultural Research Network (CCRN), which held its inaugural colloquium in Ottawa in June 1998.

I am pleased that the CCRN has chosen to meet here again five years later, in partnership with the Department of Canadian Heritage and the University of Ottawa, to examine the theme of *Accounting for Culture: Examining the Building Blocks of Cultural Citizenship*.

For the Department of Canadian Heritage, this colloquium also marks a couple of significant events: the tenth anniversary of our creation and the launch of the Canadian Cultural Observatory's new on-line service, http://www.culturescope.ca.

When the department was formed ten years ago, many wondered about the relationship between its two halves. Just what did culture have to do with citizenship? Why would anyone try to bring together the people who worked with artists and museums and broadcasters with the people who were concerned about official languages, multiculturalism, and citizen participation?

Avec l'Université d'Ottawa, je suis certaine que nous allons faire du progrès au cours des deux prochains jours pour répondre aux questions que je viens de poser.

It is important that we think hard about this because there is a growing realization among cultural policy-makers that economic justifications of cultural and heritage activities are no longer adequate (if they ever were) for policy and advocacy purposes.

We are increasingly concerned with the social and citizenship dimensions of culture. The social dimension does not just mean better measures of consumption and demand for cultural goods. It means understanding how Canadian culture affects citizens and how Canadian citizens interact with and shape their culture. It means understanding cultural diversity, citizen participation, and community building.

As Canada becomes a more diverse place, the sources and kinds of cultural expression become more diverse. We need to understand these cultural changes if our policies are going to help us to benefit from this diversity. We need information on the characteristics of cultural change, and on the effects of cultural participation on people and the motivations which drive them.

Cultural participation is one of the key tools people use to build their sense of attachment and connection to each other. Cultural participation also bridges fault lines and builds common understandings where only difference existed.

Engagement with culture is hard to distinguish from community development and the growth of citizenship. When people engage with culture, they necessarily engage with each other, with people like them in some way, and inevitably with people who are different.

Cultural policy has the potential therefore to reach out beyond the traditional realm of industry, art, and museum to influence citizenship, values, tolerance, and the very construction of Canadian society.

To support these new policy directions, we obviously need different data than we have now. But our needs go beyond data. We need scholarship to understand the relationship between culture and society. We also need theory to link culture to its social effects, and we need conceptual frameworks to help us focus in on the indicators that will really tell us what is going on.

That is why I find the dual themes of this colloquium so interesting and so timely.

Under the *Accounting for Culture* theme, you are going to look at new tools to support planning, reporting, and assessment of cultural policies and actions. And under the *Cultural Citizenship* theme, you are going to link these new tools to "rebuilding the case for culture," specifically, examining culture's role in supporting new understandings of citizenship and civic participation.

I think that by doing this alone you are breaking important new ground. However, you are doing even more. By inviting the participation of both researchers and policy-makers at this colloquium and by focusing clearly on "knowledge transfer" as a key element, you are building a bridge between those who think about cultural citizenship and those who will have to address the new policy imperatives of diversity and inclusion.

In the coming months, as Ottawa undertakes the "changing of the guard," I believe that there will be a huge appetite for new ideas, for creative approaches to persistent problems, and for what David Zussman of the Public Policy Forum has termed "a more evidence-based approach to public policy."

I view this colloquium as an important step in creating those ideas and building the evidence base that we will need to address the emerging issues surrounding cultural citizenship.

Une autre partie très importante du colloque, et un événement marquant pour le ministère du Patrimoine canadien, est le lancement du service en ligne de l'Observatoire culturel canadien, http://www.culturescope.ca.

L'Observatoire culturel canadien est une initiative du ministère du Patrimoine cana-dien, avec le support du programme Culture Canadienne en ligne. Sa mission est de suivre les développements, disséminer l'information et procurer des occasions de réseautique à ceux qui abordent le genre de problèmes et de questions qui seront soulevés au colloque durant les deux prochains jours.

Culturescope.ca est destiné à devenir le "guichet unique" de l'information culturelle au Canada. Et j'espère que ça deviendra une des grandes ressources de la base de preuves à laquelle je me référais plus tôt, de même qu'un outil pour soutenir l'échange continu de connaissances entre les communautés de la recherche et des politiques.

Le développement de culturescope.ca a tiré bénéfice de deux ans de réactions en provenance de la communauté culturelle du Canada. Et il forme une collaboration grandissante entre tous les niveaux de gouvernement, et entre des partenaires privés et sans but lucratif.

Jusqu'à maintenant, culturescope.ca est soutenu grâce à la participation de plusieurs partenaires, incluant Statistique Canada, Bibliothèque et Archives Canada, la Conférence canadienne des arts, le Réseau des villes créatives et le Réseau canadien de recherche culturelle, pour n'en nommer que quelques-uns.

En fait, le Réseau canadien de recherche culturelle a accepté de participer en donnant une période d'essai à culturescope.ca, par la création de groupes de travail de politiques en ligne qui reflètent les thèmes discutés durant les deux prochain jours. J'espère que culturescope.ca va effectivement élargir le débat, les discussions et le "momentum" jusqu'à la prochaine occasion de se rassembler.

With that, it gives me great pleasure to launch both this colloquium and culturescope.ca and to invite you all to participate in the knowledge transfer and mobilization that will take place in the next two days.

Thank you and have a great colloquium. Merci. Je vous souhaite un colloque formidable.

JUDITH A. LaROCQUE
Deputy Minister
Department of Canadian Heritage

Foreword

The Canadian Cultural Research Network (CCRN) was pleased to present, in partnership with the Department of Canadian Heritage and the University of Ottawa, the colloquium to which the chapters published here contributed. *Accounting for Culture: Examining the Building Blocks of Cultural Citizenship*, held in Gatineau, Quebec, on November 13-15, 2003, marked the fifth anniversary of the CCRN and the tenth anniversary of Canadian Heritage.

Accounting for Culture was the fourth colloquium convened by CCRN since its founding in 1998. The theme of the inaugural colloquium was *Cultural Policies and Cultural Practices: Exploring the Links Between Culture and Social Change*. The second colloquium was held in Edmonton in 2000 in conjunction with the CIRCLE/CCRN Round Table on *Culture, Connectedness, and Social Cohesion. Cultural Development in Canada's Cities: Linking Research, Planning, and Practice* was the focus of the 2002 colloquium held in Toronto.

Beginning in 2002, the CCRN came to understand itself as a network concerned with knowledge mobilization. At our colloquium that year, we invited leading proponents of knowledge transfer and exchange to present the state of research and practice pertaining to knowledge mobilization strategies in their sectors. The following year, we offered a one-day workshop on knowledge transfer and exchange in the cultural sector. Putting into practice principles of knowledge mobilization, Dr. Greg Baeker conducted an extensive consultation on the themes of the colloquium, then arranged Web- and telephone-based seminars in the weeks leading up to the event.

CCRN is a bilingual network of Canadian cultural researchers which promotes the sharing of information and research on trends, challenges, and opportunities in the cultural sector from a variety of disciplinary perspectives. It encourages co-operation and collaboration among Canadian cultural researchers and provides a point of contact for international cultural research networks. Membership is open to both users and producers of cultural research: government policy-makers and researchers, private-sector consultants, and researchers and decision-makers in industry associations and producing organizations. Practical research support and networking services available to members include an on-line directory of members, notice of publications and events of interest, access to a listserv of members and to on-line dialogues, member discounts on colloquium registrations and publications, and a customized Web-based information retrieval tool. In 2002, CCRN established an award recognizing excellence in cultural research and named it in honour of John Meisel. The Meisel Award for Excellence in Cultural Research was presented in its inaugural year to Dr. Meisel and in its second year to André Fortier.

As you prepare to delve into the debates that enriched the 2003 colloquium, I would like to recognize the intellectual leadership of Caroline Andrew, Greg Baeker, Sharon Jeannotte, Monica Gattinger, and Will Straw in focusing the colloquium topic and convening an outstanding group of presenters to lead the dialogue.

DONNA CARDINAL
President (2001 – 2003)
Canadian Cultural Research Network

Contributor Biographies

(in alphabetical order)

CAROLINE ANDREW is a professor in the School of Political Studies at the University of Ottawa. Her research areas include municipal social policy, urban development, and the role of women in local government. Her recent publications include a volume co-edited with Katherine Graham and Susan Phillips entitled *Urban Affairs: Back on the Policy Agenda* (2002). Community activities include membership in the City for all Women Initiative with the City of Ottawa, co-president of the City of Ottawa's Advisory Committee on French-language Services and member of the boards of the Lower Town Community Resource Centre and InterPares. She is currently the dean of the Faculty of Social Sciences of the University of Ottawa.

GREG BAEKER has a Ph.D. and is the managing director of EUCLID Canada. Prior to founding EUCLID Canada in 1998, he worked in senior leadership positions in the cultural sector for twenty-five years, as executive director of the Ontario Museums Association; executive coordinator of the Ontario Heritage Policy Review for the Government of Ontario, senior policy analyst for the Ontario Ministry of Culture, and lecturer in Arts Management, University of Toronto. He completed a doctorate in Urban Cultural Planning at the University of Waterloo in 1999. Recent EUCLID projects include *A Think Tank on Culture in the City* for the Governments of Quebec and Ontario (2003); the *Municipal Cultural Planning Project*, a research and networking strategy linking twenty-five Canadian municipalities (2001-02); the *Arts Leadership Network*, leadership development strategies for senior arts managers in Canada (2002); the *Council of Europe Study on Cultural Policy and Cultural Diversity* (2001); and *Municipal Cultural Forums*, four leadership forums for cultural leaders in Ontario (2004).

DONNA CARDINAL is an independent consultant, researcher and educator in the fields of cultural development and community based decision making. As an associate of The Futures-Invention Associates International headquartered in Denver, she has facilitated envisioning projects and workshops in community, church, government, and not-for-profit settings in Canada and the US for the past fifteen years. Donna pioneered the use of the Futures-Invention envisioning practices online in the Cultural Leadership Development Project. Ms. Cardinal taught cultural policy at the University of Alberta for 18 years and now teaches a Web-based course in citizen engagement and consultation for municipal administrators across Canada sponsored jointly by Dalhousie University and the University of Alberta. Donna serves on the Editorial Working Group of Culturescope.ca, an online resource for cultural policy professionals within the Canadian Cultural Observatory, and is a Member of the Canadian Commission for UNESCO's sectoral commission on Culture, Communication and Information. Donna is Past President of the Canadian Cultural Research Network.

STUART CUNNINGHAM is a professor at the Queensland University of Technology in Brisbane, Australia and the director of the University's Creative Industries Research and Applications Centre. He is an experienced researcher and research manager in the fields of media, communications, cultural policy, higher education and in what is now called the "creative industries." He is known for his policy critique of cultural studies, *Framing Culture* (1992), and for the co-edited *New Patterns in Global Television* (1996) and the co-authored *Australian Television and International Mediascapes* (1996). Others who worked with him on the chapter within this volume include TERRY CUTLER, the principal of Cutler and Company, a high-level communications consultancy based in Melbourne; GREG HEARN, a professor and a research and development coordinator; MICHAEL KEANE, an Australian Research Council postdoctoral fellow in the Creative Industries Research and Applications Centre at the Queensland University of Technology; and MARK DSVID RYAN, a doctoral candidate.

NANCY DUXBURY is the director of research and information of the Creative City Network of Canada, a national non-profit organization she co-founded that facilitates sharing of knowledge and expertise among municipal cultural staff in over 125 communities across Canada. She is also a member of Statistics Canada's National Advisory Committee on Culture Statistics, and special projects editor of the *Canadian Journal of Communication*. From 1995-2003 she was a cultural planning analyst at the City of Vancouver's Office of Cultural Affairs, and from 2000 to 2002 she was a board member of the Canadian Cultural Research Network. She holds a doctorate in communication and a master's in publishing from Simon Fraser University, and a bachelor of commerce degree in management from Saint Mary's University in Halifax. In 2001, she was awarded the Dean of Graduate Studies Medal for Research Excellence for the Faculty of Applied Science at Simon Fraser University.

JOHN A. FOOTE was born in Vancouver, B.C. and received a bachelor of arts with majors in political science and history from the University of British Columbia in Vancouver, a master in international affairs with a major in American foreign policy in Latin America from George Washington University in Washington, D.C., and a doctorate in international relations from the School of Advanced International Studies at Johns Hopkins University in Washington, D.C. His doctoral dissertation was entitled, "Political Communications in Canada's Prime Minister's Office: the Trudeau Governments, 1968-1974." He has worked in the federal government since 1974, after working for several years in the Prime Minister's Office while researching his dissertation. He has worked in a number of policy capacities, including federal-provincial relations, international relations, and arts policy, both at the Department of Communications and the Department of Canadian Heritage. Since 2001, he has been the manager of research integration and planning for the Strategic Research and Analysis Directorate of the Department of Canadian Heritage. He has taught courses at Concordia University and the University of Montreal and was seconded to the Department of External Affairs from 1977 to 1979 where he worked in the Energy Transportation and Communications Division. He is an ex-officio member of the Board of the Canadian Cultural Research Network. His principal interest is in linking cultural policy with cultural research.

ROSAIRE GARON détient une maîtrise en sociologie décernée par l'Université Laval. Il effectue des recherches au sein du ministère de la Culture et des Communications du Québec depuis plus de trente ans. Ses principaux travaux, au cours des dernières années, ont porté sur les pratiques culturelles de la population, sur la conception d'indicateurs de développement culturel et sur l'évaluation des politiques culturelles. Il s'intéresse également au financement de la culture et aux professions culturelles. En plus d'avoir collaboré à la rédaction de plusieurs articles dans des revues scientifiques, M. Garon a rédigé, pour le ministère de la Culture et des Communications, plusieurs ouvrages relatifs à la culture québécoise. Signalons la publication récente d'un document important, écrit en collaboration avec Lise Santerre, qui trace l'évolution des pratiques culturelles au Québec au cours de la période de 1979 à 1999, *Déchiffrer la culture au Québec, vingt ans de pratiques culturelles*, paru aux Publications du Québec.

MONICA GATTINGER is an assistant professor in the School of Political Studies at the University of Ottawa. Her principal areas of research inquiry concern public policy, public administration, and governance, and her main research interests pertain to business-government-society relations, public consultation, and the influence of globalization on public policy and public administration. Her research projects and publications examine these themes principally in the fields of cultural policy, energy policy and regulation, and Canada-United States relations. She is co-author, with Bruce Doern, of *Power Switch: Energy Regulatory Governance in the Twenty-First Century* (2003).

ALLAN GREGG is one of Canada's most respected and influential pollsters and political commentators. Over more than two decades, he has brought his skills to bear on every major social, political, and economic issue. His insight is highly sought after by chief executive officers, political leaders and the media, and he consults widely in the business community on issues ranging from corporate image and reputation to communications and marketing challenges. Allan was a pioneer in the integration of consulting, public-opinion research, public affairs, and communications. He not only has an intimate knowledge of the dynamics of policy-making but also a deep understanding of the communications processes necessary to forge a public consensus around government initiatives. Much sought after for his analysis, he is widely published and quoted. He appears on a weekly CBC National News panel, and is the host of two popular and respected talk shows—*Gregg and Company* and *Allan Gregg In Conversation With*. Currently chairman of The Strategic Counsel, a Toronto-based market research and consulting firm, he was a co-founder of Decima Research, one of Canada's largest polling firms. He is also an entrepreneur with diverse interests in the entertainment industry, for example, in which one of his companies manages the Canadian rock band The Tragically Hip.

M. SHARON JEANNOTTE is the manager of the International Comparative Socio-Cultural Research unit in the Strategic Research and Analysis Directorate of the Department of Canadian Heritage. Since 1996, her primary research focus has been on social cohesion as a horizontal public policy issue affecting Canadian society as a whole. She has produced research reports on a variety of subjects, such as the impact of value change on Canadian society, international definitions of social cohesion, the points of intersection between cultural policy and social cohesion, the role of cultural participation and cultural capital in building sustainable communities, culture and volunteering, the use of gambling revenues to fund culture, the role of culture and heritage in everyday life, and youth "on-line" culture. During her long career in the Government of Canada she has been a corporate strategic planner in both the Department of Canadian Heritage and the former Department of Communications. She has held positions as a social policy analyst, a program officer providing grants for information technology applications in the cultural field, and a writer and editor in several other government departments.

KARIM H. KARIM is an associate professor at Carleton University's School of Journalism and Communication. He is currently a visiting scholar at Harvard University (2004-05), and is leading an international project on intellectual debates among Muslims. He has published internationally on issues of culture and citizenship. He is editor of *The Media of Diaspora* (2003) and author of the award-winning and critically-acclaimed *Islamic Peril: Media and Global Violence* (2000). Prior to July of 1998 he was a senior researcher at the Department of Canadian Heritage and chaired the Federal Digitization Task Force's Access Policy Group. He attended Columbia and McGill universities.

JUDITH A. LAROCQUE holds a master of arts in public administration and an honours bachelor of arts in political science from Carleton University. She has a broad and varied experience in government. She started her career in 1979 at the Public Service Commission. She was a procedural officer at the House of Commons from 1982 to 1984. She has occupied the positions of chief of staff to the Government Leader in the Senate and minister of state for federal-provincial relations, and she has also been the executive assistant to the minister of justice and attorney general for Canada. From 1990 to March of 2000, she was the secretary to the Governor General, secretary general of the Order of Canada, secretary general of the Order of Military Merit, and herald chancellor for Canada. In April 2000, she became an associate deputy minister of Canadian Heritage. In April 2002, the prime minister appointed her deputy minister of Canadian Heritage.

JOHN MEISEL is the Sir Edward Peacock professor of political science emeritus at Queen's University in Kingston. His first paper on cultural policy, "Political Culture and the Politics of Culture," appeared in the *Canadian Journal of Political Science* in 1974. He has kept a watching brief on cultural policy ever since. In the early 1980s he was chair of the Canadian Radio Television Commission. In 2002 he was chosen as the first winner of the John Meisel Award for Excellence in Cultural Research. Contrary to appearances, it was not he who established the award.

COLIN MERCER is the managing director of Cultural Capital Ltd, a company specializing internationally in strategic research and development for the cultural sector. Formerly he was the U.K.'s first professor of cultural policy and director of the Cultural Policy and Planning Research Unit at Nottingham Trent University. From 1984-1998 he worked in Australia where he was director of the Institute for Cultural Policy Studies and associate professor in Cultural Policy and History at Griffith University. He is co-author of *The Cultural Planning Handbook* and many other publications in the field of cultural policy and cultural studies and has been responsible for a number of urban, regional and community cultural mapping, policy and planning frameworks which repositioned the arts and cultural resources in strategic and mainstream contexts. Most recently he has been project director and author of the book *Towards Cultural Citizenship: Tools for Cultural Policy and Development*, commissioned by the Bank of Sweden Tercentenary Foundation and the Swedish International Development Cooperation Agency (SIDA) and published in November 2002.

CATHERINE MURRAY is an associate professor of communication at Simon Fraser University. She is currently a member of the National Action Research Roundtable on Managing Communications and Public Involvement, the Board of Governors for SFU and on the Board of BC Film. She edited the inaugural conference proceedings of the CCRN and co-authored *Researching Audiences* (2003). She is a frequent public commentator on media and cultural issues.

GILLES PAQUET is a professor emeritus and senior research fellow at the School of Political Studies at the University of Ottawa. He has authored and edited a number of books and published a large number of papers on economics, economic history, public management, and governance issues. He is the president of the Royal Society of Canada and the editor-in-chief of http://www.optimumonline.ca. For additional information, see his Web site, http://www.gouvernance.ca.

CHRISTIAN POIRIER is a postdoctoral researcher at the School of Political Studies at the University of Ottawa. His research interests include policies of ethnic diversity management, cultural policies, interest groups, and the relationship between citizens and the state. He is the author of *Le cinéma québécois. À la recherche d'une identité?, Tome 1*; *L'imaginaire filmique, Tome 2*; and *Les politiques cinématographiques* (2004), and has contributed several chapters to other books and articles published in scientific journals. A native of Quebec City, he has a doctorate in political science from l'Institut d'Études Politiques de Bordeaux.

TOM SHERMAN is an artist and writer. He works in video, radio and live performance, and writes all manner of texts. His interdisciplinary work has been exhibited internationally, including shows at the National Gallery of Canada, the Vancouver Art Gallery, the Musée d'art contemporain, the Museum of Modern Art, Documenta, and Ars Electronica. He represented Canada at the Venice Biennale in 1980. In 2003 he was awarded the Canada Council's Bell Canada Award for excellence in video art. He performs and records with Bernhard Loibner in Vienna in a group called Nerve Theory. His most recent book is *Before and After the I-Bomb: An Artist in the Information Environment* (2002). He is a professor in the Department of Art Media Studies at Syracuse University in New York, but considers the South Shore of Nova Scotia his home.

DICK STANLEY is the former director of the Strategic Research and Analysis Directorate of the Department of Canadian Heritage of the Government of Canada, where he directed a team of social science researchers exploring issues of social cohesion, cultural diversity, and citizenship and identity. He is currently a visiting scholar at the Robarts Centre for Canadian

Studies at York University, and manager of the Initiative to Study the Social Effects of Culture, a research partnership of Canadian Heritage, University of Ottawa, and the Canadian Cultural Research Network. He has written on such diverse topics as economic development in the third world, management information systems, outdoor recreation demand, and measuring the non-market values of wilderness areas. His current interests include the role of social cohesion in producing social well-being, and the effects of cultural participation on social development. He is a graduate of Carleton University and the New School for Social Research in Sociology.

WILL STRAW is an associate professor within the Department of Art History and Communications Studies at McGill University. He is on the editorial boards of *Screen*, *Cultural Studies*, *The Canadian Journal of Communications*, *Social Semiotics*, *Space and Culture* and numerous other journals. He is the co-editor, with Simon Frith and John Street, of the *Cambridge Companion to Pop and Rock*, and, with Jody Berland and Dave Tomas, of *Theory Rules: Art as Theory, Theory and Art* (1996). His articles on music, film, and culture have appeared in several anthologies and journals. Currently, he is a member of a five-year research project on *The Culture of Cities*, which is funded by the Social Sciences and Humanities Research Council of Canada under their Major Collaborative Research Initiatives Program. His current research focuses on the print culture of scandal and exposé in the 1920s and 1930s.

Introduction

Accounting for Culture:
Thinking Through Cultural Citizenship

CAROLINE ANDREW AND MONICA GATTINGER

This book, like the conference which gave life to it, represents a partnership between people interested in research on culture and people interested in cultural policy. But much more complex and interrelated than that, it brings together people interested in rethinking cultural policy in the light of understanding changes in culture, changes in relationships between citizens and governments, and changes in ways governments operate. Its objective is to look both at the bases of cultural policy in this changing environment and the interrelations between statistical tools and conceptual tools. Therefore cultural indicators and cultural citizenship form the poles around which, and between which, ideas bounce. This introductory chapter's aim is not to describe the content of the discussions—the individual chapters are there to do that—but to articulate at somewhat greater length the ambitions of this project to rethink the basis for cultural policy.

The first question we want to explore is why the present moment seems so particularly well chosen to re-examine the bases for cultural policy. We would argue that there are a number of separate, but interrelated, transformations that make this kind of very broad rethinking both necessary, and exciting. Without for the moment trying to explain their interrelated nature, one can point to changes in governance (or the transformation of the ways societies take decisions and particularly in the number and types of actors taking part in these decisions), changes within government and in the relations between government and citizens, and changes within culture, both in terms of cultural products and cultural participation. Each one of these transformations is, by itself, a massive field to map and analyze, and understanding their points of intersection and reciprocal influence adds to the complexity.

We start with governance, used in the sense of designating a shift to societal decision-making processes that involve a large number of actors, not only governmental but also from the private and non-profit sectors. In addition, governance refers to processes of decision-making using information flows and networks of relationships between the relevant societal actors. The shift to governance has been explained in a number of ways, from social actors wishing to be more involved in decisions, to governments wishing to be less involved, to the influence of globalization and the ways in which the rescaling of political and social action is taking place at the present time.

Governance obliges governments to connect in new ways with non-governmental actors and to create the networks and structures for successful decision-making. As Gattinger points out, this is an extremely important area and one that requires clear and strategic thinking on the part of governments and civil society. As she points out, engagement in the process is essential and the importance of engagement has often been underestimated. Building trust relations between participants is a necessary stage, particularly in fluid, network-based decision-making structures and this can never be an automatic process.

The delicate balance of government engagement without government domination is one of the major challenges of governance processes. Paquet insists on the importance of this for the cultural field as his argument, is that governments should "tread lightly" in this field, recognizing that the major actors are those directly involved in cultural activities. Paquet argues that government's role is important but that government must recognize that culture can't be imposed by the state.

The exact nature of the relationships to be established needs more systematic reflection and analysis. Gattinger's case studies begin the work of understanding how leadership exercises itself, and how civil society and government can engage.

Another way of understanding governance in the cultural area is suggested by Straw's analysis of pathways and patterns of interaction that create networks of meanings. His case studies suggest the ways in which elements of cultural policy, Canadian content for example, bubble up from the interactions of creators and intermediates. By following these pathways, understanding the energy created and the networks of meanings, the context for cultural policies can be understood. Drawing on Straw's use of inertial and accelerative trends, governance structures such as those studied by Gattinger, can be understood in terms of their use of the known patterns of interaction (inertial) or of structures that attempt to transform previous patterns of interaction (accelerative). Thinking in terms of governance, decision-making can be understood as well from looking at creators and intermediaries (Straw) as from government policy-makers (Gattinger).

Governance also incorporates the new demands of citizens and groups to be involved in decisions that affect them. This creates challenges for governments, as we have discussed, in thinking about appropriate structures and processes, but it has also changed the methods of citizen involvement. If citizens and civil society groups want to have influence, they have to make use of techniques that governments can understand. As Mercer so eloquently puts it, counting is crucial. This is one of the interesting points of possible interaction of government and citizens—governments being under pressure for greater accountability and transparency and citizens wanting ways of intervening that have resonance with the bureaucracy as well as with elected representatives. At the federal level, this can be seen in the increasing emphasis on performance measurement and the development and use of results-based management and accountability frameworks. The push for greater accountability is well described by Poirier, particularly the *adéquation* (correspondence) or not of government objectives and evaluation tools. As he describes, Quebec's cultural policy combines economic, social, and national identity and other dimensions and yet the indicators have been almost exclusively economic. The European, and particularly the United Kingdom's, experience has been towards greater *adéquation* of objectives and measurement, having gone further in the formulation of evaluation criteria that are not uniquely economic.

Another way of understanding the intersections of governance and the field of culture is to think in terms of policy paradigms and the shifting policy paradigms that capture policy-making, good policy, and good cultural policy. Policy paradigms offer a way of understanding shifts in governance, shifts in the aim of public policies, and shifts in our understandings of culture. Mercer talks about the movement from data to information to knowledge, and finally to wisdom, as a way of understanding the path from statistics to policy. Duxbury discusses the paradigm shift from quality of life to community indicators. Others, including Mercer, also reflect on the significance of policies being seen as place-based. Cunningham looks at the transformation of the production of culture, arguing that the cultural industries paradigm had been replaced and/or should be replaced by an innovation paradigm as this was the best entrance into active government intervention for industry shaping. Whereas other authors move from economic justifications to quality of life paradigms, Cunningham's suggestion is to remain in an economic development paradigm (as being the language of government action) but to shift to innovation and the creation of a knowledge-based society. Murray describes paradigm shifts with three potential policy paradigms competing in the cultural field: social capital, cultural diversity, and cultural citizenship, a rights-based formulation.

The articulations of paradigm shifts both permit further understanding of governance processes and the roles played by government actors, cultural creators, civil society groups, the private sector, and citizens. Policy paradigms must engage governments, both politicians and policy-makers, and they must also engage the other participants in the governance process. Governments have to be engaged, in order to commit resources (monetary, legal, and political) and other participants have to be engaged, to commit their resources which include the time, energy, and mobilization to put sufficient political pressure on governments to convince them to commit public resources. At the federal level, government-wide interest in developing social capital and building social cohesion in Canada can represent a meaningful opportunity for the cultural sector. The potential contribution that cultural policy and programming can make to the development and strengthening of social capital and social cohesion can serve to attract policy-makers' interest in supporting and resourcing cultural policy.

Policy paradigms also allowed participants to link the discussion of governance processes with reflections on cultural processes, or the transformations in cultural practices. Policy paradigms are likely to change along with changes in culture. Straw's use of inertial and accelerative trends emerges in a variety of ways, highlighting the continuation of past practice and transformative elements. The transformative nature of information technology is highlighted in this volume in a number of ways, from Cunningham's description of the producers of culture, to Garon and Foote with their analysis of factors transforming patterns of cultural consumption. Garon reports on the major shifts in patterns of cultural consumption in Quebec over the past twenty years, illustrating the importance of generations, of policies of democratization, of information technology, and of education. Although there has been a major decline in traditional practices, cultural practices are still a marker of social distinction. Garon sees possibilities for culture being a way to link to the recent immigration in Quebec and therefore playing a role of integration.

Karim takes a less optimistic view of the possibilities of integration of recent immigrants through culture. Indeed, for him, culture is the zone of exclusion for those not of the dominant cultures. Increasing diversity in Canada has led to exclusions as cultural competencies define themselves in speech, in jokes, and in the full range of daily life. Recent arrivals can only hope to operate in what Karim considers "public sphericules," as full public space is closed to them. Cultural diversity is transforming Canada but equal access to public space is not a reality. Changing culture, as changing policy paradigms, is explained by a variety of factors: technological, economic, increasing ethno-cultural diversity, demographic shifts, changing patterns of interaction between creators and intermediaries and by, to quote Cunningham quoting Lash and Urry, the "culturalization of everyday life."

After a discussion of this rich mix of changing patterns of culture, policy paradigms, government strategies, and governance strategies it seemed that this was a moment for rethinking the basis of cultural policy. Not that everything was known or understood about these shifts—right away the research agenda began to take form—but there did seem to be a convergence around the interest of reflecting on cultural citizenship. This idea resonated with the shifts we have been describing, the idea of citizenship being linked to processes of participation, to building feelings of belonging and identity, to the kind of processes described as governance. There is a tension in citizenship, between a movement from below and action from above and, again, this tension resonated with the shifts described earlier. The shifts in culture also create interesting links to citizenship in the suggestions about links between cultural participation, social capital and feelings of identity.

Therefore the second major task of this book is that of thinking through cultural citizenship, in the light of all the shifts described. For some of the authors, cultural citizenship refers to an attribute of an individual. For Karim, it is a capacity to participate as an effective citizen, a set of cultural competencies that individuals had or did not have. Garon's typology is also linked to individual traits but the different categories in his typology related also to class, gender, and age characteristics. His category of the engaged citizen makes the link between cultural participation and cultural citizenship in that the engaged citizen not only goes to cultural events but creates institutions and projects that involve his or her community in cultural participation. Murray, too, sees cultural participation, not as cultural citizenship, but as a building block to cultural citizenship. For her, cultural citizenship has a collective dimension that goes beyond individual participation. Sherman's dialogue with cultural citizenship also espouses this link between individual participation and culture, exploring the interest of artists in engaging with the culture and communities around them, thereby shaping and contributing to the cultures they live in and to notions of cultural citizenship.

Different dimensions that help to construct a concept of cultural citizenship are not only individual and collective, they can also relate to different intellectual traditions. For example, Jeannotte's analysis of social and cultural capital allows her to compare the formulations of Putnam and Bourdieu and, equally importantly, those authors following on Putnam and Bourdieu. This comparison allows a rich analysis of the role of social and cultural capital in the production of citizens and, in this way, supports the interest of continuing to theorize cultural citizenship. Jeannotte highlights the role of cities in creating the meaning of cultural citizenship. A concrete example of this comes from Straw's examination of the alternative press as an example of milieus of social energy and networks of meaning. The alternative press, an urban phenomena, is, as Straw describes, breaking down the distinctions of night and day and in this way creating a more inclusive urban public space, one in which a greater number of urban residents can integrate their work, family, social, political, and cultural lives. The patterns of interaction described by Straw reinforce networks of meaning and create spaces and processes that can lead to greater feelings of inclusion, to greater cultural citizenship.

Throughout the struggles to think through cultural citizenship, the very meaning attached to culture varied from author to author. Stanley makes the most systematic attempt to define different meanings of culture, using a typology of three faces of culture. The three meanings for Stanley are culture in the sense of everyday life meanings, culture in the sense of heritage (the best of human achievement), and culture as creativity. For Stanley, culture is a strategic good in that it increases the capacity of citizens to manage change and therefore to govern themselves. It is this kind of role in building cultural citizenship that, for Stanley, offers a justification for government to invest in culture and formulate cultural policy.

Indeed, a number of the authors think through cultural citizenship by contrasting traditional, or earlier, rationales for cultural policy and for government support for culture to emerging paradigms such as cultural citizenship. Stanley's argument is that the new rationale offers a continuation of traditional rationales, both continuing and strengthening the argument for cultural policy. Meisel, on the other hand, begins his text by contrasting traditional and recent visions but ends by arguing that a fusion of the two is possible, exemplified for him by the Kingston KISS project. Cunningham, as noted earlier, feels that economic development arguments are the best to elicit government support but feels that innovation, and the construction of a knowledge-based society, is a better rationale than the earlier cultural industries argument. Gregg offers a rationale, not unrelated to cultural citizenship, whereby culture could be used to rekindle Canadians' faith in politics. His argument is based on the relationship between two sets of facts: public support for investment in culture and the arts is very low and public confidence in politics is at an all-time low. Making an economic argument for culture is pointless, according to Gregg; a citizenship argument has more reality and more weight. Canadians need to feel that governments can be productive, that public action can lead to the goal of a more progressive society, the goal Canadians want to see. Participation in culture can lead to greater feelings of confidence in public action and the efficacy of citizenship.

For Mercer, new policy rationales differ from the traditional ones, not so much by content but by method and process. For him, the essential difference needs to be one of rigour, of making arguments that can be empirically substantiated. It is only in this way that governments will, and should, pay attention to the culture community. Governments are increasingly faced with difficult financial choices and with pressures for greater accountability. In this context arguments for greater public support for culture have to be made in a way that public officials can understand. In this way Mercer links the discussion of new policy rationales to that of the tools for building cultural policy, cultural indicators. What is the state of cultural citizenship? What is the state of cultural participation? What is the impact of public policy? All these questions call for indicators so as to know where we are, in order to know where we are, or should be, going.

But indicators play an even more central role in the book and in the conference, and, as was stated earlier, cultural citizenship and cultural indicators are the two poles around which theorization built. This reflects an intellectual stance, research in the context of practice, which is a very strong thread across the participants and which implies a curiosity about the ideas behind the tools and the practices implied in the concepts. The project of thinking through cultural citizenship involves thinking about cultural indicators—what they now indicate, what they should measure and how they influence the formulation of policy.

This turns out to be an area that greatly expands the agenda of research that needs to be done. Duxbury reviews both the evolution of the lens for cultural indicators—from quality of life and sustainability to community indicators, with culture as one area within community indicators. Based on her review of studies from the United States, she argues that there is no conceptual research base for work on indicators. Given their importance, this is definitively a research priority.

Poirier also makes an argument for more research on indicators with his analysis of the *adéquation* between the objectives of Quebec cultural policy and the indicators used to examine it. Clearly more work needs to be done on establishing indicators that can correspond to the social, national, and identity-building objectives of the policy.

Finally, indicators link back to governance and to relationships between citizens and governments. Indicators are important to governments in trying to meet new pressures of accountability and transparency. Indicators are important to citizens, particularly groups that want to actively participate in policy-making, because they offer a way of talking to governments, of talking truth to power. To the extent that good indicators, the kind more research will allow us to get closer to, can facilitate the kind of trust relations, of engagement in governance that Gattinger describes as crucial, they are indeed steps to cultural citizenship.

The book is organized in four sections. The first examines the evolution and broadening of cultural policy rationales in recent years, focusing attention on the shifts in substantive focus for government intervention in the realm of cultural policy. The second section offers reflections from some notable voices in the cultural sector who have been involved as commentators, scholars, creators, and policy-makers. In the third segment of the book, the chapters examine new practices and approaches in a changing cultural environment, including contributions on innovations systems, social and cultural capital, cultural competencies, and pathways of cultural movement. The volume's final section focuses attention on governance and indicators, with chapters on each of these topics, respectively. The volume also features an annex that chronicles enduring debates and evolving research priorities for the cultural sector, and serves to give additional context to the colloquium from which this volume emerged. The concluding chapter reflects on the volume as a whole, drawing out the paradoxes and contradictions of cultural citizenship and offering potential pathways forward for cultural policy.

Part
I

The Evolution and Broadening of
Cultural Policy Rationales

1.

From Indicators to Governance to the Mainstream:
Tools for Cultural Policy and Citizenship

COLIN MERCER

The arguments presented below are designed to address a range of issues being taken up by the colloquium but, essentially, I can summarize this chapter by suggesting that there is a need to move along and up the "knowledge value chain" from *data* (statistics), to *information* (indicators), to *knowledge* (benchmarks), to *wisdom* (policy).

We need to know more about "culture"—however we define it in local, regional, national, and global contexts—both quantitatively and qualitatively. We need to improve the *quantitative baseline* (cultural statistics) and the *qualitative baseline* (evidence on "social impacts," the relationship between culture and quality of life, social cohesion and inclusion, etc). We need more numbers, more facts, more indicators, more benchmarks in both quantitative and qualitative terms.

This will require a research and knowledge-development culture which is *stakeholder-based* in the terms suggested above in our advocacy of cultural mapping, involving both "top-down" research expertise and "bottom-up" local knowledge, expertise, and ownership. This will require great efforts in "translation" and application from the best conceptual and theoretical work in the field—in cultural studies, anthropology, development economics, economic, social and cultural geography, social theory—into policy-relevant and policy-enabling forms.

The environmental movement has done this, partly by re-inventing the concept of "environment" (on the basis of a robust and accumulated knowledge and research base), and investing it with a *strategic significance* that it never had before, and partly by developing a common understanding not of what environment "is" but, rather, of *how it connects and relates to* how we go about our lives, live in our families, run our businesses, consume products and experiences: how, in short this thing called "the environment" relates to the sustainability of our development objectives and to the quality of our lives.

The challenge for us, in the cultural movement, is the same. It is not simply (or even) to define "culture" in a universally acceptable form but, rather, to define its relationship—tension, conflict, reciprocity—the broader and bigger-picture issues of economic development, community regeneration, social inclusion, diversity, *convivencia* (learning how to live together) and, ultimately, that elusive, but measurable, *quality of life*.

When we have done that then we can begin to claim that, for the cultural field, we have brought together indicators, governance, and the strategic place of culture in public policy within a unified conceptual horizon within which an enlarged and enriched concept and ambition of citizenship is the central landmark and stake.

Preamble: Citizens

Statistics ... one of the fundamental branches of the art of government.
– The Abbé (Henri Baptiste) Grégoire[1]

The Abbé Grégoire, that most enlightened and durable of the legislators of the French Revolution, and effectively the "father" of modern cultural policy, knew a thing or two. He knew that for government—and governance—in mass and proto-democratic societies, you had to know *how to count*. More importantly, you had to know *what to count*. In his case this was books, artifacts, monuments, languages, street signs, and nomenclature, the symbols and signs of the Republic, its manners, and customs. And you had to know in what context and to what ends you were counting. In his case this was "unity of idiom" for the newly formed "One and Indivisible Republic" and "Unity of the Revolution." There was a single word for the unit, fulcrum and focus of calculation: citizen. Cultural policy, that is to say, has the strategic purpose of forming, maintaining, and "managing" citizens.

Our ambitions two centuries later are perhaps less radical, less revolutionary, less unifying, but there is a common logic to be pursued which underscores the fundamental relationship between "culture," "policy," and "citizenship" and the ways in which we can both identify and evaluate this relationship by means of "indicators."

The aim of this chapter is essentially to map and highlight the conceptual field which does or should inform the work of building a knowledge base for the development of policy-relevant and policy-enabling indicators for cultural citizenship or, properly speaking, cultural indicators for citizenship. I do not fully engage here the array of possible indicators and/or operational issues as these are covered in my book *Towards Cultural Citizenship: Tools for Cultural Policy and Development.*[2] Nor do I dwell for too long on the actual definition, currency, or resonance of the concept of citizenship itself, as that could become too abstract for the purposes of this chapter. Rather, just as Baudelaire (no realist!) once pragmatically said, "puisque réalisme il y a," I'll add "puisque citoyenneté il y a."

It is certainly the case, as two Australian authors have recently argued, that cultural policy in general is one of the least studied but possibly most important domains for understanding what citizenship actually means and how it works. "Studies of cultural policy," argue Meredyth and Minson, "are centrally concerned with ... modes of neo-liberal governance, which work between public institutions and private lives and at both national and international levels, shaping civic or civil habits, tastes and dispositions in ways that are all the more effective for not being experienced as obtrusive...."[3]

This being so, and we strongly believe that it is—increasingly so in a globalized world—the question of "resourcing citizenries" becomes very important and strategic.

At the beginning of the nineteenth century (when cultural policy first became an "agenda item" for the institutions of governance), as at the beginning of the twenty-first century (when culture is becoming newly strategic in its connections with industry, with communications, with identity and simply "living together"), citizenship is what cultural policy is, or should be, about.

The Case and the Propositions

Are cultural indicators of citizenship therefore possible? If they are, and there is a strong case for this, then there are six propositions informing this chapter which relate to the three core themes—indicators, governance, and rebuilding the case for culture—of this book:

Indicators

1. Indicators need to rest on a robust knowledge base, both quantitative and qualitative, which is constantly refreshed by research, both pure and applied. We can call this *cultural mapping*.
2. Statistics are not indicators. They only become such when transformed—or when value is added—through a route map of policy. We can call this *cultural planning*.

Governance

3. Indicators only become "tools". for policy and governance when they are firmly related to or embedded in a policy framework or strategy from which they gain their meaning and currency. There are no universal cultural indicators independent of these specific and operational contexts of governance.
4. Governance is not the same as government. It describes, rather, our joint and uneven terms of engagement with the complex field of economic, human, social and cultural power relations in which we are all "stakeholders." Engagement with the concept and reality of governance means moving beyond the more traditional dichotomies of State and People, Government and Community, etc.—a new political rationality, that is.

Rebuilding the Case for Culture—or Mainstreaming Culture

5. Rebuilding the "case for culture" or, in other words, *mainstreaming* culture, as a central public policy issue, will entail subjecting culture and the cultural field to the same rigorous forms of research, analysis, and assessment as any other policy domain. This will entail—to return to the first proposition—developing indicators or suites of indicators which are integrated (and share a plausible common currency) with economic, social, environmental, and other policy domains. Knowledge of the cultural field, that is to say, will need to be able to "walk and talk" along with its policy neighbours.
6. There are a number of policy catalysts which can enable this work of integration and mobilization and these include *sustainable development, economic regeneration, social cohesion, cultural diversity* and, especially, the mother of all catalysts: *quality of life*.

Indicators: "Measuring Culture" or Cultural Mapping?

On the issue of the "knowledge base" for cultural indicators and its need for constant refreshing by both conceptual and quantitative research it may be useful to cite a recent example from the United States, that of the Arts and Cultural Indicators in Community Building Project conducted by the Urban Institute in Washington, D.C.

This project sought to develop indicators through a better understanding of arts and culture, cultural institutions, artists in inner-city neighbourhoods and community-building contexts, and to assess the existing data collection practices among the community-based and mainstream arts and culture organizations. According to the project's principal researcher, a Toronto-based teacher and consultant, Dr. Arnold Love:

- Mainstream definitions of "the arts" exclude the culture and values of many groups that live in the inner city and many expressions of artistic creativity have not been understood as art or culture;
- Arts and culture should not be viewed only as products to be consumed but also as processes and systems that are part of the life of the community;
- Cultural participation should be measured along a "continuum of cultural participation and not only as audience participation;
- Cultural activities are found in mainstream cultural venues and also in many other community locations; and
- "Indigenous venues of validation" must be understood by using ethnographic research methods before appropriate indicator categories can be created.[4]

This example is useful insofar as it points—prior to the actual process of data collection and analysis—to the necessity for appropriate and conceptually informed *mapping* of the specific cultural field in question in order to determine, so to speak, what actually *counts as culture* to the stakeholder communities—the "indigenous venues of validation." There is a "qualitative baseline" which needs to be engaged, that is to say, before the quantitative baseline can be constructed.

Cultural statistics and indicators, in this context, cannot simply be "downloaded" or imported from available data sets, no matter how robust these may be. Certainly local, regional, national, and international data on employment in the cultural sector, participation rates, family, or household expenditure, etc., will form an important *quantitative* baseline for any such investigation but this is *necessary but not sufficient* for the task of cultural mapping.

The quantitative baseline will need to be greatly enhanced by attention to the *qualitative* baseline of what these activities, participation rates, expenditure patterns, etc., actually *mean* to the stakeholder communities and how they might contribute, for example, to human, social, and cultural capital and capacity building, to identity and sense of place, to "social impacts." To citizenship in its fullest sense, that is.

To agree on a framework and agenda for cultural mapping in this sense, we need to be attentive to—and informed by—the special contours, features, and textures of the ground that we are surveying. This will require agreement both on appropriate and sensitive tools and approaches and on the stakeholders to be involved in the mapping process.

On both these counts, there is an urgent need for new forms of collaboration and cross-fertilization between research, community, industry, and government sectors. The research sector often has the competencies in the application and refinement of conceptual frameworks and methodologies; the community sector often has the necessary "local knowledge"; the industry and government sectors, in turn, tend to be concerned with sectoral or departmental objectives but, of course, have powers and resources for policy implementation beyond those of other actors. *None of these sectors, on their own, has the capacity to undertake cultural mapping in its fullest sense.* Cultural mapping is neither simply "pure" nor simply "applied" but, rather, is *stakeholder research.*

Cultural mapping can provide both a catalyst and a vehicle for bringing together these diverse interests and stakeholders (and thus moving towards cultural planning). Marcia Langton, an Australian Aboriginal academic, author, and activist advocates the approach in the following terms:

> *Cultural mapping involves the identification and recording of an area's indigenous cultural resources for the purposes of social, economic and cultural development. Through cultural mapping, communities and their constituent interest groups can record their cultural practices and resources, as well as other intangibles such as their sense of place and social value. Subjective experiences, varied social values and multiple readings and interpretations can be accommodated in cultural maps, as can more utilitarian "cultural inventories." The identified values of place and culture can provide the foundation for cultural tourism planning and eco-tourism strategies, thematic architectural planning and cultural industries development.*[5]

This approach clearly provides a fruitful context for the convergence of academic and other specialist research skills, local knowledge, industry and government interests, and a useful example of the sort of multidisciplinary and cross sectoral collaboration in research which is going to be so important for both enhancing traditional cultural resources and values *and* developing them in the context of the creative industries.

Cultural mapping seen in these terms responds to urgent new and integrally connected issues in the global cultural and communications economy and requires us to broaden our purview of the place of local cultural resources in that context, both recognizing and enhancing the relations between the "local" and the "global."

In our research and policy development, we will need to be more attentive to the *complex uses and negotiations* of cultural resources—artefacts, ideas, images, activities, places, institutions—which make up the cultural field. This will require much greater collaboration between research, community, industry, and government sectors to the mutual benefit of each, and there is some hard but useful work of "translation" to be done between these in order to arrive at a workable suite of indicators for *sustainable* cultural development.

In developing an agenda for such "cultural mapping" we will need to be very attentive to the fact that the ground has been well-surveyed, albeit from rather patrician heights, before and that we need to be attentive to the following issues:

- The need to develop a much broader and more inclusive approach to cultural resources and to recognize that these resources are not just commodities but also sets of relations and systems of classification. That is to say we need an active and use-oriented definition of resources accounting for the ways in which people and communities interact with and negotiate them.
- The importance of developing methodologies not only for identifying these resources but also for assessing how people interact with them and how, at the local and community level, they "hang together" and become meaningful in fields of interaction, negotiation, and consumption which often fall below the horizon of intelligibility of more traditional approaches to culture or beyond the remit of purely quantitative indicators.

- In developing this approach, there needs to be a new compact and relationship between "local knowledge" and tactics on the one hand, and the larger and strategic prerogatives and imperatives of cultural policy and service delivery on the other. This is a matter not simply of the adjustment of existing settings but also of the production of new forms of knowledge and resultant indicators through inclusive and integrated research agendas. Appropriate indicators, in this context, can provide the conditions for an effective "handshake" between local needs and interests and broader policy and strategic agendas.

In the end, of course, what we are confronted with in the development of a research agenda for cultural mapping is a theoretical horizon within which it becomes possible to reconcile a broad and inclusive approach to the forms of *production* in the cultural field with an equally broad approach to the forms and modalities of *consumption*—the cultural value production chain or the "culture cycle."[6] Indicators, both quantitative and qualitative, will be needed along this chain and throughout this cycle. A "template" which can act as a "floor plan" for indicators of this type, developed in the context of an English regional cultural strategy and research framework,[7] is presented in Appendix A.

From Indicators to Governance: Cultural Planning

As we begin to evaluate and understand the moments in the value chain or "culture cycle," and the points in between—distribution, circulation, promotion and knowledge, delivery mechanisms, access—we can also start to recognize the inherent connectedness of the cultural domain with others such as the nature of our "lifestyles" and quality of life, the quality of our built and natural environments, our capacities for creativity and innovation (our "soft" and "creative infrastructure"), and our ability to educate and train for diversity.

What might this mean in the context of "indicators for governance?" One answer to this lies in a key tool that we advocate in *Towards Cultural Citizenship*: "cultural capital assessment" or "community cultural assessment." This is a research tool that is aimed not simply at evaluating the culture of a community, or region, or nation but also at locating culture in the context of sustainable development. As Amareswar Galla said, this is with the aim of:

> [M]ore sustainable and vibrant communities, more cohesive community networks, greater community confidence and direction founded in a sense of self and place, and an increased community capacity for holistically addressing its own needs.... It requires an inclusive framework that recognises the cultural aspirations of different sections of the community, including groups that may otherwise be marginalised culturally, socially and economically.[8]

Positioning culture in this way is crucial, according to Galla, and based on his wide field experience in Australia, Vietnam, South Africa, Zimbabwe, and elsewhere, in order to:

- Strengthen and protect the cultural resource base for creative expression and practice;
- Engage the whole community in valuing and participating in cultural expression and appreciation;
- Provide relevant community infrastructure for the support of cultural activities; and
- Develop the economic framework for cultural production and promotion.

14

Crucially, for Galla—and in line with many of the arguments developed in *Towards Cultural Citizenship*, this is with the aim of developing "community grounded creative industries [which] could enable expression of culture that acts to affirm and celebrate community cultural development." It further suggests the need for "mediators of developmental projects ... to move away from the binary opposition of traditional and contemporary to a dynamic developmental continuum of stakeholder community groups."[9]

This argument about moving away from the "binary opposition of traditional and contemporary" and towards a more dynamic and interactive relationship between these cultural "poles" is crucial in the development of a cultural/creative industries agenda and momentum which will enable us to understand that a cultural policy *can also be* an economic policy without necessary contradiction. The World Music phenomenon (as it is known in the West/North) is an example of how this binary opposition between traditional and contemporary has been thrown into question and produced benefits for traditional/indigenous communities and creators from Mali, Senegal, Togo, South Africa, Cuba, and many other countries. The *Buena Vista Social Club* and Reggae from the Caribbean and, indeed, African American Blues and Rhythm and Blues stand as a testament to this potential in more developed parts of the world.[10]

Indigenous and Aboriginal visual arts and crafts from many parts of the developing world provide another example of how distinctive local content can enter into the broader cultural economy and marketplace. There are, of course, important policy and regulatory issues to be addressed in this context relating to the local control and management of cultural resources, their exploitation and, of necessity, their *sustainability*. These concern the ownership and management of intellectual property, the domination of many of the means of production and distribution by major transnational corporations and the power of consumer tastes and expenditure in the North/West. But the point is that this is a "developmental continuum" and, as the saying goes: *you have to be in it to win it*.

To be "in it" it is important to have a big picture of—and *to know*—the cultural value production chain—or "culture cycle"—from creation through production and distribution to consumption, and to identify and define policy measures which will enable an equitable place in that chain defined through intellectual property rights, fair dealing, and negotiated global conventions and instruments through agencies such as UNESCO (and the wider UN system), WIPO and WTO and, increasingly, regional bilateral and multilateral agreements.

Developing countries tend to be "content rich" insofar as they have cultural expressions, values, and products which, in a globalized cultural economy, the developed world wants to see, listen to, feel, and experience. They are strong, that is to say, at the beginning of the cultural cycle or value production chain but weak in the infrastructure and capacity for production, distribution, marketing, and the securing of intellectual property rights. But recognizing that there is a "chain" in which value is added at every stage to the original creation or content is the first step in both recognizing and engaging with the strategic context in which culture is now to be understood: as both local and global, as both "authentic" and able to be shared on agreed terms. This calls for an equivalent value chain of indicators.

To "win it" is a longer term task in a context where, in the global cultural economy there are only (subject to occasional variations) about three net exporters of cultural product—the USA, Japan, and the UK. This is both a threat and a challenge and it is the challenge with which I am more concerned here. The challenge is that of a forward-looking and strategic engagement with culture rather than a purely defensive posture which wants to defend and protect culture as it is.

There is an emphasis here on the *productive* cultural capacity of communities and individuals not just to celebrate and affirm their culture but to actually *enter into* the cultural and creative industries by recognizing, mapping, and exploiting their own indigenous cultural resources *on their own terms*. This is an invitation to the training and positioning of socio-economic and socio-cultural entrepreneurs as an outcome of projects rather than simply "beneficiaries."

The development of active *producers* (and reproducers) of culture is surely an important step (and indicator) in both building and developing the cultural resource base of communities which at the same time offers a way of addressing poverty, consolidating cultural diversity and providing conditions for *sustainable* development in the cultural field.

Cultural planning does not mean "the planning of culture" but, rather, ensuring that the cultural element, cultural considerations, culture *tout court*, are there at every stage of the planning and development process. This is what we mean by bringing culture in from the margins and into the mainstream.

If culture is about identities, lifestyles, conduct, ethics, governance, and the ways in which we go about our daily lives, this should not be too difficult to countenance. If we agree to have policies about culture or link culture to development objectives then we are also consenting, explicitly or implicitly, to a logic of planning. Planning, that is to say, is not just about "hard infrastructure" but also about soft and creative infrastructure: people and what they can and cannot do.

If it sounds odd to add "planning" to "culture" then that is because we have allowed planning to be unduly narrowed in its definition and remit and not because culture cannot be touched by the instrumentalist ambitions of planning. A few comments are necessary in this context.

- *Planning is not a physical science but a human science.* The Scottish founder of town and regional planning in the early twentieth century, Patrick Geddes, insisted that all planning must take account of the three fundamental coordinates of *Place-Work-Folk*. That is to say that planners need to be—or be informed by—anthropologists, economists, and geographers and not just draftsmen. They need to know how people live, work, play, and relate to their environment. Lewis Mumford, the great twentieth-century urban planner and theorist in North America, also saw culture at the very centre of planning as a field of study and professional practice.
- *Cultural planning is place-based cultural policy.* As Greg Baeker puts it: While many different definitions and understandings of cultural planning can be found to exist in other jurisdictions, a core characteristic shared by all is the concern with how the identification, monitoring, and utilization of cultural resources contribute to the *integrated development of place*. It is the focus on place that distinguishes cultural planning from the sectoral approaches favoured by cultural policy.[11]
- *It is crucial to "survey before planning."* We need to be able to fold and integrate the complex histories, textures and memories of environments and their populations into the planning process. We need to do some cultural mapping—tracing people's memories and visions and values—before we start the planning.
- *Cultures and communities produce citizens.* Our fundamental emphasis in planning should not simply be on the production and development of goods and commodities but on people, on citizens.

Cultural planning must be able to address the role of traditional arts and heritage resources but must also be able to address a *developmental* logic in the form of, for example, cultural tourism strategies, in cultural industry development, in leisure, and recreation planning, and it must make the connections between all of these.

It must address the issues of identity, autonomy, and sense of place but it must also be outward looking and part of a more general program for community development.

Cultural planning must be able to establish and maintain a real and effective policy equilibrium between "internal" quality and texture of life and "external" factors relating to tourism, attractiveness to potential residents and visitors (including inward investment by large and small businesses). It must be said that the latter has tended to drive thinking and priorities in many cities over the past decade, a situation that must be contested. It must recognize and *frequently rediscover* the wealth of cultural resources which are already there in communities but which haven't formed part of a community's cultural, social, or economic profile.

Cultural planning must be based upon the principle of a fully consultative and rigorous process of community cultural assessment or cultural mapping. Whatever you call it, the simple principle is that you cannot plan cultural resources unless you know what is there and what their potential is. You cannot guess at this and you cannot base your evaluation simply on arts resources (which is worse than guessing because it carries so many points of discrimination).

A community cultural assessment involves both consultation and a rigorous process of detailed research—quantitative and qualitative—into diverse cultural resources and diverse cultural needs.

There is a potentially "virtuous circle" between the assessment and audit functions of cultural mapping (indicators) and the operational objectives of cultural planning (governance). This will require new tools, new partnerships, new funding and resources, new ways of working at international, national, regional, and local levels.

Into the Mainstream: Culture as Capital

Cultural mapping and cultural capital assessment in combination with related forms of social capital assessment are ways of evaluating this resource base and identifying the strengths, weaknesses, opportunities and threats for sustainable development. It should proceed in the direction of the four sets of questions posed by Helen Gould, Director of the London-based cultural development NGO *Creative Exchange*:

1. *What are the community's cultural resources and assets?*
   - What are its key products, events, organizations, individuals, buildings and special sites, indigenous skills, cuisine, and forms of expression (music, dance, or visual arts)?
   - Who uses or creates cultural resources and how do they benefit the community?
   - Which local cultural resource people or organizations help deliver social capital?

2. *What cultural values underpin that community and its way of life?*
   - What are the traditional power structures, hierarchies, and decision-making channels?
   - How does the community see time, nutrition, spirituality, the environment, symbols, and images?
   - How does the community communicate and what values are communicated?
   - How widely are cultural values shared? Are there several sets of values at work?

3. *How can the development of social capital work with cultural values and resources?*
   - What are the cultural values which benefit or hinder the development of social capital?
   - How can cultural processes promote equitable relationships and foster inclusive approaches which enable all sectors of the community to participate and benefit?
   - How can culture build confidence, skills, capacities, self-esteem, and local pride?
   - How can culture promote cross-community dialogue and build new relationships?

4. *How can cultural capital and its impact on the development of social capital be evaluated?*
   - How does investment in cultural capital impact on other forms of social capital—economic and social benefits and drawbacks?
   - How do attitudes towards the community and other sectors of the community change?
   - What additional skills and capacities have been achieved and what impact did these have on community sustainability?
   - How has cultural capital enhanced relationships, built trust and created new networks?[12]

Answers to these questions will certainly provide important "indicators" for sustainable cultural development but they also provide a sound basis for moving forward in a context of cultural mapping and cultural planning. They mean taking culture seriously as both a "resource" and as *capital* (a resource which has been invested) and we should not be afraid of the possible historical dissonance of these two terms if we are serious about talking about cultural development and cultural industries in the same breath and also, hopefully, within the same policy settings, to encourage growth, diversity, and sustainability. This is the sort of knowledge, producing a range of possible indicators, connected to local, regional, and national policy frameworks which can enable us to get culture into the mainstream where it belongs.

Conclusion

The core argument presented here has to do with the central objective of building a robust knowledge and evidence base for "culture" in the same way that the environmental movement did it for "the environment." This is a concept which, just twenty or thirty years ago, simply meant the land, the landscape, or that which is not human or social. Now we understand more fully that it is the *relationships* between people and the environment which are crucial and the concept of "environment" has been invested with a strategic and political significance it never had before. We need to do the same for culture.

In understanding the relationships between people and culture we will also be learning more about the formative role of culture in constructing, understanding—and sometimes contesting—versions of citizenship and enhancing our definitions and practices of citizenship beyond the formal and legal definitions.

In principle, building the knowledge base, recognizing the inherent connectedness between culture and citizenship—the ways we live our lives, earn our livings, develop our lifestyles and identities, forms of conduct and behaviour—will then become more central to public policy and we will have indicators, like we have "common sense" in this field, as in the environmental and other fields.[13]

Notes

1. *Report on Bibliography*, Session of 22 Germinal, Year Two of the One and Indivisible Republic, followed by the Decree of the National Convention (1794).

2. Colin Mercer, *Towards Cultural Citizenship: Tools for Cultural Policy and Development* (Hedemora, Sweden: Bank of Sweden Tercentenary Foundation and Gidlunds Forlag, 2002).

3. Denise Meredyth and Geoffrey Minson, *Citizenship and Cultural Policy* (London: Sage, 2001), xi-xii.

4. Arnold Love, cited in Tony Bennett, *Differing Diversities: Transversal Study on the Theme of Cultural Diversity* (Strasbourg: Council of Europe, 2001), 96–97.

5. Council for Aboriginal Reconciliation, *Valuing Cultures: Recognising Indigenous Cultures as a Valued Part of Australian Heritage* (Canberra: Council for Aboriginal Reconciliation, 1994), 19–20.

6. The cultural value chain or cycle has been used to analyze the key stages in the overall system of cultural creation, production, distribution, consumption, etc. The value of the chain is to help identify different stages where different kinds of intervention could be made - with the goal of making the system work better and deliver better results. The value chain also helps offset the traditional focus on specific art forms or disciplines that has dominated cultural policy making.

7. Colin Mercer, *Joining the Dots: An Audit and Analysis of Quantitative and Qualitative Cultural Sector Research in the South West of England* (Exeter: Culture South West, 2003).

8. Amareswar Galla, "Culture in Development: Subaltern Perspectives," (paper presented to the Stockholm + 5 conference, Swedish National Commis⁵ion for UNESCO, Stockholm, 4 May, 2003), 4.

9. Galla, Ibid., 4.

10. Another powerful example is provided by researchers who have studied rock music as a form of cultural production. They point out that while rock music shares some basic characteristics—repeating chord structures, specific common rhythms, etc.—these are nonetheless "adapted" in different cultural contexts through lyrics, specific themes and subject matter, etc. They conclude, paradoxically, that the very form of music often characterized as a principal culprit in "homogenizing mass culture," may in fact be a very powerful *"carrier" of culture and identity.*

11. Greg Baeker, *Beyond Garrets and Silos: Concepts, Trends and Developments in Cultural Planning* (paper produced for the Municipal Cultural Planning Project, 2002), 23.

12. Helen Gould, "Cultural Capital and Social Capital," in ed., Francois Matarasso, *Recognising Culture: Briefing Papers on Culture and Development* (Gloucester: Comedia, 2001): 74, http://www.comedia.org.uk/downloads/Recognising%20Culture.pdf.

13. The "indicator floor plan" in Appendix A provides a matrix and "thinking machine" for enabling the connections to be made through appropriate indicators.

CREATION	PRODUCTION AND REPRODUCTION	PROMOTION AND KNOWLEDGE	DISSEMINATION AND CIRCULATION	CONSUMPTION AND USAGE
• Statistical data from Standard Industrial Codes (SIC) and Standard Occupational Codes (SOC) and other sources for those professionally involved (employed or otherwise) in cultural creation broken down, as necessary, by sub-sector	• Statistical data on production turnover in the cultural sector	• Statistical and other data on marketing support, e.g., marketing trend as percentage of total spent	• Statistical and other data on audience reach and diversity for produced cultural forms	• Statistical and qualitative data on diversity of cultural forms consumed and modes of consumption and usage
• Data, statistical and other relating to training, funding and investment in cultural creation	• Statistical and qualitative data on availability of infrastructure for cultural production (facilities, infrastructure audits, etc.)	• Statistical and qualitative data on research capacity and outputs	• Statistical and other data on number of institutions and agencies for distribution of cultural product	• Statistical and other data on expenditures on cultural products per capita/family and by demographics
• Information on the existence of policy frameworks and strategies to encourage/facilitate cultural creation	• Statistical and other data on reproduction of original product	• Statistical and other data on "export" capacity (national as well as international)	• Statistical and other data on use of ICTs and Broadband as a means of dissemination	• Statistical and other data on proportions of domestic and international consumption of cultural product
	• Information on the existence of policy settings and strategies to address infrastructure and other production support needs	• Information on the existence of policy settings and strategies to address marketing, research, and promotional needs	• Information on the existence of policy settings and strategies to address dissemination and circulation needs	• Information on the existence of policy settings and strategies to address consumption and usage issues

2.

The Three Faces of Culture:
Why Culture Is a Strategic Good Requiring Government Policy Attention

DICK STANLEY

Canadian films represent only 2.1 per cent of the cinema market in Canada. Less than 15 per cent of magazines on Canadian newsstands are Canadian. Only 41 per cent of Canadian television shows are domestic, less for English television and less in prime time. The various levels of government in Canada (federal, provincial,and municipal) spend over 6 billion dollars (or two hundred dollars per capita) supporting and subsidizing domestic cultural activities.[1] Broadcast content regulations are needed to ensure that Canadian recording artists can be heard on prime time radio, and that Canadian content is seen on prime time television. The federal government even operates a national broadcasting agency, the Canadian Broadcasting Corporation. Canadian publishers are subsidized to keep them in business and allow them to publish Canadian writers. Filmmakers get tax breaks to maintain a filmmaking capacity in Canada. Symphony orchestras, museums, and other cultural institutions also get financial support.[2] This kind of intervention in the cultural sector is typical of countries all over the world.[3]

Why do governments try to shore up economically non-competitive (or worse, economically competitive) industries? Would we not be better served by getting our culture from the cheapest producers like we do wheat and cars?[4] Culture is clearly a good thing, providing as it does, pleasure, enlightenment, and self-actualization. But so does whiskey, and no one subsidizes it. In fact, governments tax it. Why do we have the notion that every society should have a culture of its own, and why do we get nervous when it is threatened?

The reason is that culture is not just about artistic creation and performance, or about museums and art galleries, it is also about what we believe are proper actions and choices. Culture is therefore a source of power.[5] If one segment of society (say, the elite) has a disproportionate role in defining legitimate culture, then it will have a disproportionate influence over the choices people make and the courses of action they believe are available to them. For example, the cultural interpretation we give to certain markers like skin colour or relative poverty can determine our acceptance of certain groups into the community and the economy, and what we allow them to do.

Our interpretations, derived from our traditions, and shaped by our arts, help determine and constrain the place of others in society. In a liberal democracy, it is a fundamental principle that all citizens have an equal right to choose their courses of action for themselves and our understandings of what are appropriate courses of action should be based on as broad a consensus of citizens as possible. Excluded groups represent a failure of democracy. If we believe that every citizen should have a voice in defining appropriate action, then all citizenship is cultural. The purpose of this chapter, therefore, is to explore the nature of culture and to argue that the real purpose for policy intervention in the cultural sector is to increase the capacity of citizens to govern themselves. In other words, this chapter explores the building blocks of cultural citizenship.

It should be noted here at the outset that this chapter will not talk about the personal uses that culture is put to. Both consumers and participants in culture, arts, and heritage obtain private benefits such as enjoyment, enlightenment, and self-actualization. It is these that are the major reasons for an individual undertaking artistic and heritage activities and consuming their products. These are, however, personal benefits which accrue primarily to individuals, and which, in a free market, individuals can decide for themselves whether to support or not. What this chapter is interested in is the additional social benefits which accrue to members of society overall, the externalities created by cultural production and consumption, which are the proper object of government support.

Three Faces

So what is culture? Unfortunately, there are a bewildering variety of definitions for what Raymond Williams has called "one of the three most difficult concepts in the English language."[6] In fact, in 1952, Kroeber and Kluckhohn documented 164 different definitions of culture.[7]

In 1871, Sir Edward Tylor defined culture as "that complex whole which includes knowledge, belief, art, morals, law, custom, and any other capabilities and habits acquired by man as a member of society."[8] A long line of scholars from Franz Boas and Max Weber to Claude Lévi0Strauss and Clifford Geertz followed with variations on this theme. These definitions can all be summed up in the now famous UNESCO definition:

> *In its widest sense, culture may now be said to be the whole complex of distinctive spiritual, material, intellectual and emotional features that characterise a society or group. It includes not only the arts and letters, but also modes of life, the fundamental rights of the human beings, value systems, traditions and beliefs.*[9]

Perhaps the most useful way to understand this concept of culture is through Ann Swidler's perspective that culture is a tool kit or repertoire of beliefs, practices, understandings, and modes of behaviour from which actors select different pieces for constructing lines of action to deal with the manifold situations they face in everyday life.[10] Let us call this view of culture "culture (S)" for culture as a set of symbolic tools.

About the same time that Tylor was writing, the poet Matthew Arnold defined culture as "the best which has been thought or said in the world."[11] He thereby articulated a justification for the nineteenth-century development of museums, monuments, national historic sites, public libraries and archives, all institutions built to satisfy the passions of the time for the social status to be earned by being civilized or "cultivated." Indeed, Tylor himself started his definition quoted above by saying "Culture *or civilization* ... is that complex whole."[12] Arnold was reflecting on a perspective on culture which reached back at least to Goethe. More recently, scholars like Bourdieu[13] have taken up Arnold's concept, if only to debunk the elite's use of such culture as a tool to enhance and maintain their power. Let us call this view of culture "culture (H)" for culture as the heritage of excellence in human intellectual and artistic achievement.

Given these two alternative perspectives, what are we to make of Alberta Arthurs's concern that "these discoveries of the importance of culture seem to exclude the most familiar use of the word—that is, the arts as culture."[14] Arthurs points out that the UNESCO definition contains the telling phrase "not only arts and letters" as if saying that to take culture seriously, we must define the arts out of it. This flies in the face of common sense usage as well as various dictionary definitions such as that provided by the *American Heritage Dictionary*: "Intellectual and artistic activity, and the works produced by it," or the *Oxford Concise Dictionary*: "the arts and other manifestations of human intellectual achievement." Culture in this sense is widely used to designate such concepts as cultural industries (film, book publishing, etc.), cultural institutions (the National Ballet of Canada, the Toronto Symphony, etc.), as well as cultural activity (writing, performing music, acting, etc.). Raymond Williams gives us the same perspective in his definition of culture as "the special processes of discovery and creative effort."[15] Let us call this view of culture "culture (C)" for culture as artistic and creative activity, and the related processes of the creative industries.

A Unified Model of Culture

Can these three perspectives be reconciled? Williams provides a clue in the full passage from which his definition was taken:

Culture is ordinary: that is the first fact. Every human society has its own shape, its own purposes, its own meanings. Every human society expresses these, in institutions, and in arts and learning. The making of a society is the finding of common meanings and directions, and its growth is an active debate and amendment under the pressures of experience, contact, and discovery, writing themselves into the land. The growing society is there, yet it is also made and remade in every individual mind. The making of a mind is, first, the slow learning of shapes, purposes, and meanings, so that work, observation and communication are possible. Then, second, but equal in importance, is the testing of these in experience, the making of new observations, comparisons, and meanings. A culture has two aspects: the known meanings and directions, which its members are trained to; the new observations and meanings, which are offered and tested. These are the ordinary processes of human societies and human minds, and we see through them the nature of a culture: that it is always both traditional and creative; that it is both the most ordinary common meanings and the finest individual meanings. We use the word culture in these two senses: to mean a whole way of life—the common meanings; to mean the arts and learning—the special processes of discovery and creative effort. Some writers reserve the word for one or other of these senses; I insist on both, and on the significance of their conjunction. The questions I ask about our culture are questions about deep personal meanings. Culture is ordinary, in every society and in every mind.[16]

Williams is referring to culture (S) when he talks about "[t]he making of a society is the finding of common meanings and directions" and "a whole way of life." This is culture as Ann Swidler's toolkit, which every individual in a society needs "so that work, observation and communication are possible." Culture (S) is obtained through "the slow learning of shapes, purposes, and meanings," from society's traditions, which is culture (H), and which is preserved in expert institutions such as libraries, museums and universities. Culture (H) resembles an original computer file, of which culture (S) is a mirror image, made so that each new generation can have its own copy to use, and which can later become updated as the inevitable modifications during use occur. The bulk of culture (H) is held as a collective social memory and is called tradition. Within tradition, and supporting and stabilizing it, is a core of information and artefacts carefully preserved and documented by experts and held in institutions (museums, libraries, etc.) which can be called, at least for the purposes of this chapter, heritage.[17]

There is, of course, an interaction between culture (H) and culture (S). Some of the new strategies for action put together out of the culture (S) tool kit become habitual behaviour, or are recognized as exemplary, excellent, or remarkable and pass into tradition (i.e., culture [H]). Culture (S) therefore evolves slowly along a path shaped by the decisions and practices of individuals within the culture. Following John Ralston Saul, we can call this path society's historic trajectory.[18]

This would be but a static world if it were left there, with traditions and heritage forever being replicated in the minds of younger generations more or less as their parents had received it, and with the slow adaptation of new habits as the only source of change. Williams's model is dynamic, however. He says society's "growth is an active debate and amendment under the pressures of experience, contact, and discovery, writing themselves into the land." This leads to "the making of new observations, comparisons, and meanings," a process he takes "to mean the arts and learning—the special processes of discovery and creative effort," or what I have called culture (C). There appears to be a natural tendency in societies, at least in large ones we call civilizations, for a group to form which makes its living creating and propagating new and challenging ideas about how we should relate to our world and each other. They use entertainment, novelty, shock, spectacle, drama, and metaphor to catch our attention and render their ideas attractive and accessible. They take inspiration from culture (H) and from trends and patterns of behaviour in culture (S) (often before the rest of us are even aware of them) to develop their new ideas. Those of their ideas which find acceptance among the members of society get passed into the tradition or culture (H). We call this group "artists." Leslie Fiedler, the American critic, is reflecting this understanding of the artist's role when he characterizes all literature as subversive.[19]

Wendy Griswold provides an example of how culture (C) fulfills this role when she describes how new plays in Jacobean London provided the aristocratic, theatre-going public with role models which helped convince young men of this class that they could, with honour, pursue profitable careers in the newly emerging and highly successful commercial sector.[20]

Milan Kundera is saying the same thing, in *The Art of the Novel* when he writes:

> *The novelist is neither historian not prophet ... [h]e is an explorer feeling his way in an effort to reveal some unknown aspect of existence. ... Novelists draw up the* map *of existence by discovering that human possibility. Thus* both *the character* and *his world must be understood as* possibilities.[21]

And Paul Klee wrote, "I do not wish to represent the man as he is, but only as he might be."[22]

A model of culture which makes sense of the three faces of culture would then have to look something like Figure 1. We use culture (S) as a tool kit of meanings to understand

Figure 1: Model illustrating how the three perspectives of culture (S: symbols and meaning in everyday life; H: excellence in human achievement preserved as heritage; and C: creativity) interact. Culture (S) is illustrated as a shape in the mirror image of Culture (H), reflecting the idea that Culture (S) is a faithful copy for the current generation of society's traditions. Culture (H) is illustrated as having a central core (unshaded) which represents the formally documented and preserved part of tradition which we are calling heritage.

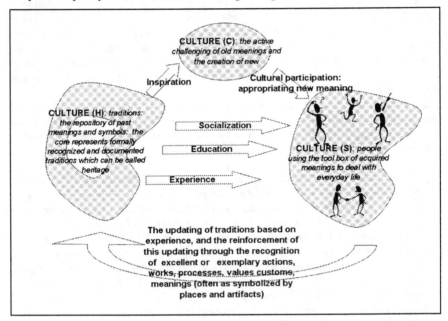

issues in our daily lives and develop strategies to deal with them. We obtain this tool kit through education and socialization which draws on our traditions and heritage: culture (H). We introduce major new meanings and test them through the creative arts, culture (C), to ensure that we can adapt our actions to the world around us.

Adapting to Change

Society exists in a real world constantly bombarding it with change.[23] How does culture help us cope? Consider the following examples.

In the popular 1980 South African film *The Gods Must Be Crazy*,[24] which many readers will remember, a pilot flying over the Kalihari desert throws an empty Coke bottle out the window, and it lands at the feet of a native tribesman. The Coke bottle is the first the natives have ever seen, and while they do not know what it is, they interpret it as a gift from the gods. When the artefact creates dissension in the tribe, they depute one of their members to find the gods and return the gift to them. This task brings him into contact with white culture for the first time, but, through a series of misadventures and misunderstandings, he eventually succeeds in getting rid of the bottle. The bottle is a cultural intrusion from outside the tribesman's own culture (S), and the tribesmen use their cultural tool kit in trying to cope with it. The misadventures arise from the incongruity between the tribesman's reality and ours.

Lest you think such cultural intrusions are merely amusing pieces of fiction, consider the death of Captain Cook, as explained by Marshall Sahlins.[25] Cook's arrival in the Hawaiian Islands in 1778 and again in 1779 coincided with the mythical annual arrival of Lono, the god of peace. In Hawaiian mythology, Lono's visit ushers in a period of feasting and a suspension of tribal warfare. At the end of his visit, he ritually dies, and leaves the Islands to return the next year, and warfare and normal life resume. Because Cook visited at a time and in a manner consistent with the myth, he was identified with the god. Unfortunately, he also returned unexpectedly a few weeks after his second visit, and this was, according to Sahlins, interpreted by the Hawaiians as an attempt by Lono to disrupt the cosmic order and take over the role of the other gods. Lono (Cook) had therefore to be ritually killed. Captain Cook, who did not share the same mythic beliefs as the Hawaiians, actually died as a result. A cultural intrusion can have serious personal consequences.

Cultural intrusions can have consequences for whole societies too. Jared Diamond asks the question how Pizarro, with 167 men, captured the Inca Empire which had forces numbering 80,000 warriors, or how Cortès captured Mexico against similar odds. Among several proximate explanations, he offered the following underlying one:

> [T]he miscalculations by Atahuallpa, Chalcuchima [Inca leaders], Montezuma, and countless other Native American leaders deceived by Europeans were due to the fact that no living inhabitants of the New World had been to the Old World, so of course they could have no specific information about the Spaniards. Even so, we find it hard to avoid the conclusion that Atahuallpa "should" have been more suspicious, if only his society had experienced a broader range of human behavior. Pizzaro too arrived at Cajamarca [site of the defeat of the Incas] with no information about the Incas…. However, while Pizarro himself happened to be illiterate, he belonged to a literary tradition. From books, the Spaniards knew of many contemporary civilizations remote from Europe, and about several thousand years of European history. … [L]iteracy made the Spaniards heirs to a huge body of knowledge about human behaviour and history. By contrast, not only did Atahuallpa have no conception of the Spaniards themselves, and no personal experience of any other invaders from overseas, but he had not even heard (or read) of similar threats to anyone else, anywhere else, any time previously in history.[26]

The Inca's lack of cultural resources, of the symbolic wherewithal to interpret new phenomena, opened the way for the Spanish colonization of Peru and the destruction of the Inca Empire. Culture is critical to sustaining a society in the face of change.

As the example of the Incas indicates, the consequences of a society not being able to deal on its own terms with cultural change from outside can be disastrous. At the very least, inability to deal means that the society no longer determines its own historical trajectory but surrenders to outside events. This is something that most of us would not welcome, and explains why even nations living under brutal dictators can mobilize citizens in defence in times of war and invasion.

These examples were not chosen to demonstrate the difficulty "primitive" cultures have in coping with "modernity" or change, or how cultural interpretations benefit societies. They were chosen to point out that culture shapes interpretation of new experience and the action taken to cope with it. The choice of examples that feature encounters between cultures serves to show how different cultures produce dramatically different interpretations, and even misinterpretations, of the same event, which lead to actions that can have significant repercussions incomprehensible in terms of the original interpretation.

Unfortunately, cultural encounters happen all the time. The whole history of humankind is a history of global cultural change and diffusion, from the initial expansion of homo sapiens out of Africa one million years ago, to the displacement of hunters and gatherers by agriculturalists starting 9000 years ago, to the spread of civilizations from China to the Andes starting about 6000 years ago, to the discovery and colonization of the new world by Europeans, the industrial revolution,[27] and the present globalization of communications, entertainment, and commodities. The historic trajectories of every society have always been buffeted and modified by these flows, and always will.

The cultural changes assaulting a society are rarely as drastic as conquistadors showing up on the doorstep, however. They are more likely to show up as images on the television screen, albeit in sometimes threateningly massive doses. Liebes and Katz studied the reactions of different cultures across the world to the television show *Dallas*.[28] They showed that understanding a cultural flow from an outside source is a process of reading and interpreting what is seen in terms of one's own culture. They discovered that groups with different cultural backgrounds came to quite different conclusions about what *Dallas* meant, and were influenced by it in much different ways. In other words, the cultural background of each group led them to appropriate the cultural message differently, even though it was the identical message. Although the program made viewers think, and had the potential to change attitudes and even possibly values and behaviour, viewers used the symbolic and meaning tools provided by their own culture to read and understand the message. Without this form of cultural "literacy," this ability to read between the lines of the new, foreign cultural message, and judge it for themselves, they would either have missed the message or accepted it uncritically, that is, given up control of their historic trajectory.

How does a culture avoid the fate of the Incas and become sufficiently literate to sustain itself in the face of the constant cultural change flowing into it? In terms of the model in Figure 1, the culture needs a rich and diverse culture (H) which provides it with what Diamond called the "huge body of knowledge about human behaviour and history" and other symbolic resources to "read" and interpret the changes realistically and appropriate them as beneficially or at least as harmlessly as possible into society's historic trajectory.

It takes time to build and diversify culture (H). Furthermore, if all society has is culture (H) as a resource, it is limited to reproducing it as is. The result is a very static society with an unchanging culture (H) (or one that adapts too slowly to cope usefully with outside cultural intrusions).

Culture needs a relatively nimble mechanism for adaptation if it is to sustain itself. Cultural adaptation can come from three sources. First, obviously, cultural flows from outside bringing new information, new interpretations, and new world views. But this does not solve the problem since it is precisely these outside flows that the society needs the adaptation mechanism to cope with. The problem cannot be the solution or it is not the problem. Of course, the flow can bring useful new symbolic tools in the long run, but the problem of adaptation is in the short run. The cultural intrusion must be coped with in the culture's own terms. So the nimble, short run adaptation mechanism must come initially from within.

The second source of adaptation is the very creativity of ordinary members of society who are daily using the symbolic resources of culture (S) to come to terms with everyday variability in their lives. They are skilled users of Swidler's toolbox to constructing lines of action to deal with the manifold situations they face in everyday life, of which the cultural intrusions are a part. They contribute to culture's evolution and enrichment through, in Williams's words, "an active debate and amendment under the pressures of experience, contact, and discovery, writing themselves into the land ... the testing of these in experience, the making of new observations, comparisons, and meanings."

Explaining cultural adaptation, enrichment, and appropriation of new and foreign meanings as a by-product of the small and quotidian adaptations of individuals in their daily lives may not be nimble enough however. Williams talks about "the *slow* learning of shapes, purposes, and meanings."[29] We are as likely to feel overwhelmed by massive doses of cultural change from outside as we are to feel inspired to decode and appropriate them.

Fortunately, there is a third way: culture (S) and the "literacy" we need to understand cultural flows from outside that are enriched through the workings of culture (C). Williams hinted at this previously when he suggests that the word culture can mean "a whole way of life—the common meanings ... [and also] the arts and learning—the special processes of discovery and creative effort." Society's artists and creators actively seek to understand and articulate the new, the strange and the menacing that confront us. In fact, they may even be its advocates. They experiment with meaning, and if we (or at least our teachers) pay attention to the arts, we will be influenced by them. If they are our own arts, created by artists who are working within our own cultural ambiance, the new tools and resources they develop will be easier for us to appropriate than the new information from outside, because, even though they are themselves new information, they arise out of a tradition we all share in common.

The consumption of culture (C) also cultivates within us a greater critical capacity to read between the lines of any new idea or concept, and to assess it for its relevance to our lives. The presence of a lively cultural (C) sector, and active participation by members of society in it, results in a literate, sceptical body of cultural citizens ready to confront any cultural change flowing toward them from outside. They will certainly not be immune to change, confusion, and doubt, but they will be in a position to manage the change, and will not lose control of their society's historic trajectory.

The Inca clearly did not have sufficient cultural resources to reach realistic conclusions about the Spaniards. Not only were they isolated, but they likely did not have a rich tradition of critical arts in the sense that European cultures do. It is important to note that the Europeans did not have nearly the easy conquests in Asia that they did in the Americas, which they reached at about the same time. In Asia, they met civilizations with cultures vastly more diverse than the Incas' and more able to interpret European intentions, strengths, and actions realistically. These cultures were able to formulate responses which did a much better job of appropriating the flows they were faced with.[30]

The existence of a culture (C) in almost all countries of the world today may be why we have not seen the emergence of McLuhan's global village as a single, homogeneous, worldwide culture, even though the technology makes it much more feasible than it was in McLuhan's 1960s.[31] Instead we see, as Crane observes,[32] the rise of regional cultural expressions in Latin America, Asia, and Europe in spite of the supposed economic dominance of U.S. media conglomerates.

Culture as a Strategic Good

A strategic good is a good on which the very existence of a nation is thought to depend. If the nation were to be deprived of the good, it could no longer sustain itself, or more particularly, defend itself against potential enemies. It is therefore critical that it retain capacity for production of this good within its borders, even if that production is economically inefficient.[33]

For example, if a nation imports all its oil or munitions from other nations, it may be cut off from these goods when it is attacked by an enemy, either because the enemy is the supplier or because the enemy nation can prevent imports. The nation then loses the ability to defend itself and is defeated. To avoid this possibility, a nation will ensure that it has production capacity for strategic goods under its own control.

Typical strategic goods are armaments and high technology products, and mineral resources such as oil and specialized metals. Categorizing a good or resource this way is a justification for protecting its production with subsidies, exempting it from trade agreements, or banning its export outright. Whether the concept of a strategic good is still valid in this day and age, most countries nevertheless have regulations dealing with strategic goods.[34]

The Incas should have considered culture a strategic good. Their lack of exposure to a broad and diverse range of world traditions and history made it difficult to conceive of the Spaniards as enemies, whereas the Spaniards had no difficulty figuring out the Incas' weaknesses. The Israeli respondents to the Liebes and Katz study used their culture as a strategic good when interpreting the content of *Dallas* in their own ways and re-formulating the ideas to suit their particular social circumstances.

Daniel Schwanen takes up this theme when he argues that the ability of people to make informed choices is critical to the proper functioning of a modern economy, so that information is a valuable good in itself. He cites Kenneth Arrow to suggest that if the information available to a collectivity (in Arrow's case an organization, but he is making a generalizable point) does not contain elements that are relevant to its very existence, the collectivity risks becoming "non-agenda" to its members, ensuring its ultimate demise.

Arrow's analysis means that information specifically aimed at Canadians creates a virtual meeting place for them. As long as they are interested in maintaining the possibility of a national character and institutional underpinnings that differ from those that would sustain other countries or communities (i.e., maintaining our capacity to control our own historic trajectory) they must have convenient access to information that contains at least some Canadian content and references. Otherwise, the basic elements necessary for making informed choices— political, educational, and others— disappear or become muted and Canada risks becoming "non-agenda" to many of its citizens.[35]

Schwanen also cites philosopher Will Kymlicka who argues:

[T]he only valid reason for protecting and promoting the right to cultural membership is to protect the "context of choice" for individuals. ...[36]

The three part culture that is described above is the mechanism by which "convenient access to information that contains at least some Canadian content and references" or the "context of choice" is maintained. Without this relevant information, citizens of a democracy will not have the cultural "munitions" to protect their capacity to direct the historic trajectory of their nation to the ends they desire. Their demise is then at least as certain as that nation's which did not keep within its borders a sufficient capacity to produce defensive armaments.

On a more commercial note, Greg Landry argues that new ideas are the fuel of corporate profit and innovation is the key to economic development.[37] Communities must be creative in order to prosper economically, and a community's creativity is fostered by policy intervention to invest in cultural assets and arts education, encourage cultural diversity, and promote community cultural encounters, such as arts festivals.

Appadurai extends Schwanen's notion of the strategic role played by information with his idea that culture provides a people with the capacity to aspire.[38] Culture embodies not only the past (habit, custom, heritage, and tradition) but also the future (plans, hopes, goals, and targets). It enables the collectivity to model a future for itself and develop consensus around solutions and action strategies. Culture provides a community with the symbolic resources needed "to debate, contest, and oppose vital directions for collective social life as they wish ... [this is] virtually a definition of inclusion and participation in any democracy."[39] The poor, he goes on to argue, remain trapped in poverty because they lack the cultural resources to give voice to their needs and aspirations, that is, "to express their views and get results skewed to their own welfare in the political debates that surround wealth and welfare in all societies."[40] Amartya Sen argues the same thing when he identifies culture as a critical contributor to the capacity for political participation, social solidarity and association and social evolution.[41]

Culture is a crucial element in the maintenance of a society's capacity to manage change. It provides the symbolic resources that people need to appropriate new meanings and skew them to their own welfare. Culture (H) provides citizens with benchmarks against which to test the consequences of new ideas, and culture (C) provides citizens with the new formulations of ideas needed to devise appropriate action strategies. Culture (S) depends for its adaptability on a dynamic balance between culture (H) which provides stability and confidence, and culture (C) which provides flexibility and innovation. Without them, as Arrow suggested, demise will occur.

It is in this sense then that cultures (H) and (C) are strategic sectors producing strategic goods. They are critical for society's survival. Governments are therefore justified in implementing policies that sustain the vitality of a domestic culture (H) and (C) as the source of the cultural diversity and literacy that a society needs to determine its own future and direct its own historic trajectory.

Notes

1 Department of Canadian Heritage, Strategic Research and Analysis Web site, based on 2000 Statistics Canada data.

2 For a complete review of Canadian cultural policy, see Johns Foote, *Federal Cultural Policy in Canada* (prepared by the Strategic Research and Analysis Directorate for the Department of Canadian Heritage, Ottawa, SRA-723, 2003).

3 Diana Crane, "Culture and Globalization," in ed.. Diana Crane, Nobuko Kawashima, Ken'ichi Kawasaki, *Media, Arts, Policy, and Globalization* (New York: Routledge, 2002), 14–15.

4 Keith Acheson and Christopher Maule, *Much Ado about Culture* (Ann Arbor: University of Michigan Press, 1999).

5 Don Mitchell, *Cultural Geography: A Critical Introduction* (Oxford: Blackwell, 2000).

6 Raymond Williams, *Keywords* (London: Fontana, 1976), 87.

7 Alfred L. Kroeber and Clyde Kluckhohn, *Culture: A Critical Review of Concepts and Definitions* (a Harvard University Peabody Museum of American Archeology and Ethnology Paper, Cambridge, Massachusetts, 1952), 47.

8 Edward B. Tylor, *Primitive Culture* (New York: Harper, 1871).

9 UNESCO-sponsored definition of culture, quoted by Ismail Seralgadin, "Introduction," *Culture and Development in Africa* (Washington, DC: World Bank, 1994), 2.

10 Ann Swidler, "Culture and Social Action," in Phillip Smith, ed., *The New American Cultural Sociology* (Cambridge: Cambridge University Press, 1998), 171–87.

11 Matthew Arnold, *Culture and Anarchy and Other Writings*, J. Dover Wilson ed. by (Cambridge: Cambridge University Press, 1961), 6.

12 Ibid. Emphasis mine.

[13] Pierre Bourdieu, *Distinction: A Social Critique of the Judgement of Taste* (London: Routledge & Kegan Paul, 1989).

[14] Alberta Arthurs, "Taking Art Seriously," *American Art Quarterly* 10, no. 3 (Fall 1996).

[15] Raymond Williams, "Culture is Ordinary," in Ann Gray and Jim McGuigan, eds., *Studying Culture: An Introductory Reader* (London: Edward Arnold, 1993), 5–14.

[16] Ibid.

[17] Ibid.

[18] John Ralston Saul, *LaFontaine-Baldwin Symposium Inaugural Lecture* (lecture given at the Royal Ontario Museum, March 23, 2000), available at http://www.operation-dialogue.com/lafontaine-baldwin/e/2000_speech.html.

[19] Leslie Feidler, *What Was Literature?* (New York: Simon and Schuster, 1982).

[20] W. Griswold, "The Devil, Social Change, and the Jacobean Theatre," in P. Smith, ed., *The New American Cultural Sociology* (Cambridge: Cambridge University Press, 1998), 126–40.

[21] Milan Kundera, *The Art of the Novel* (New York: Grove Press, 1986).

[22] Paul Klee, *On Modern Art* (London: Faber and Faber, 1963), 53.

[23] Dick Stanley, "Coke, Cook and Conquistadors: Cultural Flows and their Consequences" (paper prepared for the Strategic Research and Analysis Directorate, Department of Canadian Heritage, Ottawa, SRA-739, 2003); Arjun Appadurai, "Disjuncture and Difference in the Global Cultural Economy," *Theory, Culture and Society* 7 (1990): 295–310.

[24] *The Gods Must be Crazy*, directed by James Uys (Los Angeles, CA: 20th Century Fox, 1980).

[25] Adam Kuper, *Culture: The Anthropologists' Account* (Cambridge, MA: Harvard University Press, 2000), 177–84.

[26] Jared Diamond, *Guns, Germs, and Steel* (New York: W.W. Norton, 1999), 80.

[27] Ibid.

[28] T. Liebes and E. Katz, *The Export of Meaning: Cross-Cultural Readings of Dallas* (Oxford: Oxford University Press, 1990).

[29] Italics mine.

[30] Andre Gunder Frank, *ReOrient: Global Economy in the Asian Age* (Berkeley: University of California Press, 1998).

[31] Crane, "Culture and Globalization," 8–9.

[32] Ibid., 12–17.

[33] W. Baumol, *Economic Principles and Policy* (Toronto: Harcourt Brace & Company, 1994), 386-87.

[34] Department of Foreign Affairs and International Trade, Canada, "Military Technology and Miscellaneous Exports," *Export Control List*, (2004), available at http://www.dfait-maeci.gc.ca/trade/eicb/military/gr5-en.asp; Natalie Johnson, "Strategic Minerals of the United States" (2004), available at http://www.emporia.edu/earthsci/amber/go336/natalie/newindex.htm. See also the official government Web sites of the governments of New Zealand, Ireland, Singapore, and others for further examples.

[35] Daniel Schwanen, "A Room of Our Own: Cultural Policies and Trade Agreements," *Choices* 7, no. 1 (April 2001): 2–25, 5.

[36] Ibid., 16.

[37] Greg Landry, "Measuring Community Creativity," *Plan Canada* 44, no. 2 (Summer 2004).

[38] Arjun Appadurai, "The Capacity to Aspire: Culture and the Terms of Recognition," in eds. V. Rao and M. Walton, eds., *Culture and Public Action* (Palo Alto, CA: Stanford University Press, 2004), 59–84.

[39] Ibid., 66.

[40] Ibid., 63.

[41] Amartya Sen, "How Does Culture Matter?," in V. Rao and M. Walton, eds., *Culture and Public Action*, 37–58.

3.

Cultural Participation:
A Fuzzy Cultural Policy Paradigm

CATHERINE MURRAY

Google the term "cultural participation" and a researcher is likely to find 5.4 million hits. Something that generates this amount of activity on the Web is likely to generate heat, but not light. Is cultural participation a basic building block of cultural citizenship, or a way to measure it?[1] This chapter will argue that it should be a basic building block, suggesting that the term is better thought of as a means but not an end of citizenship. Unfortunately, as several analysts have argued, studies of cultural participation are often treated as baseline data but do not play a strategic role in policy-relevant research or cultural planning.[2] Thinking about cultural participation systematically seems most directly to imply a model of participatory democracy in cultural experience, if not policy-making. The problem has been an under-theorization of the cultural in participatory democracy. Cultural participation studies without clear cultural policy frameworks aim to defeat, manage, and corral rather than liberate creative cultural practice. It is time to claim the ground.

What is cultural participation? Defined as an umbrella term to denote activities of individuals and groups in the making and using of cultural products and processes, cultural participation has progressively widened in definition of the activities it includes, as a result of social and cultural change.[3]

Why is cultural participation important? Many states design their cultural policies to promote the value of enhancing cultural participation for their citizens to conform to international practice. Article 27 of the *Universal Declaration of Human Rights* sets out a right to participate in the cultural life of the community as a basic human right. In Canada, there is no similar right entrenched in the *Charter of Rights and Freedoms*. Yet historically, Canada had some experience with a participatory cultural policy paradigm during the Gérard Pelletier era primarily in the late 1960s and early1970s. Gilles Provonost argues that this ideology has been implicit in cultural policy at federal and provincial levels ever since.

With the inception of the Department of Canadian Heritage in 1993, widening of participation has been an important goal for federal Canadian cultural policy, regularly cited in strategic plans,[4] considered one of the central pillars of policy, and indeed, increasingly used as a measure of program evaluation—such as the Museum Assistance Program. Such a heightened federal policy concern with mapping and modelling of cultural participation emerged in the 1990s as a result of three convergent trends:

1. Growing dissatisfaction with the reliability and utility of audience research methods in the traditional cultural industries as competition for leisure time increases and new media absorb more time;
2. An ideological tilt to "demand" side rather than "supply" side measures in stimulating cultural policy and a push from arts donors to measure results of philanthropic spending; and
3. An emerging critical and theoretical concern with "popular culture" as an antidote to the perception of increasingly remote and elitist cultural policy in the 1990s.

So, how do policymakers go about "accounting" for cultural participation? The first problem in mapping cultural participation is how to measure access to cultural activities. In most basic terms, this is defined as access to performances, public museums or venues, or other types of cultural services. Yet, as Gilles Provonost points out, "there is as yet little consensus on the international level as to the choice of categories of cultural activities."[5] We may chart disciplines, institutions, or genres. As Colin Mercer suggests, we need a better identification of the unit of analysis of access to a strategic cultural resource: is it the "artifact, idea, image, activity, place or institution?"[6] With the advent of federal culture-on-line initiatives, new questions are raised. Does access imply physical or virtual access? Can the latter meaningfully supplant responsibility to supply the former? Access of course may not imply use: and use (or attendance) may not imply deeper engagement.

The second problem is deciding which activities to include in the measurement of behaviours, time use, or patterns of frequency among cultural activities as well as their impacts. Analysis of cultural participation in Pelletier's time involved mapping characteristics of amateur, community, and creative activities in a narrow range of modes (playing a musical instrument, or dancing, or singing), eventually slightly widening to include more popular modes (photography, crafts, and so on). Such activities are highly decentralized, local, and regional. Not surprisingly, cultural participation rates have apparently trended upward in most industrial states as the eligibility of the number of activities composing "cultural participation" has loosened. At the same time the definition has also moved away from a passive set of indicators to more active or interactive ones. Some analysts[7] suggest it is more useful to think in terms of segmentation of the stakeholders in cultural participation, suggesting that there are three types of participants, *creators*, *audiences*, and *stewards*, which are basic to all strategic frameworks for arts participation. While most countries account for the number of artists, consumers, and volunteers for comparative participation rates, these are not yet systematically compiled into any aggregate national index. Here it is also important to focus on non- or infrequent participants, to understand potential audiences.

The third problem in mapping cultural participation is to place it in the context of everyday life, to avoid a culture-centric world view. Culture in this view is not a product but a process, intersecting with daily work, play and sport, in social and natural environments. Colin Mercer suggests a research agenda for cultural mapping must include statistical and qualitative data on the diversity of cultural forms consumed, modes of consumption and usage, expenditure on cultural products, geo-territorial predisposition to "consumption sheds" or "walled cultural gardens," and information on the existence of democratic strategies to address consumption and usage issues.[8]

The fallacy that Mercer argues against is to conceive of cultural participation as "for its own sake," a kind of disconnected, dead-end activity in consumption terms—that is, as ticket buying or attendance—as it was even in the Pelletier era despite best intentions. In reaction to this fallacy, an emerging theoretical component of participation studies involves the idea of "creative consumption" where identity and meaning is forged through consumption, and consumption transitions to expression. In this view, cultural participation also involves the productive side: it may be creative, but it may be collective, with the goal of "engaging the whole community in valuing and participating in cultural expression and appreciation," calling citizens to "enter into" cultural and creative industries on their own terms, according to Galla.[9] Cultural participation studies must be attentive to the complex uses and negotiations of cultural resources, in Mercer's view, and are a necessary, but not sufficient condition for translation into meaningful cultural planning.

Mercer's helpful framework for mapping the cultural value chain demonstrates that theoretically, the analysis of cultural participation is related to emerging concerns about cultural rights, progressive social policy in the transition to the so-called knowledge society, the role of culture in maintenance (or destabilization) of social cohesion, and the intersection and complementarity of cultural and social capital, democratic and cultural interaction, and cultural diversity. Yet the millions of sources obtained on Google rarely rigorously question the logical and theoretical frameworks of cultural policy that must underpin the analysis of cultural participation in its myriad forms.

The object of the balance of this chapter is to set out the contending frameworks, and explore several examples of interesting "beta tests" for cultural participation studies in Canada. The goal here is not to be exhaustive, but rather to highlight important analytic cultural policy problems and see how studies of cultural participation seek to address them. To what end should participation be directed? Is all participation equal? What are the generational tendencies? What is current thinking suggesting about the capacities, the places, and the changing modes of participation? Finally, what connection is there between participation, designing indicators, and cultural policy? This chapter will conclude that we need a Canadian consortium to advance both the theory and method for Canadian cultural participation studies.

Participation for What End?

Currently there seem to be three different paradigms at war in Canadian cultural policy networks struggling for dominance. Where the early 1990s saw fascination with social cohesion in the Policy Research Initiative (with the creation of an interdepartmental social cohesion network), now the term has been supplanted by a *social capital* approach to policy. There is now also a *cultural diversity* approach—lent all the more credence, internationally at least, with the signing of a convention at UNESCO. The final approach struggling to emerge but by no means with anything other than a minority foothold is a *cultural citizenship or rights-based* one, which may overlap but not coincide with any of the others. Different policy frameworks, of course, call for different approaches to measuring participation.

In defining the grounds for these frameworks, I am referring to the overarching ideologies, values, or discourses involved primarily at the federal level. Equally important is a critical movement in thinking about appropriate cultural policy space—switching from the federal to the local or municipal level—and in thinking about appropriate policy action. Colin Mercer and Greg Baeker's work in setting out the new trends in cultural planning in Europe is extremely useful and best considered as a holistic overlay to the policy process (and an important heuristic for policy-makers) to the paradigmatic tendencies.

Social Capital

Since de Toqueville, social scientists have accepted the idea that it is primarily through interaction in voluntary organizations that citizens learn the skills of democratic participation and the civic virtues of trust and reciprocity.[10] Participation then, breeds social capital. Social capital turns on the trust and norms of reciprocity required in a society to cultivate social networks.[11] Social capital may lead to social bonding (within group identity), or bridging (between group identities), or linking (hierarchical status). Primarily a North American concept developed by Robert Putnam and now extended, the idea of social capital speaks to the way associational links function in society. Social capital is a finite "public resource" from which all members may draw. It must be refilled, or the common stock will diminish. To test this insight, Putnam measured community organizational density, newspaper readership, and voter turnout. More "civic" communities—defined by higher levels of social capital—corresponded with more effective governance than those with more economic capital.

Sharon Jeannotte's *Just Showing Up: Social and Cultural Capital in Everyday Life*[12] outlines Bryant and Norris's typology to assess social capital holdings that is of direct relevance to this discussion. Borrowing from Jenson's paper on cultural citizenship, these Statistics Canada analysts set up several main dimensions in the *predisposition* to cultural, social, or political participation (but in no particular order):

- *Sense of belonging*, civic engagement, political action, or other voluntary social movement surrogate;
- *Efficacy*, or confidence, life satisfaction, perception of degrees of political opportunity;
- *Resources*, or social networks, supports and depth of other cultural relationships; or *capacity to participate*, that is, the acquisition of basic cultural codes or ritualistic markers that enable participation or basic cultural literacy; the amount spent on cultural activities; and
- *Perception of shared values*, trust and confidence in institutions and perceptions.

It is very telling that of these measures, Statistics Canada's own study of multiculturalism in Canada operationalizes only the first dimension, that is, whether immigrants feel a sense of belonging.[13]

If we adopt a social capital approach to cultural policy, then it is important to design socio-metric studies (which focus on the individual's web of social relationships) to map the flow of cultural participation: from consumption, to creation, to action. A social capital approach to cultural policy is heuristically rich[14] and has the benefit of easy conversion into a policy instrument and benchmark.[15] For example, federal governments can impose a requirement to use intercommunity partnerships to be eligible for funding, and chart if the transactions between these partners improve or increase in frequency over time.

Yet there are a number of weaknesses in the social capital conception. It seems tautological, since associational memberships are correlated with the rise and fall of the stock of social capital, but not sufficient to cause it in multiple study comparisons drawn from the World Values Survey, for example. It is not clear what the relationship between cultural and civic capital may be. And it appears blind to differential class access to associations, or, for that matter, emerging forms of non-traditional associational activity.[16]

What do we know about the impact of social capital on civic capital? As Jeannotte states:

> *The researcher, Francois Matarasso ... documented several instances where participation in the arts increased the confidence of individuals, enriched their social lives, and helped them build the skills needed to find better jobs. Matarasso also recorded in some detail how participatory arts projects reinforce social cohesion by promoting partnerships, co-operation and intercultural understanding. Such involvement, he maintains, strengthens communities by encouraging people to become more active citizens and to get involved in their neighbourhoods.*[17]

Jeannotte's own analysis of the General Social Survey in Canada finds that those who attend cultural performances, visit galleries, or participate in a cultural activity such as singing in a choir are much more likely to volunteer for social as well as cultural activities in the community than those who did not and it is from these networks of social relations that we find predictors of future action.[18] Participation in creative cultural activities then, has positive effects on health, community development, social cohesion, and individual well-being.[19]

Perhaps one of the most vexing findings in social capital analyses is that it is not cultural aspiration that explains cultural participation. A survey by Environics of the motivation for cultural consumption in 2000 (like the 1992 Canadian Arts Consumer's Project) suggests that aesthetic value as a motive for cultural participation plays second fiddle to instrumental social bonding.[20] Conclusions were similar in a more rigorous academic study conducted in Australia. A study by Tony Bennett, Michael Emmison and John Frow called *Accounting for Tastes: Australian Everyday Cultures*[21] intended to contribute to the international policy debate over the development of "cultural life chance" indicators that can assist in evaluating the equity objectives of national cultural policy. In their study the researchers confirm that it is social capital—not cultural capital—that Australians want from their children's arts education. In general, they hypothesize, it is economic capital and social capital that play the major role in transmitting an advantage to the next generation and reproduce class inequality in Australia, not cultural capital.[22] Such findings are also confirmed in the U.S. The study *Informal Arts: Finding Cohesion, Capacity, and Other Cultural Benefits* found that "otherwise normative patterns of hierarchy (class, race, status, gender roles, age, or seniority) did not operate as much in the (cultural) communities of action they studied."[23]

Can we move beyond social citizenship to the political? Jeannotte cites a 1998 study by Stole and Rochon which explores the relationship between participation in cultural associations and generalized social trust and self-sense of political efficacy, finding a positive correlation. In their study of informal arts participation in the Chicago area, the team of ethnographers who produced *Informal Arts*[ß] regularly found a cross-over in local community political and arts involvement among about a third of their participants (suggesting, in other words, higher incidences of social activism than is found among other constituents), one that is harder to demonstrate at national levels of study.

However, few arts studies look for general predisposition to political action, whether through formal political institutions or non formal social movements (the latter of which are not a proxy for associations as Stole and Rochon seem to suggest). *From Reggae to Rachmaninoff*, an interesting U.S. study of cultural participation, bases its framework on the model of civic voluntarism created by Sidney Verba, the noted American political scientist.[24] But the problem has been that even such models probe associational membership as a black box in which all associations are equal (when evidence from Milner and others suggests they are not) with little understanding of the exercise of cultural leadership or franchise.

What all these "social capital" studies share is what Diana Crane has called a sociological view of culture as micro and macro tool kits in the development of individual identity, civic literacy, and collective community. Is culture just a means?

The conceptual danger in a social capital approach is that *it buries the cultural*: treating it either as a by-product or enabler of bonding, bridging, or linking functions. But cultural capital is not a synonym for social capital. Cultural capital is not yet central to the lexicon of cultural policy, but it originates with the theories of Pierre Bourdieu.[25] In Bourdieu's work on cultural practice in France, cultural capital refers to cultivated competence, knowledge of classificatory schemes, codes and conventions, and the ability to display such knowledge to social advantage. There is both a literacy component and a performative component (or, as Dick Stanley suggests both a tool box and a heritage lens to culture). What is at stake, for Bourdieu, is not simply differences in taste, but the ability of the dominant class to impose some differences as "legitimate" and others not.[26] Cultural capital is reproduced across generations by family and schooling, but is not solely structurally determined. The *Everyday Cultures Project* in Australia led by Tony Bennett defines cultural capital more simply as skill in making cultural distinctions, later expanding their definition to include skill in making *social* distinctions:

> *Cultural choice positions us: it tells us and others who we are. And it defines for us and for others who we are not. It sorts us into "kinds" of people … that sorting is done by us as we shape and elaborate a social place that is partly given and partly chosen in the open-ended formation of our lives. The choices are always constrained.*[27]

Indeed, the theoretical challenge is to prove when and under what circumstances, cultural capital can *improve* social capital (or the converse). This is an important point. If there is something to be gained from academic surveys of the kind Tony Bennett and colleagues are contributing, it is to the understanding that cultural capital may improve life chances … that social capital, by contrast, is more tied to reinforcing economic, vocational, and educational class than cultural capital: that cultural capital *works* on the social.

The Australian team found that cultural participation in venues of more public culture—featuring arts events or experiences outside the home such as art galleries, botanical gardens or libraries or public broadcasting supported by a mostly public tax base—can indeed contribute to social mobility and more democratic distribution of cultural resources. Cultural capital they argue *may* provide a means of social mobility within and across generations: how, and under what conditions is the main analytic challenge. Is this not the goal of culture: betterment of life?

If analysts continue to use social capital as a framework for cultural policy, then cultural capital has to provide a new—epistemologically different—category to *bonding, bridging, or linking* ("bbl") which has become au courant in social capital studies. More to the point, analysts must develop an alternative conceptual framework building on the analogy to "bbl," by arguing that cultural capital contributes to societal networks because it *directs the social connectedness*: its function is diversifying, contextualizing, imbuing with meaning. Dick Stanley has argued the difference of cultural capital from social capital is found in the way we think about the world around us, the way we bond, in the cognitive, evaluative, ideological dimension.

Cultural capital now, unlike its analysis during Bourdieu's era, offers many more venues for its accumulation today than forty years ago. Increasingly cultural capital may be acquired through non-formal means, outside of school, in self-formed cultural communities as Diana Crane has identified or as the Chicago analysts have identified (in myriad sectoral specific studies of the popular cultural phenomenon of the reading club).[28] Where there are richly promising applications of cultural capital approaches in cultural planning,[29] it is interesting that participation is synonomous with consumption and treated as one of four indicators, linked to diversity, to lifestyle, to identity, and to ethical governance. Yet cultural capital is only one element of participatory democracy, or a citizen model for cultural policy, and it is ideologically constructed. Clearly, much more theoretical and empirical inquiry into the intersection of social and cultural capital in mediating participation is needed.[30]

Cultural Diversity

The second emerging cultural policy paradigm is around cultural diversity. Bennett identifies four overlaying principles as key to the development of this new vocabulary:

> *The first consists in the entitlement to equal opportunity to participate in the full range of activities that constitute the field of culture in the society in question. The second consists in the entitlement of all members of society to be* provided with the cultural means of functioning effectively *within that society without being required to change their cultural allegiances, affiliations or identities. The third consists in the obligation of governments and other authorities to* nurture the sources of diversity *through imaginative mechanisms, arrived at through consultation, for sustaining and developing the different cultures that are active within the populations for which they are responsible. The fourth concerns the obligation for the* promotion of diversity *to aim at establishing ongoing interactions between differentiated cultures, rather than their development as separated enclaves, as the best means of transforming the ground on which cultural identities are formed in ways that will favor a continuing dynamic for diversity.*[31]

In this view, the analytic focus of cultural participation switches from activity to mode of its address: awareness of cultural differences, tolerance of cultural differences, and experience with cultural difference in cultural practice, even diversity of cultural tastes. The ability to function effectively, balanced by measures of social dysfunction (feeling out of place and so on) become central in understanding the predisposition to cultural participation and its practice.[32]

Several representative studies, such as the social cohesion study conducted by Environics, or others with Decima, and which have accounted for a significant federal investment in recent years, have made a great effort to identify attitudinal factors friendly or hostile to cultural diversity. Fully eighty-six percent of Canadians state that they are interested in arts in other cultures according to the Environics study, while fifty-three percent seek to eliminate barriers and involve citizens and individuals in all walks of everyday life. Cultural diversity implies a high value on heterogeneity and pluralism of cultural participation, and it is these measures which become the chief framework for analysis. Explicit models such as Bennett, Frow, and Emmison develop an index around the variety of activities participated in as an important focus of analysis—finding "omnivores" and so on. Other models (in the Chicago group) prefer to think along a continuum between informal (or personally performative) and formal (to the more classic audience model). But neither model, as yet, embeds in it the social category of race or ethno-cultural identity explicitly.

Thinking through such normative models of diversity, it would be important to probe linguistic competence, experience living in other cultures, travel, attendance at festivals, and a range of other measures of participation in "most similar" and "most different" cultural venues or experiences (awareness and reading of the new canonical non-white Canadian authors, for example). These ideas probe the functional prerequisites to local attachment, global citizenry, tolerance, and national adjustment. The federal government's formation in 2003 of the Interdepartmental Committee on Public Education and Diversity which is geared to interdepartmental partnerships promoting shared citizenship, cross cultural understanding, and the elimination of racism and discrimination, will pioneer benchmark measures to see how their interventions change cultural participation.

Whatever the intensity of the policy commitment to embrace cultural diversity as a policy paradigm—and the rhetoric is running high at home and internationally—it is difficult to see how analysts of cultural participation can develop meaningful insights into diversity as lived (or as given) and the impact of policy interventions defined to affirm it over time. If diversity affirms difference, then participation gives it meaning. How? The job of cultural participation analysts is to unmask such "pluralist" assumptions to determine progress overcoming systemic and racist barriers to such participation.[33] Often implicit in early discussions of cultural diversity is either fear of old assimilationism, or a high value placed on liberal cultural cosmopolitanism: tolerance and experimentation with a wide array of cultural activities. In this view, diversity becomes a proxy for "cosmopolitanism" or mutual adaptation in complex, multicultural societies, but so too might be acquisition of multiple language skills, travel to other countries, or interest in the cultural "other."

It is important to recognize that the idea of diversity can play to this "social justice" or "critical multicultural agenda" just as much as it can to a neo-liberal one, which argues that diversity generates economic vitality.[34] Richard Florida's book *The Rise of the Creative Class*[35] continues work in the latter tradition with an almost Schumpeterian notion of cultural diversity, looking for the mobility of new global classes (young urban, highly educated professionals) dubbed the "new creatives" who import their cultural tastes and push for change in American cultural landscapes.[36] Florida maps density of associational links like Putnam, but adds a bohemian index (evocative of Bourdieu's preoccupation with the artistic vanguard), a gay index (as a proxy for liberal social values) and foreign-born or ethnic diversity and several other key measures to predict city vibrancy and the power to attract "new creatives" in social and economic development. Is the Florida model guilty of being a branding exercise for urban gentrification? It is based on a rejection of the utility of mere cultural tolerance and calls for a neo-liberal view that "differences" can add value in social capital or economic productivity. New efforts by others, such as Stuart Cunningham on Australian Creative Clusters, broaden the creative class definition away from an industry focus to a new labour definition to include a wider array of performing artists, cultural industry workers, and design professionals (including architecture, software, advertising, and so on).[37] To do so, they implicitly draw on Michael Porter's theory of endogenous economic growth of geographic clusters. These initiatives, while working loosely in the cultural diversity paradigm, are hampered by state statistical agencies which are struggling to catch up with new contours of the cultural services.

Moving quite beyond Florida is the perspective of Benjamin Barber, who writes about how to make society civil and democracy strong. Barber sets out a platform for the renewal of participatory democracy which includes a commitment to cultivating the arts, in which he advocates treating artists as citizens and citizens as artists, thereby focusing on arts education. In Barber's liberal-humanist view, participatory democracy requires us all to be a creative class.

Clearly, despite over five years of intensive domestic and international discourse on these issues, it is just as difficult today to set a normative or operational definition of diversity measures in cultural participation today as it was then. Why? Much of the policy discourse just treats cultural diversity as a reified "thing"—it is there or it is not, leaving it difficult to see it as anything other than an inert resource. Or frequently the arguments are really determined by the interests of the traditional cultural industries from a supply-side perspective who are motivated to find compelling public discourses to resist free trade in cultural services. What is really needed is a more complex model of cultural participation, which roots individual cultural rights in some way with the community and *in the collective democratic deliberations of that community*.

Cultural Rights and Citizenship

A central theoretical hurdle is to accept the axiom that cultural participation is directed to some end. Tracing its political provenance to Montesquieu and others, the concept of participatory democracy holds the ideal of active cultural citizenship in high esteem— valorizing dedication to the cultural and a sense of cultural responsibility.[38] In this view, cultural participation then is a *proxy for citizenship in the nation state—or, increasingly global agency*. It is a way of "measuring" the realization of cultural citizenship. As a consequence, it is important to chart participation over time to look for increases or changes in direction and intensity. The twentieth anniversary of the *Canadian Charter of Rights and Freedoms* led to creative reflection about the kind of society we are building, and focused a lot of attention on the theory of citizenship. The Charter is not explicit about full cultural rights, but there are a range of sections of explicit language (equality rights, notwithstanding clause, right to freedom of expression) which construct a space for cultural citizenship. International covenants may be pushing Canada farther along. If analysts adopt a cultural rights/citizenship model, different dimensions to cultural participation matter in their measurement. There is no *a priori* assertion of pluralist equality as there would seem to be in cultural diversity models. Instead, the conditions of equity become central to the exploration of participation. The right to participate in this view has a range of meanings:

- *Expressive*: implying that people have a basic right to tell stories in their own language or to practice everyday life in different ways, to create and disseminate their work in the language of their choice;[39]
- *Normative*: referring to the civil values of treatment with respect, tolerance, or establishing the security of being, that is the right to live in freedom from fear of arbitrary cultural genocide;[40]
- *Instrumental*: compelling the State to provide the informational tools, education, or capacity to function as cultural citizens in a manner that fully respects their cultural identity. Conversely, the State may guarantee access to cultural resources to all regardless of income or geographic location;
- *Procedural*: including grounds for *protection of minorities* as an ethical imperative, inseparable from respect for human dignity. It implies a commitment to human

rights and fundamental freedoms, in particular the rights of persons belonging to minorities and those of indigenous peoples; and

- *Deliberative*: that is, setting out the principles of recognition of cultural status, representation in cultural decision-making, or control over cultural self-determination.[41]

Of the five meanings explored above, the normative and the procedural are probed to some degree in a range of federal studies, such as Reinventing Government, the Ethnic Diversity Survey, and the Metropolis Project, but there has been little exploration of deliberative, expressive, and instrumental meanings. It is important not to underestimate the discomfort policy planners may feel with a return to the moral agenda of equity and social justice concerns, which is evocative of the old UNESCO battles over cultural development.

While there are many problems in hammering out the conceptual uniqueness of a cultural rights approach at least this paradigm asks: to what end? What democratic benefit? And what balance between cultural right and responsibility? A concern with theoretical and substantive, rather than methodological elements of participation is bound to be more theoretically productive.

Inherent in such a normative approach is also a basic political conception of deliberative cultural action. We may think of any approach to participation as predicated on an implicit model or hierarchy of democratic *political* participation or engagement. Sidney Verba and others, in a study of civic voluntarism, have found that the decision to participate is based on the interplay among personal resources, motivations, and paths of recruitment.[42] If we were to translate his political framework for action into a cultural one, citizens may attend the opera, they may donate to the arts, they may belong to organizations, they may sign petitions, they may volunteer their time, and they may aspire to creative contribution for their own pleasure or those of others. Or they may protest or participate in cultural management or governance, they may support arts in the schools, or they may express other political views on the role of culture around them, and on the relative trade offs they are prepared to make in their conceptual view of culture as a "universal health care" policy for the collective soul and betterment of quality of life. Each mode of cultural participation, then, may be seen to differ according to whether it can be read to convey the individual's cultural preference, or applies pressure for cultural compliance, if it is directed toward a broad cultural outcome, if it involves conflict, relative effort, and co-operation.[43] Recognizing the differential investments of energy, efficacy, and opportunity that involvement in both formal and informal cultural organizations presupposes, is what Colin Mercer talks about in his review of the Urban Institute of Washington, DC's *Arts and Cultural Indicators Project*. Putnam's own work into the differential contribution of strong ties and weak ties in social relationships (where the latter serve a more pro-social function) hints at this, and it is precisely in these kinds of questions where we have weaknesses in comparative cultural interpretation.

Is All Participation Equal?

Jane Jenson argues in her seminal 1998 work, *Mapping Social Cohesion*, that while some social scientists have said that social inclusion is strongly correlated with participation, others refute this and suggest any participation (regardless of income, class, or race), is sufficient for belongingness. Her proposed research agenda sets out a challenge (still not addressed in any coherent fashion) which asks us if programs that seek to engage individuals in *any* form of community are as effective as those which also include meaningful and recognized redistribution of economic resources to enable participation.[44]

As Kymlicka and Norman have identified, faith in the automatically educative function of participation may be overrated. They ask if civil society theorists have demanded too much of voluntary associations by expecting them to be the main school for democratic citizenship. In this, they are partly upheld by the *Final OECD Report of the International Adult Literacy Survey*, which finds associations between literacy skills and participation in voluntary activities, while minimally statistically significant " seem quite small ... compared to the strength of the relationship between literacy skills and initial educational attainment and the labor market."[45] The anomaly is that in regression analysis of the literacy trends, participation in voluntary activities is found to be one of the top four explanatory factors in Canada and Poland among the participating nations— but still a weaker predictor in most other countries around the world.

From the days of Bourdieu, cultural capital has been conceived as primarily transmitted over generations by class and education. Policy analysts subscribing to theories of participatory democracy may value cultural mobility: that is, social movement across the cultural field and the acquisition of new cultural "habitus" or resources, to paraphrase Bourdieu. A central challenge for the Australian researchers was to decide how to look for intergenerational class assimilation—without the luxury of a longitudinal, or rolling periodic, study like the Media Panel Project directed by Karl Rosengren and colleagues in Sweden.[46] Like Bourdieu, the *Everyday Cultures Project* researchers relied heavily on the respondent's account of his or her parent's occupation and education to look at upward or downward social mobility. They also relied on questions about where children are sent to school (private or public systems) and how much emphasis their children's school places on art and musical training as passports to distinction.[47] The effects of more formal education, they find, are more pronounced for private patterns of cultural consumption than any other. Second ranked in exclusivity is public culture— museums, libraries, or galleries—and third is subsidized culture. By contrast, public broadcasting proves the most open and accessible of all—even though only thirty-one percent of those with primary education cite ABC as their regular channel.[48]

A common assumption in many participation studies is that ritual differentiations between elite and mass status groups are hypothesized to decline. Tony Bennett and his team's *Accounting for Taste* (AFT) speculates that we are entering a period of cultural declassification with the advent of a widespread commodification of culture. The chief conceptual difference in cultural capital revolves around scale and diversity: number of activities, and diversity among them. AFT finds that the working classes and especially manual workers have a clear cultural disadvantage, but it stems less from their exclusion from "high" culture than from the relatively more restricted ambit of their cultural practice overall.[49] The authors argue that taste cultures of contemporary society have shifted to an urban landscape more adequately contrasted as omnivore and univore.[50] An omnivore has the ability to adapt and appropriate meaning from a wide range of cultural pursuits.

The authors conclude the data suggest there is a "publicness" to public culture, if we use egalitarian tests of participation. Because education serves as a gateway to virtually all forms of cultural participation, the authors conclude that public investment in education of a kind and level capable of offsetting the effects of different social backgrounds is crucial to any government concerned with enhancing the cultural life chances of its citizens. The World Bank's studies on governance around the world also underline the importance of investment in primary education, for civic development around the world.

42

Yet, ironically and perhaps because of the jurisdictional divide between cultural and educational policy in Canada's constitution, there are few studies of the efficacy of certain "cultural curricula" in and outside of the schools in mediating cultural participation. A new Canadian coalition of arts educators is collaborating with UNESCO in Canada on the assessment of various educative initiatives. Important new work in political participation is exploring the interaction of political knowledge (defined as both factual information and cognitive capacity) and tendency to vote, or participate in other civic associations[51] and finding sharp differences in levels of political knowledge among young and older citizens.

The venue for surveys of cultural participation must shift to the young and to those in school, to understand how cultural capacity is built, and how cultural citizenship formed over time. We urgently need a longitudinal study of children and their acquisition of cultural skills, cultural participation, and citizenship. In a very interesting article, Marie McAndrew explores educational policy in the context of the Metropolis' project on immigration, integration, and urban dynamics.[52] She acknowledges that most provinces are trying to promote a set of broad, common values known today as citizenship education in mandatory curriculum not only as a specific subject, but horizontally as a skill that must be acquired throughout the educational process. Such efforts aim at balancing rights and responsibilities and favour developing civic skills rather than · simply acquiring knowledge. In British Columbia, such programs also seek to increase youth volunteerism, which other studies have shown to be perilously low in Canada. The impact such educational policies and programs will have on patterns of cultural participation is open to conjecture. States McAndrew, "it is still difficult to evaluate the type of citizenship education 'cocktail' found in various schools." She identifies a vital need for comparative analyses of educational options and the impact of this trend on diversity in education (still not met, as far as I could find).

The final blind spot in the study of equity of access/equality in patterns of cultural participation is the study of immigrants, people of colour, or new minorities. Just one in ten are found to belong to a cultural association, apparently lower than white populations.[53] Is race a predictor of lower or higher rates of cultural participation overall? Of more "omnivorous" patterns of consumption or not? There are some hypotheses that there are different modes of participation in different cultural and familial structures, but how do these translate into cultural capital and cultural citizenship and how do they change with length of time in Canada? Statistics Canada and the Department of Canadian Heritage have joined forces to try to study these and other questions with their path-breaking Ethnic Diversity Survey. Participation in Canadian society increases with time lived in Canada. But what is the impact on cultural activity? The Longitudinal Survey of Immigrants may further deepen these understandings. A study of cultural tourists within Canada finds them, for example, more likely to be new Canadians,[54] but these citizens are less likely to travel far distances.

Participation: What Generation?

While youth or senior studies are still relatively rare across a number of nations, they share a concern about the creeping commercialization of youth media realms (video games, Internet, new specialty youth channels) and their implications for cultivating cultural practices, cultural tastes, and building cultural citizenship.

In measuring capacity for cultural identification, the *Everyday Cultures Project's* researchers used open-ended questions to identify respondents' favorite films, television programs, or books. In three major areas of consumption—television, music, and literature—*Accounting for Taste* finds that younger Australians prefer American programs, musicians, and authors. No other demographic factor accounts for as much overall variation in tastes as age.[55] Television showed the highest convergence of tastes to a top thirty list. About half of the television schedules available show imports, and fifty-three percent of the top thirty cited by Australians surveyed are Australian in origin. The rest are mostly from the U.S. or U.K. When age is introduced into the analysis, however, the incidence of preference for American television grows to seventy-seven percent among those eighteen to twenty-five. Because of the gendered pattern of program consumption—sports and factual programs preferred by men are more often indigenous in orientation—it is women who are more likely to select genres and series from the U.S. This is quite different from trends in Europe[56] but similar to Canada.[57] The authors' definition of "youth," however, revolves around the young adult in the making, not the "tween." Other studies of Internet usage suggest six- to seven-year-old boys are the most international in orientation.

The data suggest not only that young Australians inhabit cultural worlds saturated by American materials, but that they are more likely to prefer this material.[58] Do such findings play up old cultural industry rhetorical concern about cultural imperialism and cultural assimilation? But it is important that even such "hybridized" global tastes may NOT lead to crude assimilation. Exciting studies of world music as a genre note how rock uses traditional modal structures, but adapts these to different cultural contexts successfully. Such theoretical work is probably better aided by ethnographic studies to probe meaning derived from such patterns of cultural consumption.

Without longitudinal data the researchers cannot speculate if "global" tastes among youth are a life cycle phenomenon—conditioned by age or family status—or one in which we may see a trajectory of cultural taste, entailing movement from the active, spectacular, physical, and entertainment-oriented cultural pursuits to the more contemplative, informative, or cerebral. But equally theoretically important, if not touched due to political incorrectness, is the question of cultural decay, that is, decline in cultural standards and taste, and the understanding of the dynamics that may come into play to correct this. Only discourses about renewal and reconciliation in aboriginal cultures make issues of decay, or decomposition of cultural values explicit, and the federal government has leaped into the breach with a number of remedial, if ad hoc programs (such as dedicated aboriginal envelopes in cultural industry spending on television production, for example).

Capacity, Competence, Taste, and Participation

There is a certain irony in the preponderance of studies of cultural participation which ignore the issue of capacity to participate. What is the nature of cultural competence required to function in our culture today? How is it acquired?

Provonost has identified a central problem with state-led surveys of cultural participation:

> There is often an explicit cultural bias in the choice of activities selected in surveys, a bias very often based on community standards (one chooses activities that imply a reference to what is "active" rather than "passive" even if this distinction is, in fact, virtually impossible to make), or on social class choices (why museums and not the contemplation of nature?). Take the example of "amateur practices" again. A recent French survey ... refers to a dozen

activities linked to the so-called "noble" domain (playing a musical instrument, writing, plastic arts) while the 1997 American survey refers to pottery, embroidery and photography. These choices were not strictly made by chance, but rather in terms of different cultural universes.[59]

It is almost tautological, and indeed, predictable, to state cultural participation is related to education across most of these studies. But education as a reported category of analysis is weakly conceived, tested, or understood as a measure compared to cultural literacy in certain conditions, according to Bourdieu or his legion of followers fascinated with the emergence of the avant-garde or what Richard Florida has called the new "bohemians."

If this hypothesis is right, the fact that there is a resistance to finding a way to empirically explore the idea of cultural literacy in Canada is lamentable. A central determinant of cultural participation is acquired cultural knowledge, predisposition, and judgment of taste. While mediated by education and class, there is an element of life chance here, which should become central to the analysis. Inspired by Bourdieu's seminal approach, the *Everyday Cultures Project* includes a section on *cultural judgment* across a number of arts and media (how subjects for a photograph may be classified, as clichéd or interesting, and so on), and on *cultural knowledge* (whether a list of musical works is known, and if the composer of a given work can be named). Like Bourdieu's survey, the questions probe aesthetic preferences, tastes in music and reading, and political views against their social and class backdrops; indeed, the dynamics of subculture and style.

How did the authors select the "canon" on which they based their analysis?[60] There are two ways to do this. One approach used by historians, relies on a peer jury to identify the certain historical events or political or cultural "facts" a citizen is deemed to "need to know" and benchmark "progress" against that. Canons may be defined as "essential" to citizen literacy, or pleasure derived from the practice for its own sake, as the Eurobarometer survey is careful to identify in its study of reading patterns. Or conversely, researchers can build a factorial quantitative model across a very large array of practices in which to probe awareness, liking, and aversion, or conduct qualitative studies of cultural discourses to explain cultural preferences.

Perhaps the French are furthest along in thinking through these lines, producing a typology of seven canonical universes (of cultural exclusion, destitution, of juveniles, of the average, of the classic cultured, of the modern, of the "in" post-modern) and so forth.[61]

As Canadians continue to attain higher levels of education (climbing to over forty percent of the population aged fifteen and over who have graduated from post secondary institutions), the slow conversion of the "educated" into active cultural citizens is increasingly a problem. There must be an intervening variable of social practice and acquisition of cultural taste. By contrast, monitoring the reach of cultural practices among the one quarter of Canadians who are functionally illiterate is critical to democratic cultural policy. In various arms of the federal government, there are basic civic instructional tools developed[62] which may or may not have been peer reviewed as a kind of civics course in culture, but which may provide a framework for testing citizen knowledge—or at least a prod to provinces to develop some kind of harmonized standard about citizen education together with the federal government.

The final area where there has been descriptive, but not analytic, inquiry into cultural capital is the field of language. Statistics Canada has produced a report describing different cultural orientations in participation among language groups, but has not explored linguistic facility as a door opening wider vistas of culture. Such studies of the role of language as a cultural passport to participation are urgently needed (and while largely positive in French-language literature, lead to negative conclusions in English-language studies).

The *Reggae to Rachmaninoff* study in the U.S. identifies a useful set of what they call "participation skills" which exert a very powerful influence over frequency and type of cultural participation. They include awareness of opportunities to participate; knowledge of music, drama, dance, and visual art; understanding of cultural standards, practices, histories, and ideas; interest in and knowledge of other times, cultures, and communities; and knowledge of the range of possible responses to artistic and cultural experiences.[63]

Such focus on competence, literacy, and capacity to manipulate symbolic codes should not overlook the voluntary, acquired, or providentially learned aspect of taste. The *Everyday Cultures Project* researchers define cultural capital simply as skill in making cultural distinctions,[64] or policing the boundaries of taste. To explore some of the dimensions of *distaste* the researchers develop batteries of more indirect questions such as "Which type of music do you most *dislike*?" or "Could you indicate in few words what good and *bad* taste entail?" Patterns of distaste are rarely explored in studies of Canadian cultural participation, yet provide important contextual meaning to the construction of identity, by age, gender, or race. Definitions of cultural competence in the Canadian case urgently need peer review.

Participation and Place

Bennett, Emmison, and Frow argue that choice between domestic and international media output implies explicit symbolic negotiations between known and unknown narrative repertoires and formal signs, social conventions, and world view.

Certainly, the *Accounting for Tastes* study did not conclude that widespread preferences for American popular productions indicate that young Australians are turning into Americans. When asked "which country was the most important in making you the person you are today," an overwhelming majority of youth between eighteen and twenty-five say "Australia." Most also agree that a distinctively Australian culture exists, with young people citing a "multicultural heritage" as a more important defining Australian cultural characteristic than their older cohorts, even if they cannot then go on to make the connection to cultural products and their personal consumption.

Methodologically, the researchers are vulnerable because the other side of "global village" identification is not posed. How can we theoretically reconcile such seemingly contradictory but concurrent taste and belief systems among young people? Is the thesis of cultural imperialism borne out by the youth data in this study? Or is this "multiculturality" which bridges to the more complex process of intermixing of identities and hybridity today? *Accounting for Tastes*, despite asking about trends in immigration, personal, and collective identification with ethnic groups, and so on, does not foreground this kind of analysis. Arguably, such work may be better developed in ethnographic venues[65] before it can translate into the more standardized forms of questioning and comparison with more "informational or educative" genres and entertainment sources of practical reasoning. Understanding these processes is key to public debates about the changing nature of national and civic identities, and future global cultural institutions.

Changing Modes of Participation

If analysts have abolished simple dichotomies of "high" or "low," "elite" and "popular" frameworks for analyzing cultural activities, it is not clear if new models are emerging. A number of American studies have identified that there is a tendency to single-ticket, spontaneous purchase among audiences, and that:

Audience research suggests that cultural consumers aren't very interested in boundaries ... but freely graze as cultural omnivores among a range of choices from country music to opera, beadwork to Cezanne, experimental film to the latest DVDs.[66]

Bennett, et al., would have us replace this univore/omnivore conception with a new aesthetic category: "documentary" or active and spectacular, versus the contemplative and aesthetic (a kind of McLuhanesque body and mind dichotomy, or conversely, a spectacular and contemplative one). The researchers argue that the more democratic of subsidized cultural forms tend to revolve around documentary cultural forms (museums, festivals, and so on) and attract the widest participation, rather than aesthetic culture (art galleries and operas). Documentary cultural practices offer a greater degree of bodily involvement: walking and seeing and direct experience rather than sitting and listening and spectatorship.[67]

Teachers are far more involved in these participatory/documentary realms of public culture—generating benefits whose public effects are multiplied as they are relayed, via the classroom, more widely through the public education system. The institutions of such "documentary" public culture then present a stronger case for government support than do those of subsidized culture, where the authors conclude openness may mask social closure. Conversely, Bennett, Emmison, and Frow find the idea of *public versus private consumption* an important organizing feature. The Chicago Group's work on *formal and informal modes of cultural participation* provides another rich continuum, and what is unique about this study is that the informal modes are clearly more important in understanding cultural action and that the "body" or performative, documentary levels of involvement here are equally intertwined. In this area of participatory research, the international museum movement is definitely in the vanguard. A recent pilot project at a museum of natural science used ubiquitous computing instruments to map museum goers in their interaction with an exhibit, and to customize the "navigational" content provided for each user.[68] The potential richness of such observational data in the design of exhibitions and the understanding of cultural engagement is mind-boggling, and it is fair to say Canadian policy-makers are on the brink of a quantum leap in the amount of information about cultural participation available—but perhaps advancing in a rear-ward formation when it comes to understanding why it is important or what it means.

Clearly, studies of participation are looking for changes in orientation to cultural activities, and increases and decreases or substitution across types of activities. Principal here is the idea of the emergence of mediated consumption of culture—on line, or by other means. Here Canadian arts researchers have a fairly robust set of data banks. Technology has had a marked impact on use of free time, but still more than half of leisure time is spent on cultural pursuits. But the big news is the drop in participation rates for over half of thirty listed activities.[69] Reading, borrowing, music, or festival participation—even museum or art gallery attendance—went down between 1992 and 1998, but zoos, gardens, and nature parks rose, as did visits to historical sites and public art galleries.

There are sharp regional variations in patterns of participation, and it is only in Quebec where there is a marked preference for the performing arts.[70] Spending on cultural goods and services over the period slightly outpaced growth in other household spending (four percent over three percent). Yet not since 1992's *Canadian Arts Consumer Profile* has consumption of mediated cultural activities been analyzed for its relationship to supplanting or supporting cultural participation: and here, the relationship may not be negative.[71] In other words, depending on the access to the kinds of television available, such pursuits can increase consumption of cultural goods, as we can see from the Quebec precedent. The veracity of this finding sorely needs to be tested, in view of the massive investments in culture-on-line projects, which surely deserve evaluation of their impacts on participation rates.

Perhaps one of the most interesting ideas to emerge in looking at the changing modes of participation arises out of the *Reggae to Rachmaninoff* study, and a few other American ones, which note a *"local" preference in modes of consumption*: a retraction geographically in where one wants to experience a live performance. In this view, the opportunity to experience local social networks is a good predictor of participation, suggesting even major metropolitan organizations should develop touring in their suburbs.

Connecting Policy and Participation

Cultural participation as a policy tool may be said to have arrived when a researcher can find it as one of the key societal indicators used by Canada's Treasury Board as an indicator of the strength of a community. Treasury Board is unabashed in the liberal-humanist goal that participation should broaden experience, introduce new ideas, and encourage understanding.[72] The four main measures they use to "track progress" on community strength are: attendance at heritage institutions, attendance at performing arts, use of reading, and access to technology such as the Internet. The inadequacy of these indicators is obvious. One is also tempted to ask: what happens if there is no change in participation rates? A further retraction of cultural spending? Or conversely, a reward of those whose participation rates are the highest? Such sweeping policy implementations of cultural participation as a benchmark in the study raise Foucauldian nightmares of what may happen in a new Martin/Liberal Party regime.

There are a range of policy initiatives which have undertaken participatory strategies, and it is instructive that the most well-developed and practical seem to stem either from the local level, or from the level of the arts organization. Over the decade since the early studies of cultural participation[73] there has been an explosion of practical marketing primers on how to gather intelligence on audiences, build them, and design participation strategies at the micro level, but no breakthrough at the macro level.

Grassroots initiatives like the Oregon Art Commission's effort to build community cultural coalitions leading to a successful cultural trust being established by the State Legislature begin by asking: what do citizens want the cultural life in the community to be? They then ask how best to realize this vision, and how to remove barriers to cultural expression. If explicit goals are set to increase participation (for example, among at risk youth) then the policy planners must conceptualize how various quantitative indicators (spending on programs for youth at risk) and qualitative indicators (youth perception of quality of cultural life, satisfaction with programs) may be employed to benchmark progress.

From a planning perspective at the organizational level, cultural decision-makers have identified that they are faced with three main ways they want participation to change. They may want to *broaden participation*, to *deepen it* (by serving fewer but in a more frequent or intense manner), or to *diversify participation*—that is, draw in new audiences (for example, as in the case of the Harlem Nutcracker cited by Moore). It is instructive that this sort of Harvard Business School case analysis is of course American. Unasked is how should cultural participation improve? Why would Harlem have to meet the Nutcracker, anyway? What are the ethical and democratic objectives?

Cynics may question why policy-driven studies of participation (*Accounting for Taste, the Canadian Arts Consumer Profile*) often legitimate a broad ambit of popular participation in the arts and heritage and in the services of the cultural industries, but may also rationalize a contraction in state cultural spending in neo-liberal times. Why? In the Australian case only professionals or those who have completed a tertiary level of education favour public subsidy for "the arts." Manual workers and those with primary education are less likely to support state funding (and less likely to use state-funded cultural activity). Nonetheless, fractions of Australians with less formal education do indeed participate in forms of public culture, and the possibility of converting these "light users" of public culture to supporters of public arts policy is rarely explored in participation studies.

Despite the empirical proof that cultural activity, or participation in cultural associations may not lead to "affirmative cultural citizenship." there are sufficient grounds[74] to conclude that cultural participation is a basic building block for cultural citizenship but not a synonym for it. The critical need is to understand the tools citizens need to have before we can say they have the capacity to participate, to recognize that not all participation is equal, and that participation and place is increasingly important in its construction.

However helpful early efforts may be in thinking through patterns of cultural mobilization analogous to democratic or political participation, the defect is of course that there is not the same summit: what would be the cultural equivalent of the exercise of the democratic franchise in our current representative system during elections, equal, free, and informed? Or how may citizens' assemblies or alternative direct democracies provide the ground for cultural "votes?" Or can we conceptualize of such a value summit, such a democratic rendezvous over cultural governance?

Perhaps it is because I am writing from British Columbia, where the first national experiment with a citizen's assembly is underway, that this idea of creating a model to understand and evaluate cultural citizenship has become quite important. In fact, many of the local grassroots coalition approaches to building cultural participation, presuppose the creation of such citizens coalitions or assemblies (for example in Oregon) but do not reason through either the *representative function*, the *deliberative one*, or the *accountability one*. Yet we know that there are important issues for citizens' juries to evaluate. They routinely rule on matters of community standards of taste, or offensive content in certain of the cultural industries, or oppose censorship of certain books on school boards or conversely, serve on municipal councils as advisory arts committees, or other sorts of "deliberative" bodies making planning decisions which effect cultural outputs. They may even be asked to advise on intractable issues such as hate and intercultural conflict in the implementation of the dark side of the new national security policy.[75]

Yet we know little about this process of cultural judgment making, or conversely, what contributes to the predisposition to cultural action, and direct participation in "votes" with collective consequences. In some utopian views, cultural citizens even, some day, may participate in the International Criminal Court where crimes such as cultural genocide may routinely be tried—with fundamental social consequence for all nations. Or conversely, social justice agendas may bridge from social to natural worlds, enjoining the problems of cultural sustainability to environmental sustainability. Certainly there is something in the Nordic model of cultural participation which routinely functions as democratic and political reinforcement of everyday life, but it is notably poignant that few scholars or practitioners yet can identify it. Yet researchers must address these and other gaps in order to understand how cultural governance contributes to creative and sustainable communities in all their complexity.

Conclusion

As this chapter has argued, there may be more heat than light in policy talk about the concept of cultural participation. There most certainly remains a disconnection between cultural participation research and cultural policy. We are as yet not clear on what policy interventions most profitably increase the quantity and quality of cultural participation. Part of the problem is the lack of consensus over a *cultural capital, cultural diversity*, or *cultural rights* based approach to cultural policy frameworks (or perhaps an even better alternative?) which imply very different goals in cultural participation measurement.

For practitioners, there are signs of faint hope. There have been a number of exciting cases of "better practice"[76] studies in measuring cultural participation, from the international *Everyday Cultures Project*, to the Work sponsored by the Wallace Foundation, to Canada's very own Ethnic Diversity Survey underway. Yet many of the studies are cross-sectional, ad hoc efforts to "map" cultural participation, without modelling it. Where models are developed (for example, in *From Reggae to Rachmaninoff*) they seem crudely borrowed from behaviorist American political science. The studies are not conducted over time, they do not conceive of cultural capital, and they rarely address issues defining cultural competence, cultural mobility, or its collective benefits. They are certainly not grounded in a theory of cultural citizenship. A new consortium of practitioners, theorists, and policy-makers is needed to design research and develop the concept of cultural participation as a basic building block of cultural citizenship, an indicator in policy evaluation, and to better connect policy to participation. This chapter argues that a research agenda on cultural participation must include the following:

1. A deepening of Gilles Provonost's "meta analysis" of cultural participation studies in Quebec and across Canada which reviews principal contributions using a wide array of methods, and in particular, addresses the critical exploration of what Provonost calls the "cause and effect link" between intervention by public authorities and popular participation.
2. The design of a longitudinal cultural participation study which identifies the capacity to participate, the predictors of participation, and the evaluations of the personal, social, and future cultural participation based on the *Everyday Cultures Project* model conceived of by Tony Bennett, John Frow, and Michael Emmison conducted in Australia.
3. A focus on educational and cultural policy intersections: what citizenship/curricula best advance cultural awareness, knowledge, capacity, and participation?
4. A generation agenda: why do successive studies show different patterns of cultural participation and openness to multiculturalism by age? What implications does this have for citizenship, cultural participation, and social change?
5. A more critical political agenda: what forms of cultural association/participation lead

to "pro social" political attitudes, mobilization on cultural issues and exercise of the democratic cultural franchise for collective cultural governance?

Perhaps the biggest challenge facing such a consortium is simply to prove that research in cultural participation matters and can be effectively linked to cultural policy studies. However important the theoretical interventions of the *Everyday Cultures Project* and a myriad of others on cultural participation, they raise more questions than they answer. Gilles Provonost is not alone when he states that the "cause and effect link" between intervention by public authorities and popular participation is not established.[77]

Does that mean policy makers can afford to ignore cultural participation in their bid to "get on with it?" Not likely. But it does place a high priority on co-ordinating efforts to design, develop, and evaluate cultural participation studies in this country and around the globe. The worst thing in the world is to have the audience all in their seats, but cultural policy-makers without a clue why they are there, or what the performance should be about.[78]

Notes

[1] For a fuller review of cultural research methods, see Kim Schroder, Kirsten Drotner, Stephen Kline, and Catherine Murray, *Researching Audience* (London: Arnold, 2002).

[2] Dr. Mark Schuster argued in favour of a narrower definition at the UNESCO International Statistics Conference held in Montreal in October 2002, but acknowledged the populist thrust to broaden definitions as a popular force will not abate.

[3] How do we define culture? In Canada, we exclude sport and nature activities from the definition of participation. This has gender effects, but it also flattens understanding of the interaction of participation and its flow through these parts of everyday meaning. The Eurobarometer study (a face-to-face survey of 16,000 Europeans conducted in 2001) includes sports and natural recreation activities in their definitions of cultural activities to yield a participation rate. Among Canadian policy-makers, the holy trinity of heritage, arts, and cultural industries still raises hot infighting about appropriate definitions, languages, and values (with heritage often the poor sister).

[4] http://www.pch.gc.ca, 2003-04.

[5] Gilles Provonost, "Statistics in the Wake of Challenges Posed by Cultural Diversity in a Global Context: a Review of Surveys on Cultural Participation" (2002), 3.

[6] Colin Mercer, *Towards Cultural Citizenship: Tools for Cultural Policy and Development* (Stockholm: Gidlunds Forag, 2002), 5.

[7] Michael Moore, *Rethinking Participation: A Framework for Change* (New York: Wallace Foundation, 2003).

[8] Mercer, *Towards Cultural Citizenship*, 7.

[9] Amareswar Galla, "Culture in Development: Subaltern Perspectives" (paper presented to the *Stockholm + 5 Conference*, Swedish National Commission for UNESCO, Stockholm, May, 4, 2003), 4, cited in Mercer, *Towards Cultural Citizenship*, 9–11.

[10] Henry Milner, *Civic Literacy: How Informed Citizens Make Democracy Work* (Hanover, NE: Tufts, 2002), 16.

[11] Simon Szreter, "A New Political Economy: The Importance of Social Capital," in Anthony Giddens, ed., *The Global Third Way Debate* (London: Polity Press, 2001), 290–99.

[12] Sharon Jeannotte, "Just Showing Up: Social and Cultural Capital in Everyday Life," chap. 9 in this volume.

[13] Jane Badets, Jennifer Chard and Andrea Levett, "Ethnic Diversity Survey: Portrait of a Multicultural Society" (study prepared for Statistics Canada, 2002, catalogue number 89-593-XIE), available at http://www.statcan.ca/english/freepub/89-593-XIE/free.htm.

[14] Milner, *Civic Literacy*.

[15] There is a certain tautology to Putnam's theory, however, as Milner argues. If the main attributes of social capital (associational density and interpersonal trust) also explain how social capital comes to be built up and depleted, then attribution of causality is difficult. Rather than the abstract term social capital, Milner argues the better term is civic engagement. Milner, *Civic Literacy*, 18.

[16] Russell J. Dalton, *Citizen Politics* (New York: Seven Bridges Press, 2002), 45.

[17] Francois Matarasso, *Use or Ornament? The Social Impact of Participation in the Arts* (London: Comedia, 1997), cited in Jeannotte, "Just Showing Up."

[18] Ibid.

[19] Dick Stanley, "The Three Faces of Culture: Why Culture is a Strategic Good Requiring Government Policy Attention," chap. 2 in this volume.

[20] Environics, Social Cohesion Survey (2001), http://www.pch.gc.ca/special/dcforum/pubs/opinion_e.cfm.

[21] A single cross-sectional survey of 2756 adults published in 1999, the *Everyday Cultures Project* is now underway in Britain, and is being considered in a number of other countries. Innovative for its blending of statistical agency and academic interests, the project is a useful exemplar for Canadian policy-makers.

[22] Tony Bennett, Michael Emmison, and John Frow, *Accounting for Tastes: Australian Everyday Cultures* (Cambridge: Cambridge University Press, 1999), 268.

[23] Alaka Wali et al., "Informal Arts: Finding Cohesion, Capacity, and Other Cultural Benefits" (study conducted for the Chicago Center for Arts, June 2002), http://www.artspolicy.colum.edu/researchreports.

[24] Sidney Verba, Kay Lehman Schlozman, and Henry E. Brady, *Voice and Equality: Civic Voluntarism in American Politics* (Cambridge, MA: Harvard University Press, 1995), fn. 9.

[25] Pierre Bourdieu, *Distinction: A Social Critique of Taste* (Cambridge, MA: Harvard University Press, 1984).

[26] Bennett, Emmison, and Frow, *Accounting for Taste*, 10.

[27] Ibid., 8.

[28] http://www.artspolicy.colum.edu/pub.html.

[29] Mercer, *Towards Cultural Citizenship*.

[30] The problem is the following: is the debate over cultural capital replaying the debate over education of the 1950s? Mass education is intended to contribute to middle class mobility, and ratchet up the gifted from the poorer classes, but has, in many regimes, failed miserably given the contraction of state spending.

[31] Tony Bennett, "Transversal Study of the Theme of Cultural Policy and Cultural Diversity" (paper prepared for the Council of Europe's Study on Cultural Policy and Cultural Diversity, February 2000), 62–63.

[32] Badets, Chard and Levett, "Ethnic Diversity Survey," 589–93.

[33] Greg Baeker, *Cultural Policy and Cultural Diversity in Canada* (prepared for the Council of Europe Study on Cultural Policy and Cultural Diversity, 2000), citing Tator and Henry on democratic racism.

[34] Nan Weiner, *Making Diversity Work* (Toronto: Carswell, 1997), 35.

[35] Richard Florida, *The Rise of the Creative Class* (USA: Basic Books, 2002).

[36] Such a "global" class fraction is not new: it stems from early studies by Armand Mattelart, Manuel Castells, and Saskia Sassen.

[37] Stuart Cunningham et al., "From 'Culture' to 'Knowledge': An Innovation Systems Approach to the Content Industries," chap. 8 in this volume.

[38] David Held, *Democracy and the Global Order: From the Modern State to Cosmopolitan Governance* (Stanford, CA: Stanford University Press, 1996).

[39] United Nations Educational, Scientific and Cultural Organization, *Universal Declaration on Cultural Diversity*, Article 1.

[40] Ibid., Preamble.

[41] Catherine Murray, "The Third Sector: Cultural Diversity and Civil Society," in Nancy Duxbury, ed., "Making Connections: Culture and Social Cohesion in the New Millenium," *Canadian Journal of Communication* 27, no. 2 (special issue) (2002): 331–50, citing UNESCO.

[42] Verba, Schlozman, and Brady, *Voice and Equality*.

[43] Dalton, 33.

[44] Jane Jenson, *Mapping Social Cohesion: The State of Canadian Research* (prepared for the Policy Research Network, Ottawa, 1998), 30.

[45] The *Final OECD Report of the International Adult Literacy Survey* (2000), xiv.

[46] Karl Rosengren, ed., *Media Effects and Beyond: Culture, Socialization and Lifestyles* (London: Routledge, 1994).

[47] Bennett, Emmison, and Frow, *Accounting for Taste*, 265.

[48] Ibid., 233.

[49] Ibid., 268.

[50] Ibid., 187.

[51] Henry Milner, *Civic Literacy: How Informed Citizens Make Democracy Work* (Hanover: Tufts University Press, 2002).

[52] Marie McAndrew, "Changes in Canadian Educational Policy and Integration of Young Immigrants," *Horizons* 5, no. 2 (2002): 6–9.

[53] Environics, "Social Cohesion Survey," http://www.pch.gc.ca/special/dcforum/pubs/opinion_e.cfm.

[54] http://www.pch.gc.ca/progs/arts/pubs/research-culture/al_e.cfm (site now discontinued).

[55] Bennett, Emmison, and Frow, *Accounting for Taste*, 217.

[56] Kirsten Drotner, "Global Media Through Youthful Eyes," in Sonia Livingstone and Moira Boivill, eds., *Children and their Changing Media Environment* (Mahwah, NJ: Lawrence Erlbaum Associates, 2001), 289.

[57] Catherine Murray, Roger de la Garde, and Claude Martin, *Starwars: Canadian TV Fiction in The Eurofiction 2000 Report* (Florence: Council of Europe, 2001).

[58] Bennett, Emmison, and Frow, *Accounting for Taste*, 221.

[59] Provonost, "Statistics," citing Olivier Donnat, *Les amateurs, enquête sur les activités artistiques des Français* (Paris: ministère de la Culture, 1996).

[60] "Canon" here is not intended to retreat to a universalizing, Eurocentric vision of a singular "high art" place of appreciation. Canon may be much more complex. But it refers to a "body of knowledge" or "cultural facility in interpretation" which is crucial to the study of cultural participation.

[61] As has Olivier Donnat, cited in Provonost, "Statistics," 70.

[62] See, e.g., the *About Canada* series.

[63] Verba, Schlozman, and Brady, *Voice and Equality*, 16.

[64] "Every Day Cultures Project," 3.

[65] Carol J. Greenhouse and Roshanak Kheshi, eds., *Democracy and Ethnography* (Albany: State University of New York, 1998).

[66] http://artsusa.org.

[67] Bennett, Emmison and Frow, *Accounting for Taste*, 242.

[68] See the "Echo" Project, Ron Wakkary, Marek Hatala, Kenneth Newby, Dale Evernden, Milena Droumeva, *Interactive Audio Content: An Approach to Audio Content for a Dynamic Museum Experience Through Augmented Audio Reality and Adaptive Information Retrieval* (paper prepared for Museums and the Web 2004), http://www.archimuse.com/mw2004/papers/wakkary/wakkary.html.

[69] Lucie Ogrodnik, *Patterns in Cultural Consumption and Participation* (Cultural Statistics Program of Statistics Canada, December, 2000).

[70] Ibid.

[71] Decima Research and Les Consultants Cultur'inc Inc., *Canadian Arts Consumer Profile 1990-91: Findings* (May 1992).

[72] http://www.tbs-sct.gc.ca/pubs_pol/sipubs/comm/comm1_e.asp#con.

[73] See, for example, the 1992 *Arts Consumer Project*.

[74] Bennett, Matarasso, Jeannotte, and others.

[75] http://www.canadianheritage.gc.ca/progs/multi/pubs/police/practice/page5_e.cfm, April 2004.

[76] It is premature to argue that "best practices" have been reached.

[77] Provonost, "Statistics."

[78] Other helpful sources include Benjamin Barber, "How to Make Society Civil and Democracy Strong," in *The Global Third Way Debate*, Anthony Giddens, ed., (London: Polity Press, 2001); Bill Bulick et al., *Cultural Development in Creative Cities* (prepared for Americans for the Arts, available at http://www.americaforthearts.org, October 13, 2004); Diana Crane, "Cultural Globalization from the Perspective of the Sociology of Culture" (prepared for the UNESCO International Statistics Conference, Montreal, October 2002); Mark A. Hager and Mary Kopczynski, "The Value of the Performing Arts in Five Communities: A Comparison of 2002 Household Survey Data for the Greater Metropolitan Areas of Austin, Boston, Minneapolis-St. Paul, Sarasota, and Washington, DC" (prepared January 31, 2004), available at http://www.urban.org/url.cfm?ID=410941; Jane Jenson, "Place Sensitive Citizenship: The Canadian Citizenship Regime until 1945," in Dirk Hoerder et al., *The Historical Practice of Diversity* (New York: Berghahn Books, 2003), 221–39; Will Kymlicka and Wayne Norman, "Return of the Citizen: A Survey of Recent Work on Citizenship Theory," in Ronald Beiner, ed., *Theorizing Citizenship* (NY: State University of New York Press, 1995), 283–315; Catherine Murray, *The BC Arts Consumer Profile* (prepared for the British Columbia Ministry of Tourism and Culture, Cultural Services Branch, 1994); Simon Szreter, "A New Political Economy: the Importance of Social Capital," in Anthony Giddens, ed., *The Global Third Way Debate* (London: Polity Press, 2001), 290–99; Statistics Canada, "Profile of Languages in Canada: English, French and Many Others" (2001 Census), available at http://www12.statcan.ca/english/census01/Products/Analytic/companion/lang/contents.cfm. The following Web sites may be helpful: http://www.artservemichigan.org; http://www.wallacefoundation.org; http://www.oregonartscommission.org/pdf/culturaldev.pdf; http://www.ozco.gov.au; http://www.policyresearch.gc.ca; http://www.policiesforculture.org.

Part
II

Voices

4.

The Chameleon-like Complexion of Cultural Policy:
Re-educating an Octogenarian

John Meisel

There are two kinds of fools.
One says, "This is old, therefore it is good."
The other says, "This is new, therefore it is better."[1]

Research in the cultural sector sometimes invites a cross-over mode of scholarship: it must be methodologically and theoretically rigorous while at the same time it benefits from an understanding of, and perhaps even empathy for, culture. Its "science," in other words, ought also to reflect the aesthetic world of the arts. Accordingly, this chapter adopts a format not normally associated with the dry mode of scholarly reports. It seeks to preserve some of the flavour of the original oral presentation—an art form—with a reasonably disciplined exploration of certain facts and propositions.

Situated somewhere mid-point between a cyber-peasant and a wannabe-geek (closer to the c-p than the w-g), I eschewed power points but resorted to the (to me) daring innovation of using overheads. I shall occasionally reproduce these here in a form echoing the original atmosphere of my message. This vestige of what is to many an archaic mode of communication fits perfectly my status as a mature student seeking to come to terms with emerging realities—the leitmotif of my presentation.

A careful perusal of the literature provided to the participants of the colloquium on *Accounting for Culture: Examining the Building Blocks of Cultural Citizenship* revealed to me not only that what I understood by "culture" was a far cry from the meaning espoused by the pre-conference intellectual leaders, but also that there was widespread inconsistency and ambiguity with respect to the vocabulary of the discourse.

The most effective way of grappling with this situation seemed to be to trace my own peregrinations through the cultural landscape and then bring the fruits of what I have learnt from them to bear on the conference agenda. In some ways, therefore, this is a fragment of what the Germans call a *bildungsroman*.

Figure 1

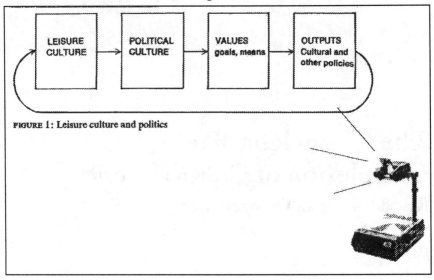

FIGURE 1: Leisure culture and politics

Figure 2

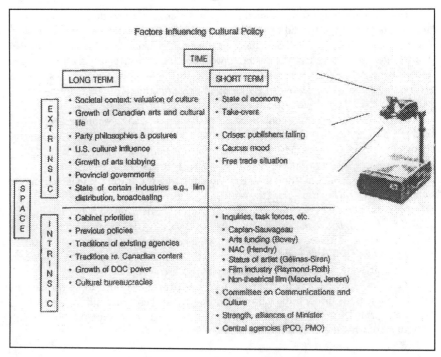

A political scientist and political sociologist, I first ventured explicitly into the cultural area in 1974 by urging my professional colleagues to recognize that an important relationship existed between politics and culture—leisure culture, as I defined it at the time.[2] The schematic presentation was simple but surprising to my professional colleagues.

The underlying assumption was that cultural experiences have an impact on one's general values, including those related to politics. Thus culture affects, through one's normative predilections, how one evaluates political phenomena and how one makes political choices, including voting decisions. These in turn determine the make up of governments and hence, as the feedback loop indicates, the stance taken by the state towards leisure culture, including the arts. The resulting cultural policies in turn have an impact on one's values, and so on and on and on.

A few years later, as chair of the Canadian Radio-television and Telecommunications Commission (CRTC), I became deeply immersed in communications policies and particularly in the broadcasting sector of the newly dubbed "cultural industries." Cultural nationalism—an approach I found congenial—was a burning issue affecting many of the arts and permeating a great many of the Commission's decisions. These affected popular culture more extensively than "high" culture but had a strong bearing on both. When I returned to the academy after my stint as a cultural regulator I wrote a lot and taught courses exploring government involvement in the arts.

A typical exercise was a review of cultural policies when Flora MacDonald was the responsible minister in the Mulroney cabinet. This 1988 paper, "Flora and Fauna on the Rideau: the Making of Cultural Policy,"[3] sought to map the societal, political, and administrative factors influencing cultural policy in Canada. Even a casual perusal of Figure 2, which encapsulates its scope, shows that by cultural policy I meant the government's position vis-à-vis the arts and the cultural industries.

At about the same time, an analysis I did of the cultural scene in Canada and its policy context, the title of which was inspired by one of Northrop Frye's classic papers,[4] appeared in an American book whose tell-tale subtitle was "Government and the Arts in Europe, North America and Japan."[5] In the subsequent ten years, and beyond, I wrote and taught about cultural policy, *always* meaning by the term what governments do (or not do) to support the arts. The context was usually that of high culture although occasionally I would venture into the popular field. My approach has been "arts-centric," a perspective I since discovered to be suspect or even unacceptable to some of the current students and practitioners of cultural policy, including important movers and shakers of our colloquium.

Figure 3

The late 1990s brought about a rude awakening. Three publications, whose covers are portrayed in Figure 4, graphically tell the story.

Each of the three works, while, to different degrees, allowing that culture has something to do with the arts, attaches a central place in cultural policy to decidedly non-artistic factors . Readers familiar with the literature will immediately recognize the volumes, respectively, of the first United Nations Environmental Scientific and Cultural Organization (UNESCO) Culture Report in 1998 and in some respects, the kindred exploration of culture and development by the Council of Europe in 1997. Some will also greet another old friend—the proceedings of the Canadian Cultural Research Network's (CCRN's) 1998 colloquium, edited by Catherine Murray.

The subtitles convey which way the wind was blowing. Whereas the volume containing my late 1980s paper included the words "government and the arts" in the subtitle (see Figure 3), the UNESCO and Council of Europe tomes' explanatory captions highlight *markets* and *development*, whereas Murray's focuses on *social change* (see Figure 4). My initial assumption that the de-emphasis on the arts and the shift to something else resulted from the well-known inbred mind-sets of UNESCOcrats and EUROcrats received a jolt when I realized that some Canadians had also adopted the new meaning. Not only Catherine Murray's work, but also Sharon Jeannotte's showed this, although almost all *operating* Canadian cultural organizations still saw their central *métier* as the arts. There seemed a divergence between bureaucrats and critics on the one hand, and creators on the other.

Jeannotte's Report from the Second Annual International Conference on Cultural Research in New Zealand bears the highly significant title *Fractured Discourse*[6] and observes that "cultural policy and cultural policy research are currently undergoing a paradigm shift of major proportions."[7]

It was clear that my long established and deeply rooted view of what cultural policy was all about was not universally shared and that other perceptions were abroad. Was the position I thought I had acquired more or less with my mother's milk (or after having digested the Massey Report[8]), and held unthinkingly ever since, outdated? If I were to

---

Figure 4

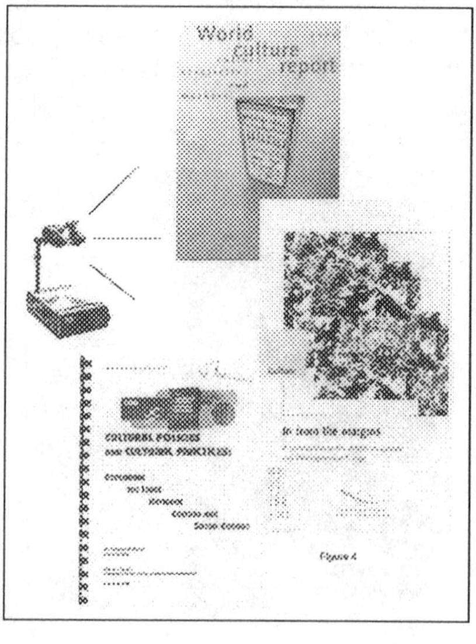

remain on speaking terms with my colleagues, did I need to embark on a steep learning curve and did I need to dive into a severe regime of retrofitting?

To answer these questions I started to peruse a good deal of the relevant literature and, particularly, as the opening of this colloquium approached, the rich material prepared for it. I entered into lively exchanges with their authors, usually through e-mail or the telephone. Greg Baeker was a generous, indeed an inexhaustible and indulgent helper who, through personal exchanges and his Web-seminar did his utmost to set me straight. But I did not stop there. A very large number of people deeply immersed in the cultural sector, in various jurisdictions, and holding diverse ranks, shared with me their understanding of our universe. Lest they become tainted with a tarnished brush, I shall not name them here but note that their backgrounds are in the creative world, the bureaucracy, granting agencies, and the academy. A lot of schmoozing has gone into this chapter!

The upshot of all this palaver was that while I was not willing to abandon my basic view of the nature of culture and of cultural policy, I did need to broaden my definitions somewhat and to learn to explore are as *related* to the traditional meaning of culture and the arts. It became apparent that a deep chasm exists between various views of what is meant by culture and about what the purposes of cultural activity should be. At the core of the debate, or more accurately of the often unexamined and un-addressed Babel-like profusion of meanings, is the question: "what is the raison d'être of cultural policy?" One camp sees support for artistic creation—arts policy—as the focal point. Others view cultural policy in a much broader context concerned with community cultural development and assisting individuals to be empowered, fulfilled citizens. The former places the highest value on aesthetic results, the latter on social goals.

The difference is nicely highlighted in the following episode, one of several similar ones I have encountered. The conference planners sent out invitations to some members of the cultural community suggesting themes for a "virtual" pre-conference discussion. One proposed topic was identified as "Rebuilding the case for culture at a time when old rationales no longer hold." One recipient categorically asserted that the old rationales are as valid as ever. The rationales hold: it is the policy responses to them that require examination.

The incident pinpoints a state of affairs that cannot be swept under the rug: a strong, persistent thread in conference literature (and elsewhere) is that support for so-called "arts-centric culture" has lost its legitimacy. But, on the other hand, there are also numerous creators and others who vehemently disagree. To many, a cultural policy which is not "arts-centric" makes absolutely no sense.

Two Cultural Models

Other issues have of course been identified as requiring scrutiny. Many of them are tackled in these pages. But, to my mind, how we define culture and the relative importance we attach to various forms of cultural expression are of absolutely central relevance and make an inescapable starting point for a discussion of the matters addressed in this volume.

Given the heat likely to be generated by what follows, a word of caution is in order. You may consider it unnecessary, but those who think it superfluous are usually most in need to be reminded of it. Virtually all of us—and this certainly includes your author—become imprisoned by our mental universe, by our customary system of thought, which is perpetually reinforced by our like-minded associates. This is especially so in circles which seek to promote or defend a particular cause. The cognitive straightjacket reduces our capacity to see and read developments realistically and may also lead to an inappropriate choice of instruments chosen to further a project we wish to promote.

In the cultural universe, there are naturally numerous positions and divergences of opinion among and across students, policy-makers, practitioners, and even passive folk just enjoying the fruits of the available goodies. I dwell here on only one area needing clarification because of its primordial importance. It turns, as I have noted, on what some see as the incongruence or even antithesis between artistic creation and community or social goals. The difference is complex and finely nuanced. For the sake of exposition I have reduced it to a simple dichotomy of Weberian ideal types, naming each after its champions. They are:

1. Arts-centred *traditionalists*, and
2. Society-focussed *innovators*.

In what follows I describe, in perforce simplified form, some virtues (+) and liabilities (-) of each and then seek to ascertain how the two stack up against one another. They are laid out in Figure 5.

Figure 5

Figure 5

TWO IDEAL TYPES
(1) Traditional

(+)	(-)
Arts centred	Only partial coverage
	Libraries ? archives? literacy ?
Quality focussed	
Sucessful	Circumscribed reach
western canon	
post-Massey Canada	Only partial response to demographic change
Strengthens national identity	
other face of globalization	Aloof from social context
	Structural rigidities (admin., org'l.,
Enjoys legitimacy	inadequate linkages)
pleases key	
constituency	Top down
Top down	

(2) Innovative

(+)	(-)
Social issues centred	Imprecise definition
	What is covered ? what is
Egalitarian	not?
Addresses some failures of (1)	May undervalue, short change, arts
Responsive to technological	Divert arts towards intrumentalism
and demographic	
change	Beggar traditional canon
Compatible with globalization	Dumbing down of arts
Exciting intellectual quest	Lack of fit with current structures
Raises critical questions	Urban bias
Bottom up	Bottom up

The Arts-Centred Traditional Ideal Type: Plusses

We begin, in the top half of the figure with the traditional (or my) view of culture and cultural policy. The left-hand column lists the positive features of this perspective and the one on the right enumerates what is seen by some as the down side.

The traditionalists' quintessential position is its unflinching and overriding focus on the arts and their dominant aesthetic promise. The *sine qua non* of cultural policy must be support for the arts. Traditionalists, often seen as elitist, also place strong emphasis on high quality performance. "Their" culture has produced the Western canon, not only in literature but also in the plastic arts, music, and architecture. Domestically, it consists of the artistic achievements foreshadowed and facilitated by the Massey Commission and then subsequently supported by the all-important Canada Council. It has become inseparably, but by no means exclusively, associated with the notion that Canadians have the right, and need the opportunity, to express their experiences, sensitivities, stories, pictures, and music in their own way and in a manner that suits their shared national and particularly their regionally and locally relevant experiences. It is deeply rooted in the British and French traditions, but more recently has started to respond vigorously to the riches of our new demographic cornucopia. The artistic community prizes it increasingly as United States and global influences tend to occupy Canadian space and markets and as some of them threaten to crowd out indigenous voices. Much of Canadian culture and cultural policy thus become linked to the question of how Canadians define themselves collectively and how they view their own identity, or identities. This aspect is increasingly relevant in the face of globalizing pressures engulfing the world.

Both the Western canon, and Canadian cultural works, have acquired awesome legitimacy and are considered in Canada and abroad as the highest forms of our artistic achievement and of our civilization. They are admired and accepted as towering and lasting treasures, branding our civilization. As such, they are internalized and loved deeply by numerous individuals and groups, if not always by huge majorities. They engage mature and older people more than they do youngsters.

As their respective labels imply, compared with pop and folk culture, the traditionalists' culture has a top-down, rather than a bottom-up quality, in the sense that it does not always spring up spontaneously from the people. Some of it does, but much also emerges as the result of stimulation and support from important institutions like powerful religious and secular organizations, often including the state. This has meant, over the years, that considerable emphasis was placed on the arts measuring up to the highest standards and maintaining criteria established by a cosmopolitan and international milieu of experts.

The Arts-Centred Traditional Ideal Type: Minusses

The first item noted in the top right-hand quadrant of Figure 5, listing some problems of the traditionalists' position, refers to the scope of what is normally embraced by culture. In addition to the puzzling and awkward grey zone between crafts and arts, there is the question of the appropriate niche for various activities and experiences arising from what might be termed the para-literary domain. Libraries, archives, questions of literacy come to mind. The last-named, in particular, invites comparisons between the definitions used by traditionalists and those of the innovators. To what extent should cultural policy concern itself with the collection, storage of, and providing access to written or pictorial records, literary works, plays, etc., and should it cover the teaching of skills needed to utilize them? Where does cultural policy end and some other policy field begin?

Traditionalists are also found wanting by some with respect to the degree that "their" culture fails to speak to certain sections of the population. For diverse reasons, among them the need to bring an experienced and sophisticated eye or ear to certain art forms, if they are to be appreciated, traditional culture is perceived by some as being elitist. It certainly appeals to some people more than to others, and thus has a circumscribed reach. Among other things, the income, schooling, age, and ethnic origin of potential participants sometimes introduces social distinctions between the cultural community and others, causing it to be seen as elitist. This aspect, among others, can produce political obstacles to government support for culture. "Cultural abstinence" by young age cohorts in particular, and some ethnic and linguistic features, have been particularly important in triggering calls for a re-examination of the appropriate scope of traditional culture in contemporary society. Some of these arise from the realization that there is reticence about spending public funds on activities of interest only to some sections of the population, although this restraint has seldom been applied to non-cultural areas awash in public subventions.

A related criticism follows from the fact that it is usually the old, well-established and even privileged groups in society who are most involved in traditional culture and that the latter is slow in adapting to new demographic realities. Culture is seen as catering to the old elites and to speak little or not at all to new groups emerging, often at the margins, of society. Recently very considerable steps have been taken in Canada on many fronts to compensate for this past tendency but, in the eyes of some, much more is needed, including the re-definition of what is meant by "culture" and "cultural policy."

Traditional cultural policy, as has been suggested, is intended to enhance the presence, quality, and availability of works of art in various forms. Its primary focus is the quality of what emerges from it, not the socio-economic conditions of the practitioners. While most "traditionalists" no doubt recognize that cultural works depend in some way on their socio-economic contexts, issues and policies related to the latter are deemed to be the responsibility of programs and agencies other than the cultural ones, who are better qualified and endowed to deal with them. This aloofness or seeming insensitivity is deemed a major failing, and constitutes one of the most important distinguishing features of the "Traditional" and "Innovative" camps.

An emerging, more fluid, conception of what constitutes the arts is causing strains within the cultural community. Among the many manifestations, those related to libraries and archives noted above, as well as museums, are particularly evident. Most contemporary cultural institutions are expanding their horizons and are engaging in activities which exceed their former mandate and spill into related areas. This leads to overlap of responsibility among various operating, controlling, and regulatory agencies, as well as to conflict and jurisdictional dispute. The heritage and industry ministries, the CRTC, museum corporations, the CBC, and other involved agencies within the central governmental apparatus or as various arms-length bodies, are all in the game, but their roles are not always clearly defined with respect to the cultural sphere. One of the consequences is that pressure is rising for the re-definition of the cultural sector and of the respective responsibilities within it. Calls for an enlarged conception of culture therefore arise because of new realities in the art world and in the institutions traditionally and newly involved with it.

I noted above that the top-down quality of the traditional arts contributes to their living up to generally recognized standards. But there may also be disadvantages: elitism, particularly when not handled sensitively and responsibly, can lead to lack of concern for certain individuals, groups, interests, and even art forms. Some traditional cultural institutions give an aloof or even snobbish impression which is deeply off-putting and which severely restricts their reach.

The aforementioned broader perspective of the innovators leads them to define culture less narrowly than the traditionalists. They see it very much in its social, political, and economic contexts and therefore are less arts-centric. Their position can, in fact, be described as being social issues oriented, rather than being arts driven. It is not too far-fetched to assert that whereas for the traditionalists, culture is the independent variable, with all other aspects being dependent on it, the innovators make social factors the independent variable; the arts are dependent on, and secondary to it.

The Society-Centred Innovative Ideal Type: Plusses

The linking of social issues to the cultural area is not only its most characteristic, but also the most commendable feature of the society-centred innovative model. It is also, as we shall see, one making it vulnerable. By linking culture to the social conditions which affect its content and nature as well as how it is received, the innovators operate within a more holistic setting than the traditionalists and they consider more seriously how various cultural artifacts are perceived and "utilized" by members of the public. Furthermore, they shed light on how the artistic and aesthetic phenomena affect one's general condition of life, how one is socialized, perceived by others, and how one relates to them. The present volume provides numerous examples, and specifically explores cultural citizenship.

Because it exceeds the traditional framework of "arts culture" and embraces so much more, including creative activities that have little to do with the canons of aesthetics, the innovative model is far from being elitist. It is, therefore more accessible and egalitarian. It does so at a price, but it does it. Its social reformist impulses also make it more sensitive to some of the implications of rapid social change. Its scope, therefore, includes art forms and activities which appeal to Canadian newcomers more than to established groups, and to younger cohorts who are entirely comfortable in cyber-space and the art forms associated with it.

As noted earlier, the traditional arts in Canada are often infused with national consciousness and with Canadian nationalism. This is in some contrast to the new approach of the innovators and its greater inclusiveness and potentially greater appeal to recent arrivals. The latter encourages links between Canadians of varied ethnic origins and similar groups in other countries. This affinity and the intercourse it facilitates make Canada more adaptable to a globalizing planet. Thus cultural policies facilitating the development and empowerment of ethnic minorities are likely to enhance Canada's compatibility with the new globalizing realities.[9]

The challenge the innovators present to the traditional definition of culture confronts the cultural community—and others—with a series of important and exciting issues crying to be tackled by thoughtful and concerned citizens. Critical dilemmas are at stake, of equal importance to the artistic world and to civil society. The differences of opinion before us are a salutary invitation to pose questions about the nature of society, the place of the arts in it, and the place of public policy in their resolution.

We have noted the egalitarian nature of the society-based perspective and its eponymous emphasis on the societal dimension of the arts. Unlike the more elitist school it is, therefore, a bottom-up phenomenon in which policy often arises as the result of societal needs and not because of governmental priorities intended to bring about some desired public good or because of the demands of cultural elites. This, while also offering hazards to culture, prompts desirable public policy with consequences going a long way beyond the arts.

The Society-Centred Innovative Ideal Type: Minusses

A major problem of the society-centred definition of culture is that it is exceedingly broad. By so closely linking arts policy to socio-economic conditions it moves way beyond the sphere of the arts and embraces all of society. Cultural policy, therefore, in this perception, is involved in income levels, standards of living, social adjustment, citizenship, the economic, social and psychological status of various groups, etc. The new definition is not only impractical but also poses immense problems of clarity.

At the present time, federal cultural policy is predominantly under the aegis of the Department of Canadian Heritage. If culture were defined according to the optic of the society-centred innovators, it would have to fall under virtually every ministry; cultural policy would then also become social policy, economic policy, and policy for everything else affecting the population.

The broader definition, in other words, makes the term "cultural policy" meaningless. Its adoption would create administrative chaos not only in culture but throughout government. It is only a small exaggeration to argue that cultural policy would have to cover everything—all ministries combined would have to form a super cultural portfolio.

Furthermore, when the arts are lumped together with numerous other fields, their importance is likely to become watered down. Their unique character, contribution, and needs may consequently be undervalued and short changed. Since its champions tend to be less numerous, and involved in areas eliciting less heart-rending cries for assistance than others (health and poverty, or regional economic catastrophes, for instance), they are in danger of being crowded out in the intensely competitive struggle for government attention. A purely arts-centred organization is more likely, therefore, to field effective spokespersons than bodies in which the arts are merely one of several competing interests. There is indeed the question of whether the umbrella-like character of the Department of Canadian Heritage is not in danger of diluting its arts portfolio. Being responsible for sports, heritage, citizenship, and multiculturalism inevitably means that the Arts Policy Branch must compete with other players for funds and the attention of the minister and senior interlocutors. The reorganization which created the Department may, therefore, have unwittingly placed structural obstacles in the path of champions of the arts.

Loosening and extending the meaning of culture, and including para-aesthetic activities in its orbit, may also lead to the neglect and beggaring of the traditional canon. Voices among the advocates of a less restricted view of culture all too often include those denigrating the legacy of dead white European males, as if the storehouse of classical culture had become irrelevant. This is, of course short-sighted, if not blind, madness. This is, to me, ridiculous, and the dismissal, in some of the pre-conference literature of arts-centric policies as being irrelevant, strikes me as plain silly.

Efforts to endow culture with a substantially wider appeal are timely and welcome, but they may come at a cost. If they lead to the dumbing down of the whole enterprise, they may end up being more destructive than helpful. The contrast between serious historiography and storytelling is instructive. While both are important, to impoverish the former for the sake of the latter is counterproductive in the long run. While extending the reach of the arts is salutary, to do so at the expense of their depth and integrity is not.

At the practical level, the innovative model also poses some serious problems. If cultural policy were to concern itself not only with culture as it is generally understood, but also with the improvement of the human condition, it could not be the responsibility of a single department like the Department of Canadian Heritage. As was noted above, virtually all government activities and agencies would have to become involved and a completely new administrative structure would be required. This could, of course, be achieved in due course, but the teething problems would be immense, and the consequences for all policy areas incalculable.

There is a strong presumption in much of the innovative literature that cultural activities and processes are essentially urban, even metropolitan. The rural and small town dimension receives short shrift. This is not a fatal or irremediable failing but one that, in the short run at least, impoverishes the case for a revised approach.

Finally, as I observed above, the bottom-up character of the society-centred model, while making it more inclusive and egalitarian, also courts the downgrading of quality. To excise the nasty elitism of tennis, as someone said, is to take down the net.

Reconciling the Opposites?

Where does this grand tour of the world of culture leave us? What have I learnt from it? My scoreboard (Figure 5) reveals that although there is a fundamental difference between the concepts of culture of each approach, the two nevertheless complement one another in several ways. In a sense, the innovators' culture compensates for some of the weaknesses of the traditional model, and vice versa. My original impression that the society-centred perspective should be categorically rejected has been replaced by the view that it offers some useful correctives. But it needs to be clarified and contained.

The society-centric approach makes culture more widely accessible than the arts-centric one, and encourages a closer link between cultural (aesthetic) concerns and the general well-being and effective functioning of society. Traditionalists, on the other hand, strengthen the emphasis on creative artistic activity of a high order, and seek to ensure that the arts-context will be nourished and not overlooked in the pursuit of more mundane goals.

Now, it is clear that the two are in a sense mutually exclusive and that government can adopt either one or the other of the approaches. But remember that, for the sake of exposition, I here presented ideal types which, by virtue of this, represent extreme positions. In the real world, it is possible to modify each and so arrive at a definition of culture and of cultural policy which to some extent embodies characteristics of both. I can espouse the innovators' cause if it can be achieved without degrading effective arts support. Similarly, if traditional arts policy can enhance social well-being, I can only applaud.

I have the impression—and it is at this stage no more than that—that the extent to which the two spheres mesh depends in large part on the scope of the activities involved. It is more difficult to embrace both orientations at the level of *grande politique* when big and complex projects are at stake than to fuse arts- and society-centric programs at the smaller and more intimate community level. It is an intriguing question why the size and complexity of the activity should affect its character and type. Considerably more research than is now available is required for an understanding of this phenomenon.

The Fusion Model

Several months after I presented the original draft of this chapter to the colloquium, I stumbled upon a deliciously apposite example of what, for lack of a better term, we might call the fusion model—a meeting ground of the two perspectives. It illustrates and reinforces the tentative impression just noted. I would likely not even have noticed its significance had the colloquium not prompted the educational odyssey reported in this chapter. And "stumbled" is the *mot juste* under the circumstances. On one of my periodic post-prandial visits to the Agnes Etherington Art Centre at Queen's (it happily lies between the University Club and my office), I was astonished to find its imposing atrium resemble a Bedouin settlement breaking camp. Only it was not tents that were being dismantled but stalls, exhibits, and installations. This was the parting KISS, so to speak, where the acronym stands for a daring project of the Kingston Arts Council, called Kingston In SightS.

Ten artist-facilitators each worked with a community group to produce art in a variety of media, always starting off with photography and always relating the artistic content to the group's nature, interests, location, or preoccupations (see Figure 6).[10] In all cases art was the point of departure reaching out and permeating the following community groups: vendors (and hence also producers) at the famous Kingston market; Barriefield community—a one time picturesque village, now part of Kingston; construction workers; Kingston collectors (of anything); funeral directors; former federal prison inmates; residents in a well defined area; a neighbourhood close to the downtown core, called Swamp Ward; users of a local park; a native community with its dance and drum tradition, as well as others; and a group of street people. The groups worked

Figure 6

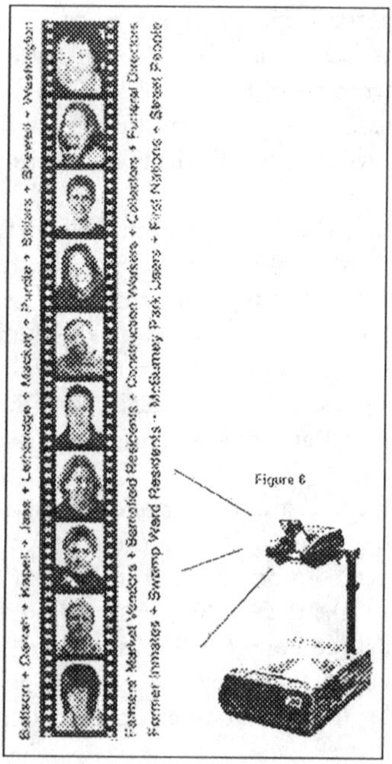

together for a long period of time until they presented the results of various forms of community art-making at the exhibition and during a discussion forum. Many of the multi-media productions ranged widely across the boundaries of traditional and emerging art forms.

A *retrospective*, fascinating, lavishly illustrated, forty-eight-page catalogue was produced on CD, months after the event (see Figure 7).[11] It could not, of course, be assembled until after all the pieces of the ten projects came together and were presented at the Agnes Etherington atrium. Ian Hodkinson, retired professor of art conservation and KISS project director, in the preface to the catalogue encapsulates how this planned happening is a prototype of our fusion model. "KISS," he writes "is aimed at developing community awareness through art and awareness of art throughout the community."

The venue of the "performance," "exhibition," or "presentation," is exceedingly interesting and illustrative in the context of the present discussion. The culminating event was held at the Queen's Gallery, but not as part of its normal program or in its principal galleries. Since it was not curated (if that's a word) by the gallery it was not, strictly speaking, a gallery event and it was not announced in the gallery literature. Its site in the atrium—a sort of grandiose ante-chamber—physically attested to the somewhat marginal status of something neither quite fish nor fowl, but an exemplar of the emergent fusion model. The venue had become a metaphor for the event. While it was not the sort of initiative for which Canada Council support would have been sought, it was a community-based, arts-centric undertaking.

Several of the artists involved have high reputations and the event benefited from support from the Ontario Arts Council and, *mirabile dictu*, from the otherwise notoriously philistine City of Kingston. The KISS project involved a large number of

Figure 7

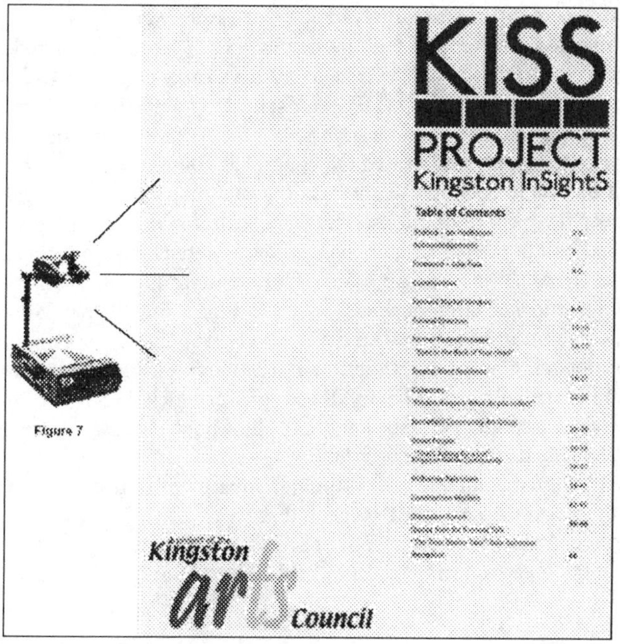

individuals and groups and the exhibition and forum were very well attended. It was deemed a huge success by the Kingston Arts Council and was welcomed by the gallery. It is, likely, the first of many future—and growing—collaborations between a traditional gallery and a community arts project. It is also a vivid illustration of a widely manifested contemporary phenomenon: boundaries of artistic and cultural activities are in a fluid state undergoing continuous change.[12] I have made much of it here because it is a wonderful example and illustration of the emerging new image of what constitutes a cultural event. Not, in itself, frightfully important in the great scheme of things, it serves here as a snapshot of just one development in the vast panorama of social and cultural change. For every KISS there are innumerable similar initiatives—perhaps not all of them so successful—attesting to the evolving and beneficial convergence of aesthetic and community-oriented human endeavours.

How to Tread Through a Profusion of Cultures

As we have found, the cultural community inhabits a vast tent, holding many tribes. I have identified two modal definitions of culture: the arts-centric and the society-focused. A third, mixed-perspective, emerged in the just-described fusion mode. It tends to be evident more at the community than at the national level.

Does the recognition of these types facilitate the formulation of appropriate and effective government policies and the creation of suitable administrative structures and procedures? I believe that it can contribute quite a bit, if certain practices and even principles are deduced from an examination of each model. It is these deductions which retain us for the remainder of the paper. They have their source in two quite distinct aspects of the case. The first is roughly laid out in Figure 5; the other arises from my subjective attitude to, and evaluation of, the cultural domain. Since both the scoring in Figure 5 and my judgment in this area are intensely personal, I make no claim for presenting some sort of pristine universal law but rather warn the reader that what is offered is one person's perception and guideline. That person has studied and thought about the issues involved for many years and from a variety of perspectives. In addition, he has from time to time descended into ("risen to" is actually the more appropriate term) the ubiquitous fray of cultural warriors, as a regulator, activist, and citizen. He has written extensively on a host of related issues and has come to adhere to his stance with some passion. *But*, he is as fallible as the next guy and offers views in a field notoriously guided by a deep diversity of opinions. The term "culture wars" carries many meanings.

The pivotal point of departure, unchanged by my intensive recent course of study, is that the *traditional creative arts* are sacrosanct. Our existence as civilized, mentally healthy, and alive beings and societies depends on their flourishing. Whatever enlargement emerges of the definition of culture—and there will certainly be some—it must not lead to the diminution of support for traditional arts activities. On the contrary, more is needed. Furthermore, in my vocabulary, these activities include not only music, dance, theatre, and plastic arts but also publishing and all of book culture, as well as the rest of the hazardously named cultural industries.

A number of *related cultural areas*—notably museums, archives, and libraries—are equally worthy players. Ways need to be found to fit them into a coherent and all-embracing policy arena in which overall approaches are developed to the needs of all participants. Both "creative" and "institutional" aspects must be covered.

Community Based Creative Activities also rightfully claim a place in the sun. They include such fields as architecture, archaeology, streetscapes, folkloric ventures, buskers, or the beautification of a variety of urban and rural spaces. They are as legitimate as the others mentioned here but may require a somewhat different institutional support system. And, since there is often a considerable overlap in focus and in the creative media employed, flexibility is of the essence. Individual cases to some extent command specific policy and institutional responses.

This massive (dare I say crushing?) panorama of activities and enterprises presents too lush and bustling a jungle to fall within a single policy framework. What we have, but need to refine, is a variety of policies and policy fora. The benefits of these to the cultural community and the public will be optimized if consistency, compatibility, and congruence are achieved among them, rather than if they exist at cross purposes. At the same time, individuality and variety are of the essence. No monolithic policy environment should or could ever be developed. But an appropriately flexible and congruent policy *setting* will protect and enhance creative Canada. To move towards the creation of propitious needed conditions requires that we see and understand the whole cultural situation in Canada and that we learn how the various parts can best interact. A great many useful programs are now in place and constitute a promising point of departure for a possible new inquiry. Their examination would become part of an inventory of the component parts and of a mapping of how they relate to one another.

The task involved would be colossal, requiring the mobilization of huge and well endowed human and monetary resources. It would, further, need the collaboration of a wide variety of actors, some of them seemingly marginal to culture. Since, insofar as public policies are concerned, federal, provincial, and local jurisdictions would have to become involved, all levels of government would have to be included. The ever-growing importance of the private sector in culture furthermore dictates that its participation also be scrutinized and guided.

We need, to put it in another way (and now you had better sit tight!), a new Massey Commission—one built on the scale recently associated with government inquiries into major national problems. I am not even sure that a royal commission or some such body will be best or whether a new creature ought to be invented—a joint public-private inquiry of a kind heretofore unknown and imagined by neither man nor beast. The recently created Council of the Federation might be approached as a possible partner in the cultural probe.

That is a very tall order indeed; so tall that one needs to approach it most cautiously and carefully. A gargantuan enterprise on this scale will require a careful and slow build-up. The time for its completion should be reckoned in many long years, if not decades. But unless a beginning is made nothing at all will happen. It is well to remember the Chinese saw that even the longest journey must begin with a single step. The CCRN might take the initiative in the early exploratory probes but need not be the prime catalyst. A helpful start would be to convene a workshop or conference of manageable size bringing together some of the principal interests: the CCA, the Department of Canadian Heritage, some homologous provincial organizations, the Canada Council, artists' organizations from diverse fields and regions, some leading arts personalities, and certainly people representing the arts-centred, society-oriented schools and the fusion model should be involved from the start. Experts on business links to the arts will be essential and, it goes without saying, representatives of the scholarly community must play a part. The challenge will at first be to ensure that the launching pad be small enough to get things done, and large enough to contain most of the principal interests.

Conclusion

The reader with a sense of shape and symmetry will be struck by our having come full circle. I embarked on an educational venture, a sort of refresher course, bringing me up to date on the current perceptions of the arts and of arts policy in Canada. While, as the foregoing shows, I have learnt a few things, I appear to be entering a new stage in my education, to be provided by another inquiry laying bare the facts and identifying future options.

In concluding my original paper at the opening of the conference, I was upbeat about the political environment in Canada. The federal Liberals had acquired a new leader, the Harris era was over, and the municipalities were beginning to flex their muscles. This, I thought, could become a promising time for the arts, if they made a strong plea for themselves. They had not, however, managed to put together a coherent, overriding case, and as I indicated at the outset, could not even agree on what was embraced by the arts and arts policy. I wistfully suggested, as my final slightly facetious thought, that "if we knew what we wanted, this would be a good time to go for it."

A little over half a year later, Canada looks quite differently, seeking to re-learn how to make the most of a minority government. While this situation may inhibit innovation in cultural policy, it can nevertheless provide opportunities. The Martin Liberals, while not attaching high priority to the arts, are considerably more concerned than the new Conservative party. The Bloc, on the other hand, and also the NDP, on whom the minority government will from time to time have to depend, have the best record of the parties with respect to the arts. There may be an interregnum in which the idea of some sort of re-invented Massey II might receive favourable attention. One never knows what initiatives may come in handy during the fluid deal-making associated with minority governments. Irrespective of that, a time will inevitably come when the cultural community will again be able to rely on solid public and private support. It will be well to start preparing for that day now rather than wait for the advent of a dazzlingly promising conjuncture of the stars. So I return to the earlier admonition and, more tentatively than before perhaps, again conclude by urging that we consider starting to go for it.

Notes

[1] Laurence J. Peter, cited in the "Thought du Jour," *The Globe and Mail* (September 14, 1999).

[2] "Political Culture and the Politics of Culture," *Canadian Journal of Political Science* 7, no. 4 (December 1974): 601–15.

3 John Meisel, "Flora and Fauna on the Rideau: The Making of Cultural Policy," Katherine A. Graham, ed., *How Ottawa Spends, 1988/89: The Conservatives Heading Into the Stretch* (Ottawa: Carleton University Press, 1988), 49–80.

[4] John Meisel and Jean Van Loon, "Cultivating the Bushgarden: Cultural Policy in Canada," in eds., Milton C. Cummings, Jr. and Richard S.

Katz, *The Patron State: Government and the Arts in Europe, North America and Japan* (New York: Oxford University Press, 1987).

[5] Cummings and Katz, *The Patron State*.

[6] M. Sharon Jeannotte, "Fractured Discourse: A Report from the Second International Conference on Cultural Policy Research—'Cultural Sites, Cultural Theory, Cultural Policy'" (prepared for the Department of Canadian Heritage conference, January 23-26, 2002). See also M. Sharon Jeannotte, "Singing Alone? The Contribution of Cultural Capital to Social Cohesion and Sustainable Communities," *International Journal of Cultural Policy* 9, no. 1 (2003): 35–49.

[7] Jeannotte, "Fractured Discourse," 4.

[8] Royal Commission on National Development in Arts, Letters & Sciences, 1949-1951, *Report* (Ottawa: Edmond Cloutier, Printer to the King's Most Excellent Majesty, 1951).

[9] John Meisel, "Human Rights and the Transformation of the Multicultural State: The Canadian Case in a Global Context," in K. Kulscar and D. Szabo, eds., *Dual Images (Multiculturalism on Two Sides of the Atlantic* (Budapest: Institute for Political Science of the Hungarian Academy of Sciences, 1996), 19–40.

[10] My purist self is now in a quandary. As you have noted, to remind the reader of the oral delivery in which the present ideas were first voiced, I have reproduced the overheads here accompanied by a little icon showing an old fashioned projector. Figures 6 and 7, however, came to my attention only *after* the colloquium and should, therefore, logically, not be accompanied by the projector. But, for the sake of consistency I have retained the image.

[11] Kingston Arts Council, Draft Retrospective Catalogue, KISS Project.

[12] Subsequent to the KISS exhibition, two shows in the Agnes Etherington Art Centre further attested to the ongoing broadening of horizons of traditional, arts-centric curators. One, "Art in Bloom," contrived by the Gallery Association of volunteers, invited florists and horticulturalists to "select works in the galleries and design floral creations based on them." Several artists were chosen, including some members of the Group of Seven and Rembrandt. The purpose was primarily to raise funds and bring in visitors to the gallery. The latter was more successful than the former. But there was no doubt that the aesthetic dimension met with great success.

The other exhibition, "Ah Wilderness! Resort Architecture in the Thousand Islands," was put together by a very imaginative scholar, Pierre du Prey—a professor at Queen's, well known for his important work on architecture in Canada and abroad. The exhibition was inspired by him and executed by him and members of one of his courses. The show recreated the life, history, and architectural legacy of the remarkable Thousand Islands.

Information on both these exhibitions can be found in the Agnes Etherington Arts Centre, *Currents* 20, no. 2 (Summer 2004).

A very handsome catalogue is available for the Thousand Island exhibition. It is entitled "Ah, Wilderness! Resort Architecture in the Thousand Islands" and is published by, and available from, the Agnes Etherington Art Centre, Queen's University, Kingston, Ontario, Canada. See also http://www.queensu.ca/ageth.

5.

Reframing the Case for Culture

ALLAN GREGG

Allow me to start with a confession. I am neither an expert on public policy or culture. Rather, it has been my lifelong interest in politics and the arts—and particularly music—that has caused me to explore alternatives to existing cultural policy and a different way to frame the case for culture. More specifically still, it was a growing concern that both politics and the arts are imperiled in today's environment that gave me impetus to venture into territory where common sense, if not expertise, would suggest I had no entitlement to explore. Over the last two decades, we have seen a systematic disengagement of citizens from public life.

As recently as 1984, over sixty per cent of Canadians reported that they had at least a somewhat, if not very favourable impression of politicians. Today, more Canadians believe Elvis is alive than hold that particular point of view. This disengagement is also reflected in not merely their attitudes but also in public behaviour and patterns of political participation. In 1984, federal voter turnout was 75.3 per cent. Since then we have seen a steady and systematic decline, to an all time low of 61.2 per cent in the 2000 election. Generationally, the pattern is even more alarming and suggests things will get worse, rather than better, over time. In the 2000 national election study conducted for the chief electoral officer, voters under twenty-five were only half as likely as those over forty-eight years of age to report a belief that voting was "essential" (twenty-four per cent versus forty-four per cent).

The state of affairs in the arts appears to be not one wit healthier. Not only does the average creator in this country earn under $15,000 per year, but if you ask the average Canadian what their priorities are for government spending, they routinely will tell you that funding for the arts and culture is at the bottom of their hit parade (it routinely wrestles for last place with foreign aid).

Anyone intimately involved in the sector however will know that the response of the "average" citizen masks deep differences within the total population on the deemed importance of public support for the arts and culture. While the wisdom of funding symphonies, book publishers, museums and their ilk may be lost on the braying masses, there is a whole legion of cultural crusaders, mavens, and volunteers who seem to spend a considerable part of their day marshalling the case and lobbying policy-makers on the essentialness of more funds for the arts. Indeed, while it is rarely in the forefront of public debate, there is an argument that no single issue divides elites and the general masses more than this question.

Yet as someone who has run numerous political campaigns, chaired film festivals and, as my failing hearing will attest, attended more rock shows than you can imagine, I have come to believe that the two endeavours are not unrelated.

The arts have the power to bring citizens together in a shared experience and sense of community. Politics give citizens the necessary expression to translate values into the kind of community we collectively seek. The question for me therefore became "could the decline in faith in our political process and the lack of support for culture, be related?" And more proactively, "Can culture be used to rekindle faith in politics?"

As far as we can tell, the decline in faith in political authority has its root in the late 1970s when the great experiments of post-war liberalism began to show some early cracks. The creation of a seamless welfare state failed to eradicate poverty, a collection of publicly-owned agencies and corporations were unable to deliver services or compete effectively with their private sector counterparts, and the limitless opportunities of the 1950s and 1960s began to shrink at the very same time that the public sector accelerated its interventionist activities. In its wake, governments were left with bloated deficits, taxpayers' discretionary income shrank as government revenues grew, and problems believed to be in the purview of government deepened and became more complex. As they looked to themselves rather than to government and government-sponsored solutions, this increasingly well-educated electorate became more efficacious and defiant. Their attitudes were further fuelled by a vigilant and aggressive press, with a greater emphasis on investigative journalism that routinely exposed the shortcomings, foibles, and missteps of our elected leaders.

As E. J. Dionne observed some years ago in *Why Americans Hate Politics*,[1] people were willing to tolerate a great deal of unpleasantness in politics when they saw the political process as productive. However, by the 1990s, Canadians had come to conclude that politics' productive capacity had virtually collapsed. By the end of the millennium, rather than look to government to guide the public interest, all that was demanded was that government become more "efficient." In the process, peripheral and non-essential government services and programs became not only the victim of spending cuts, but for many, actually associated as a handmaiden to the problems Canadians were experiencing.

For whatever their failures, however, politicians and governments have never lost their ability to read the shifting public mood and the temper of our times. Rather than defend them and paddle against the current of public opinion, politicians have fed this cynicism. Government has responded by scaling back the scope of its activities to correspond more closely to the public's reduced expectations.

Far from reversing the loss of faith in public institutions, giving the public what it asked for has simply reinforced the notion that politicians are venal and that governments are incapable of acting as positive agents of social change. The entire process has resulted in what Thomas Frank refers to as "the train wreck ideal": persuade the public that government is bad by giving them spectacularly bad government. Today, fifteen years of government responding to the lowered and cynical expectations of the public with lower and more cynical performance has served little purpose other than to excavate an even larger chasm between government and the electorate. Moreover, I would argue that there is a strong case to be made that governments in retreat have a deleterious effect on not just the quality of public policy but also on the quality of citizenship.

I asked Naomi Klein, author of *No Logo*,[2] the best selling screed against growing corporatism, for her opinion as to why a whole new generation of activists, protesting against everything from child labour practices to environmental protection to gay rights, chose to eschew politics, party, and parliament and instead channel their activism into single interest groups, non-government organizations, and other vehicles of so-called "civic culture." Her answer was devastatingly simple. She said that in her entire adult life she could not recall one government initiative that she admired and was proud of. Voters under thirty-five who share her passion for societal improvement feel that the State not only fails to share that passion, but actively aids and abets those who oppose them. Small wonder then that in the last federal election, seventy-three per cent of first-time voters in the province of Québec chose not to cast a ballot.

Even if you accept this analysis, it still begs another set of inevitable questions: "Why should we even care about this?" "Who wants to return to the bad old days of excessive government intervention and decision-making by elite accommodation?" "Are we not better off—more independent and self-reliant, less deluded—by coming to the realization that we had misplaced our faith in governmental authority and instead began turning to a new found reliance on ourselves?"

The answer is, of course, that when we come to view government and government initiatives as irrelevant, we cease to make demands on government to improve our lives and communities—we create an almost complete disconnect between the public and the output of public policy. Even worse, we lose the capacity to use ethical considerations to judge the output of government and how we are being governed. From there, it is a small step before we stop asking what kind of community we want and value. In the end, we cascade toward a society of meaninglessness.

Think about it.

Any poll I might care to conduct would find that Canadians, virtually to a person, report that they want homelessness eradicated, the environment protected, and disparities between the richest and poorest reduced. This being the case, how then do we explain the continued presence of the homeless in our midst; the systematic degradation of our environment and scare resources, the stunning accumulation of individual wealth in the face of heartbreaking third world poverty?

Given the reputed power of public opinion, why does government not respond to these wishes with concerted effort and bold measures? Even more curiously, if this is what the public wants, why do we not hear a hue and cry when these problems persist and become more intractable? The fact is that while these may be the responses given in polls, they are rarely heard in public debates or translated into direct demands on government for action. Rather, what we find is a public who has come to accept that the homeless are just "there," the deterioration of environment is accepted as part of the normal course of events, and the world is just "as it is."

Canadians—at least at an intellectual level—know what kind of community and society they want but seem to have stopped asking for it. Additionally, they have concluded that government is incapable or unwilling to produce the results they desire. Consequently, we not only fail to express these views, we have ceased to even frame these questions as part of our civic dialogue.

This is the cascading effect of turning our back on the government as the principal vehicle through which society's major aspirations are satisfied. It begins with cynicism toward our institutions, grows into indifference toward their outputs, and robs us of the desire to make ethical considerations an essential part of political debate. Rather than feel we have a kinship and responsibility to that homeless man on our street corner, we step around him. Our sense of and capacity for civic virtue has been eroded. Canadians may still view themselves as a "just person," but they have become "bad citizens."

It is against this backdrop that cultural policy is currently framed. The arguments in support of cultural funding however are many, varied, rarely coherent, and most often revolve around questions of which constituency within the arts and cultural community is in most need or who would benefit most from this support. Writers, painters, filmmakers and musicians argue that they need financial aid in order to create their art. Book and magazine publishers, film producers, and record companies make the case for tax-based assistance so that they can build an indigenous cultural industry that will create jobs, expose the Canadian creator community to the public, and keep the American cultural wolf away from our door. Public broadcasters, museums, and other cultural "spaces" espouse a variation on these themes and attempt to make the case that they are the necessary conduit through which the Canadian voice and Canadian stories can be heard and told, without which we would be unaware of our common history, land, and peoples. Rarely stated, but always implicit in these pleas, is the premise that Canadian culture (at least at this point in time) is not economically or commercially viable. Not even whispered, however, is the further admission that Canadians and the average citizen are not sufficiently interested in any of these forms of cultural expression to pay—either through their tax dollar or at the box office—the freight for our creator community, cultural industries, or the public institutions that exhibit and host cultural events.

Although I can hear my various invitations to exclusive film galas and gallery openings being ripped up as I speak, given the basic manner and form in which the case for culture is most often argued by the arts community, you have to ask yourself, "why would anyone expect otherwise?" The average Canadian is unschooled in the arcana of Rachmaninoff, Patterson Ewen or for that matter, even David Cronenberg. For their part, the cultural community does not seem to be overly concerned about this state of affairs. In fact, today, "great art," "serious music," and "true cinema" are not even deemed to be aimed at the mass market or suitable for consumption by the average Joe.

Yet the same cultural community that believes art is so essential that they ask the many to reach into their pocket to fund their pursuits also sees their art as suitable for only the few. It should be of no surprise to any clear thinking person, therefore, that the conceit of the defenders of culture is met by passive disinterest or active disdain by the very people who are supposed to subsidise the arts.

The fate of "low" art and the popular entertainment industry fares no better in the court of public opinion. If the aim of our book publishers, film producers, and record distributors is to create cultural products that will garner mass appeal, then the response of the taxpayers is "if the only benefits you generate are economic—either in the form of jobs or profits, I say good luck, but you're on your own. Why should I subsidize your industry any more than any other?"

By this point, my cultural friends have not only taken me off their guest lists, but have me pegged as a knuckle-dragging troglodyte. Pigeon-holing notwithstanding, the fact is that there is another and different case for culture that is available, and there is a credible argument that the population would support, and in the end, the creator community would actually benefit much more than it does under the current regime of endless subsidies and fruitless failures.

This view starts from a perspective that is normally absent from the current debate over support for the arts—namely, focus not on why cultural support is important for the various (cultural and non-cultural) constituency groups who are the recipients of funding, but ask instead, "What purpose does culture serve in terms of society and citizenship?" For example, there is no "rational," economic argument that a painter warrants state support any more than a plumber, for the intrinsic economic "value" of a painting is no greater than that of a toilet. The reason to support the painter and not the plumber therefore, is not for the painting that is produced, but for the effect that the painting has on the community. The effect, in turn, is to stimulate debate, create a common bond, inspire citizenship, and bring members of a community in closer proximity to one another—something a toilet can rarely do, but great art almost always does. In short, the "value" of cultural should not be measured as the end product of art but as the means by which art is exposed to and invigorates community life.

Viewed in this way, the worth we place on art, as a society, need not be measured on the basis of either its input costs (i.e., paint, canvas, labour) or its market value as a product (i.e., the price it may command for commercial sale) but in terms of its galvanizing effect on citizenship.

Similarly, it is all well and good to correlate the relationship of economic prosperity to cultural diversity (as the likes of Richard Florida have done quite convincingly), but the mere presence of a creative class alone offers no guarantee of greater community cohesion or civic virtue. In fact (as I'm sure many of you know) there is increasing evidence that many communities with the highest "bohemian indices" also score surprisingly low on measures of social capital. Indeed, the central focus of the original epistemological debates surrounding culture and citizenship that go back to the time of the Greeks demanded that creator and citizen must come in contact in a common sense of community. Why did the ancients create amphitheatres where politicians would hold court and spectacles would be produced? Why was the public square an essential part of the architecture of the earliest cities? Why did the Medicis build grand monuments to house the works of the artists they patronized?

The rationale for all these early initiatives to "support culture" was to enrich the democratic ethos—a rationale that seems to have been obscured in modern times. Today, public support for culture has been reduced to a necessary substitute for shrinking private philanthropy or the grist of one of many industrial policy options. The end result is that we are left with the State (and taxpayers) subsidizing private enterprise on one hand or propping up "high" culture, which cannot support a commercial audience in its own right, on the other. By weighing the primary task of cultural development on a scale which measures how well art is disseminated to the public, rather than funding cultural products as an end unto itself, the value of this endeavour can be evaluated and embraced in a different way. "How the hell do we put a price tag on that?" we might well ask. The answer, of course, is that we cannot. Once that conclusion has been reached, however, it is a small step to recognize that culture, by definition, is not commercial, industrial, or economic—any more than we calculate the costs of free speech, justice, or democracy. It is an essential ingredient of civil society and its cost is an essential part of citizenship.

The modern day rationale for reframing the case for culture in this way is rooted in the growing body of evidence concerning what is happening not just to the arts or to voter turnout but to the "social capital" of modern day western societies. Our propensity to "bowl alone" extends not just to the number of bowling leagues and teams but also to the frequency of family get-togethers, having friends over for dinner, memberships in parent-teacher associations, and almost any other group bridging and bonding activity that may bring citizens together into a sense of community. Television and the Internet, suburban commuting, two-career families, and increased mobility have all been linked to the diffusion of citizen contact and the increasing atomization of modern-day society.

More than a nostalgic harkening back to a better time, this research suggests that a growing social capital deficit leads to the erosion of mutual support, co-operation, trust, and institutional effectiveness. In a more optimistic way, the evidence also indicates that when citizens actually are brought in contact with one another towards a common cause or purpose there is less violent crime, higher educational performance, lower levels of teen pregnancy, better health, and even higher personal incomes.

This notion is neither revolutionary, speculative, nor new. De Tocqueville, almost two centuries ago, noted that when "a citizen ... isolate(s) himself from the mass of his fellows and withdraw(s) into the circle of family and friends, with this little society formed to his taste, he gladly leaves the greater society to look after itself."[3] Indeed, the entire hollowing out of our democratic institutions, loss of faith in political leaders and even declining voting turnout has been traced back to our less frequent social intercourse with our neighbours.

While I have very little doubt that these two things are related, I wonder whether the social capital theorists may have confused cause with effect. In other words, there is a very strong argument that it is not our increasing tendency to "bowl alone" that has led to our loss of faith in the political system, but instead, it is our growing cynicism about the utility of our governments and the effectiveness of our elected leaders that leads to our increasing isolation from one another, and to our reluctance to tackle the problems we share as members of a community.

Gathering together to satisfy human needs is, of course, the central integrating concept modern civilization has used to pursue collective goals and move society forward—it is nothing less than the basis and rationale for creating communities and governments. In fact, while you rarely hear anyone talk about it anymore, organizing ourselves into groups also has an ennobling effect on our individual character and behaviour. Jean-Jacques Rousseau eloquently made this point 340 years ago when he wrote The Social Contract:

> [T]he passage ... to civil state produces a very remarkable change in man, by substituting justice for instinct in his conduct and giving his actions the morality they had formerly lacked. Then only, when the voice of duty takes the place of physical impulses and right of appetite, does man ... find that he is forced to consult his reason before listening to his inclinations.[4]

An explicit part of the "contract" Rousseau immortalized was that in exchange for the benefits of community, we must voluntarily surrender some of the unbridled freedom we would otherwise possess if we lived apart. We erect a stop sign that delays our arrival to our desired destination, but we do so willingly ... to avoid head-on collisions.

As I advise clients or comment on current events, I am struck by how often people I otherwise admire, seem to give short shrift to this fundamental aspect of our social organization—that community, duty, and restraint produces not only more efficient results than we could achieve alone, but it also breeds better citizens and better human beings—that there is a moral imperative that forms the basis of our gathering together and not simply a utilitarian and practical one.

Culture viewed in a different way—from the perspective of the galvanizing effect it can have on our sense of shared experience, rather than as mere "products"—uniquely, has the properties required to be the glue that brings citizens together, and bonds them into a sense of community. And there are real life examples in the culture field already available that illustrate how this can happen—examples that afford an alternative perspective of how the State can support art to the benefit of not only the cultural community but to all Canadians.

In 1988, a young man named Cameron Haynes launched a film festival in, of all places, Sudbury. Against all odds and in the face of much skepticism from the film community, it became (in his words and in the estimation of virtually everyone I know who has attended) "an overwhelming success." Encouraged by the response of a community that had never experienced the opening of a Canadian film before, he started the northern film circuit in 1992. By coming to Toronto and getting film distributors to give him pictures, he took these movies (and often their directors—the likes of Atom Egoyan, Bruce MacDonald and Patricia Rozema) on a "tour" of centres such as Kirkland Lake, Timmins, and Sault Ste. Marie. In almost every case, the films sold out and the directors were treated as visiting royalty. He then did the same in southern Ontario in towns like St. Catherines, Woodstock, and Stratford. Today, the film circuit encompasses one hundred Canadian cities and has just been expanded to twenty centres in the United Kingdom. Forty new cities in Canada and eight in the United States are scheduled to join the circuit this year. Every year, since its inception, audience attendance has doubled and now totals a quarter of a million patrons. In Canada, twenty-eight per cent of attendees watch Canadian films. In the U.K. and the United States, the number is one hunred per cent. This compares to less than two per cent of commercial movie attendance in Canada and virtually nothing outside of our borders.

For years, Mr. Haynes received no government support for his efforts, whatsoever. Today, approximately fifty per cent—or $300,000—of his budget is state supported and the box office he generates earns the film industry $1,500,000 per year. Compare this to Telefilm Canada which spent almost $200 million last year to fund 782 feature, short, and documentary films which virtually no one saw. In fact, the economic effectiveness of the two approaches, while telling in its own right, is almost irrelevant to the point being made. The fact is that Cam Haynes's film circuit not only creates a real audience for Canadian films, it also uses arts and culture as a means to congregate Canadians together, and in doing so gives them a greater sense of sharing, common experience, and yes, citizenship.

So, does this heroic tale of success (for that is most definitely what it is) mean that every creator with a paint-brush or manuscript, or every budding cultural entrepreneur with a good idea or innovative business plan should be the beneficiary of state largesse? Not necessarily. The case for cultural democracy, while willfully non-economic, is surprisingly hard-headed when it comes to "who gets what, when, and how." By viewing art and cultural expression in terms of its effect on citizenship (rather than the constituency groups who are involved in the "products" of culture), the criteria for funding also become crystal clear. While I realize this is outright heresy for many, it is my belief that artists will create whether or not they have state support. In fact, I would submit you could pass a law banning artistic expression, and creators would still paint, sing, dance, and make films. Cultural businesses will survive based on their ability to find audiences for their products. The State has no need to support either the creation of cultural products or the overheads of profit-making enterprises.

If, in the end, the case for culture rests with its essentialness to community, then the beneficiary of cultural support must—either directly or indirectly—be the citizen.

This means support must be offered to citizens—like Cam Haynes—who aspire to be not just cultural entrepreneurs but also community builders, to volunteer-based groups who want to bring creators into their midst, and to public institutions who provide space for citizen interaction to take place.

In practical terms, it also means authors or publishers who want to host a reading series in senior citizen homes should be eligible for funding. The landlord who wants to put a revolving art installation in the lobby of his building should get support. Churches, schools, and recreation centres—public spaces that sit empty most times of the day— should have public moneys set aside to hold gatherings and discussions around art, music, and literature. Festival holders, concert promoters, museums, and libraries would be the principal financial beneficiaries of this new funding criterion.

And where would this leave our impoverished creators? First (and to address the issue of poverty), with a paying audience (if need be, subsidized by the State) to whom they can expose and sell their art. And even more importantly, in terms of cultural democracy, with a community that was immersed and surrounded by art, and over time, which would come to see our painters, writers, musicians, and performers as an essential part of its community rather than (as is so often the case today) as something tantamount to unworthy welfare recipients. And out of that community, I believe, would come not only better citizens, but real patrons of the arts, and real people who would better appreciate the meaning of art to their lives and who, in the end, would be far more ready to reach into their pocket in recognition of value they placed on the creators (nay, not simply creators, but now, neighbours) in their midst.

Far from reducing funding for the arts, these changes would involve significant investments in infrastructure, public spaces, and events that disseminate art and bring culture closer to the taxpayer. If I'm right, it would also produce a citizenry that places cultural funding not at the bottom of its priority list, but closer to the top.

In the end, this is a case not for retrenchment, but for cultural democracy—a public policy regime where instead of mimicking private philanthropy or aping industrial policy, public funding would be invested in communities, institutions, and organizations working to clasp art and citizenship to a single bosom.

Notes

[1] E. J. Dionne, Jr., *Why Americans Hate Politics: The Death of the Democratic Process* (New York: Simon & Schuster, 1991).

[2] Naomi Klein, *No Logo: Taking Aim at the Brand Bullies* (New York: Picador USA, 2000).

6.

Artists' Behaviour in the First Decade

Tom Sherman

Someone asked me what I thought of the idea of cultural citizenship.[1] The first thing I thought of was whether or not I belonged to a specific culture. I guess I could claim my birthright. If I were born and raised in a specific locale, I would have the right to participate culturally without inhibition, and hopefully with some sophistication, in the culture I was born into. If I inhabited that locale for a sustained length of time, my citizenship would undoubtedly be strengthened. If I decided to move or I was uprooted for some reason I would still carry the sensibility of my original culture forever.

If by chance I landed somewhere worthwhile and decided to invest in a new culture, I suppose I'd have to work harder than the locals to earn my new cultural citizenship. But I would already have an idea of what it's like to belong somewhere. I could apply my previous experience to my new context. I would be that much richer having two cultural identities. Eventually I would learn to blend my duality into something special. When I would travel the world I would have a choice of expressing the sensibilities of my first or second culture. Depending on my day-to-day position in transit, it would be interesting to see which citizenship made more sense in this place or that, with different kinds of people, or when I was alone in a foreign landscape. Even a couple of cultural citizenships can be confusing. Where would my allegiances lie?

In the first decade of the new millennium people are conflicted about a lot of things. Distances separate children from parents, workers from offices and co-workers, people from the landscapes they belong to. Everyone I know is networked in a profound way. The glue isn't a familiar place where everyone knows the rules and shares a water cooler, or a whiteboard, or a vegan menu. Telecommunications devices facilitate the connections that people make today. People connect through devices like telephones and computers, and speakers and screens, with the goal of eliminating the distance between each other.

Sure people still meet and press the flesh. Meeting people in person is great as long as you wash your hands frequently. There is still something to be said for a sense of smell and our rusty instincts. But in such unusually intimate circumstances people find it reassuring to be augmented by cameras, recording devices, and surrounded by all kinds of supplementary memory.

Flipping back to my thoughts on cultural citizenship, I suppose I have an opinion on such an abstract, slippery concept because I'm an artist. Artists are usually oblivious to the fact that they are out of their depth. Artists are very comfortable with the notion of cultural environments because they are obsessive, compulsive consumers of information. My eyes bleed and ears ring every third day. I'm a voyeur and I can't get enough of the things people say, and the way they dress and act and display their relationships with machines. That's my particular fetish: person-machine relationships.

As an artist, as a general rule, I never trust a sociologist,[2] or anyone who poses as one. I buy into the idea of cultural citizenship because as an artist I contribute to the cultures I am living in through my work. I'll even go so far as to claim special status as I participate far more than the average citizen. I take pride in my work, although most of the people who appreciate my efforts do so from a distance. I meet almost total indifference in my immediate physical environment. In fact, when I display my work locally it seems to make my associates very uncomfortable. They pretend I don't exist. Sometimes I'm happy to hear that most theorists agree that the meat body is disappearing in the digital age. I'm certainly uncomfortable in mine when people don't know how to respond to the things I make. Thankfully I'm networked to a string of kindred spirits residing in other jurisdictions.

I think the root of this indifference bordering on hostility has to do with my inability to accept thanks or the gift of art in return. I'm learning how to give and receive art, but I've been conditioned by the culture at large to be competitive. As an artist I go to great lengths to try to give back to a culture that steadfastly refuses my gifts. I vomit in the face of a culture dominated by industrial crap: the waves of violent, titillating cinema; the wasteland of totally banal formulaic music; the blanket of broadcast propaganda, state-issued or private. Our media environment is structured as a one-way, top-down, irreversible flow of manufactured instruction sets on how to act and look and feel and consume. Our radio, television, and newspapers invite our response, our participation in call-in, talkback forums, or letters to the editor or through text messaging or audience polls via the World Wide Web. This formal reversibility of the media, the apparent "interactivity" of the culture, couched as a utopian fantasy of true reciprocity, is nothing more than a repeated exercise in controlled feedback, a spectacle of cybernetic manipulation. The power always resides with the one who can give *and cannot be repaid*.[3]

But surely we can vote with our dollars, our consumer power, or ultimately through our indifference. After our letters to the editor are rejected or our calls put on hold—after our submissions by e-mail are acknowledged by avalanches of spam—we tend to pull back and withdraw. Who needs the rejection and subsequent harassment? Everyone knows the only feedback the media will accept is that which demonstrates obedience. Talk back to the media critically and you will face public humiliation. The audience is thus trained to accept a culture designed to be received by a polite, compliant populous conditioned to accept programming determined by the lowest common denominator. Pabulum for the pabulum eaters.[4]

As an artist I am left stranded with all those rejected by the predominant culture. Misery loves company. There are a great number of us. I understand that power always resides with those who can give *and cannot be repaid*, and admit that I am suspicious when people identify with and tell me they appreciate my work. My first instinct is to mistrust and reject positive feedback. If people can identify with and embrace what I'm doing, I fear it must be too close to standard fare. It is hard to be a good citizen when one is locked in such a double bind. I beg for attention and space in the culture, and yet when I get some respect I tend to want to bite the hand that feeds me.[5] This double bind used to inevitably shorten my relationships with curators and producers, but since I've shifted my work from objects and installations and the kind of things that make sense in relation to bricks and mortar architecture, institutions like museums and galleries have stopped being interested. I have made concept-based video and audio and performance art for over thirty years.

I have found institutions, most of the museums and galleries and broadcast media, to be dreadfully slow to evolve. I used to be ahead of my time. Now I'm smack dab in the middle of a burgeoning media culture supported by a decentralized infrastructure of networked personal computers. These computers are connecting people through opportunities to exchange art. Sometimes the screens are big. Sometimes they're small. Opportunities to display to audiences are suddenly everywhere. I'm finding it a lot easier to give and receive in this new environment.

Let me describe the media saturated world I'm living in. First, let me say I hesitate to use the phrase "new media" because it is a business term being used deviously to extend the reach of converging broadcast, publishing, communications, and security industries into our communities, our homes, and our personal gear. Saturation is the name of the game. There are only so many hours in the day. The "new media" bridge the gaps between movies, live performances, and recordings while in transit. Content is diluted so everything can be overlapped. We surf the Web while we talk on the phone. We listen to recorded music while we converse over ambient television. If we're not talking, we're doing something else with our mouths, like eating or drinking or smoking. Talking across distances is very popular. Talking while doing something else is as big as it gets. The more things we can do at the same time the better. High-density overlaps are a generational thing. Multi-tasking is the primary skill set of youth.

Camcorders, notebooks, downloading players, and personal digital assistants help us manage our information flow. All of these devices are getter smarter and have even begun "talking" to each other. People are getting so stressed out managing their personal information; they have to take a break from time to time. Video games offer an escape. Video games are immersive. They demand our complete attention. That's the limiting factor with the interactive forms; you can't do anything else at the same time. Camcorders are different. They transform live experience into opportunities for documentation. Your immediate world is cloned in real time, appearing in the camcorder's LCD screen while it is being recorded. We can save our experiences for later on. With our computers we can organize our recordings, mixing and matching downloads and streams, and shuffling files to make something new out of ordinary experience. When you double your experience, you can end up with a lot of unmanageable time. These information appliances are turning us into very stylish librarians![6]

Today's personal media environment is the hot turf of contemporary art. The idea of the pro-sumer, the complete synthesis of the *pro*ducer and con*sumer* of information, fostered by Japanese consumer technology firms in the 1980s, is now fully realized. Well-equipped individuals are producing and moving information around at unprecedented rates. Artists are bypassing anachronistic institutions such as museums, galleries, broadcasters, and publishers. Individual artists manage to compress pre-production (research), production, distribution and exhibition, once discrete and specialized time-consuming functions, into the same week. Middlemen and middlewomen everywhere are being cut out of the loop. Artists are aligning themselves strategically into co-operative groups. Co-operation replaces collaboration in an effort to conserve and enhance personal autonomy. Playing in parallel beats compromise.

There is little money involved at ground zero in the twenty-first century information economy. The rush is in the open exchange of information. Art, like science before it, is now functioning as a gift economy.[7] One's status among peers is based on giving away things that are useful to the community. Science has been a gift economy of ideas for a long time. Scientists *give* papers and openly share research findings, hoping to make significant, lasting contributions with their "gifts." The scientist who contributes the most to his or her field is held in the highest esteem. Scientists have been able to sustain their gift economy because institutions like universities and research institutes have supported them.

Artists have been supported by different kinds of institutions. Museums, galleries, and publishers "commodify" art by being selective and exclusive. There is a collective, open-source mission in every art scene, but these institutions force so much redundant, unattractive, competitive behaviour. Arts councils have been better at supporting art as a gift economy. Governments have tended to spread their funding across a wider spectrum of activity, mainly because public officials tend to get in trouble when they interfere with businesses trying to make a buck. The number of practicing artists has exploded over the past three decades, and the proliferation of digital media art (video, photography, animation, interactive installation, net.art) has increased the volume and circulation of contemporary art to a whole other level. Institutions still trying to function as gatekeepers are moving too slowly and will never catch up with the excellent work swirling through regional and international gift economies.[8]

Universities have been busy credentialing artists with M.F.A. degrees and most recently through Ph.D. studio/theory programs. The art gift economy is now composed of a mix of university-based artists and independent, institutionally unaffiliated artists working day jobs as designers, technicians, computer programmers, cooks, waiters, carpenters, models, etcetera, etcetera. Young artists have always done whatever they needed to do to support their art habit. Digital media art scenes are trans-generational. The unknown mingle freely with the notorious. What you've done in the past doesn't matter as much as what you're doing now. The technology and media are ubiquitous and inclusive. International work is freely exchanged in shows, screenings, and festivals. Local scenes make use of artist-run spaces, ad hoc-quick hit galleries, vacant storefronts, music clubs, community centres, cafés, restaurants, and bars (any "third place" between work and home). On-line shows link any variety of third places with homes, libraries, schools, and wireless laptops.

Despite the efforts of universities, museums, and publishers to privilege a select group of professional artists, in fact the speed of change and complexity of activity in the digital media arts sector is having a leveling effect on all active participants. Reputations are hard to maintain when the technology is evolving quickly and the territories and jurisdictions are fluctuating between popular culture, underground art, technosocialism, and the expansive hybridity of recombinant aesthetics. Cultural citizenship today must be established through local commitment and presence, along with simultaneous international initiatives and recognition abroad, technical competency, increasingly refined media literacy, punctuated by occasional successes in expanding audience by crossing-over into the spotlight of pop culture.

A university education will definitely help one stay afloat in such a complex world, but degrees in themselves will not insure professional status. Everything rests with accomplishment in the arts, and with the digital media arts you are only as good as your latest work. Media art history is sketchy and poorly known. The DIY (do it yourself) culture holds the sophisticated amateur in the highest esteem. As sexy trends and the sheer velocity of change undermine the notion of professionalism, young artists emerge very quickly, self-taught, self-promoted, self-screened, and self-streamed. Information on how to be a digital media artist is abundant. The tools of the trade are everywhere. Is it really possible to be a folk artist in the information age?

This elevation of the amateur and the devaluation of professional status are in line with relentless attacks on the elitist status quo launched repeatedly by the avant-garde throughout the twentieth century. Marcel Duchamp's initial attack on retinal art, Dada's spirited critique of the bourgeoisie, the ridicule of abstract painting by the nouveaux realists, the anti-establishment message of Fluxus, and conceptual art's assault on object-based art have taken their toll on the status of the individual creative genius and the institutions that perpetuate this myth. Andy Warhol and Joseph Beuys, extremely prominent artists in the 1960s, both proclaimed that everyone is an artist and that anything can be art. Warhol went so far as to state that he wished he was a machine (and not an artist). Beuys, in his sermons on social responsibility, said everyone, in all walks of life, was obliged to be creative. Art could no longer be separate from life. This rhetorical bravado signaled the dawn of a post-modern chaos that has now spanned five decades and shows no sign of abating. Artists have enthusiastically embraced this black hole of freedom (absolutely anything goes) and have recently dumped the whole delicious mess into a transcontinental blender called the digital revolution. Total fragmentation doesn't begin to describe the current state of affairs.

To close I would like to touch on the idea of cultural citizenship in this era when institutional, economic, and aesthetic order in the arts continue to collapse. Artists will lead their societies into a future where the consumption of art and culture is balanced with real creative output by a majority (not a minority) of its citizens. Artists will be respected as skilled managers of information, not individual creative geniuses, and art will be seen and valued as information. Artists will no longer be defined by medium or discipline. They will work with media appropriate to the task at hand. Practically everyone works with a computer these days. When the problems or opportunities call for different technologies or media, artists will adapt and alter their approach accordingly. National borders will continue to fade, but exact geophysical positions will be as crucial as dates and times in defining point of view and intent. Global positioning systems (GPS), and Geographic information systems (GIS), will anchor psychological, social, and spiritual exposures physically and statistically. Artists will continue to think locally and globally. Regionalism will be redefined as micro-regionalism. Contemporary art history will be tracked like the weather is today, by information scientists, using computer models to predict the near future. Museums, galleries, publishers, and broadcasters will keep trying to ride out the storms.

The gap between personal and industrial culture will continue to widen. Corporate and government media will hammer away at social and psychological anomalies, attempting to control perception and ideology cybernetically.[9] Artists, in the broadest sense of the profession, will respond with combinatorial play, playing in parallel, improvising with recombinant strategies. Power will reside with the one who gives and receives in equal measure. Initially these human "transceivers" will be heavily mediated, simulated, and virtual, but registered and tracked by micro-region. Security issues will slow real social change. Mediated behaviour can be tagged with less risk. The psychologists, sociologists, and economists will get their data. Corporations and governments will attempt to maintain their gag orders on artists through the enforcement of copyright law. Gordon B. Thompson, the renowned engineer and theorist at Bell-Northern Research, once told me "copyright is theft."[10] He knew that intellectual property law would be used to sew up the media environment, restricting the two-way flow of information by preventing reciprocity of manipulation (i.e., talking back to the media using the actual media environment as the subject and substance of discourse). Consumer rights advocates ultimately defending the rights to personal autonomy, free speech, and privacy will protect the personal media domain.

Collage, in visual art, and montage in cinema, set the stage for sampling and the remix in music. Video, the supreme reproductive technology of the twentieth century, has been incorporated into the twenty-first century's maturing digital media forms whose principal advantage is endless reproducibility without loss of quality. Digital, non-linear editing has engineered the increasing use of repeat structures in audio and video. "Phrases" of images and sound are recombined to establish the form and substance of video compositions. The analogies for all digital media are minimalist musical structures, or more profoundly genetic recombination, where the building blocks of DNA are reassembled in seemingly endless combinations to yield the diversity of life. The recombinant aesthetic strategy is environmentally friendly in that it permits the recycling of used mediated content into fresh new permutations of message.[11] The finished work of art is a thing of the past.[12]

Artists' behaviour in the first decade of the twenty-first century is characterized by a desire to interact in tight local communities, rubbing shoulders through exchanges in gift economies, in two-way, back and forth exchanges, whether these exposures[13] are comfortable or not. The analogy of collective, open-source programming is transformed into a prescription for social change. These exposures, live and mediated in degrees, or mediated across distances through networks, will be most effective in the long run if registered by micro-regional origins (GPS, GIS data: exact time and place). Tracking and measuring the volume and describing the nature of the flow will yield important insights into the psychology and behaviour of artists. The practice of recombinant aesthetics will permit a direct, critical discourse with a toxic industrial media culture, and foster a healthy disregard for corporations and governments attempting to repress this discourse.

The concept of cultural citizenship will only be useful if the public understands and embraces it. The first question artists will ask is whether or not they belong to a specific culture. Time and place, in this era of dematerialization, dislocation, and alienation, are extremely important. Being able to get and keep one's hands on the actual substance of the media environment, to probe, reconfigure, and cleanse the ether of this place, is crucial.

Notes

[1] Colin Mercer, *Towards Cultural Citizenship: Tools for Cultural Policy and Development* (Hedemora, Sweden: Bank of Sweden Tercentary Foundation and Gidlunds Forlag, 2002).

[2] Art & Language is an English group of conceptual artists founded in 1968 by Terry Atkinson, Michael Baldwin, David Bainbridge, and Harold Hurrell. In May of 1969 they established the journal *Art–Language*, and began issuing multiples in various media, including a phonograph record where one of them issued the warning: "never trust a sociologist."

[3] Jean Baudrillard, in response to Hans Magnus Enzensberger's "Constituents of a Theory of the Media," a discussion of a concept that might be called interaction. See Hans Magnus Enzensberger, "Constituents of a Theory of the Media," *New Left Review* 64 (Nov.-Dec. 1970): 13–16, reprinted in Stuart Hood, trans., *The Consciousness Industry* (New York: Seabury Press, 1974). See also Jean Baudrillard, *For a Critique of the Political Economy of the Sign*, Charles Levin, trans., (Saint Louis, MO: Telos Press, 1981), 164–84, from the French *Pour une critique de l'economie politique du signe* (Paris: Galliard, 1972). Baudrillard states: "On a more practical level, the media are quite aware how to set up formal 'reversibility' of circuits (letters to the editor, phone-in programs, polls, etc.), without conceding any response or abandoning in any way the discrimination of roles. This is the social and political form of feedback. Thus Enzensber-

ger's 'dialectization' of communication is oddly related to cybernetic regulation. Ultimately, he is the victim, though in a more subtle fashion, of the ideological model we have been discussing."

⁴ This phrase was issued by the group General Idea (A. A. Bronson, Felix Partz, Jorge Zontal) in the 1970s. I don't know where they picked it up, but it was used to describe a culture based on the lowest common denominator. Probable source: *Press Conference*, a video recording made at the Western Front in Vancouver, British Columbia, March 10, 1977.

⁵ *Cultural Engineering*, was the title of a solo exhibition of my video and text-based installations at the National Gallery of Canada, Ottawa, May 19-July 10, 1983. *Cultural Engineering* was an existential portrait of the artist (Tom Sherman) as product of the combined cultural policy of the Federal Government of Canada. The exhibition featured a series of photo/text works featuring configurations of the logos of Canadian agencies in 1983: The National Film Board, The Canada Council, The Canadian Broadcasting Corporation, The Science Council of Canada, and The Department of Communication (the split-Canadian flag logo covered many additional departments).

⁶ For a full description of the contemporary media environment, see Tom Sherman, *Before and After the I-Bomb: An Artist in the Information Environment*, in Peggy Gale, ed., (Banff: Banff Centre Press, 2002).

⁷ Lewis Hyde, *The Gift: The Erotic Life of Property* (New York: Vintage Books, 1983).

⁸ Tom Sherman, "Museums of Tomorrow," *Parachute*, No. 46 (March, April, May, 1987).

⁹ Tom Sherman, "Artificial Perception as Reality Check: Thinking About MIT's Tangible Bits," in *HorizonZero* 3 (Banff, AB: Invent, 2002), available at http://www.horizonzero.ca/textsite/invent.php?is=3&art=0&file=14&tlang=0.

¹⁰ Gordon B. Thompson, *Memo from Mercury: Information Technology is Different* (Montreal: Institute for Research on Public Policy, June 1979, Occasional Paper #10). Besides being a senior engineer at Bell-Northern Research, Gordon B. Thompson speculated in music copyrights. Having discovered that the rights of the Canadian national anthem had lapsed and were available, he purchased it. He then informed the Federal Government of Canada that they were violating his copyright. After making his point, Thompson sold the anthem's original score (back) to the Government of Canada for one dollar.

¹¹ Tom Sherman, "An Addiction to Memory [and the Desire to Annihilate Images]," in *NOEMA.lab, technologie & societa* (Universita di Bologna, Italy 2002), http://www.noemalab.com/sections/ideas/ideas_articles/sherman_memory.html.

¹² Tom Sherman, "The Finished Work of Art is a Thing of the Past," in *C*, no. 45 (Spring 1995); and as "L'œuvre d'art 'achevée' est un concept du passé," in *Où va l'histoire de l'art contemporain?* (Paris: l'Image et l'École Nationale Supérieure des Beaux-Arts, 1997).

¹³ Cary Peppermint, a performance artist, calls his performances (and Web-based photo/text works) "exposures," a compression of the idea of personal, psychological disclosures with the act of exposing photographic film to the light of day.

Part
III

New Approaches in a Changing
Cultural Environment

7.

The Changing Environments of Cultural Policy and Citizenship in Canada

John A. Foote

Culture and citizenship in Canada are shaped and influenced by a broad range of contextual factors that are changing rapidly at home and around the world. While system change is nothing new, the scope and power of current changes are transforming the way we live, cultural and citizenship-related activities, and our capacity to identify, measure, evaluate, and understand their effects and implications. In this chapter, it is argued that both culture and citizenship, as well as the points where they intersect, can be shown to be heavily influenced by rapid and extensive change in their surrounding environments. We define culture as ways of life including the mix of professional and amateur elements of the cultural sector. We define citizenship as the rights and responsibilities of citizens in relation to their country and the state. Cultural citizenship, therefore, refers to the points where cultural expression forms part of one's role as citizen such as identity, belonging, diversity, advocacy, and different arenas of participation. This chapter addresses these concepts and issues pursuant to the ground-breaking analysis of Colin Mercer who spoke of "the ongoing and indissoluble connection between culture and economics, culture and social relations, culture and power, culture and identity, culture and rights, and culture and human development."[1] The emphasis of this chapter is clearly on culture rather than citizenship, given the large amount of quantifiable information available for the latter. The approach described in this chapter can also be applied to future discussions of citizenship.

Environmental scanning is a recently introduced tool that helps researchers, policy-makers, and stakeholders understand where we have been, where we are now, and where are we going. It is a technique based on a variety of traditional disciplines such as history, economics, sociology, and political science as well as more frontier methods including futures analysis, pyschographic studies, organizational behaviour, and impact assessment. The methodology draws on existing trend lines, identifies and assesses both the beneficial and risk-associated impacts of current innovations or system changes, and projects probable "futures" under a variety of scenarios of environmental configuration. It follows closely on the first environmental scan prepared in the Department of

Canadian Heritage[2] which was intended to prepare policy-makers for major change in each of the above environments including governance and political change.

This chapter applies the concepts and information associated with globalization, social and demographic change, economic change, and technological innovation (loosely based on the traditional STEEP model which includes social, technological, economic, physical environmental, and political factors) to the cultural sector including those areas in which culture intersects with citizenship. Selected issues are linked to this panorama of change to help demonstrate how the new environment affects us as creators, producers, or consumers of cultural content, as well as citizens. The reader will observe that we have *not* included change in other important realms such as governance and political change, bio-technology, the physical environment, transportation and energy, or nano-technology, to cite only these examples. However, we contend that change in one or more parts of our global environment does, indeed, contribute to the shaping of all interdependent systems, including those of culture and citizenship. The chapter is structured according to what we do and do not know in regard to how cultural change is affected by environmental changes and how culture and citizenship might better inform and intersect with each other to promote cultural and civic engagement.

What Do We Know?: Key Issues and Trends

Evidence of change in our multiple environments is obvious to us all. While there is nothing radically new or novel in change—all systems undergo change or do not survive—the pace and scope of change, as well as its implications, are increasingly difficult and complex to track and forecast effectively. Nowhere is this truer than in the cultural sector, which is beset by constant change at every stage of its functional chain, from the creative artist, through the production and distribution of content and services, to the consuming and participating citizenry and back again in ubiquitous feedback loops. The changing context for cultural policy requires us to broaden our policy research horizons accordingly. In this opening section of the chapter, we are going to look at the "New Canada" from the perspective of change in globalization, socio-demographics, economics, and new technologies. We will be looking primarily at trends rather than statistical snapshots wherever possible.

Globalization

Globalization is resulting in major power shifts around the world through the introduction of new players and the changing roles of traditional interests. National autonomy and borders are more fluid and subject to international compromise or negotiation based on the development of global rules. The term "intermesticity" has been coined to refer to the intensified exposure and vulnerability to world crises and the increasing international interdependence dominated, in the case of Canada, by growing North American economic integration. For example, World Trade Organization (WTO) rulings which ran counter to certain existing federal cultural policy instruments in 1997 placed limits on the capacity of governments to secure international legitimacy for formerly sovereign initiatives, some of long standing such as the postal subsidy for Canadian books, periodicals, and newspapers. In any event, according to Victor Rabinovitch: "Retaining a formal sovereign right to develop cultural policies is no longer adequate if program and structural measures put in place by a country are constantly assessed (or challenged) against the standards set for trade in commodities and services."[3]

All things cultural are subject to global variation in mode and nature of expression, access and market power. Globalization affects the nation-state, the region, and locality. The old slogan, "go glocal" still resonates, recalling the strong interconnections of culture embodied in local everyday life, global trade in goods and services, and immigration that typify the modern profile of the "New Canada." Trade liberalization has contributed to a huge increase worldwide in the movement of goods and services, as well as investment and people, the latter referring to the continuing high levels of sustained immigration and travel (tourist and business). Numbers have remained high in immigration (Canada accepted 235,000 immigrants in 2003, far more than the 100,000 in 1987), although tourism has dropped off rather precipitously in response to the fall-out from 9/11 and other global crises, most recently SARS and West Nile.

International trade has increased one thousand per cent since 1945 while the global GNP has increased only five hundred per cent during that same period. Canada's trade to GDP ratio increased from fifty-one per cent in 1990 to eighty-one per cent in 2001. In simple terms, trade is fundamental to Canada, a country historically dependent on trade. The same is true for culture where historically, the country's dependence on cultural imports was much stronger than its proven record of exporting domestic output. The gap between Canadian cultural imports and exports grew smaller from 1996 to 2000, during which period exports of Canadian culture grew by fifty per cent to reach the current level of almost five billion dollars.

There is a lop-sided dependence on the United States as both a foreign market for culture produced in Canada and a source of the still larger volume of cultural imports (seven-and-a-half billion dollars in 2000, up twenty-three per cent for the period between 1996 to 2000). Given the limited economies of scale in Canada's small domestic market, the longer term viability and competitiveness of Canada's cultural sector will increasingly depend on taking full advantage of international business opportunities. In principle, globalization or the global reach of digital technology such as satellite and the Internet should allow for greater long term diversification of demand by non-Canadian customers for Canadian content. To date, however, this diversification and a potentially more balanced profile of foreign markets for Canadian content have yet to take place in any significant way.

While globalization holds out the promise of eventually diversifying our cultural markets abroad, Canada continues to run the risk of commercial challenge at home, largely but not entirely US-based, to Canadian cultural policies such as foreign investment limitations and regulatory provisions that distinguish between foreign and Canadian content. The foreign share of Canada's domestic cultural economy remains high and dominates most cultural industries. Foreign content is pervasive in Canada's domestic market as the following selected indicators demonstrate: forty-five per cent of book sales, eighty-one per cent of English-language consumer magazines on Canadian newsstands, seventy-nine per cent of retail sales of tapes, CDs, concerts, merchandise and sheet music, eighty-five per cent of film distribution revenues and incredibly, more than ninety-five per cent of theatrical screenings of feature films are foreign-controlled in Canada's cultural sector.[4]

From the Canadian perspective, globalization not only occurs in the North American context but also represents WTO negotiations in services affecting trade and culture and the current drive towards gaining international acceptance for a new international instrument to protect cultural diversity. Canada has demonstrated leadership by being involved with the International Network on Cultural Policy in establishing a new instrument that is now being taken up by UNESCO, pursuant to UNESCO's October 2003 decision to develop an international convention on cultural content and artistic expression. It is also important that Canada retain its historically close relations with the United States under any administration including those which might tend to ignore or exploit Canadian cultural vulnerabilities. While Canada cannot ignore the very real impact of the United States on the Canadian cultural economy and psyche occasioned by the continuing forces of continental integration, it must not fail to maintain and solidify the country's sovereign capacity for choice.

The continuing close interaction of Canada and the United States should not mask the profound change in values held by Canadians concerning foreign policy and globalization in which Canada's so-called third pillar of foreign policy (which many critics argue is still ill-defined and under-appreciated) is projecting our values and culture outside the country. While it does not constitute a full-scale review of Canadian foreign policy, the 2003 *Dialogue on Foreign Policy* with Canadians conducted by the Department of Foreign Affairs and International Trade found that many Canadians believe that while increasing global interconnections facilitate trans-national networking, they may also provoke social tensions over the erosion of political and cultural sovereignty.[5] Many are concerned that Canada is losing influence and should work to strengthen our international presence. While Canadians support freer trade, they also want to be assured that bilateral and multilateral international agreements are consistent with human rights, cultural diversity, and ecological sustainability and that they explicitly protect essential public services in Canada, especially Medicare and education. Notably, the *Dialogue on Foreign Policy* report states that "public confidence in the value of globalization will be sustained only if its benefits are fairly shared." Culture, and Canada's growing cultural diversity are strong "calling cards" in promoting Canadian values and interests abroad. Without fuller and more strategic exploitation and "branding" of Canadian cultural assets through trade and international exchanges, culture as the third pillar will never assume its rightful place in the country's foreign policy.

Socio-Demographic Trends

Canadian society is changing fundamentally towards greater diversity. This is true in respect to an aging population as medical advances continue their revolutionary enhancement of baby boom longevity. Canada's population exhibits growing levels of ethno-cultural and linguistic diversity brought about largely by society-transforming patterns of immigration. The continuing relevance of place to a country as diverse and extended geographically as Canada is reflected in growing regional alienation of perimeters from the centre and the continuing growth of urbanization and mega-cities leading to a concomitant decline in rural populations. There are some apparent anomalies present in the trajectory of social change in the New Canada including, for example, a slow decline in the fertility rate of much of the Canadian population and the rapid birth rate of Canada's Aboriginal population (more than one-third of Aboriginals in Canada are fourteen years old or under.)

Let us look at some of the indicators of demographic change first. By 2021, seniors could account for almost one-fifth of the Canadian population (they currently represent thirteen per cent). Regionally, Quebec and Atlantic populations are likely to age more rapidly than those in the Western provinces including the Territories, Manitoba, and Saskatchewan (each with large Aboriginal youth cohorts), and Alberta and B.C. with their steady immigration of working age populations. At the same time, significant numbers of Canada's youth (eighteen and under) are becoming increasingly marginalized as their respective share of the population declines. This marginalization is quite apparent in voting turnout where Canadians eighteen to twenty-four are consistently between ten per cent and twenty-five per cent below that of the general voting population.

In 2001, Canadians reported more than 200 ethnic origins: forty-seven per cent of the population reported ethnic origins other than British, French and Canadian, making these latter groups a decided minority in the New Canada. Five ethnic origins (German, Italian, Chinese, Ukranian, and North American Indian) currently report populations of over one million each. The visible minority population (defined as persons other than Aboriginal peoples, who are non-Caucasian in race or non-white in colour) has grown from just 4.7 per cent of the Canadian population in 1981 to 13.4per cent in 2001 and is expected to reach twenty per cent by 2016. Currently, three of ten visible minorities were born in Canada and thus, are not solely the result of first generation immigration. Immigration continues to redefine the face of Canada and is expected to provide some eighty per cent of Canada's population growth by 2030. Immigrants continue to face challenges however, including substantially lower earnings than other Canadians even after ten years in the country, regardless of education. Recognition in Canada of foreign credentials also remains problematic. The impacts of these trends are felt primarily in Toronto and Vancouver and to a lesser extent, in Montreal. eighty-seven per cent of visible minorities are concentrated in these three cities today, up over twelve per cent from 1996.

Linguistic diversity is also growing in the new Canada. In 2001, Canadians reported 100 languages as mother tongue. Close to thirty per cent of immigrants and refugees aged fifteen and up do not know at least one of Canada's official languages, although the longer immigrants remain in Canada, the more likely they are to speak English or French at home. Official language minorities are over-represented in aging population cohorts and the bilingual capacity amongst young Anglophones (fifteen to nineteen) outside Quebec declined from 16.3 per cent in 1996 to just 14.7 per cent in 2001 and from 12.9 per cent in 1996 to just 11.5 per cent in 2001 for those aged ten to fourteen.

Social change is broader than demographic change. It can also extend to identity where twenty-two per cent more census respondents reporting Aboriginal origin (712,000 in 1986, 1.3 million in 2001) self-identified as Aboriginals.[6] In respect to attachment, public opinion surveys report higher percentages of Canadians who feel more attached to their province than to Canada (from twety-nine per cent in 2000 to thirty-eight per cent in 2003) while those who professed attachment primarily to Canada declined slightly from sixty-one per cent in 2000 to fifty-eight per cent three years later. The decline in Canadian attachment is most marked in Alberta where respondents are ten per cent less attached to the country in 2003 than they were six years earlier.

Trends in the cultural behaviour of individuals, notably cultural attendance, consumption and participation, including voluntarism, show interesting signs of rapid socio-demographic change in Canada. The environmental scan can help to identify and understand cultural consumption and participation patterns inside and outside Canada. It can also help policy developers select from among the most persuasive evidence-based research. Finally, the scan can help to plan and develop future strategic policy research priorities. In 1998, Canadians over the age of fifteen had at their disposal only 6.2 hours of free time per day, only five minutes more than 1992.[7] The importance of culture in everyday life is demonstrated by the fact that Canadians spent fifty-five per cent of their leisure time on culture-related activities, thirty-one per cent on socializing with family and friends, eight per cent playing sports and six per cent on volunteering.[8] Clearly, changing demographics have a very important impact on time use. Canadian-born residents of Canada are more likely to visit traditional heritage institutions such as museums whereas those born outside Canada report a higher rate of visits to zoos, aquaria, planetaria, etc. Geographically, participation differs considerably among the provinces. Higher numbers of individuals with post-secondary education attend theatre, symphonies, and dance performances. Looking at age, young people fifteen to twenty-four spend only .2 hours per day volunteering while older adults fifty-five to sixty-four spend .6 hours per day.[9] Today's teens are well connected: In 2003, eighty-nine per cent had access to home computers while fifty-nine per cent had access to high speed Net service.

In regard to voluntarism, studies have shown a strong correlation between volunteering and other forms of participation such as philanthropy, group membership, and voting. However, here the picture is not altogether rosy: voluntarism in 2000 declined thirteen per cent from 1997 (although still accounted for over one billion hours of work) and a small core of volunteers (seven per cent of all Canadians) contributed almost three-quarters of all voluntary hours. With respect to donations, the other principal participation category, only 2.4 per cent of Canadians donate money to cultural organizations. Education remains the most important determinant of who donates while income determines how much to a significant degree. It is interesting that rural and small town Canadians give proportionately more to the cultural sector than do urban Canadians.[10]

The values held by Canadians are, of course, also subject to considerable stress and change as well. Declining deference to authority in the "New Canada" represents a sea-change from that of the "Old Canada." For example, demand for accountability is on the rise while there is a concomitant decline in trust in public and private sector institutions and interest in quality of life issues is expanding in the post-materialist Canadian society. As North American economies are converging, Canadian and American values seem to be diverging somewhat.[11] As another recent article extolling the "New Canada" noted, young adults in the two countries tend to hold rather opposing attitudes on such values as collective social responsibility and post-materialism; in other words, Canadians are the Venus to the American Mars.[12]

As noted above, the results of social change can be negative such as the growing disengagement of Canadians in civic institutions and practices. The digital divide has become a very real and significant trend in the information age to the detriment of "unplugged" Canadians. Among indicators showing enduring disparities in Canada are economic security (income polarization, poverty, unemployment, homeless, and at risk populations), lifestyle changes (average leisure time, quality of life index), co-operation, participation (religious attendance and affiliation, social involvement and networking) and literacy. In regard to the latter, forty-two per cent of Canadians ages sixteen to sixty-five did not have the literacy skills to participate fully in the knowledge-based economy in 2001.

Technological Trends

Technological innovation continues its inexorable evolution but over a shorter time span than heretofore and with greater economy- and society-wide consequences. Technological change is having a profound impact on the cultural sector where new tools for the expression of creativity, enhanced production values such as special digital effects in film and broadcasting, the ubiquitous development of new media and the greatly enhanced capacity to distribute cultural content are now common place. Technological change is also altering citizenship in good ways such as the creation of virtual communities and multiple identities and the rise of e-government while broadening the gamut of interactive communications between citizens and governments including electronic voting in elections and referenda. It can also affect citizenship in more negative ways such as the alienation of disengaged youth and the growth of "smart mobs" with the use of mobile communications and computing devices.[13] The period of time between invention/innovation and popular uptake by the population is narrowing considerably.

The social, economic, and political potential of interactive, high speed, and unlimited volume of information distribution and manipulation is immense and growing daily.

While Canada has always been at the vanguard of developing and accessing new technologies such as cable, microwave, and satellite, their long term use in creating, transmitting, and receiving cultural content as well as in messaging is perhaps better known. New technologies allow new players to enter the cultural marketplace, increase competition among traditional players, and expose vast amounts of digital content to interested consumers. Cultural industries must use new technologies to remain competitive but in so doing, there is always a significant investment cost and risk involving the same problems of national scope and scale associated with the traditional media. However, this technical advancement, which will be felt at each end of the cultural chain, is sure to continue its rapid acceleration with the spread of information and communication technologies (ICTs) throughout the economy, especially by miniature chips imbedded in goods and services rendered increasingly more efficient, interactive, and reliable.

Along with the electric light bulb, the telephone and computers, the Internet is yet another "tipping" innovation which has already begun to transform all who use it. The Net exemplifies the major convergence of several new technologies with its rapid creation of new opportunities for the dissemination of cultural and other forms of content. Creators, producers, and distributors of Canadian content are pressed to secure prominent places on the Internet in the face of massive real-time global information flows. Policy issues affecting both culture and citizenship that are associated with the introduction of the Internet and its rapid diffusion to users include the impact of the Net on traditional media such as books and broadcasting, questions involving violations of privacy in monitoring Net usage, the unchecked carriage of pornography and violence on the Net (as in digital television on demand), regulatory limitations, (based on the technical difficulties involved in controlling aspects of the Internet), the need for enhanced digital copyright protection, the need to bridge the digital divide as a public policy priority and to support on-line services through constantly expanding e-commerce. Yet another issue pertinent to Canada is the continuing low level of French-language content on the Net, resulting in a differential in utilization, e.g., forty-four per cent of French-speaking Canadians used the Net in 2001 compared to fifty-eight per cent of English-speaking Canadians.

Economic Trends

The global and Canadian economies are subject to the same abundant and relentless change as are each of the other environments discussed here. Notwithstanding the small downturn or slowdown in growth since 9/11 throughout the Western world, Canada has enjoyed a relatively long period of what Peter Schwartz and others have called "The Long Boom" in terms of economic growth prior to 9/11.[14] Schwartz et al. refer to the years between 1980 and 2020 as a period of remarkable global transformation in the economy marked by an incredible confluence of technological change, economic innovation, global integration, and spreading democratization. They believe that this transforming period of global economic growth and integration is the first stage of a more complex social and political integration anticipated as the twenty-first century evolves. They also believe that technological change and globalization are fundamental to this period of economic change. However, notwithstanding the long-term relevance and reliability of this analysis, global economic growth prospects have deteriorated somewhat since 2000-2001 owing to a previously over-heated technological marketplace and, of course, global crises such as 9/11.

Canada fared relatively well in economic terms during the first half of the boom, especially over the last decade. GDP per capita increased on average by almost three per cent annually from 1995 to 2000 compared to .2 per cent annually during the first half of the 1990s. Canada's real disposable income gained on average 2.3 per cent annually between 1997 and 2000. 560,000 jobs, sixty per cent full-time, were created in 2002, the largest number in history. Although unemployment rates declined steadily from 1993 to 2000, they have inched back upwards since and currently stand just over seven per cent. On an international scale, according to the Government of Canada's most recent *Report to Parliament on Performance*, Canada led the Group of Seven industrialized countries in economic growth for two of the first three years in the new millenium.[15] Moreover, Canada is the only G7 country that had both a federal budget surplus and a surplus in trade in 2002. It is also noteworthy that Canada has not lost as many jobs per capita as did the United States following the collapse of the high tech dot-com financial markets in the late 1990s. While Canada outpaced the United States over the past four years based on several economic indices, it has not, however, narrowed the gap in regard to productivity where the gap between the two countries grew from 12.5 per cent in 1981 to 16.1 per cent in 2000.

Owing to global and hemispheric ties, Canada is impacted strongly by foreign competition. This is particularly true in the case of Canadian cultural industries with economies of scale limitations compared to the large scale advantages of their larger American counterparts. Canada's cultural organizations have not been immune from downsizing and mergers/acquisitions as part of a continuing restructuring required for effective global competition. Concerns about multi-media ownership are recurring once again after an earlier flurry of public interest in the 1970s. These concerns extend the effect of mergers and consolidation of ownership on diversity of content, independence of editorial content within multi-media conglomerates, and foreign ownership regulations. While the rush of mergers and acquisitions has slowed down since the late 1990s, the results can be seen in the following figure for 2000-2001 in Canada: five private television companies accounted for eighty-eight per cent of total industry revenues, five firms accounted for seventy-eight per cent of daily newspaper circulation as well as sixty per cent of community newspaper circulation, five cable television firms generated eighty-five per cent of all cable revenues, five pay and specialty service operators captured seventy per cent of total pay and specialty revenues and five private radio operators accounted for fifty-seven per cent of total radio revenues. The report of the House Standing Committee on Canadian Heritage addressed the issues of concentration of ownership and foreign ownership in broadcasting.[16] Cultural consumption is yet another area that measures aspects of the sector's economic impact. Cultural consumer spending in Canada, totalling $21.3 billion in 2001, was more than three times larger than total government spending in culture by all three levels of government ($6.2 billion) and grew more quickly (twenty-six per cent) than overall consumer spending (twenty-three per cent) between 1997 and 2001. Cultural spending accounts for approximately four per cent of total household spending in Canada or almost one dollar out of every thirty dollars spent by Canadian consumers.[17] Consumer spending on the live arts and heritage grew by ten per cent from 1997 to 2001, more than double the rate of increased spending on sporting events. Spending also increased in motion picture admissions (forty-six per cent), home entertainment (thirty-three per cent), and photography (twenty-eight per cent) during the same period.[18] Again, there are strong regional variations in cultural consumption as well as differences between urban and rural spending.

Other economic trends bearing on the cultural sector in Canada as well as the economy as a whole, include the rising Canadian dollar (relative to the declining American dollar), the growing impact of culture on the Gross Domestic Product, and the growth of the "new media" industry. While the recent rise in the Canadian dollar has not yet registered a definitive impact on Canadian cultural exports, a dampening influence on the pattern of multi-year growth could develop. The economic impact of culture in Canada was most recently measured for 1996-1997 although a more recent study was released in 2004 by Statistics Canada.[19] The GDP impact of culture has grown from five billion dollars in 1981, or 1.7 per cent of total GDP, to $22.5 billion, or 3.1 per cent of the GDP in 1996-1997. New numbers expected in 2004 concerning the economic impact of culture in Canada will undoubtedly show a continuing pattern of growth in GDP attributed to it. Moreover, this pattern of growth is also demonstrated in the number of new media companies in Canada—many of which are content-based—which doubled in just one year from 1999 to 2000. Every major cultural industry firm in Canada is currently competing to deliver content electronically and many are currently planning major roll-outs of digital services such as digital television and high definition television.

The cultural labour force in Canada is also growing rapidly but it remains one of strong regional and occupational variations in income levels and age distribution: sixty-eight per cent of writers were over thirty-five in 1997 while forty-five per cent of employed performing artists were under thirty-five. Some 640,000 jobs were estimated to have been generated by the cultural sector in 1996-1997, up from 186,000 in 1981. Continuing trends on the cultural labour front include higher than average educational levels of cultural workers: over sixty per cent in writing and heritage/library occupations had a university degree in 1997 in contrast to just twenty-two per cent for the entire labour force.

What Don't We Know?

Knowledge gaps are the substance of futures research from the short-term to the long-term. Futures can be defined as the science of measuring and predicting change. When this change risks negative consequences, we are warned by Alfred Sauvy that "il faut prévoir pour ne pas voir."[20] From the perspective of promoting the public interest in enhanced and more democratic cultural and citizenship participation, futures analysis can be used, with varying levels of success, to identify and project ahead trends in key variables and system change. It is not unusual that research on major gaps in cultural data can be joined up with evidence-based policy analysis to help address the scope of change, prepare scenarios for different types of change, and chart the course of change to come. The collection over time of meaningful longitudinal data used in determining aggregate society- or economy-wide impact requires long-range commitments, sizable research budgets, and carefully designed research instruments such as surveys and electronic tracking. The recent work of Ted Gordon on the development of improved futures scenarios through the State of the Futures Index (SOFI) is an especially instructive use of futures on a global scale.[21]

The following gaps are only a brief statement of selected areas among many requiring further research.

Social Change and Motivation

Among our biggest gaps in cultural research are those that lie in the area of social change, especially the motivations underlying social behaviour and which condition the social impact of culture. Cultural and civic participation are notable types of social behaviour although, for the most part, the motivations and necessary or conducive conditions underlying their engagement are neither widely known nor understood. Consequently, more work is needed to gather and analyse data on the motivations that bear upon participation in culture and leisure activities. Similar research might be undertaken in citizenship engagement. The two areas could then be compared and points of intersection described. Some possible topics in common might include time use, formats (live or mediated), effects on identity and quality of life, and contributing factors (income, education, family structure, region, age, gender, diversity).

While social gaps are notoriously difficult to fill, impressive steps are being taken in addressing aspects of social impact such as the role of culture in enhancing social cohesion and attachment. Work is under way to isolate a manageable but meaningful set of indicators, with the help of constantly evolving environmental scans, among other measures. Parallel to this search for social indicators is the vital work of conceptual development and related theoretical framing of the field of enquiry. A coherent and targeted research program dedicated to studying the social impact of culture would certainly constitute a useful contribution to the current and future cultural research agenda. Again, the relationship of culture and citizenship, and their interrelationships, could form a critical part of the work on social impact. Indeed, there is increasing evidence of a positive correlation between cultural participation and health, well-being and quality of life.

Economic Issues

Detailed statistics are not always available concerning all aspects of trade in cultural goods and services, global and domestic investment flows for the cultural industries, the constantly changing profile of mergers and acquisitions in the cultural and communications industries, the development of new media economic applications, and the central role of consumers of cultural hardware, software, and content in system development and change. Other data gaps include the lack of fully harmonized estimates of the cultural labour force which vary significantly depending on the data source(s) used (e.g., Census, Monthly Labour Force Survey, Cultural Surveys, Economic Impact Analsysis). Yet another economic data gap is our paucity of knowledge of Canada's productivity in the cultural sector where extensive, ongoing investment and integration of new technology applications are key to the future viability of the cultural industries. Finally, from an economic perspective, it is always tempting to join together the cultural and information industries in an effort to portray the growing size of the information economy. This is largely a question of classification but involves the inclusion of both hardware and content in this larger construct.

New Technologies

The latest developments in Internet-related technological applications are high speed access and mobile interconnections. Both are well under way in various parts of the world. Canada has one of the world's highest penetration rates of high speed access over both telecommunications and cable. In Japan and Europe, text messaging over wireless telephones connected to the Net is taking off and creating what Howard Rheingold has labelled the "smart mob." We have little real information yet on how new forms of mobile communications and information will, indeed, usher in profound social and economic change. However, there can be little doubt that both the cultural and civic agenda will be altered in ways that cannot always be fully appreciated faced with the rapid, inexorable change of new technologies.

Social science research is required in regard to the effect of new technologies in helping to forge new visions of culture and citizenship in Canada. As Manuel Castells stated, "[T]here is an extraordinary gap between our technological over-development and our social under-development."[22] John Petersen demonstrates how new "tipping" technologies often take the form of unforeseen "wild cards" that can trigger massive change in the environment or cause major system change.[23] The challenge is to develop proactive scenarios that incorporate a serious assessment of risk to help counter the impact of wild cards. One of the most important elements of reducing the risk of technological determinism is moving away from technological *forecasting* to technological *foresight*.[24]

Creativity

Creativity is used in a variety of circumstances but is generally understood to have something positive or purposeful to contribute towards reaching a desired end. As the U.S.-based Council of Scholars said over twenty years ago, "The need is for a more precise definition of creativity, one which comprehends innovation and tradition and which is applicable across disciplines and fields."[25] While the Council of Europe has referred to "cultural and creativity as the cornerstones of the information society,"[26] little in the way of focused research has been undertaken on creativity either from the perspective of its direct and ubiquitous presence throughout the cultural sector—especially at the creative end of the cultural process chain—or its broader societal implications. For example, the role of psychology in the creative process, usually mediated by institutions such as the family, society, church and school, is a well-studied phenomenon but not often applied to the formation of artistic creators. Similarly, the role of creativity in planning has been neither rigorously nor imaginatively explored.

The thrust of these changes has been to elevate the importance of creativity as a defining part of each of the four basic functions represented in the cultural economic chain—creation, production and distribution (including marketing and advertising), consumption and participation, and preservation. Creativity is critical to the work of artists who provide the research and development for the cultural economy. The increasing use of the term, "creative industries" in Europe provides evidence of the increased recognition of a strong link between the cultural industries and creativity. Creativity will also become more visible at the consumer stage through the use of interactive digital technologies and services in ordering and consuming. Using new media and multiple mobile ways of interacting and interfacing will soon become normal activities of our culture in everyday life. The uses to which they and other new media are placed will be determined in part by the creativity of their users as well as by the functionality and efficacy of the devices.

Implications: Possible Effects on Culture and Citizenship

We are looking for a conceptual approach that helps us move away from the marginalization of culture or cultural policy towards a greater recognition of its fundamental role in encouraging active cultural and civic participation and in bridging inter-cultural differences. Canadians can and must engage more actively with their fellow citizens and either directly or indirectly with the peoples and cultures of the world. Governments are beginning to change their roles and rethink their mandates in light of this period of hastening change. There are likely to be major changes in the process of policy development and the structure of programs that are occasioned by rapid change in the global, social, economic, and technological environments. Some examples of changes in policy development triggered by changes in the environment are already evident in respect to cultural diversity both at the regulatory and policy level. Other recent examples where technological and economic change is at the fore of successive reviews of culture in Canada include the Public Hearings and Final Report by the House Standing Committee on Canadian Heritage[27] and the Senate Standing Committee on Transport and Communications.[28] There are many more examples of similar policy reviews that are closely associated with major changes in the global environment. Some of these also result in program re-structuring such as the significant upgrading of audience research as part of program components intended to stimulate demand.

Power and governance relations are shifting. Some functions previously carried out by the state are being transferred to business. Shifts are also under way in civil society where voluntary organizations are beginning to assume certain responsibilities. There will be increasing numbers of players and enhanced decentralization of functions among governments, industry, the voluntary sector, civil society, and individual citizens. Simultaneously, demand is growing for more accountable governance mechanisms that will allow for and indeed promote more extensive citizen involvement in policy development with the benefit of evidence-based evaluation. "Intermesticity" has become the norm as issues are increasingly borderless and the lines among nations, jurisdictions, and departments are more and more blurred. The importance in a federal state such as Canada of an ongoing exchange of information, consultations, partnerships, and joint ventures among all levels of government, including cities which are a creative powerhouse behind cultural development, will become more pronounced. The expanding role of communities, both geographical and of interest, must also be taken into fuller account for it is there that policies hit the ground. New technologies also facilitate, some might say, "drive" many of the independent environmental changes.

In its initial applications, environmental scanning helps build a mental model of the environment and naturally tends to focus on coping with information overload by grouping and categorizing information and by drawing trend lines over time.[29] Environmental scanning ideally should be able to track things quantitatively, qualitatively and perhaps even intuitively in each sphere of the total environment using the STEEP model or a variation thereof. Morgan argues that futures studies can only gain by the application of its methods and techniques to so-called "fringe" areas of enquiry.[30] We believe that while the social sciences, and culture and entertainment in particular, may have been cast as fringe areas, they are likely to provide insights that would be useful in environmental scanning exercises and to serve as creative laboratories for understanding change now and in the foreseeable future.

In conclusion, the strong conceptual linkages between citizenship and culture, posited as one of the fundamental themes of this book, must be deepened in order to guide researchers in the direction of a strong policy research effort that may ultimately explain the causation of changing environmental realities. Moving towards "cultural citizenship" will benefit from the application of environmental scanning methods and approaches and their inclusion of both quantitative and qualitative evidence, organized and explained according to different disciplines, in the form of trend lines from the past, through the present, towards the future.[31]

Notes

[1] Colin Mercer, *Towards Cultural Citizenship: Tools for Cultural Policy and Development* (Hedemora, Sweden: Bank of Sweden Tercentenary Foundation and Gidlunds Forlag, 2002).

[2] First environmental scan prepared in the Department of Canadian Heritage (2003).

[3] Victor Rabinovitch, "The Social and Economic Rationales for Canada's Domestic Cultural Policies," in Dennis Browne, ed., *The Culture/Trade Quandary* (Ottawa 1998).

[4] Ibid.

[5] Department of Foreign Affairs and International Trade, *Dialogue on Foreign Policy* (Ottawa, 2003).

[6] Statistics Canada, *Census of Canada* (Ottawa, 2001).

[7] Statistics Canada, *Changing Patterns of Cultural Consumption and Participation* (Ottawa, 2000).

[8] Statistics Canada, *Canada Survey on Giving, Volunteering and Participating* (Ottawa, 1999 and 2001).

[9] Statistics Canada, *Changing Patterns of Cultural Consumption*.

[10] Statistics Canada, *Canada Survey on Giving*, (2001).

[11] Michael Adams, *Fire and Ice: The United States, Canada and the Myth of Converging Values* (Toronto: Penguin Books, 2003).

[12] Allan Gregg, "Strains Across the Border," *Maclean's* (December 30, 2002).

[13] Howard Rheingold, *Smart Mobs: the Next Social Revolution* (Cambridge, MA: Perseus Books, 2003).

[14] Peter Schwartz, Peter Leyden, and Joel Hyatt, *The Long Boom: Vision for the Coming Age of Prosperity* (New York, 2000).

[15] Treasury Board of Canada, *Canada's Performance: Annual Report to Parliament* (Ottawa, 2003).

[16] House Standing Committee on Canadian Heritage, *Our Cultural Sovereignty, The Second Century of Canadian Broadcasting* (Ottawa, 2003).

[17] Statistics Canada, *Survey of Household Expenditures* (Ottawa, 2000).

[18] Ibid.

[19] Statistics Canada, *Economic Impact of Culture in Canada* (Ottawa, 2004).

[20] Jean-Claude Guillebaud, *Actes du congrès AIUTA* (Geneva, 2001).

[21] Ted Gordon, "State of the Future Index," *Futures Research Quarterly* 19, no. 2 (Summer 2003).

[22] Manuel Castells, *End of Millenium: The Information Age—Economy, Society and Culture, Volume 3* (London: Blackwell Publishers, 2000).

[23] John Petersen, *Out of the Blue: How to Anticipate Big Future Surprises* (Lanham, MD: The Arlington Institute, 1999).

[24] Zhouying Jin, "The Fourth Generation of Technology Foresight and Soft Technology," *Futures Research Quarterly* 19, no. 2 (Summer 2003).

[25] John Foote, "Research on Creativity" (unpublished paper, 2002), citing Council of Scholars, *Creativity: A Continuing Inventory of Knowledge* (Washington, DC: Library of Congress, 1981).

[26] Council of Europe, *In From the Margins* (Strasbourg, 1997 and 2001).

[27] House Standing Committee on Canadian Heritage, *Our Cultural Sovereignty*; see also Government of Canada, *Response to the Report of the Standing Committee on Canadian Heritage, Our Cultural Sovereignty* (Ottawa, 2003).

[28] Senate Standing Committee on Transport and Communications, *Fourth Interim Report on the Canadian News Media* (Ottawa, 2004).

[29] Andy Hines, "Applying Integral Futures to Environmental Scanning," *Futures Research Quarterly* 19, no. 4 (Winter 2003).

[30] Matthew J. Morgan, "On the Fringes: Future Opportunitites for Futures Studies," *Futures Research Quarterly* 19, no. 3 (Fall 2003).

[31] Other helpful resources include John Foote, "The Cultural Policy of Canada," in Council of Europe, ed., *Compendium of Cultural Policies* (Strasbourg 2003); Helen Gould, "Cultural Capital and Social Capital," in François Matarasso, ed., *Recognizing Culture: Briefing Papers on Culture and Development* (London: Comedia, 2001), cited in Colin Mercer, *Towards Cultural Citizenship*.

8.

From "Culture" to "Knowledge":
An Innovation Systems Approach to the Content Industries

STUART CUNNINGHAM, TERRY CUTLER, GREG HEARN,
MARK DAVID RYAN, AND MICHAEL KEANE

Culture is very much the home patch of us content proselytizers—where many of us grew up intellectually and feel most comfortable. It has been around as a fundamental rationale for government's interest in regulation and subsidy for decades. The "cultural industries" was a term invented to embrace the commercial industry sectors—principally film, television, book publishing, and music—which also delivered fundamental, popular culture to a national population. This led to a cultural industries policy "heyday" around the 1980s and 1990s, as the domain of culture expanded. (In some places it is still expanding, but is not carrying much heft in the way of public dollars with it, and this expansion has elements trending towards the—perfectly reasonable—social policy end of the policy space, with its emphasis on culture for community development ends.)

Meanwhile, cultural policy fundamentals are being squeezed. They are nation-state specific in a time of WTO and globalization. Cultural nationalism is no longer in the ascendancy socially and culturally. Policy rationales for the defense of national culture are less effective in the convergence space of new media. Marion Jacka's[1] recent study shows that broadband content needs industry development strategies, not so much cultural strategies, as broadband content is not the sort of higher-end content that has typically attracted regulatory or subsidy support. The sheer size of the content industries and the relatively minute size of the arts, crafts, and performing arts sub-sectors within them underline the need for clarity about the strategic direction of cultural policy (John Howkins[2] estimates the total at $US 2.2 trillion in 1999, with the arts at two percent of this). Perhaps most interestingly, and ironically, cultural industries policy was a "victim of its own success": cultural industry arguments have indeed been taken seriously, often leading to the agenda being taken over by other, more powerful, industry and innovation departments.[3]

The core concept of cultural citizenship has come to the fore even as, and perhaps even because of, the need to negotiate such "squeezing" of cultural policy fundamentals. It is this chapter's perspective, and its distinctive contribution to the debate on cultural citizenship, that culture is best grasped through *propagation* into the future—its active insertion into both mainstream and cutting-edge public policy—rather than only *preservation*. A renewed focus on genuine production diversity (beyond the charmed circle of professionalized production enclaves), the fundamental role of cultural consumption in driving innovation, and the responsibility of government and thought leaders to take culture into the mainstream of public policy are some of the perspectives derived from this approach. The themes of the colloquium from which this volume has come included "rebuilding the case for culture" and "new public interest discourses in cultural policy." The colloquium sought—and this volume seeks—to address "the changed context for cultural policy." By advancing an industry development and innovation approach to cultural production, we contribute to these aims.

And Services ...

This doesn't get talked about much in the cultural/audiovisual industries "family," but it's *sine qua non* in telecommunications and in, well really, pretty much the rest of the economy. Many of the content and entertainment industries—especially the bigger ones such as publishing, broadcasting, and music—can be and are classified as service industries. But the broader and larger service industries, such as health, telecommunications, finance, education, and government services are needing more creativity through increased intermediate inputs, and it is here that much of the growth opportunities for content creation is occurring. Just as it has been received wisdom for two decades that society and economy are becoming more information-intensive through ICT uptake and embedding, so it is now increasingly clear that the trend is toward "creativity-intensive" industry sectors. This is what Lash and Urry[4] refer to as the "culturalization of everyday life" and why Venturelli[5] calls for "moving culture to the center of international public policy."

It is not surprising that this is where the growth opportunities are, as all Organization for Economic and Cultural Development (OECD) countries display service sectors which are by far the biggest sectors of their respective economies (the services sector is in the seventy-eighty percent range for total businesses; total gross value added; and employment across almost all OECD economies), and that relative size has generally been growing steadily for decades.

To Knowledge and Innovation

How and why might content industries qualify as high value added, knowledge-based industry sectors, and from where has this new macro-focus emerged? In part, it's been around for some time, with notional sub-divisions of the service or tertiary industry sector into quaternary and quinary sectors based on information management (fourth sector) and knowledge generation (fifth sector). But the shorter term influence is traceable to new growth theory in economics which has pointed to the limitations for wealth creation of only micro-economic efficiency gains and liberalization strategies.[6] These have been the classic service industries strategies.

Governments are now attempting to advance knowledge-based economy models, which imply a renewed interventionist role for the state in setting twenty-first-century industry policies, prioritization of innovation and R&D-driven industries, intensive re-skilling and education of the population, and a focus on universalizing the benefits of connectivity through mass ICT literacy upgrades. Every OECD economy, large or small, or even emerging economies (e.g., Malaysia) can try to play this game, because a knowledge-based economy is not based on old-style comparative factor advantages, but on competitive advantage, namely what can be constructed out of an integrated labour force, education, technology, and investment strategies.

The content and entertainment industries don't, as a rule, figure in knowledge and innovation strategies, dominated as they are by the science, engineering, and technology sectors. But they should. Creative production and cultural consumption are an integral part of most contemporary economies, and the structure of those economies are being challenged by new paradigms that creativity and culture bring to them.

What, in outline form, is a conceptual frame that may begin to see the content industries in the context of a knowledge and innovation agenda? This is important for two reasons: it opens up dynamic and central policy territory which has been the preserve of science, engineering, and technology (SET) worldwide; and it asks new questions, outside the domain of cultural support, which may precipitate a more holistic approach to the content industries.

The Nature of the Innovation System

The nature of R&D and innovation within the creative and content industries generally has not been closely examined. This largely reflects the sorry fact that these industries have tended to be, at best, *at the fringes* of national discussions about science and innovation policy, and of related funding and industry programs. A further complication is that there is little systematic data about the extent and nature of R&D activity and funding in the content industries in general and for digital content production in particular.

In part, this is a result of "category confusion" which has given rise to numerous ways of approaching this sector around the world.

Figure 1: The Category Confusion with Content Industries

CREATIVE INDUSTRIES	COPYRIGHT INDUSTRIES	CONTENT INDUSTRIES	CULTURAL INDUSTRIES	DIGITAL CONTENT
Largely charac- terized by nature of labour inputs: creative individuals	Defined by nature of asset and industry output	Defined by focus of industry production	Defined by public policy function and funding	Defined by combination of technology and focus of industry production
	Commercial art	Pre-recorded music,	Museums & galleries	
Advertising	Creative arts	recorded music	Visual arts &	Commercial art
Architecture	Film & video	retailing	crafts	Film & video
Design	Music	Broadcasting &	Arts education	Photography
Interactive	Publishing	Film	Broadcasting &	Electronic games
software	Recorded media	Software	film	Recorded media
Film and TV	Data processing	Multimedia	Music	Sound recording
Music	Software	services	Performing arts	Information
Publishing			Literature	storage &
Performing arts			Libraries	retrieval

This category confusion means that it is extremely difficult to gather accurate, authoritative, and timely data about the sector and that it is subject to unfocused analysis and intervention. Having said this, it is a problem generic to much of the service sector. Despite the problems, it is important to establish why digital content should be an important area of focus within a national innovation system. There are several reasons why the content industries in general and digital content in particular are important.

- This industry cluster is economically significant. In 2000, sector turnover in Australia represented nineteen billion dollars, or 3.3 per cent of GDP. Comparison with the U.K. and U.S., where GDP shares are five per cent and 7.8 per cent respectively, shows that the potential significance of the sector in Australia is even greater.
- The creative industry is a high growth sector. A survey of a cross-section of countries (see Figure 2) shows that the content industries have been growing faster than the rest of the economy. In the U.K. and U.S., average annual growth rates for the creative industries have consistently been more than twice that of the economy at large. This translates directly into jobs and economic growth.
- The content industries and digital technology are becoming important enablers as intermediate inputs to other industry sectors. Digital content is becoming an important enabler across the economy, and especially in the services sector. This translates directly into the competitive advantage and innovation capability of other sectors of the economy.
- The creative industries fuel the creative capital and creative workers which are increasingly being recognized as key drivers within national innovation systems.

All these reasons support the contention that digital content and creative industries sector clusters matter, both in their own right and within the context of national innovation capabilities.

Figure 2: Cross-Country Comparisons of the Economic Value of Content Industries

COUNTRY	YEAR	% GDP	AVG ANNUAL GROWTH (content industries/ overall economy)	VALUE ADDED	EXPORT	% NATIONAL EMPLOYMENT
US	2001	7.8	6.9/3.2 (1997-2001)	US $708B	US $89B (Core Copyright only)	6
UK	1997/8	5	16/<6 (1997-1998)	STG 113B	STG 10.3B	5
Australia	1999/2000	3.3	5.7/4.8 (1995-2000)	AU $19B	AU $1.2B	4
Singapore	2000	2.8	13.4/10.6 (1986-2000)	S $4.8B	S $4B	3.4

Source: Singapore, *Creative Industries Development Strategy, 2002*
Note: *Treatment of industry statistics varies slightly across countries.*

Innovation and innovation systems approaches are a relatively new public policy framework, which means that general definitions of innovation are subject to contest and reformulation. "Business innovation is the process whereby ideas are transformed, through economic activity, into sustainable value-creating outcomes or a measurable change in output" is a working definition of innovation which has gained currency.[7]

The conventional wisdom (and normative framework) for policy on innovation resides in the OECD's Oslo Manual.[8] What matters within such a framework is how we understand the dynamic processes giving rise to systemic effects and industry outcomes. Despite the difficulties in shoehorning content and entertainment industries into innovation frameworks—designed as they are fundamentally for the manufacturing sector—it is beginning to occur, as innovation and R&D policies evolve. Lengrand and others[9] talk of "third generation" innovation policy, while Rothwell[10] contemplates five generations of innovation. The trend is the same, however. Earlier models are based on the idea of a linear process for the development of innovations. This process begins with basic knowledge breakthroughs, courtesy of laboratory science and public funding of pure/basic research, and moves through successive stages—seeding, pre-commercial, testing, prototyping—until the new knowledge is built into commercial applications that diffuse through widespread consumer and business adoption. Contemporary models take account of the complex, iterative and often non-linear nature of innovation, with many feedback loops, and seek to bolster the process by emphasizing the importance of the systems and infrastructures that support innovation. This model can be cross-referenced well enough, without too much mutilation either way, with industry models like Michael Porter's representations of industry and cluster competitiveness. Both attempt to chart non-linear and multi-causal systems.

Figure 3: The Elements of a Digital Content Innovation System[11]

COMPONENTS	RELATIONSHIPS	ATTRIBUTES
The operating parts of a system:	Linkages between system components:	• economic competencies
		• organizational (integrative or co-ordinating) ability
• organizations (firms, universities, research centres, research agencies, industry associations, cultural agencies, funding agencies, regulatory agencies, customers and users);	• market transactions	• functional ability
	• non-market linkages	• learning (adaptive) ability
	• information flows	
	• technology transfer	
• properties and assets (technology, IP, human capital, skills, finance, infrastructure, repositories);	• capital flows (people; capital)	
• Institutional regimes (IP law, rights management, content and market regulation consumer protection, competition law)		

While this migration is from a simplistic "technology push" model of innovation driven by upstream R&D to the more real-world characterization of industry markets as complex systems, old paradigms die hard. This is because science and research institutions change slowly. This has also been compounded by the false dichotomy between "hard" science and manufacturing policy on the one hand, and the "soft" research of the social sciences and the relative neglect of the services sector—within industry policy—on the other. Digital content production falls within this gap.

One of the shortcomings of most embedded models of innovation and their related policy programs is that many of these were established within the context of stable, relatively mature industries, primarily in the primary production and manufacturing sectors. The challenge is how to adapt and extend thinking about innovation systems to the services sector and to emerging, technology-based firms in service industries. Addressing this challenge has shifted the focus to the dynamics of industry change and structural adjustment within a globally turbulent environment and shifted attention to new levels of granularity in seeking to understand innovation processes in terms of dynamic feedback loops, non-linear change processes, and the learning processes associated with organizational and institutional adaptiveness.

Any system is defined by the relationships between the component elements. The nature and calibre of those linkages will be determined, *inter alia*, by various organizational attributes.

Analyzing the Innovation System

Having regard to the limits and criticisms of innovation system thinking just canvassed, the key for conceptualizing such a system for digital content is to marry innovation frameworks with proven industry development paradigms.

Michael Porter's work in progress on assessing key parameters to cluster competitiveness provides an industry lens for identifying potential requirements of an innovation system as well as linking this to what successful innovation *outcomes* might involve. It should be noted that linking a situation analysis with possible outcomes is about optimizing identified prerequisites for industry competitiveness and success. As an aside, it is noteworthy that the role of government and of chance (for which we can read externalities) features increasingly strongly as Porter has concentrated more and more on applying his industry diagnostics to the issue of industry clusters. In the context of innovation systems, the arrows representing interactions and linkages in this model are as important as the component building blocks. The analysis of industry innovation involves the examination of both the component building blocks and the network processes—the links.

Modelling the drivers of competitiveness and innovation specific to digital content production against the wider industry systems of either creative or content industry descriptors provides a comprehensive—albeit complex—picture of the mapping required to elaborate a policy framework for innovation systems affecting digital content production.

We will exemplify this model of an innovation system by treating Australia as a case study.[12] (In this chapter, it will only be possible to focus on a few key elements of the system. In particular, we have chosen to focus on weaknesses in certain key components of the system as this is where most research has taken place.)

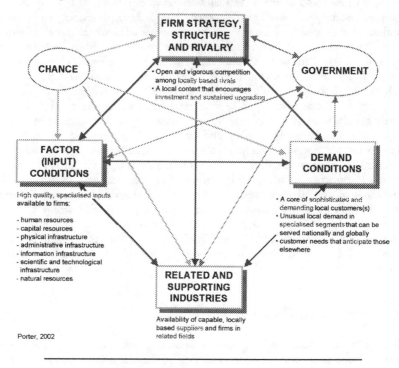

Figure 4: Porter's Determinants of Industry Cluster Competitiveness

FIRM STRATEGY, STRUCTURE AND RIVALRY
- Open and vigorous competition among locally based rivals
- A local context that encourages investment and sustained upgrading

CHANCE

GOVERNMENT

FACTOR (INPUT) CONDITIONS

High quality, specialised inputs available to firms:
- human resources
- capital resources
- physical infrastructure
- administrative infrastructure
- information infrastructure
- scientific and technological infrastructure
- natural resources

DEMAND CONDITIONS

- A core of sophisticated and demanding local customers(s)
- Unusual local demand in specialised segments that can be served nationally and globally
- customer needs that anticipate those elsewhere

RELATED AND SUPPORTING INDUSTRIES

Availability of capable, locally based suppliers and firms in related fields

Porter, 2002

Figure 5: Overview of Elements in Cluster Competitiveness in Digital Content Production

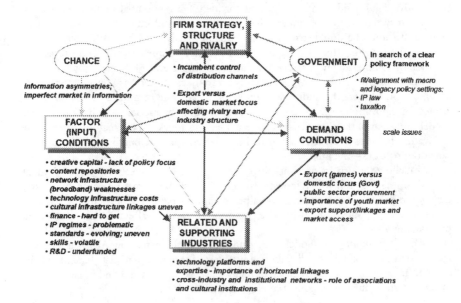

FIRM STRATEGY, STRUCTURE AND RIVALRY
- *Incumbent control of distribution channels*
- *Export versus domestic market focus affecting rivalry and industry structure*

CHANCE

Information asymmetries; imperfect market in information

GOVERNMENT

In search of a clear policy framework
- *fit/alignment with macro and legacy policy settings:*
  - *IP law*
  - *taxation*

FACTOR (INPUT) CONDITIONS

- *creative capital - lack of policy focus*
- *content repositories*
- *network infrastructure (broadband) weaknesses*
- *technology infrastructure costs*
- *cultural infrastructure linkages uneven*
- *finance - hard to get*
- *IP regimes - problematic*
- *standards - evolving; uneven*
- *skills - volatile*
- *R&D - underfunded*

DEMAND CONDITIONS

scale issues

- *Export (games) versus domestic focus (Govt)*
- *public sector procurement*
- *importance of youth market*
- *export support/linkages and market access*

RELATED AND SUPPORTING INDUSTRIES

- *technology platforms and expertise - importance of horizontal linkages*
- *cross-industry and institutional networks - role of associations and cultural institutions*

Components: Organizations

Firms

The market is characterized by few large players—usually deriving their market position from strong incumbency in established traditional content industries or related markets, and a large, fragmented base of small enterprises. Few companies occupy the middle ground.

The distinctive economics of creative industries makes for unusual organizational forms and a viral form of growth and activity that is often hard for industrial age statistics and strategies to accommodate. A recent study[13] of the shape and trends in European businesses in the sector points to high levels of employment volatility (apart from the echelon of senior executives and managers), concentration of power amongst a small number of large multinational companies at the distribution and aggregation end of the value chain, and an "hourglass effect" (see the diagram below) in the distribution of employment, with much smaller employment in medium sized businesses than is normal for industry sectors in general, which exhibit a pyramidal rather than hourglass shape. "The difference between [the creative industries] and other industries is the result of public support inflating the number of larger organizations and the difficulty and lack of propensity of small scale enterprises to grow into medium sized ones."[14]

A major issue is the undeveloped linkages between large and established firms and SMEs, as is the issue of linkages across related markets (supplying or using inputs). The industry fragmentation, production specialization, and the small domestic market all act to reinforce weaknesses in collaboration, clustering, and resource pooling. Remoteness from international deal-making centres and time-zone factors contribute to marginalization within the global value chain.

The market focus of firms varies widely. Games is a "born global" business with a strong focus on the youth market, whilst many multimedia Web services are more domestically focused as input services in areas such as education, advertising, and marketing. An export orientation appears to foster firm collaboration, and clustering influences the "mindset" and development of firm capabilities. The question is how strategies can be developed that enhance the capacity and propensity of firms to

Figure 6: Firm Size in the Content Industries

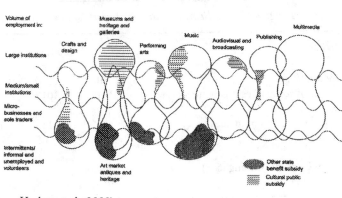

(*Source: Hackett et al., 2000*)

compete in global markets. The following figure gives a sense of the content industry's participation in Australia's major SME export facilitation scheme, Austrade's Export Market Development Grants. (Austrade is the Australian Government's statutory trade promotion body.)

While the industry's share of export support funding is roughly commensurate with its share of GDP, the base is soberingly low for a sector characterized by high growth and increasing trade deficits in intellectual property. In addition, the bulk of sector applications comes from one segment, the export oriented games industry. If the contribution of games companies is discounted, it is clear that most digital content activity pursued in conjunction with Austrade is incremental to domestic market turnover.

The domestic market focus in most segments of the industry creates barriers to collaboration because firms are competing for share within a small market. There is little sharing of infrastructural resources, reflecting a lack of maturity, or trust, in inter-firm relationships and transactions. Emerging firms are commonly staying in one niche rather than venturing into related fields (such as digital content producers moving into education and e-learning). There are widespread weaknesses in vertical and horizontal linkages. In particular, technology spinoffs or technology by-products often risk becoming stranded assets because of the lack of horizontal market linkages or paths to technology diffusion.

Universities and R&D

The creative industries appear to be marginal within university-based research. University research strategies do not embrace content readily (in contrast to their emphasis on ICT and biotechnology). The many different research fields involved with creative industries do not relate to each other well and the potential linkages are seldom articulated into an R&D strategy involving the linkages between ICT, creative content, and educational and services industry content. University research assessment systems rarely specifically reward industry collaboration or inter-disciplinary and multi-institutional activity.

Digital content and applications appear underweight in national competitive research funding under the Australian Research Council's (ARC's) industry "Linkage" program,[15] receiving funding of only five per cent of projects funded under the Humanities and Creative Arts category (nine out of 172 projects) for the period 1998 to 2003.

Figure 7: Digital Content Share of Austrade's Export Grants Scheme

EMDG scheme	2000/1	2001/2	2002/3
Total Funding ($m)	150	150	150
Total number of companies receiving a grant	3214	3018	3795
No of Digital Content companies	143	136	151
as % of total	4.5	4.5	4
Total Digital Content funding ($m)	7.1	8.3	6.7
as % of total funding	4.7	5.5	4.5

Source: Austrade; QUT and Cutler & Company analysis.

Australia's National Research Priorities, announced first in December 2002, included "[f]rontier technologies for building and transforming Australian industries." In this priority area there are key statements such as "research is needed to exploit the huge potential of the digital media industry," and a number of examples of content applications such as e-commerce, multimedia, content generation, and imaging are mentioned for priority research and development. This has been strengthened by the more recent inclusion of a related priority goal of "maximizing Australia's creative and technological capability by understanding the factors conducive to innovation and its acceptance." We must wait and trust that these new priority areas will be "cashed in," as the research culture and administration frameworks continue to marginalize research into content and related interdisciplinary research.

R&D in content involves a shift in research focus from the supply to the demand side environment, consistent with the feedback systems characterizing an effective innovation system. Within a consumption-driven, innovation-led new economy, R&D into the contexts, meanings, and effects of *cultural consumption* could be as important as *creative production*. Major international content growth areas, such as on-line education, interactive television, multi-platform entertainment, computer games, Web design for business-to-consumer applications, or virtual tourism and heritage, need *research* that seeks to understand how complex systems involving entertainment, information, education, technological literacy, integrated marketing, lifestyle and aspirational psychographics, and cultural capital interrelate. They also need *development* through trialing and prototyping supported by test beds and infrastructure provision in R&D-style laboratories. They need these in the context of ever shortening innovation cycles and greater competition in rapidly expanding global markets. The centrality of consumption is one of the realities of the new economy that brings the research traditions of cultural and communication studies into mainstream and sharp relief. An innovation agenda would seek to facilitate hallmark work such as Bennett, Emmison, and Frow's *Accounting for Tastes: Australian Everyday Cultures*[16] and in-depth industry intelligence such as Saatchi & Saatchi's report to the Australia Council (the Australian Government's statutory arts funding body), *Australians and the Arts: What Do the Arts Mean to Australians*)[17] being regularly updated.

The creative industries are supported by a mix of fields of study based in the ARC discipline cluster of Humanities and Creative Arts, but crossing over to the Information Sciences discipline cluster as well as into the business disciplines in the Social Sciences. Many of these are typically young academic disciplines with marginal to negligible profiles within the wider research community. The ARC could more actively support the creative arts disciplinary array at the intersection of the information sciences and the creative arts through new incentives for cross-disciplinary activity and strategic investment in emerging industry innovation.

A clear example of how current models penalize digital content and creative industry outputs in university research is the Higher Education Research Data Collection (HERDC) process administered by the Department of Education, Science, and Training (DEST) which measures—and rewards—research outputs. Research output data is collected in only four "proxy" categories out of more than two dozen recognized research output categories. These four are authored research monographs, book chapters, refereed journal articles, and refereed conference proceedings. Designs, patents, major creative works, and contributions to professional communication are not included and are thus subject to informal discounting as academic behaviour "follows the framework" of recognition. An innovation system more supportive of the creative industries would seek to weight these discounted outputs differently.

Universities and Post-graduate Research

Current higher education research policy, administered by DEST, discriminates against digital content in terms of the Research Training Scheme (RTS) which awards funding for research and funded places for research training based on the dollar value for grants won (rather than, for instance, valuing them on the basis of numbers of grants won or weighting them to take account of the much higher dollar amounts required to conduct research in traditional science and technology areas), and thus creates significant differences between high cost and low cost higher degrees in terms of the dollar value for their completion to the university from which the student graduates. This formula produces a regressive outcome whereby it is impossible for digital content and the wider humanities, creative arts, and social sciences disciplines to advance their funding base no matter how hard they try and, indeed, succeed in their own terms. Universities may be constrained to focus RTS places into areas which perform well in terms of the DEST formula, none of which are digital content areas. Unfortunately, this is not necessarily into areas that will, in turn, drive innovation.

The Cooperative Multimedia Centre (CMC) scheme from the mid-1990s was one initiative aimed specifically at a development and training focus on digital content. Six centres were funded at $1.375 million per annum over the period 1996-1998, and this funding was extended in 1998 to 2002. This scheme notably failed to achieve sustainable linkages between the higher education sector and industry. Instead of paralleling Cooperative Research Centre (CRC) processes, which enjoy significant public funding triggered by industry involvement, the scheme became in effect a localized vocational education and training service for those few CMCs that remain standing.

The ARC, through its Networks, Centres, and Projects programs could seek to address key lacunae in the innovation system for DCA by connecting early career researchers with industry skill sets to the research and development system through cross-disciplinary initiatives and encouraging research mentorship whereby a major advance in the R&D credibility and competence of next generation emerging talent in the digital content supporting disciplines is achieved.

Universities and Careers

Placement and role of creative industry graduates in "out of field" jobs tends not to be captured by higher education employment surveys, thus discounting the market value attributable to career paths outside the sectors which creatives are traditionally employed in. There appears to be real data gaps about the career and vocational choices increasingly available to creative workers and talent in the broader service industries as creative solutions are now increasingly sought in domains such as government and financial services, education, tourism, and health. Some jurisdictions, notably the U.K., have implemented national initiatives to promote the wide and innovative career options arising from a background in the creative industries.[18] Of course, much excellent research is done to track the career prospects and actualities of creatives.[19] However, it tends to focus on employment in the creative sectors as such. There is evidence that there are at least as many (and, given the problematic status of much of the data, probably many more) "creatively skilled" people outside the actual sectors recognized as creative industries as inside them.

Co-operative Research Centres

The key university-industry-research agency linkage program, the Co-operative Research Centres (CRC) program, has been running for over a decade and more than seventy CRCs have been awarded. Despite this program being a lynchpin of R&D linkages between university and industry sectors, it has programmatically excluded from its purview the DCA and related sectors, permitting only science, engineering, and technology disciplines and related industry sectors to apply. While a few CRCs (Smart Internet, Sustainable Tourism) have contained slivers of the social sciences, and Interaction Design was funded in the last round, it remains the case that CRC support for digital content and applications is extremely limited. In addition, the focus of CRCs does not appear conducive to the three way linkage between universities, industry, and cultural institutions that appears highly desirable in the field of digital content and the creative industries.

Industry Associations

There has been an untoward balkanization of collective association within the content industries. The digital content industry is specifically addressed in two industry associations: the Australian Interactive Media Industry Association (AIMIA) and the Games Developers Association of Australia (GDAA). The ICT industry is variously represented by the Australian Information Industry Association, Internet Industry Association, the Australian Computer Society, and numerous professional bodies. There is little connection between the content and technology bodies. The potential role of AIMIA is limited by the lack of participation by large players and the parochial interests of its small enterprise membership base. It tends to be a meeting place for emerging SMEs and a platform for entrepreneurial individuals. The GDAA on the other hand has been an effective and tightly-knit group with a strong focus on industry development activities, reflecting its strong state (or provincial) government funding and support base.

Traditional content industries are represented by numerous associations, usually representing fields of practice and including the Australian Society of Authors, the Screen Producers Association, the Federations of Commercial Television and Radio Broadcasters, the collection agencies which act as industry organizers, as well as the industry trade union, the Media and Entertainment and Arts Alliance. These bodies are paralleled by numerous special interest (for example Arts Law) or guild-like organizations.

There is little integration of digital content activities in established content industry associations, limiting the impact and agenda on both sides. There is a general fragmentation along lines of special interests, and a lack of national co-ordination.

Government Support Agencies

There are numerous government agencies with specific industry support and funding charters involving digital content at national, state, and local levels. Apart from main agencies with specific charters relating to content industries sectors, a range of other government programs could be relevant to support of the sector. These include various "Sustainable Regions" programs (2001); the already-mentioned Austrade; the federal Department of Foreign Affairs and Trade (through bilateral cultural exchanges); the main national industry development agency, AusIndustry. As a general observation, available data appear to support the finding that digital content is systematically under-represented in generic industry support schemes run by such bodies—that is, industry support not specifically targeted at a particular sector. We have already cited the example of Austrade's EMDG scheme; Figure 8 shows that it is also the case with the key tax concession scheme for R&D as well.

Government Support Funding

There is evidence of a variety of support for digital content over the past decade by government agencies administering funding programs. However, it should be noted that, apart from specific programs (such as the Co-operative Multimedia Centres, the Australian Multimedia Enterprise, and the Learning Federation) which have delivered one-off surges of funding into the sector, the base level funding remains extremely low when compared to the funding allocated to so-called "critical infrastructure" (telecommunications infrastructure, digital television conversion) and mainstream R&D like biotechnology.

Government Procurement

A fundamental issue for innovation systems is that of government and agency approaches to the administration of intellectual property (IP) and Crown Copyright. Unlike the U.K. and Australia, the U.S. *Copyright Act* explicitly excludes coverage of works produced by government. In the U.K. there were detailed reviews of Crown Copyright in 1998, resulting in a White Paper[20] which sets out a new policy to open up access to government content and to streamline administrative processes for access. A good Australian example of how treating government content as a public domain resource supports digital content development is in the area of legal resources. Following the shaky beginnings of digital legal databases in the early 1980s, subsequent relaxation of access and re-use rules applying to statutes and case law across Australian jurisdictions has led to a very successful online service called AUSTLII. In other areas, digital content producers continue to complain that policies on Crown copyright within government procurement practices create barriers to the commercialization of sector innovation.

Figure 8: Registrants for R&D Tax Concession

ANZSIC SECTOR	1998–99		1999–2000		2000–2001	
	No. of registrants	% of total	No. of registrants	% of total	No. of registrants	% of total
Printing, Publishing & Recorded media	35	0.2	38	0.3	31	0.3
Cultural, sporting, etc.	42	0.5	36	0.7	30	0.6

Source: AusIndustry, IR&D Board Annual Reports
Note: Reporting by industry code is in aggregated categories. Separate and specific tax concessions apply in the film industry.

Customers and Users: Intermediate Use

Preliminary analysis of national industry input/output tables[21] suggests that there is increasing use of digital content and applications as intermediate inputs by traditional content and creative industries and especially by the wider service sector industries. Lags in statistical publications limit dynamic trend analysis. For example, the latest published input/output tables are for 1996/97, with the following year's data released only in mid-2004. Against this several-year lag in the relevant data, it is hypothesized that the emerging trends identified will have strengthened significantly in the subsequent period of major development for the content industries.

Intermediate industry use of content industry outputs outweighs final consumption in each broad segment of the content industries—as captured by ANZSIC statistical codes—except in the case of the more traditional arts and cultural institutions.

The following tables (Figures 9 and 10) highlight the main industry sectors reliant on content industry outputs. The Australian data is consistent with findings in other jurisdictions.[22]

In addition, the intra-sectoral patterns of intermediate use within the creative industries themselves reinforces observations about the importance of cluster development for the creative industries and digital content. The emerging statistical evidence of growing intermediate use, supported by qualitative evidence, should put an increased spotlight on the way digital content is becoming an important enabler across the economy, and especially in the services sector. This observation highlights the growing importance of digital content within the wider context of national innovation systems.

Figure 9: Use of Sector Outputs (1996-97)

ANZSIC CODE	SUPPLYING INDUSTRY SECTOR	TOTAL INDUSTRY USE AS % OF TOTAL SUPPLY	TOTAL FINAL CONSUMPTION AS % OF TOTAL SUPPLY
2401	Printing; services to printing	89	11
2402	Publishing; recorded media	65	35
9101	Motion picture; radio etc.	65	35
9201	Libraries; museums; arts	27	73

Source: ABS Input Output Tables, 1996/7 *(ABS 2003)*

Figure 10: Utilization of Creative Products by Major Industry Users

USER INDUSTRY (I-O SECTOR)	1996/7 %	USER INDUSTRY (I-O SECTOR)	1996/7 %
Wholesale trade	2.4	Scientific research	2.5
Retail trade	6.7	Legal & Accounting	5.6
Hotels & restaurants	1.8	Other business services	6.2
Communications	6.6	Government	2.5
Other property	2.6	Education	10.7
		Sport; gambling	3.3

Source: ABS Input Output Tables, 1996/7 *(ABS 2003)*

Components: Assets

Technologies

The chronic lack of venture capital for commercialization in the content sector restricts invention. The finance sector's wariness of content investment is compounded, in Australia, by the smallness of the domestic market and the lack of a critical industry mass to justify investor attention. Other impediments include the high cost of access to broadband and other equipment inputs, which limit the capacity to nurture R&D at the SME level where it is most productive.

Digital content firms are underweighed in government industry R&D support. Analysis of Industry Research and Development Board *Annual Reports* show that they represented two per cent of the main federal scheme, the R&D Start Grant, in 2000-01 and one per cent in 2001-02, and received three per cent and 0.5 per cent respectively of total funding for each year. This situation largely results from the fact that standard definitions of R&D used in grant guidelines and for tax concessions discriminate against "soft" technologies, and this has been raised as an issue to be addressed in several jurisdictions, including the U.K. and New Zealand.[23]

Intellectual Property

Intellectual property issues go to the heart of the sector's business models and value chains, and the hotly contested issue of which parties capture disproportionate shares of the value added. It is often bundled—unnecessarily or inappropriately—with the matter of the protection of corporate or commercial information. The Australian government has shown an awareness of copyright and digital-rights issues (as evidenced in copyright reviews and the Department of Communications, Information Technology and the Arts'

Figure 11: The Access Lockout of Inactive Copyrights

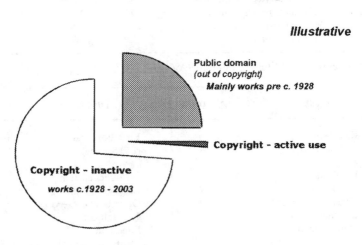

Illustrative

Public domain
(out of copyright)
Mainly works pre c. 1928

Copyright - active use

Copyright - inactive
works c.1928 - 2003

Source: Author's (Cutler & Company) analysis, 2003

release of a Digital Rights Management Guide). There remains an inherent risk that established interests—not innovators—will capture the agenda in reviews of IP regimes. There continues to be a lack of robust policy debate around this crucial topic.

At the heart of this debate is the imbalance of market power between distributors and publishers on the one hand, and content creators and users—and re-users—on the other. The fundamental debate is over the balance of private and public rights and interests in the control of copyright content, particularly that ninety-eight per cent of copyright content estimated to be not under active commercialization or use.

The availability of "source content" is a powerful innovation and industry driver; its lack, a major inhibitor. There has been but limited attention to the issue of possible licensing regimes for more open content repositories. Whatever the licensing models, there needs to be a system of digital rights management that is flexible, transparent, secure, and allows user customization and micro-management of content. In general, the lack of clear and certain IP parameters adds to transaction costs and discourages innovation and development.

Human and Creative Capital

Richard Florida's[24] work on creative workers has recently highlighted the wider economic significance of creative capital, especially in under-pinning high technology industry development. An overall creativity index comparing Australia and the United States on the parameters of population diversity, high-tech output, innovation, and human capital was prepared by National Economics,[25] with the following results, see Figure 12.

Thus, ranked against U.S. cities, Sydney and Melbourne would have come in at seventh and eighth places.

As a percentage of the population, Australia's "super creatives" are outranked by the U.S. by about two percentage points, but the reverse holds for the second-tier creative professionals in business services, health, and education. Australia also out-performs the U.S. on the "Bohemian" Index of arts workers as a proportion of population, and also on the Diversity Index. Where we lag significantly in this comparative study is in Innovation (patents per capita), human capital talent (percentage of population with a higher degree), and high technology production.

Figure 12: Creativity Index: Top Ten Regions—U.S. and Australia

REGION: AUSTRALIA	SCORE	REGION: USA	SCORE
Global Sydney	992	San Francisco	1057
Melbourne Inner	985	Austin	1028
ACT	831	San Diego	1015
Perth Central	744	Boston	1015
Adelaide central	735	Seattle	1008
Sydney inner West	733	Raleigh-Durham	996
Brisbane City	720	Houston	980
Melbourne South	606	Washington-Baltimore	964
Sydney Outer North	535	New York	962
Melbourne East	519	Dallas	960

Whilst the Australian survey confirms and replicates Florida's U.S. findings about the correlation between concentrations of creative populations and the location of high tech industries, it is also apparent that Australia is not successfully leveraging its creative capital into economic outcomes as successfully as the US. This suggests there are significant points of failure in Australia's national innovation system.

Skills

Most of the people working in the sector are highly skilled with a high proportion of youthful energy. It has been observed at an industry level that university graduates often lack industry readiness, indicating a lack of career preparation pathways. A widespread industry view is that universities cannot structure research and teaching around a multi-disciplinary focus, limiting the competencies of graduates.

The skills requirement in this sector is not straightforward. The skills typically needed in digital content sectors include creativity, a risk taking and innovative mindset, integrative problem solving abilities, high levels of technical knowledge and applications ability, and entrepreneurial business acumen. The split between higher and further education, between mass undergraduate, boutique coursework post-graduate, and R&D post-graduate, and the deep silos representing the discipline clusters from which these skill sets might be nurtured (ICT, creative arts, and social science disciplines) makes planning for skills development for the digital content sector a particularly difficult feat. This inherent challenge is compounded by the embryonic nature of some of the sector, and its inherently volatile nature.

Despite a somewhat negative public image of entrepreneurial activity in mainstream business culture, the "creative entrepreneur" is a different class of actor than the corporate buccaneer. As Leadbeater and Oakley[26] point out in their study of knowledge entrepreneurship in Britain, the knowledge entrepreneur acts collectively and is data- and evidence-driven in order to sense new opportunities in extremely volatile emerging fields based on new knowledge.

The lack of critical linkages between the education and training sector and the digital content industry sector needs means that skills development is not yet fully co-ordinated for maximum value. There is but patchy support for a suite of suitable and widely accepted credentials in the industry analogous to the situation with nursing prior to the development of a nationally accepted and co-ordinated credentialing system.

Conclusion: Improving the System

The preceding gives some sense of the components of a content industry innovation system. There are many *elements* of such an innovation system in place. There is a very large education and training sector providing skilled graduates and trainees into the sector. There are large market organizers and industry players, both in the public sector (broadcasters, funding agencies, and cultural institutions such as museums and galleries) and in the private sector (commercial broadcasters, publishing houses, telecommunications firms, and advertising). There is strong and growing demand, both in retail consumer demand and in the role of digital content as an enabler across a growing range of industries, particularly in the services sector.

However, the *quality of linkages* and the *lack of clear public policy signals and frameworks*, together with a number of other critical issues mark the innovation system as embryonic at best. Public policy needs to address the significant framework shifts required to capture the innovation potential of digital content industries by moving, for example, from a situation of unrelated cultural policy and higher education policy to a more fluid, dynamic but more challenging mix of more co-ordinated program initiatives.

In particular, the scale of investment in innovation in and through digital content appears significantly underweighed relative to the funding of other industries. Given the growing economic importance of the creative industries, increased investment in innovation through digital content initiatives is key to capturing future national benefits.

There are several possible strategies for improving the innovation system for content industries.[27] There is clearly a need to develop an industry action agenda to establish a framework for the alignment of existing policy regimes with digital content industries and an emerging agenda. A primary focus of the innovation agenda is better to align cultural policies with industry development and R&D policies. Nationally-funded centres of research designed to promote university and industry linkages need to encompass *tripartite* interfaces between cultural institutions, universities, and content industries. This initiative would create incentives for, and legitimize the role of, cultural institutions in research collaborations. Such an R&D initiative might invite participating industry sectors to pay levies to fund innovation, which would then trigger government funding. The industry levy could be limited to content industry firms with turnover above a floor level, to exempt emerging SMES. The levy might apply to broadcasters, publishers, and distributors. Levy contributions could offset, or replace some or all of existing broadcasting licence, and other imposts. The scheme could be extended in the event of any major changes to cross-media or ownership rules, off-setting any windback of existing local production requirements which might become obsolescent. An essential element of such a centre (or R&D corporation) would be a national information and resource brokerage centre for the sector addressing the serious and endemic information asymmetries and structural weakness in the innovation system.

A suite of reforms to research and higher education policies to accommodate digital content and the creative industries is necessary; as are educational and PR campaigns targeting school-age young people with the message that knowledge entrepreneurship—a "creative career"—is a viable and attractive option. Supporting and promoting an export orientation is important as the only way the sector can scale to realize sustainable growth. Equally important, only evidence of sustainability and scalability will make the sector investable over the long term, breaking the vicious cycle of under-investment.

Broadcasting and broadband's role in the innovation system is crucial, as the gateway between established and emergent *content creation* (major popular entertainment and informational formats transmigration to interactivity and mass customization) and *industry structure* (highly centralized distributional models to more networked and distributed models). Understanding the interaction between the potent legacy of broadcasting and the potential of convergent broadband media is the key to positioning innovative opportunities in content creation if they are to remain close to the mainstream of popular cultural consumption rather than being siphoned off into science or art alone.

Major technology-related reforms such as national investment in content and metadata standards and supporting systems (thus limiting the huge transaction costs for both producers and users created by the current "bottom-up" approach to standards) and tax credits for R&D investment in technology infrastructure in emerging content areas, are crucial pieces in the innovation jigsaw.

Open content repositories, or public domain digital content, are the content industries equivalent of open source software. They *selectively* addresses barriers to production and unintended cultural outcomes of prevailing copyright and IP regimes through an alternative *opt in* model which can operate in parallel with existing regimes. As such it can be a powerful structural mechanism to support a rich "digital sand pit" for creative content producers. The measure facilitates the active re-purposing and re-use of digital content assets. Misuse of this public domain material would be protected under the provisions of a general non-exclusive public licence scheme.

An innovation systems approach to the content industries is important for two reasons: such an approach opens up dynamic and central policy territory which has been the preserve of science, engineering, and technology worldwide; and it asks new questions, complementary to contemporary notions of cultural citizenship and cultural capital, which may precipitate a more holistic approach to these industries. Both a cultural citizenship approach and an innovation systems approach seek to move culture into mainstream policy calculation—the former by emphasizing the central role that cultural literacy and diversity play in undergirding inclusive participation in contemporary society, the latter by connecting culture to the most trenchant current rationale for active government involvement in industry shaping.

Notes

[1] Marion Jacka, *Broadband Media in Australia: Tales from the Frontier* (Sydney: Australian Film Commission, 2001).

[2] John Howkins, *The Creative Economy: How People Make Money From Ideas* (London: Allen Lane, 2001).

[3] Stuart Cunningham, "From Cultural to Creative Industries: Theory, Industry, and Policy Implications," *Media Information Australia Incorporating Culture & Policy*, no. 102 (February 2001): 54–65; T. O'Regan, *Cultural Policy: Rejuvenate or Wither?* (Griffith University lecture given in 2001), http://www.gu.edu.au/centre/cmp/mcrlpublications.html#tom (site now discontinued).

[4] Scott Lash and John Urry, *Economies of Signs and Space* (London: Sage, 1994).

[5] Shalini Venturelli, "From the Information Economy to the Creative Economy: Moving Culture to the Center of International Public Policy" (Washington, DC: Center for Arts and Culture, 2002), available at http://www.culturalpolicy.org.

[6] Brian Arthur, "Increasing Returns and the New World of Business," in John Seely Brown, ed., *Seeing Differently: Insights on Innovation* (Boston: Harvard Business Review Books, 1997), 3–18; Paul Romer, "Interview with Peter Robinson," *Forbes* 155, issue 12 (1995): 66–70; Paul Romer, "The Origins of Endogenous Growth," *Journal of Economic Perspectives* 8, no. 1 (Winter 1994): 3–22.

[7] Catherine Livingstone, "Managing the Innovative Global Enterprise" (Warren Centre Innovation Lecture, given to the Commonwealth Scientific and Industrial Research Organization, 2000), 3.

[8] Organization for Economic and Cultural Development Oslo Manual (Paris, 1997).

[9] Louis Lengrand & Associés, PREST and ANRT, "Innovation Tomorrow: Innovation Policy and the Regulatory Framework—Making Innovation an Integral Part of the Broader Structural Agenda" (innovation paper no. 28 prepared for the Directorate-General for Enterprise, Innovation Directorate, EUR report no.17052, European Community, 2002).

[10] Roy Rothwell, "Towards the Fifth-Generation Innovation Process," *International Marketing Review* 11, no. 1 (1994): 7–31.

[11] Cf., Bo Carlson, Staffan Jacobsson, Magnus Holmén, and Annika Rickne, *Innovation Systems: Analytical and Methodological Issues* (1999).

[12] The Australian Government's Creative Industries Cluster Study (http://www.cultureandrecreation.gov.au/cics)

conducted through the Department of Communications, Information Technology and the Arts and the National Office for the Information Economy in 2001-2003, resulted in the announcement of a Digital Content Industry Action Plan in February 2004. This case study is drawn from the authors' "Research and Innovation Systems in the Production of Digital Content and Applications," one of the reports within the Creative Industries Cluster Study.

13 Keith Hackett, Peter Ramsden, Danyal Sattar, and Christpophe Guene, *Banking on Culture: New Financial Instruments for Expanding the Cultural Sector in Europe* (Manchester: North West Arts Board, September 2000).

14 Ibid., 1.

15 The ARC is the Australian Government"'s statutory research funding body. This finding is based on estimates derived from data supplied by the ARC to the ARC Learned Academies Special Projects grant "Partnerships in the Humanities," based at the University of Western Sydney. For a general orientation to Humanities and Creative Arts ARC Linkage outcomes, see Ien Ang and Elizabeth Cassity, *Attraction of Strangers: Partnerships in Humanities Research* (report prepared for the Australian Academy of the Humanities, 2004), available at http://www.humanities.org.au/Final%20full%20report.pdf.

16 Tony Bennett, Michael Emmison, and John Frow, *Accounting for Taste* (Cambridge: Cambridge University Press, 1999).

17 Australia Council, *Australians and the Arts: What Do the Arts Mean to Australians?* (report prepared for the Australia Council, Saatchi & Saatchi, Surry Hills, N.S.W, 2000).

18 for a good international literature survey. see, e.g., the National Advisory Committee on Creative and Cultural Education's report, All Our Futures, published in 1999, and the U.K. Goverment's statement of progress made following the original recommendations of the naccce Report, in January 2000, available at http://www.dfes.gov.uk/naccce/).

19 See, e.g., http://www.ifacca.org/files/040527/ResearchingArtists.pdf.grep.

20 "The Future Management of Crown Copyright" (HMSO White Paper, March 1999).

21 Australian Bureau of Statistics, *Australian National Accounts: Input-Output Tables 1996/1997* (document 5215.0, 2003), available at http://www.abs.gov.au/Ausstats/abs@nsf/Lookup E3B034F5DBFCE899CA256888001F4C26.

22 Singapore Ministry of Trade and Industry, *Economic Contributions of Singapore's Creative Industries* (2003), available at http://www.mti.gov.sg/public/PDF/CMT/NWS_2003Q1_Creative.pdf?sid=40&cid=1630.

23 HM Treasury, Department of Trade and Industry and Inland Revenue, "Defining Innovation: A Consultation on the Definition of R&D for Tax Purposes" (U.K., July 2003); "R&D Strategy for Creative Industries—a Discussion Paper" (discussion paper prepared for the Foundation for Research, Science, and Technology, New Zealand, 2003).

24 Richard Florida, *The Rise of the Creative Class* (USA: Basic Books, 2002).

25 National Economics, *State of the Regions Report 2002* (Canberra: Australian Local Government Association, 2002), Table 6.21. Chapter six of this report has an extensive analysis of creative capital.

26 Charles Leadbeater and Kate Oakley, *Surfing the Long Wave: Knowledge Entrepreneurship in Britain* (London: Demos, 2001).

27 Creative Industries Research and Applications Center and Cutler & Company, "Research and Innovation Systems in the Production of Digital Content" (report prepared for National Office for the Information Economy, September 2003), available at http://www.cultureandcreation.gov/au/cics/Research and innovation systems in production of digital

9.

Just Showing Up:
Social and Cultural Capital in Everyday Life

M. SHARON JEANNOTTE

> To paraphrase the American filmmaker and comedian Woody Allen:
> *eighty percent of social capital is just showing up.*[1]

This chapter is intended to be a synthesis of current knowledge about social and cultural capital and their relationship to questions of citizenship. Its aims are to identify the role that these forms of capital play in the construction of cultural citizenship and to suggest how a conceptual understanding of them is useful to our understanding of the formulation of cultural policies. The chapter is structured as follows: Section One describes what we know about social and cultural capital and includes definitions, analytical approaches, and an overview of research findings and critiques of current approaches. Section Two focuses on knowledge gaps with regard to social and cultural capital and the construction of citizens, and Section Three discusses the implications for policy and decision-making, based on current knowledge and the analysis of knowledge gaps in Section Two.

In reading this synthesis, it should be kept in mind that despite the deluge of literature and the huge policy interest in social capital in recent years, there is no consensus on research findings. By contrast, policy interest in cultural capital and its relationship to social capital is of quite recent origin and, since researchers have only begun to explore what this relationship might mean for cultural policy, agreement is nowhere on the horizon. In both the social and cultural capital research fields, definitional issues are still being debated (although researchers and policy-makers appear closer to consensus in the case of social capital). As analytical approaches tend to follow from the definitions of social and cultural capital adopted by researchers, it is important to understand just which elements of social or cultural capital are being discussed. Therefore, Section One of this chapter will begin with a focus on definitional issues.

What We Already Know[2]

Definitions of Social Capital

The definition of social capital most often used is the one made popular by Robert Putnam: "social networks and the norms of reciprocity and trustworthiness that arise from them."[3] Putnam has made a further distinction between "bonding" and "bridging" social capital. The former refers to social networks that reinforce exclusive identities and homogeneous groups, the latter to networks that are outward looking and encompass people across diverse social cleavages (forging so-called "weak ties," as opposed to the strong ones that characterize "bonding" social capital).[4] Recently, some scholars have added a third type of social capital to this list—"linking" social capital—which refers to vertical links between different strata of wealth and status.[5] It has been suggested that "linking" social capital is key to leveraging resources and information from formal institutions beyond the community.[6]

Another popular definition of social capital is the one used by the Organization for Economic Cooperation and Development (OECD) which characterizes social capital as "networks together with shared norms, values and understandings that facilitate co-operation within or among groups."[7] Many scholars go beyond these fairly abstract definitions to deconstruct the elements of social capital. One study, done in Australia, used factor analysis to identify eight dimensions of social capital:

- generalized trust;
- social agency (capacity to seek information and make decisions);
- tolerance of diversity;
- value of life (empowerment);
- community connections;
- neighbourhood connections;
- family and friends connections; and
- work connections.[8]

In another example, a Canadian study on ethnicity and social capital analyzes social capital along four dimensions: interpersonal trust, political trust, formal participation, and informal social interaction.[9] Helen Gould, a researcher looking at social capital in the context of cultural development, defines social capital as "the wealth of the community measured not in economic but in human terms," where each transaction "… over time, yields reciprocity and sustainable improvements to quality of life."[10] Both Colin Mercer and Gould suggest, however, that the "currency" of these transactions is "relationships, networks and local partnerships."[11]

Definitions of Cultural Capital

The extensive work of Pierre Bourdieu, a French sociologist, has shaped contemporary thinking on the subject of cultural capital. He has defined cultural capital as "the disposal of taste" or "consumption of specific cultural forms that mark people as members of specific classes."[12] Bourdieu's conceptualization of cultural capital is complex, but in its simplest terms consists of three elements: 1) embodied capital (or habitus), the system of lasting dispositions that form an individual's character and guides his or her actions and tastes; 2) objectified capital, the means of cultural expression, such as painting, writing, and dance, that are symbolically transmissible to others; and 3) institutionalized capital, the academic qualifications that establish the value of the holder of a given qualification.[13]

For a long time, the investment yields from cultural capital, as defined by Bourdieu, were viewed as primarily personal. However, in the context of cultural development theory, some scholars have begun to define cultural capital in collective terms. Gould has observed that "when a community comes together to share cultural life, through celebration, rites and intercultural dialogue, it is enhancing its relationships, partnerships and networks—in other words, developing social capital."[14] In this vein, I have suggested that while cultural capital has traditionally been thought to contribute to "bonding" social capital by reinforcing ideologies, values and social differences, and by strengthening ties between intimates, it may also play a role in "bridging" social capital by promoting social solidarity (or commitment to a larger whole), social integration (or linkages between functional elements), and sustainable communities (patterns of social and spatial interaction distinguishing a collective).[15]

An additional definitional angle has been introduced by David Throsby, an economist who distinguishes between tangible and intangible cultural capital. In his view, *tangible* cultural capital is "an asset that embodies a store of cultural value, separable from whatever economic value it might possess; the asset gives rise to a flow of goods and services over time which may also have cultural value." He places most heritage buildings and artifacts in this category of cultural capital. *Intangible* cultural capital, in his view, consists of "ideas, traditions, beliefs, and customs shared by a group of people, and it also includes intellectual capital, which exists as language, literature, music and so on."[16]

Relationships Between Social Capital and Cultural Capital

At a workshop on "Social Capital Formation and Institutions for Sustainability" that was held in 1998 at the University of British Columbia, participants explored the differences between social and cultural capital. "This distinction is important," they stated, "because one can have a society rich in social capital; however, due to the nature of its cultural capital (as represented, for example, by a 'frontier economic' mentality) such a society may be unsustainable. Cultural capital may determine the *quality* of social capital."[17]

Researchers have pointed out that both social and cultural capital are embedded in complex social systems that are in many ways the human equivalent of natural ecosystems. Social and natural systems, some suggest, are not separate, but are intertwined in ways that are still not understood. From this perspective, cultural capital can be viewed as an asset that "provides human societies the means and adaptations to deal with the natural environment and to actively modify it."[18] According to this notion of sustainable development, how people view the world and the universe, their environmental philosophy and ethics, their traditional knowledge, and their social and political institutions will dictate how they function within their environment. Embodied cultural capital, or habitus, therefore lies at the base of this concept.

Analytical Approaches to Social and Cultural Capital

As noted above, the analytical approach taken in social capital research usually depends on how it is defined by the investigator. Bryant and Norris of Statistics Canada have developed a useful thematic typology to organize the agency's social capital data holdings which also serves as a concise summary of the main analytical categories:

Theme 1: Social Participation, Social Engagement, and Commitment (participation in voluntary organizations, political action, civic engagement, sense of belonging to community).

Theme 2: Level of Empowerment (life satisfaction, perception of control and level of self-esteem and confidence).

Theme 3: Perception of Community (levels of satisfaction with community in areas such as quality of life, crime and safety).

Theme 4: Social Networks, Social Support, and Social Integration (contacts with friends and family, support systems, and depth of relationships).

Theme 5: Trust, Reciprocity and Social Inclusion (both trust in people and institutions, confidence in institutions, and perceptions of shared values).[19]

The Policy Research Initiative has usefully described how the four main analytical frameworks on social capital mesh with the five themes developed by Bryant and Norris. These are summarized in Table 1 below.

In the case of cultural capital, analytical frameworks have been much less clearly articulated, probably because public policy interest in the subject is so recent. To date, however, a number of themes appear to dominate.

Theme 1: Personal Empowerment (personal benefits derived from investments in cultural capital).

Theme 2: Cultural Participation (linkages between cultural participation and altruistic behaviour, such as volunteering and civic engagement).

Theme 3: Cultural Development and Quality of Life (linkages between cultural capital and economic and social development).

Theme 4: Cultural Sustainability (ways in which cultural capital supports human development and maintains the cultural life and vitality of human civilization over time).

Table 1: Analytical Approaches to Social Capital[20]

ANALYTICAL FRAMEWORK	THEMATIC FOCUS
Communitarian	Theme 1 – participation
Network Analysis	Theme 4 – resources embedded in networks; individuals' access to bridges or key resources within the network; size, density and composition of networks
Institutional	Theme 1 – civic engagement, voting, sense of belonging Theme 3 – historical and cultural context of the political and institutional environment; cleavages within civil society, economic performance
Synergy (combination of network & institutional approaches)	Theme 3 – Community capacities, relations between public and private sectors Theme 5 – relationship between citizens and public institutions

Research on cultural capital has tended to concentrate on Themes one and two. This is perhaps a logical outgrowth of Bourdieu's contention that the volume of social capital possessed by an individual depends on the size of his or her network connections and on the volume of economic and cultural capital possessed by those to whom he or she is connected.[21] While Theme one, focusing on the quantitative effects of network "investments" on personal capital, has been fairly well researched, particularly by educational sociologists, the qualitative and collective themes have barely begun to be explored. In recent years, the cultural capital and participation element (Theme two) has received a fair amount of attention from researchers working on public policy issues such as social exclusion, particularly in the United Kingdom and the United States. The cultural capital/quality of life connection has been most frequently explored by scholars working in the area of urban development and creativity. Both the World Bank and UNESCO have been active in exploring Themes three and four, but only recently have they taken a closer look at the role of cultural capital in promoting either cultural development or sustainable communities.[22]

Research Findings on Social Capital

Over the past few years, there has been an explosion of research on social capital. This section will not attempt to provide a comprehensive review of this research, but will instead focus on the characteristics and procedural elements of social capital that are thought to transmit its effects, an overview of these effects, and one of the major social capital issues that has been of interest in cultural policy analysis.

Economists have only recently begun to take an interest in adding social capital to the list of other "capitals" (natural, physical, and human) that play a part in economic growth. They have identified it as a public good, since it can only be acquired by a group of people, rather than an individual. Like many public goods, it also tends to be under-produced.[23] The major mechanisms through which social capital produces its beneficial effects have been summarized by Adler and Kwon as: 1) enhanced information flow through networks of collaboration; 2) increased influence through the quantity and quality of an individual's network ties; and 3) increased solidarity as a result of the "bonding" that takes place in closely-knit social networks.[24]

In general, social capital has been shown to be linked to improved health, greater personal well-being, better care for children, lower crime, and improved government.[25] As well, there is growing evidence that greater co-operation and trust (an outcome or possible element of social capital) are associated with both stronger economic performance[26] and more effective democratic political participation.[27] However, some researchers have pointed to several potentially negative outcomes as well. In this vein, Portes lists exclusion of outsiders, free-riding by individuals within social networks, restrictions on individual freedoms due to excessive bonding, and downward leveling of norms.[28]

One of the major social capital debates of relevance to cultural policy analysts and decision-makers concerns the impact of diversity on social capital. Several studies conducted in the United States have found lower scores on trust and participation in ethnically diverse communities.[29] However, recent Canadian research appears to suggest that other contextual factors may be more significant in explaining levels of social capital among recent immigrants and diverse ethnocultural groups. Nevitte and Bilodeau, in an analysis of trust, tolerance, and confidence in institutions among Canadian immigrants, have discovered that recent immigrants have both higher levels of general trust and higher levels of confidence in institutions than native-born Canadians, but that their levels of trust and confidence tend to converge with those of native-born Canadians over time.[30] A study of ethnicity and social capital conducted by Pendakur and Aizlewood also found higher levels of trust in government among immigrants and visible minority groups using bivariate analysis, but found that controlling for individual and contextual characteristics using survey regression methods erased most of these differences. They concluded that community size was the most significant determinant of social capital, suggesting that "... an urban lifestyle may be a more useful explanation for variance in civic attitudes and behaviours."[31]

Research Findings on Cultural Capital

In examining the research findings on cultural capital, one should keep in mind the variations in definitions discussed in Section One. Most cultural policy research tends to focus on what Bourdieu called objectified cultural capital—means of cultural expression that are symbolically transmissible to others (or what Throsby has labelled intangible cultural capital). Most educational policy research examines habitus—the embodied cultural capital that forms an individual's character and that frequently underpins his or her institutionalized cultural capital or academic qualifications. Much recent cultural development research has taken place in the urban studies field, using Throsby's definition of tangible cultural capital (or assets embodying cultural value) as a starting point (although in practice it has been difficult for researchers to separate intangible cultural capital from its physical manifestations). In general, cultural sustainability studies have used an expanded notion of both social and cultural capital which seeks to aggregate such notions as habitus and intangible cultural capital up to the community level and to examine the impact that ideas, traditions, beliefs, customs, and intellectual capital might have on the health and sustainability of collectives.

The common feature of most studies is that they concentrate on the role that cultural capital plays in the everyday lives of individuals and communities. While cultural development research has tended to focus on individuals as consumers, the individual as citizen is generally the focal point for cultural capital research on participation and sustainability.

However, because of the embeddedness of cultural capital within everyday transactions, it is often difficult to separate economically-driven activity from the social framework in which it takes place. It is this embeddedness that makes analysis so difficult and leads to fierce debates within the academy about whether trust, or civic engagement, or cultural participation, or creativity is the key factor producing positive or negative outcomes. Since there are no easy answers (and certainly no consensus) about the role of cultural capital (however defined) in reinforcing the fabric of everyday life, this section will simply provide a selective overview of research under the thematic headings identified in Section One.

Theme 1: Personal Empowerment

The field of educational sociology has extensively documented the personal benefits derived from investments in cultural capital, demonstrating that it improves academic performance,[32] family-school relationships,[33] marital prospects,[34] physical fitness[35] and children's psycho-social development.[36] In addition, there is a growing scientific literature on the benefits of arts involvement for youth-at-risk[37] and prisoners.[38]

Theme 2: Cultural Participation

In his ground-breaking study on the social impact of the arts, British researcher François Matarasso documented several instances where participation in the arts increased the confidence of individuals, enriched their social lives, and helped them to build the skills needed to find better jobs.[39] He also recorded in some detail how participatory arts projects reinforce social cohesion by promoting partnerships, co-operation, and intercultural understanding. Such involvement, he maintains, strengthens communities by encouraging people to become more active citizens and to get involved in their neighbourhoods.[40]

In the United States, the Saguaro Seminar, an organization devoted to studying civic engagement in America, has produced case study research showing the various ways that arts organizations and museums are attempting to build community connections and "bridging" social capital through initiatives such as residencies in women's shelters, music classes in impoverished areas, and community theatre productions.[41] In these cases, it is clearly the *quality* of the cultural capital underpinning the social capital that is given credit for bridging differences, as the report asserts that "we need not be of the same race, generation, gender, political party, religion, or income group to sing, act, or create together."[42]

To determine the collective impact of individual investments in cultural capital, I have used data from the Canadian General Social Survey to examine the volunteering patterns of individuals who participate (or do not participate) in a variety of cultural activities. I have found that those who attended performances, visited galleries, museums and historic sites, read books and magazines, visited libraries, and participated in cultural activity (such as singing in a choir) were much more likely to volunteer than those who did not.[43] Bourdeau has confirmed these findings and, using multivariate analysis, has determined that the correlation of cultural participation (and, indeed, sport participation) with voluntarism remains significant after controlling for socio-economic and demographic factors such as gender, income, and education.[44] The tendency to volunteer increases with the frequency of participation in cultural activities.[45]

Stolle and Rochon used survey data to answer the question, "Are all associations alike?"[46] They hypothesized that not all associations contribute to social capital to the same degree and that the effect will vary depending on the inclusiveness of the association. They found that members of cultural groups (defined as those engaged in "preservation of traditional regional, national or ethnic culture, church groups, literary, music and arts activities") scored highest on generalized trust and political trust/efficacy, and second-highest on optimism and tolerance (after social groups). They also concluded that "... some association memberships, particularly those of cultural associations, appear to exhibit a wide range of forms of public social capital."[47]

Very little research has been done on the motivations for voluntarism and community involvement, either from a social capital or a cultural capital perspective. However, a study by Bang and Sorensen on so-called "Everyday Makers"—people who engage in "small p" politics at the local level—suggests that "they do not primarily gain their political identities from being citizens of the state but from being engaged in the construction of local networks."[48]

The findings of a cultural participation survey carried out by the Urban Institute in the United States in 1998 tend to support the importance of local networks as motivations for involvement. In that study, the top three reasons why people attended arts and cultural programs and events were to socialize with friends and family (fifty-nine per cent), to support friends and family (forty-none per cent) and to support organizations or events important to the community (fortt-seven per cent).[49] The desire to socialize was also evident in a Canadian study of passive cultural participation that was conducted by Environics in 2000. That study found that the primary motivation for attending live performances and artistic events was the desire to be entertained, to relax, or to enjoy oneself (sicty=two per cent). Only small minorities mentioned other motivations, such as interest in specific performers (fourteen per cent) or to learn, stimulate, or challenge oneself (four per cent).[50] These figures suggest that the aesthetic value of cultural capital appears to be a secondary consideration for many participants and may, in fact, be serving more as a building block for social capital, although much of this social capital may be based on nothing more profound than "just showing up."

Theme 3: Cultural Development and Quality of Life

The theme of culture and development in the 1980s was primarily linked to economic development, but in the 1990s, the UNESCO World Commission on Culture and Development proposed a broader conceptualization that recognized the role of culture in relation to other societal objectives, such as "... sustaining the physical environment, preserving family values, [and] protecting civil institutions in society." This definition, the Commission suggested, should be guided by "... the fostering of respect for all cultures and ... the principle of cultural freedom."[51]

In the intervening years since the Commission's report, the focus of cultural development has shifted noticeably from a national to a local community perspective. Over the past decade or so, there has been an explosion of research on the role of culture and creativity in the development of communities, particularly urban communities. The most well-known scholar working in this area is Richard Florida, whose linkage of human capital and diversity to creative cities has received enormous attention in both the popular and scholarly press.[52] His work has prompted (at least in North America) concerted attempts by city administrations to establish the amenities and find the right cultural "mix" needed to attract knowledge workers. However, some have criticized Florida's methodology for deriving his "bohemian" and "gay" indices as unreliable.[53] Moreover, as Florida has recognized himself, recent research suggests that the regions with the strongest creative economies also have the greatest income inequality.[54]

In Canada, Meric Gertler, in collaboration with Florida and others, recently attempted to reproduce Florida's "quality of place" findings using data from a group of city-regions in Ontario.[55] In a comparison of 309 city-regions in Canada and the United States, Gertler found that Toronto, Ottawa, Hamilton, Kitchener, London, St.-Catherines-Niagara, Windsor, and Thunder Bay ranked in the top ten for diversity (on the "mosaic index"), while Toronto also ranked in the top ten on the "bohemian index" but only Ottawa ranked in the top ten on the "talent index" (within their population size categories). Gertler and his colleagues concluded that "... there appears to be a strong set of linkages between creativity, diversity, talent and technology-intensive activity that are driving the economic growth of Canada's—and Ontario's—city regions." They were also explicit about the role of cultural capital in this development, suggesting "that public policies at all three levels of government that support immigration and settlement, as well as nurturing the arts and creativity, have played a critical role in creating the conditions for successful urban economic development today and into the future."[56]

A great deal of research on this topic is also taking place in Europe. For example, in 1996 Charles Landry and his colleagues examined the role of cultural activity in urban regeneration, using case studies of fifteen European cities. Among the benefits derived from cultural programming at the community level, they identified enhanced social cohesion, improved local image, and renewed vision for the future.[57] In a similar vein, the Canada West Foundation examined the role of culture in promoting the economic competitiveness of Vancouver, Calgary, Edmonton, Winnipeg, Saskatoon, and Regina. *Qualitative* research clearly showed four categories of community benefits derived from arts investments: 1) health and well-being of citizens; 2) enhanced community identity and social cohesion; 3) community revitalization and redevelopment; and 4) economic growth. However, while the study concluded that cultural capital has an important impact on the quality of life of cities and is an important factor in attracting talent, *quantitative* evidence of this impact was still lacking.[58]

Despite the growing evidence base on the beneficial impacts of cultural capital investments in urban communities, there is still little agreement on the nature of these investments. Gertler and his colleagues have suggested that "... Ontario's and Canada's city-regions ought to reinforce and strengthen their urban character by using planning tools that encourage higher-density growth, diverse, mixed-use urban redevelopment, and the preservation and accentuation of authentic, distinctive neighbourhood character.[59]

According to many researchers, however, the type of cultural capital investment that many cities are now undertaking is anything but "authentic." In his book on "fantasy cities," John Hannigan examines the growth of Urban Entertainment Destinations (packaged and sanitized leisure and tourist attractions in cities). He also analyzes the linkages between tangible and intangible cultural capital in postmodern cities, suggesting that themed venues, which blend entertainment, fashion, sport, technology, and food represent the only truly global cultural capital. Like Naomi Klein in her widely-read book *No Logo* and Chatterton and Hollands in their book on *Urban Nightscapes*, Hannigan believes that the primary value of corporatized themed environments lies not in their tangible bricks and mortar, but in their ability to generate intangible cultural capital in the form of *brands* which can be replicated in locations throughout the world. This form of cultural capital is aimed primarily at generating economic rather than social benefits, leading to questions as to the sustainability of local cultures within such an environment.[60]

Theme 4: Cultural Sustainability

David Throsby has drawn some parallels between natural resources and cultural capital that serve as a useful departure point for a discussion of cultural sustainability. He points out that while natural capital has arisen from the beneficence of nature, cultural capital has grown from the creative activities of human beings. Both types of capital impose a duty of preservation in order to pass them on to future generations and, while complex natural ecosystems function to maintain and support balance in the natural environment, equally complex "cultural ecosystems" are required to maintain the cultural life and vitality of human societies. Throsby also points to the importance of diversity in both natural and cultural ecosystems, suggesting that the principal value of cultural capital resides in the unique and distinct nature of the cultural goods and services that comprise it.[61]

The role of cultural capital in building and maintaining communities has not received a great deal of research attention in Canada. However, a few sociological and psychological studies of Aboriginal groups suggest that cultural capital may be a critical element in sustaining communities that, in turn, support the individuals within them. Chandler and Lalonde found a significant correlation between low levels of youth suicide and Aboriginal communities that scored high in six markers of cultural continuity.[62]

Chataway's research indicates that institutions and initiatives in Aboriginal communities are more likely to succeed if they are grounded in culturally-relevant values and that a "cultural match" is related to higher levels of employment and income.[63] Graham and Peters, in examining Aboriginal communities and urban sustainability, suggest that support for diverse Aboriginal cultures and identities in urban communities must take place at the same time as poverty-reduction measures to ensure the sustainability of these communities.[64]

The type of cultural capital that sustains communities, as indicated in the discussion of cultural development above, is the subject of much disagreement among researchers. In a study of urban nightlife in the United Kingdom, Chatterton and Hollands describe the commodification of alternative lifestyles by the "coolhunters" who attempt to brand "subcultural capital" and replicate it in other communities. They suggest that in authentic venues, "... participation is more about 'active production' than 'passive consumption' and hence there is a more fluid boundary between producers and consumers through the exchange of music, ideas, business deals and networks of trust and reciprocity."[65]

This "fluid boundary" seems to apply to non-profit types of cultural capital as well. Describing the *Our Millennium* project initiated by the Community Foundations of Canada to mark the new century, Jeannotte notes that over twenty-seven percent of the lasting "gifts" that Canadians made to their communities to mark the millennium were in the domains of heritage and arts and culture. Some of these projects were traditional, such as restoration of heritage buildings in the community or the publication of local histories. Others, however, utilized various means of cultural expression as a platform for activism. For example, several groups organized concerts or film festivals to raise awareness of problems such as racism or global warming. In other cases, performance art was used as a vehicle for promoting intercultural contact and understanding, for articulating the special needs of groups such as the disabled, or for preserving and celebrating the traditions of particular ethnocultural groups.[66] Clearly, the citizens who mobilized cultural capital in this manner were using it as a vehicle to sustain the everyday life of their community and were doing more than "just showing up."

Critiques of Cultural Capital Research

Cultural capital research carried out in the past decade or so on Theme Two (cultural participation) and Theme Three (cultural development) has borne the brunt of critical commentary. Research on the social impact of arts participation has come under intense scrutiny, probably because of its profound influence on the cultural policies of the New Labour government in the United Kingdom. Paola Merli has criticized Matarasso's research, suggesting that the "research design is flawed, research methods are not applied in a rigorous way and the conceptual bases are questionable."[67] For example, she contends that "... in order to legitimately declare that an artistic programme has improved the quality of life of participants it is necessary ... to know what are, in the opinions of participants, the main constituents of 'quality of life' and the relative weights attributed to them."[68] Both Merli and Eleonora Belfiore suggest that the quantitative statistics utilized by Matarasso's survey data have been derived from ambiguously-worded questions and that, without longitudinal evaluation of the impacts of arts and cultural participation, it is very difficult to prove either positive or negative effects.[69]

Under Theme Three, the issue of instrumentality—employing research to justify using culture as a means to another end, such as economic growth or social inclusion—has come in for heavy criticism in the United Kingdom. A recent discussion paper by Adrian Ellis suggests that current cultural policy aimed at contributing to social inclusion, urban regeneration, tourism, inward investment, employment, and the development of the creative industries is "perverse" because it "… eschews value-judgments that imply a hierarchy of cultural value; emphasizes the quantitative in a field where qualitative assessments have been regarded as central; and aspires to judge cultural organizations by their efficacy in addressing social and economic agenda that could in some cases be addressed more effectively directly."[70] The biggest disconnect, Ellis contends, is in the case of the economic impact studies of cultural development which define cultural activity too generously, seldom account for opportunity costs, and almost never compare funding inputs to actual outcomes.[71] Social impact studies, however, do not escape criticism as Ellis, like Merli and Belfiore, points to the lack of strongly grounded empirical data to back up social impact claims.[72] He does concede, however, that evidence regarding locally-oriented urban cultural development appears to be more persuasive than evidence for projects aimed at attracting "fickle international capital and tourists."[73]

As indicated in Section One, the methodology for deriving the various indices on which Richard Florida bases his "Talent Model" has also come in for a fair amount of criticism. Donald and Morrow, in examining the implications of this model for social and cultural policy in Canadian city-regions, observe that the "gay index" is based on data that include same-sex households that are not gay, that the "talent index" measures only the university-educated and does not take into account other forms of post-secondary education and that the "melting pot" or "mosaic" indices fail to include minority group members that are born in Canada or the US. They are also critical of Florida's lack of attention to gender and life cycle issues and to the relationship between high-tech urban growth and income inequality, racial segregation, and social capital.[74]

What We Need to Know

The critiques of various types of research on social and cultural capital provide a hint as to some of the perceived gaps in our knowledge. It may be useful to group these knowledge gaps under several broadly overarching questions:

- What is the relationship between social and cultural capital? How does social and cultural capital work to produce beneficial (or detrimental) effects? How important are these effects in producing positive public policy outcomes?
- What are the most important elements of social and cultural capital that cultural policy research should be examining?
- How can we best measure the effects of cultural capital?

Causation Knowledge Gaps—How Does Social and Cultural Capital Work?

To quote Robert Putnam, "The causal arrows among civic involvement, reciprocity, honesty, and social trust are as tangled as well-tossed spaghetti."[75] If we are to assume, as the evidence cited above suggests, that social and cultural capital are deeply embedded in complex social and cultural ecosystems, then it may be many years before causation is fully understood.

Uslaner and Dekker, in analyzing the tangle of causality, suggest that social capital is not a single concept and cannot be reduced to a single dimension. They therefore recommend that researchers adopt Onyx and Bullen's metaphor of the cake as a starting point:

We recognize many varieties of cake that look and taste different, having been baked with different variations of a similar stock of ingredients, all of which we none the less recognize as a cake. So it is with social capital. Communities and groups differ, not only in the overall level of social capital, but also in the importance of each arena and capacity building block.[76]

They suggest that researchers begin to examine, for example, whether civic engagement leads to trust and whether all types of social ties are equally good at generating trust. They also note that levels of both trust and civic engagement appear to be lower where there is substantial economic inequality, and the relationship of these dimensions of social capital, at least, needs to be examined within the context of broader public policy interventions.[77]

In the case of cultural capital, we are even further from understanding the causal connections. Jeannotte has suggested that,

... [A] very important feedback loop may exist between cultural capital and civil society / social capital that has not hitherto been acknowledged. We do not yet understand why people who participate in cultural activity also seem to have higher rates of participation in their communities, but if this connection proves to have a robust link to social capital and the quality of community life, it may signal a role for cultural capital that goes far beyond "opera tickets for the elite."[78]

Nevertheless, understanding causality in the area of participation may not provide answers regarding other important dimensions of cultural capital, such as trust, tolerance, connections, reciprocity or social agency, which may be critical to sustainable communities. Much work remains to be done, as Gould suggests in a series of questions (and sub-questions, which are not reproduced here), aimed at describing how cultural capital sustains cultural ecosystems:

- What are the community's cultural resources and assets?
- What cultural values underpin that community and its way of life?
- How can the development of social capital work with cultural values and resources?
- How can cultural capital and its impact on the development of social capital be evaluated?[79]

To answer these questions, Colin Mercer argues that an understanding of cultural capital will entail "... an archaeological task of excavation of the relations between access to and use of cultural resources (including regimes of 'taste' and 'distinction') and the capillary structures of social and economic power."[80]

Constituent Knowledge Gaps—What Are the Key Elements of Social and Cultural Capital?

In the case of social capital, scholarly attention has begun to focus on the inter-relationships among the key elements described in Section One, but this research has been inconclusive so far. Onyx and Bullen have found that tolerance of diversity in their research correlates most with the capacity of an individual to act (social agency) and with feelings of trust and safety. On the other hand, they found that tolerance of diversity correlates least with neighbourhood connections and participation in the local community. In fact, some of the rural communities they studied scored highly on all elements of social capital except tolerance of diversity.[81]

Stolle found that people who tended to join groups and associations already scored high on trust and that membership over a period of time did not increase generalized trust.[82] She also found significant variations in trust between "joiners" in different countries and in different kinds of groups. This would seem to contradict Putnam's argument that in the social capital arising from joining an association, "the causation flows mainly from joining to trusting."[83] Other research tends to support this cultural "self-selection" thesis. Hooghe, in his research on people who do not participate, found that "[n]ot only do the privileged groups in society participate more, they also do so more intensely" and concluded that putting stress on civic participation might introduce new inequalities by favouring people with higher debating skills or time to spare.[84]

Part of the appeal of Putnam's model of social capital, according to Bang and Sorensen, may be that it succeeds in providing "... space both for those who want freedom from the 'system' (the communitarians) and those who consider the hegemony or legitimate domination of the state to be a condition for such freedoms (the republicans).[85] Onyx and Bullen found little evidence that social capital is derived from the state, inasmuch as "... government agencies do not hold a meaningful place in people's networks."[86] However, this runs contrary to Putnam's arguments that strong civic involvement correlates with well-run state and civil institutions.[87] In the United States, Putnam has run a series of multivariate regressions in which he shows strong correlations between social capital and such public policy outcomes as crime rates, health, educational performance, and economic equality.[88] He has, however, cautioned that the direction of causation is not clear: it is not certain whether social capital is a precondition for the development and maintenance of healthy public institutions, such as schools and health care institutions, or whether it is these institutions that help create the conditions that favour social capital formation.[89]

On the cultural capital side, the research of educational psychologists has confirmed the role that habitus (or embodied cultural capital) plays in improving the academic qualifications and life chances of individuals. However, there has been little research on the community-level impacts of these investments.

More to the point for cultural policy decision-makers, there are large knowledge gaps in our understanding of the impact that either tangible and intangible cultural capital might have on the development and well-being of communities (this in spite of the fact that an American study has found that "arts in community development" initiatives were the fastest growing program and service area of local arts agencies in 1996.[90] One of the few rigorous investigations in this area is the extensive research on the community impact of the arts undertaken by the Social Impact of the Arts project in Philadelphia.[91] In 1994, the project team set out to determine if cultural capital was important, not only as an instrument of class dominance by elites, but also as a means of strengthening social ties and community spirit. While the study found the usual correlations between arts attendance and higher incomes and education, it also found that the number of arts and cultural groups in the respondent's zip code was the best single predictor of participation in arts events. After examining a number of possible explanations, the researchers concluded that the ecological context in which individuals live is a powerful contributor to involvement, although the causation was not clear. While it was possible that the number of groups in a neighbourhood might encourage individuals to become more involved in the arts, the researchers suggested that "... there might be another feature of these areas—for example, the social commitment of community residents or "social capital"—that leads to *both* the creation of more groups and greater attendance."[92]

The Social Impact of the Arts project carried out similar analyses in other cities—Chicago, Atlanta, and San Francisco—which confirmed and expanded upon the Philadelphia findings. These analyses found strong correlations between neighbourhoods that were *both* economically and ethnically diverse and the number of arts groups in those neighbourhoods. This study also found that those areas of Philadelphia most likely to have experienced economic revitalization between 1980 and 1990 were *both* economically and ethnically diverse and had a large number of arts and culture organizations.[93]

Throsby maintains that cultural capital generates a time stream of both economic and cultural benefits that can be used as justification for investment. He suggests that cultural investments in *tangible* cultural capital should be based on an understanding of the social impacts that they will have on intergenerational equity (or sustainability), intragenerational equity (equity in access to cultural capital benefits across social classes, income groups, and locational categories), and maintenance of cultural diversity. He cautions that since the destruction of cultural heritage is irreversible, the role of heritage in the infrastructure of a city, region, or country must also be understood in making decisions about cultural capital investments.[94] However, it is the economic impacts of *intangible* (or objectified) cultural capital on communities, as indicated in Section One, that have tended to dominate both the research and the policy agendas. In general, huge knowledge gaps exist with regard to the social impacts listed by Throsby, both in the relatively straightforward domain of tangible cultural capital (which is mainly concerned with movable and immovable cultural property) and the much more abstract realm of intangible cultural capital (which embraces the various forms of intellectual property used by creators to express themselves).

Measurement Knowledge Gaps—How Do We Measure Social and Cultural Capital?

In recent years, there has been a flood of social science literature on social capital measurement issues. The World Bank has developed a fairly cohesive framework to guide the measurement strategies of the projects it has funded (see Figure 1). This framework is notable for its attention to both the micro and the macro dimensions of social capital, as well as to the hard (structural) and soft (cognitive) elements that may contribute to the level of social capital in a society. This has been further refined in a Social Capital Assessment Tool developed for the World Bank by Krishna and Shrader which examines not only community and household characteristics, but also structural elements, such as organizational affiliations and networks, and cognitive elements, such as trust, solidarity, and reciprocity.[95]

Putnam has suggested that in addition to analyzing micro- and macro-level data on social capital, there is also a need to compare data across countries, to do experimental work, and to develop longitudinal measures.[96] Willms has also stressed the multi-level measurement challenges and has suggested that, because social capital is about relationships among people, analysts must examine both individual and collective impacts.[97]

In comments that are also relevant to the measurement of cultural capital, Willms has argued that the quality of social relationships appear to be more important than quantity in dictating outcomes such as social integration and social support. Because "... social capital is embedded in the culture of a society and, therefore, affected by social, economic and historical factors," Willms suggests that these factors cannot be ignored when seeking to measure and understand the impact of social capital.[98]

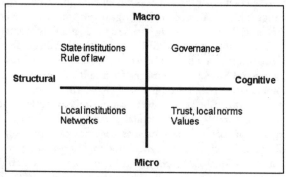

Figure 1: Measurement Dimensions of Social Capital

Macro

Structural

State institutions
Rule of law

Governance

Cognitive

Local institutions
Networks

Trust, local norms
Values

Micro

Source: Grootaert and van Basteleaer, 2002

Due to the pressure on cultural organizations in the United Kingdom to demonstrate that they are addressing social exclusion in their communities, more attention has been given to cultural indicators in that country than elsewhere. A survey report on measuring the economic and social impact of the arts, prepared in 2002 for the Arts Council of England, describes a huge range of assessment methodologies with varying levels of robustness.[99] None of these methodologies, however, explicitly uses a cultural capital lens and little effort has been made to date to develop an overall model or framework for such a lens.

An exception, however, is the work of Colin Mercer on cultural citizenship, carried out for the Bank of Sweden Tercentenary Foundation in 2002. In his book, *Towards Cultural Citizenship: Tools for Cultural Policy Development*, Mercer proposes the development of a Cultural Capital Assessment Tool, using as a base the methodology employed by Australian researchers for the *Accounting for Tastes* study. That survey methodology asked a series of questions under eight categories: household characteristics, domestic leisure practices, social activities, tastes and preferences, recreational activities, family and friends, personal characteristics, and social and political attitudes.[100] Refining and supplementing these questions with material from other researchers, Mercer suggests a framework of four sets of indicators aimed at measuring: 1) cultural vitality, diversity, and conviviality; 2) cultural access, participation, and consumption; 3) culture, lifestyle, and identity; and 4) culture, ethics, governance, and conduct.[101] He argues that the methodological "edge" given by social and cultural capital assessment is that "... they are tools that set in motion not an 'objective' process of scientific research but a mode of questioning and reflection which enable people to recognise—and potentially become stewards of—assets they may not have realised they had."[102]

The density of cultural capital existing within a community is likely much greater than policy-makers realize. A purely unscientific glance at the local "What's on?" listings in Ottawa/Gatineau, a medium-sized city, yielded 172 separate cultural and entertainment events during the August 23-29, 2003 period. These ranged from large events, such as the Ottawa Folk Festival, the Central Canada Exhibition, and the Gatineau Hot Air Balloon Festival, to small ones, such as a Heritage Ottawa walking tour of the village of Britannia, and Soundstorm, a youth video dance event. In addition, there were seventeen separate events, such as dances and workshops, for "singles" wishing to increase their social capital.

A numerical breakdown of the events by category (Table 2) provides an interesting perspective on public investment in the cultural capital of everyday life. About one-

CATEGORY OF EVENT	NUMBER OF EVENTS
Concerts	5
Theatre	5
Dance	2
Special screenings (film and video)	2
Comedy	2
Live music / Rock	7
Live music / Folk / World / Blues	18
Live music / Jazz	6
Live music / Country	6
Live music / Lounges	8
Dance clubs	11
Readings / Literary events	3
Other events (includes fairs, walking tours, historic sites)	14
Museums	41
Galleries	42
Total	**172**

third of the events—music featured in various clubs and other venues—was clearly unsubsidized by the public purse. While a significant portion of the museum events listed were likely in receipt of public support from one level of government or another, the majority of the gallery events probably were not. But even if public money may not be directly invested in the venues and events that embody everyday cultural capital, the public sector, through various urban government planning processes, definitely has an interest in the extent and shape of this cultural landscape.

Implications for Cultural Policy and Decision-Making

In a report on cultural policy and cultural diversity in Canada, prepared for the Council of Europe in 2000, Greg Baeker referred to the definitional and conceptual dilemmas in Canadian cultural policy as "longstanding and numbingly repetitive," documenting what he refers to as "recurring policy tensions": between "high art" and "popular culture," between public and private interests, between old and new institutions and between "supply-side" and "demand-side" policies.[104] He concludes that, in the face of increasing diversity, "... traditional arguments regarding national identity and cultural sovereignty are outmoded and elitist: new policy rationales are needed."[105]

Catherine Murray, in an essay on cultural diversity and civil society, frames her arguments in terms of cultural governance and suggests that "... we must also seek to create a more broadly conducive climate for the appreciation of cultural value, through more effective forms of cultural governance and coordination."[106]

From an international perspective, Mercer defines the policy challenge as one of needing "... to witness and encounter ... a much noisier 'stakeholder scenario' in which many more voices participate."[107] His prescription is to develop a set of cultural indicators that go beyond administrative performance measures in order to listen to these many voices and incorporate their point of view into the knowledge base that informs policy.

At the risk of contributing to the "numbing repetitiveness," this chapter must also add its voice to the growing chorus urging a broadening (and possibly deepening) of the conceptual base for cultural policy in Canada. Social and cultural capital are not panaceas for cultural policy dilemmas, but they are certainly useful tools for understanding those dilemmas.

Bourdieu's concepts of habitus, fields (or social spaces), and cultural capital can help us to understand the critical linkages between lifestyle and culture. Social spaces, as Chatterton and Hollands have pointed out, are "... mediated by various types of 'capital': economic—access to various monetary resources, social—resources which one accrues through durable networks of acquaintance and recognition, and cultural or informational—competence and ability to appreciate legitimate culture related, in particular, to level of education."[108] The central question for cultural policy is: who is defining "legitimate culture?"

In a recent paper on cities and polarization, Caroline Andrew connects the dots between social spaces, physical spaces, lifestyles, and public policy by asking the question, "Is the persistence and deepening poverty of poor neighbourhoods a problem because the residents cannot see other lifestyles and therefore cannot imagine changing the distribution of societal resources? Or is it a problem because these spatial distributions get different levels of public services and indeed different philosophies of public action?"[109] Chatterton and Hollands argue that the fragmentation of cultural capital into a cornucopia of "subcultural capitals" explains, in part, why certain segments of the urban landscape are ignored by public policy.[110] Those inhabiting these marginalized areas are usually left with only two options: to "invent" new forms of symbolic or objectified forms of expression or to fend for themselves on the margins with whatever cultural resources are available.

For a number of reasons (not the least of which is the increasingly urban nature of Canada), cities have become the primary site where many of the issues related to cultural and subcultural capital play out. As Russell Smith, in a recent *Globe and Mail* column, notes, "the word citizen comes from the Latin word for city—*civitas*. We would not have a concept of citizenship without cities."[111] In his monumental work, *Cities in Civilization*, Peter Hall goes further to suggest that "... a very important part of living, and the creativity that comes out of it, has consisted in finding solutions to the city's own problems of order and organization."[112] In his view, it is the collective creativity brought to bear on the problems of the *civitas* that characterize a great city—"People meet, people talk, people listen to each other's music and each other's words, dance each other's dances, take in each other's thoughts. And so, by accidents of geography, sparks may be struck and something new comes out of the encounter."[113] In the current world of instantaneous communications and international travel, cities are the conduits of global cultural flows, and local encounters frequently represent the shores over which the leading edge of these flows break and disperse.

So, what does this mean for cultural policy? For cultural policy as currently formulated, visions of dollar signs often spring to mind when the words "creative" and "cities" are used in the same sentence. However, the real meaning may lie in the more mundane and, paradoxically, more profound sphere of everyday life as lived by citizens in their communities. A first step in understanding the significance of social and cultural capital in the formulation of cultural policy may consist in applying, as Mercer suggests, a Cultural Capital Assessment Tool at the level of the local community. As he has pointed out:

... this process or "tool" of mapping, auditing and assessment of the true cultural resources of a community becomes part of the task of linking culture integrally, rather than marginally, to the development process. It makes culture part of the action rather than an incidental or bit player and stresses the ongoing and indissoluble connection between culture and economy, culture and social relations, culture and power, culture and identity, culture and rights, culture and human development.[114]

In building the case for a more deliberate and scientific "cultural mapping" of urban spaces, Mercer emphasizes that this is not simply an exercise in inventorying the "bricks and mortar," but also one of understanding how individuals and communities interact with these resources—in other words, how they are used to build and maintain social and cultural capital. In developing new cultural maps, he suggests that "... there needs to be a new compact and relationship between 'local knowledge' and tactics on the one hand, and the larger and strategic prerogatives of cultural policy and service delivery on the other."[115]

Cultural mapping, in the emerging lexicon of cultural policy, is merely a prelude to cultural planning—a process that goes beyond beautification or "producing a mask of leisure and entertainment to conceal the most profound social and economic inequalities."[116] The fundamental emphasis of cultural planning should be, as Mercer suggests, the production of citizens, rather than goods and services.[117]

The production of citizens has not traditionally been on the cultural policy agenda, but in a global cultural economy, where the means of production for cultural goods and services are increasingly in the hands of the multinationals; this may be the only remaining locus for effective state intervention. This chapter has outlined the case for linking a greater understanding of the role of social and cultural capital in the creation of citizens. It has argued that cultural, as well as political and economic practices, contribute to a sense of empowerment and belonging, foster active participation in communities, contribute to economic vitality and quality of life, and help to sustain the *civitas*—the social space in which citizenship is rooted. Cultural citizenship, in an increasingly diverse and globalized environment, may in fact be one of the most effective mechanisms for states wishing to strengthen their democratic foundations. Citizens live their lives in communities not only through rights and duties, but also through imagination and creativity. Therefore, recognition of the many forms that cultural capital takes within the multifaceted and complex social spaces of today's world is a necessary first step to the development of a vital and inclusive form of cultural citizenship.[118]

Notes

[1] Eric Uslaner and Paul Dekker, "The 'Social' in Social Capital," in Paul Dekker and Eric M. Uslaner, eds., *Social Capital and Participation in Everyday Life* (London: Routledge, 2001), 178.

[2] Certain parts of this section rely heavily on the author's previous study: M. Sharon Jeannotte, "Singing Alone? The Contribution of Cultural Capital to Social Cohesion and Sustainable Communities," *International Journal of Cultural Policy* 9, no. 1 (2003): 35–49.

[3] Robert Putnam, *Bowling Alone: The Collapse and Revival of American Community* (New York: Simon & Schuster, 2000), 19.

[4] Ibid., 22.

[5] Michael Woolcock, "The Place of Social Capital in Understanding Social and Economic Outcomes," *Isuma–Canadian Journal of Policy Research* 2, no. 1 (Spring 2001): 13.

[6] Policy Research Initiative, *Social Capital Background Paper–Conceptualization* (Ottawa: Policy Research Initiative, 2003), 8.

[7] Organization for Economic Cooperation and Development, *The Well-being of Nations: The Role of Human and Social Capital* (Paris: OECD, 2001), 41, available at http://www.oecd.org/els/pdfs/EDSMINDOCA003.pdf.

[8] Jenny Onyx and Paul Bullen, "The Different Faces of Social Capital in NSW Australia," in Dekker and Uslaner, eds., *Social Capital and Participation in Everyday Life*, 45–58.

[9] Amanda Aizlewood and Ravi Pendakur, "SRA-657: Ethnicity and Social Capital in Canada" (paper prepared for the Strategic Research and Analysis Directorate, Department of Canadian Heritage, Ottawa, June 27, 2003).

[10] Helen Gould, "Culture and Social Capital," in François Matarasso, ed., *Recognising Culture—A Series of Briefing Papers on Culture and Development* (London: Comedia, the Department of Canadian Heritage and UNESCO, 2001), 85–86.

[11] Colin Mercer, *Towards Cultural Citizenship: Tools for Cultural Policy and Development* (Stockholm: Gidlunds Förlag, 2002), 34.

[12] Pierre Bourdieu, *Distinction* (Cambridge, MA: Harvard University Press, 1984).

[13] Pierre Bourdieu, "The Forms of Capital," in John G. Richardson, ed., *Handbook of Theory and Research in the Sociology of Education* (Westport, CT: Greenwood Press, 1986), 241–58.

[14] Gould, "Culture and Social Capital," 87.

[15] Jeannotte, "Singing Alone," 39.

[16] David Throsby, "Cultural Capital and Sustainability Concepts in the Economics of Cultural Heritage" in Marta de la Torre, ed., *Assessing the Values of Cultural Heritage* (Los Angeles: The Getty Conservation Institute, 2002), 103.

[17] Asoka Mendis, "Social Capital Formation and Institutions for Sustainability" (workshop proceedings, at the University of British Columbia, November 16-17, 1998), available at http://www.sdri.ubc.ca/GBFP/soc_cap.html; italics added.

[18] Fikret Berkes, "Cultural and Natural Capital: A Systems Approach Revisited, in Asoka Mendis, ed., *Social Capital Formation and Institutions for Sustainability*.

[19] Quoted in Policy Research Initiative, *Social Capital Background Paper–Measurement* (Ottawa: Policy Research Initiative, 2003), 2–3.

[20] Ibid.

[21] Bourdieu, "The Forms of Capital," 249.

[22] Gould, "Culture and Social Capital."

[23] Christian Grootaert, "Social Capital–The Missing Link?," in Dekker and Uslaner, eds., *Social Capital and Participation in Everyday Life*, 16–17.

[24] Paul S. Adler and Seok-Woo Kwon, "Social Capital: Prospects for a New Concept," *Academy of Management Review* 27, no.1 (2002): 20–30.

[25] Organization for Economic Cooperation and Development, *The Well-being of Nations*.

[26] Francis Fukuyama, *Trust: The Social Virtues and the Creation of Prosperity* (New York: The Free Press, 1995); Stephen Knack and Philip Keefer, "Does Social Capital have an Economic Payoff? A Cross-Country Investigation," *The Quarterly Journal of Economics* (November 1997): 1251–88.

[27] Peter A. Hall, "Social Capital in Britain," *British Journal of Political Science* 29 (1999): 416–61; Robert Putnam, *Making Democracy Work: Civic Institutions in Modern Italy* (Princeton, NJ: Princeton University Press, 1993); Dani Rodrik, "Participatory Politics, Social Cooperation, and Economic Stability," *American Economic Review* 90 (2000): 140–44.

[28] Quoted in Policy Research Initiative, *Social Capital Background Paper–Conceptualization* (Ottawa: Policy Research Initiative, June 2003), 7.

[29] E. L. Glaeser, D. Laibson, J. Al Scheinkman and C. L. Soutter, "Measuring Trust," *Quarterly Journal of Economics* 65 (August 2000): 811–46; Saguaro Seminar, "Better Together–The Report of the Saguaro Seminar: Civic Engagement in America" (Cambridge, MA: John F. Kennedy School of Government, 2002), 33–39; Robert Wuthnow, *Sharing the Journey: Support Groups and America's New Quest for Community* (New York: Free Press, 1994).

[30] Neil Nevitte and Antoine Bilodeau, "SRA-747—Trust, Tolerance and Confidence in Institutions: Evidence from the Canadian World Values Surveys, 1990-2000" (prepared for the Strategic Research and Analysis Directorate, Department of Canadian Heritage, Ottawa, March 20, 2003).

[31] Aizlewood and Pendakur, "Ethnicity and Social Capital in Canada," 14.

[32] James S. Catterall, "Involvement in the Arts and Human Development: General Involvement in Music and Theatre Arts," in Edward B. Fiske, ed., *Champions of Change: The Impact of the Arts on Learning* (Washington, DC: Arts Education Partnership and the President's Committee on the Arts and the Humanities, 1999), available at http://www.aep-arts.org./highlights/coc-release.html; Paul DiMaggio, "Cultural Capital and School Success: The Impact of Status Culture Participation on the Grades of U.S. High School Students," *American Sociological Review* 47 (April 1982): 189–201; Richard L. Zweigenhaft, "Accumulation of Cultural Capital and Social Capital: The Differing College Careers of Prep School and Public School Graduates," *Sociological Spectrum* 13 (1993): 365–76; Richard L. Zweigenhaft, "The Application of Cultural and Social Capital: A Study of the Twenty-fifth Year Reunion Entries of Prep and Public School Graduates of the Yale College," *Higher Education* 23 (1992): 311–20.

[33] Annette Lareau, "Social Class Differences in Family-School Relationships," *Sociology of Education* 60 (April 1987): 73–85.

[34] Paul DiMaggio and John Mohr, "Cultural Capital, Educational Attainment and Marital Selection," *American Journal of Sociology* 90, no. 6 (1985): 1231–61.

[35] Chris Shilling, "Schooling and the Production of Physical Capital," *Discourse* 13, no. 1 (October 1992): 1–19.

[36] David R. Offord et al., "Sports, The Arts and Community Programs: Rates and Correlates of Participation," (prepared for the Applied Research Branch, Human Resources Development Canada, Ottawa, October 1998).

[37] See, for example, Catterall, "Involvement in the Arts and Human Development;" Judith Humphreys Weitz, *Coming Up Taller—Arts and Humanities Programs for Children and Youth at Risk* (Washington, DC: President's Committee on the Arts and Humanities, 1996).

[38] A. Peaker and J. Vincent, *Arts in Prisons: Towards a Sense of Achievement* (London: Research and Planning Unit, Home Office, 1990).

[39] François Matarasso, *Use or Ornament? The Social Impact of Participation in the Arts* (London: Comedia, 1997), 14–22.

[40] Ibid., vi-vii.

[41] Saguaro Seminar, "Better Together."

[42] Ibid., 35.

[43] Jeannotte, "Singing Alone," 45.

[44] Jean-Pierre Bourdeau, "SRA-672–Bowling Along: Cross-indicators of Social Participation and Local Community Belonging in Canada" (prepared for the Strategic Research and Analysis Directorate, Department of Canadian Heritage, April 2002).

[45] Ibid.; Jeannotte, "Singing Alone."

[46] Dietland Stolle and Thomas R. Rochon, "Are All Associations Alike? Member Diversity, Associational Type and the Creation of Social Capital," *American Behavioral Scientist* 42, no. 1 (September 1998): 47–65.

[47] Ibid., 61.

[48] Henrik P. Bang and Eva Sorensen, "The Everyday Maker: Building Political, Rather than Social, Capital," in Dekker and Uslaner, eds., *Social Capital and Participation in Everyday Life*, 156.

[49] Chris Walker, *Arts & Culture: Community Connections—Contributions from New Survey Research* (Washington, DC: The Urban Institute, 2002), 4.

[50] M. Sharon Jeannotte, "SRA-541–Cultural Symbiosis: Cultural Participation and Cohesive Communities" (prepared for the Strategic Research and Analysis Directorate, Department of Canadian Heritage, Ottawa, November 24, 2000), 9–10.

[51] Pérez de Cuéllar, Javier et al., *Our Creative Diversity—Report of the World Commission on Culture and Development* (Paris: UNESCO, July 1996) (summary version), 15.

[52] See, for example, Richard Florida, "The Rise of the Creative Class—Why Cities Without Gays and Rock Bands are Losing the Economic Development Race," *The Washington Monthly* (May 2002), available at http://www.washingtonmonthly.com/features/2001/0205.florida; Richard Florida, *The Geography of Bohemia* (Pittsburgh: Carnegie Mellon University, 2001); Richard Florida and Gary Gates, *Technology and Tolerance: The Importance of Diversity to High-Technology Growth* (Washington, DC: Brookings Institution Center on Urban and Metropolitan Policy, 2001).

53 Betsy Donald and Douglas Morrow, "SRA-674–Competing for Talent: Implications for Social and Cultural Policy in Canadian City Regions" (prepared for the Strategic Research and Analysis Directorate, Department of Canadian Heritage, Ottawa, May 14, 2003), 14.

54 Richard Florida, "The New American Dream," *The Washington Monthly* (March 2003): 26–33; Betsy Donald and Douglas Morrow, "SRA-674–Competing for Talent:".

55 Meric S. Gertler, Richard Florida, Gary Gates, and Tara Vinodrai, *Competing on Creativity: Placing Ontario's Cities in North American Context* (Toronto: Ontario Ministry of Enterprise, Opportunity, and Innovation and the Institute for Competitiveness and Prosperity, November 2002).

56 *Ibid.* 24–25.

57 Charles Landry, L. Green, François Matarasso, and F. Bianchini, *The Art of Regeneration: Urban Renewal Through Cultural Activity* (London: Comedia, Stroud, 1996).

58 Jason J. Azmier, *Culture and Economic Competitiveness: An Emerging Role for the Arts in Canada* (Calgary: Canada West Foundation, 2002).

59 Gertler et al., *Competing on Creativity*, 25.

60 Paul Chatterton and Robert Hollands, *Urban Nightscapes: Youth Cultures, Pleasure Spaces and Corporate Power* (London: Routledge, 2003), 28–44; John Hannigan, *Fantasy City: Pleasure and Profit in the Postmodern Metropolis* (London: Routledge, 1998), 69–70; Naomi Klein, *No Logo: Taking Aim at the Brand Bullies* (Toronto: Vintage Canada, 2000), 35–38.

61 Throsby, "Cultural Capital and Sustainability Concepts," 106.

62 Michael J. Chandler and Christopher Lalonde, "Cultural Continuity as a Hedge Against Suicide in Canada's First Nations," *Transnational Psychiatry* 35, no. 2 (June 1998): 191–219.

63 Cynthia Chataway, "Successful Development in Aboriginal Communities: Does it Depend Upon a Particular Process?," *Journal of Aboriginal Economic Development* 3, no. 1 (2002): 76–88.

64 Katherine A.H. Graham and Evelyn Peters, *Aboriginal Communities and Urban Sustainability* (Ottawa: Canadian Policy Research Networks, 2002), 22.

65 Chatterton and Hollands, *Urban Nightscapes*, 209.

66 Jeannotte, "Singing Alone," 42.

67 Paola Merli, "Evaluating the Social Impact of Participation in Arts Activities: A Critical Review of François Matarasso's *Use or Ornament?*," *International Journal of Cultural Policy* 8, no. 1 (2002): 107–18, 114.

68 Ibid., 115.

69 Ibid., 110; Eleonora Belfiore, "Art as a Means of Alleviating Social Exclusion: Does it Really Work? A Critique of Instrumental Cultural Policies and Social Impact Studies in the UK," *International Journal of Cultural Policy* 8, no. 1 (2002): 91–106, 98.

70 Adrian Ellis, *Valuing Culture* (London: Demos, 2003), 5.

71 Ibid., 7.

72 Ibid.

73 Ibid., 8.

74 Donald and Morrow, "Competing for Talent," 13–14. It should be noted, however, that Florida will be responding to some of these criticisms in his forthcoming book.

75 Putnam, *Bowling Alone*, 137.

76 Onyx and Bullen, "The Different Faces of Social Capital," 56.

77 Uslaner and Dekker, "The 'Social' in Social Capital," 179–83.

78 Jeannotte, "Singing Alone," 47.

79 Gould, "Culture and Social Capital," 90–91.

80 Mercer, *Towards Cultural Citizenship*, 51.

81 Onyx and Bullen, "The Different Faces of Social Capital," 56.

82 Dietland Stolle, "'Getting to Trust': An Analysis of the Importance of Institutions, Families, Personal Experiences and Group Membership," in Dekker and Uslaner, eds., *Social Capital and Participation in Everyday Life*, 126–29.

83 Robert Putnam, "Bowling Alone: America's Declining Social Capital," *Journal of Democracy* 6, no.1 (1995): 65–78, 66.

84 Marc Hooghe, "'Not For Our Kind of People': The Sour Grapes Phenomenon as a Causal Mechanism for Political Passivity," in Dekker and Uslaner, eds., *Social Capital and Participation in Everyday Life*, 173.

85 Bang and Sorensen, "The Everyday Maker," 159.

86 Onyx and Bullen, "The Different Faces of Social Capital," 56.

87 Putnam, *Making Democracy Work*.

88 Robert Putnam, "Social Capital: Measurement and Consequences," *Isuma—Canadian Journal of Policy Research* 2, no. 1 (Spring 2001): 41–51, 48–51.

89 Ibid., 51.

90 Gary O. Larson, *American Canvas* (Washington, DC: National Endowment for the Arts, 1997), 84.

91 Mark J. Stern and Susan C. Seifert, "Individual Participation and Community Arts Groups: A Quantitative Analysis of Philadelphia" (working paper no.1 prepared for the Social Impact of the Arts Project, University of Pennsylvania School of Social Work, 1994).

92 Ibid., 7.

93 Mark J. Stern, "Is All the World Philadelphia? A Multi-City Study of Arts and Cultural Organizations, Diversity and Urban Revitalization" (working paper no.9 prepared for the Social Impact of the Arts Project, University of Pennsylvania School of Social Work, May 1999), 8.

94 Throsby, "Cultural Capital and Sustainability Concepts," 109–10.

95 Anirudh Krishna and Elizabeth Shrader, "Social Capital Assessment Tool" (prepared for the World Bank Conference on Social Capital and Poverty Reduction, Washington, DC, June 22-24, 1999), available at http://www.poverty.worldbank.org/library/view/8150, cited in Mercer, *Towards Cultural Citizenship*, 35.

96 Putnam, "Social Capital: Measurement and Consequences," 51.

97 J. Douglas Willms, "Three Hypotheses About Community Effects on Social Outcomes," *Isuma—Canadian Journal of Policy Research* 2, no. 1 (Spring 2001): 53–62, 60.

98 Ibid.

99 Michelle Reeves, *Measuring the Economic and Social Impact of the Arts: A Review* (London: Arts Council of England, May 2002).

100 Mercer, *Towards Cultural Citizenship*, 51.

101 Ibid., 60–61.

102 Ibid., 53.

103 "Going out," *The Ottawa Citizen* (August 23, 2003), K1-K3.

104 Greg Baeker, "SRA-468–Cultural Policy and Cultural Diversity in Canada" (prepared for the Strategic Research and Analysis Directorate in the Department of Canadian Heritage, Ottawa, August 28, 2000), 39–42.

105 Ibid., 3.

106 Catherine A. Murray, "The Third Sector: Cultural Diversity and Civil Society," in Nancy Duxbury, ed., "Making Connections: Culture and Social Cohesion in the New Millennium," special issue, *Canadian Journal of Communication* 27, nos. 2 & 3 (2002): 331–50, 346.

107 Mercer, *Towards Cultural Citizenship*, 112.

108 Chatterton and Hollands, *Urban Nightscapes*, 80.

109 Caroline Andrew, "Cities and Polarization" (workshop presentation for Canadian Council on Social Development Conference on Social Inclusion, Ottawa, March 27-28, 2003), 4.

110 Chatterton and Hollands, *Urban Nightscapes*, 83.

111 Russell Smith, "Hot Town, Summer in the City," *The Globe and Mail* (August 2, 2003), T1.

112 Peter Hall, *Cities in Civilization* (London: Weidenfeld and Nicolson, 1998), 6.

113 Ibid., 21.

114 Mercer, *Towards Cultural Citizenship*, 53.

115 Ibid., 169–70.

116 Ibid., 171.

117 Ibid.

118 The following sources may also be helpful: Cindy-Ann Bryant and Doug Norris, *Measurement of Social Capital: The Canadian Experience* (country report for the OECD-UK ONS International Conference on Social Capital Measurement, London, September 25-27, 2002); Christiaan Grootaert and Thierry van Bastelaer, *Understanding and Measuring Social Capital: A Synthesis of Findings and Recommendations from the Social Capital Initiative* (Washington, DC: Forum Series on the Role of Institutions in Promoting Economic Growth, January 2002); Alejandro Portes, "Social Capital: Its Origins and Applications in Modern Sociology," *Annual Review of Sociology* 24 (1998): 1–24

10.

The Elusiveness of Full Citizenship:
Accounting for Cultural Capital, Cultural Competencies, and Cultural Pluralism

Karim H. Karim

Most discussions about cultural capital seem to revolve around the consumption or use of cultural goods and services. This chapter attempts to address some aspects of a more fundamental role that cultural capital plays in society. Adopting an anthropological perspective on culture as a way of life, it seeks to widen Pierre Bourdieu's discussion of the social exclusion that results from a person's lack of certain aesthetic dispositions to one that accounts for broader aspects of life. Cultural capital in the present discussion refers not only to the acquisition of taste and distinction, but to an individual's possession of a more extensive set of cultural competencies. They include the forms of knowledge and practices that all human beings need in order to interact with each other in society.

Sharon Jeannotte[1] succinctly summarizes Bourdieu's conceptualization of cultural capital as consisting of three elements:

> ...1) *embodied capital (or habitus), the system of lasting dispositions that form an individual's character and guide his or her actions and tastes; 2) objectified capital, the means of cultural expression, such as painting, writing, and dance, that are symbolically transmissible to others; and 3) institutionalized capital, the academic qualifications that establish the value of the holder of a given qualification.*[1]

The present chapter's inquiry is primarily concerned with the competencies that individuals hold in themselves rather than the objectified and institutionalized forms of cultural capital. Bourdieu presents "habitus" as the sociological factors (parentage, class, education) that lead to the production of a person's capacities for taste. Whereas I find his overly-structural analytical framework and its implications for the relative immutability of individual taste to be problematic, this study does draw from his idea of the embodied nature of cultural capital.

Bourdieu's well-known inquiry into this matter, published in English as *Distinction: A Social Critique of the Judgement of Taste*,[2] was motivated by the effort to identify the aspects of bourgeois culture that become symbolic of social status. The book presented his analysis of a survey that he conducted in the 1960s in France.

The survey sought to determine how the cultivated disposition and cultural competence that are revealed in the nature of the cultural goods consumed, and in the way they are consumed, vary according to the category of agents and the area to which they applied, from the most legitimate areas such as painting or music to the most "personal" ones such as clothing, furniture or cookery, and within the legitimate domains, according to the markets—"academic" and "non-academic"—in which they may be placed.[3]

The present discussion's anthropological approach to culture does not subscribe to notions of the legitimacy or illegitimacy of cultural practices. On the contrary, it involves in its ambit of inquiry broader cultural expressions such as language, humour, and communal memory. It also seeks to address the pluralism of Western societies that goes beyond the traditional idea of a culturally homogenous nation-state.

The key question for this discussion is: how does a liberal democracy strive to broaden the access to social power that some citizens have by possessing specific kinds of cultural capital? As with Bourdieu, this question suggests that cultural capital facilitates the acquisition, maintenance, and growth of other forms of capital. It is also vital to having effective citizenship. Cultural capital is to be found in the cultural knowledge and competencies that an individual holds, but which are not necessarily articulated by society in formal manners.[4]

The citizen role involves a range of forms of tacit knowledge, competence and taken-for-granted assumptions. Citizens must know how to engage in citizenship activities. They require basic working knowledge of the political system and skills in accessing and processing information, interpreting political talk, and debating public issues. All of this must be contained in the taken-for-granted knowledge which comprises their (shared) lifeworld.[5]

Jim McGuigan rightly notes that cultural citizenship vastly exceeds the ambit of traditional cultural policy.[6] It has implications for a variety of state policies, including economic policy, since those citizens who do not have certain forms of *cultural* competencies are denied access to society's resources.

Citizenship

Most contemporary liberal democracies uphold the principle of equality among their respective citizens and reflect this goal in their legislative and policy structures. Social inclusion is generally viewed as the means to ensure the benefits of citizenship for all. However, it is debatable whether *full* citizenship—the ideal of complete access to participation in social, cultural, economic, political, and spiritual aspects of national life—is attainable. According to Derek Heater,[7] the practice of such "perfect citizenship" is dependent on both the society as well as the citizen. He constructs a hierarchy in which the full citizens "have the most complete set of rights and who most fully discharge their civic duties"—this involves an active effort to be engaged with one's rights *and* responsibilities. On the second rung of Heater's schema are "passive citizens"— who have the freedom and ability to participate in society but do not do so. Below them are "second-class citizens ... who have the legal status of citizen but, because of discrimination, are denied full rights in practice." Next come the "underclass" who "are so economically and culturally impoverished that they are in effect excluded from the normal style of social and political activity which the term citizen connotes." At the bottom of the ladder are the "denizens" who are residents but not nationals in the country where they have a very limited range of rights.

Citizenship of any kind is not possible without the possession of a set of basic rights that enables an individual to participate in various sectors of society. She also has to have the inclination and the personal capability (physical, economic, cultural) to exercise those rights, as well as to fulfill her social responsibilities. Furthermore, the freedom to conduct these activities implies that they are not impeded by either structural or temporary barriers. However, it is doubtful that any one individual, no matter how privileged and active in society, is able to participate in all aspects of life. Full citizenship, if conceptualized in that manner, is an unattainable ideal. In practical terms, it may be conceived of as the freedom to carry out the socially responsible actions that express one's rights and fulfill one's duties within the range of one's areas of interests. This freedom does not imply the complete actualization of one's intentions. Even the leader of the country can only hope to participate optimally in the particular fields of life in which she is involved, rather than be engaged to the maximum degree.

The mid-1990s saw the emergence of the discussion on cultural rights,[8] which later gave rise to the contemporary debate on cultural citizenship. Among the issues that this debate is addressing is the very exercise of effective citizenship. As a tentative definition, Bryan S. Turner states that "cultural citizenship can be described as cultural empowerment, namely the capacity to participate effectively, creatively and successfully within a national culture"[9]; he then goes on to problematize this formulation with a discussion of globalization, cosmopolitanism, and contemporary communication technologies. Nick Crossley[10] suggests that the exercise of citizenship is based on the cultural recognition of communal symbols and an intersubjective relationship with others in society, without which it would be merely an ideological construct.

Effective citizenship involving participation in various areas of social life is dependent on knowing how to interpret relevant information culturally rather than merely in a technical fashion. In order to acquire the cultural competencies to operate in particular social situations the citizen has to be able to understand the subtle codes that underlie the surface appearance of a situation. "A beholder who lacks the specific code feels lost in a chaos of sounds and rhythms, colours and lines, without rhyme or reason."[11] Symbolic interactionists like Erving Goffman[12] have demonstrated the kinds of knowledge that one needs for basic societal relationships.

Having the right sets of knowledge is vital for effective participation in various spheres of life and for socio-economic and political mobility. The former are acquired through socialization, education, and interactions with others. Appropriate occupational training is supposed to open doors to opportunities for participation in economic life; however, in practical terms one needs not only the requisite bodies of knowledge necessary for performing the nominal aspects of the job at hand but also other "inside information" such as the relevant jargon to conduct informal conversations related to the work. The more adept a person is in such cultural competencies, which are often mistakenly viewed as being superfluous, the better she will perform. Whereas the technical occupational knowledge usually is the basis of being hired, relevant cultural insight is crucial for advancement. In some cases, "the right fit" into the existing office culture is a requirement for being engaged in the first place—attending a particular school, support for a specific sports team, or willingness to engage in an extracurricular pastime can be an unwritten but essential criterion. Membership in a particular religion, race,[13] class, gender, or sexual orientation can give applicants an edge over others; conversely, it can also automatically disqualify them. Such discrimination is prompted not only by the characteristics of a group but also against the cultural behaviour that is perceived as resulting from it—a person of a particular ethnicity can be viewed stereotypically as being prone to certain outlooks and actions that will not provide the right "fit" with the predominant office culture.

Business networking is usually conducted within social circles defined by group membership. Institutions such as private clubs are perhaps the most exclusive venues for the exchange of valuable information and the forming of partnerships. They have traditionally been restricted on the bases of gender, class, race, religion, and sexual orientation. Informal, but similarly exclusive "old boys' clubs" operate in a variety of ways in society to limit access to outsiders. They have an adherence to similar sets of values derived from common social backgrounds—this sustains bonds of trust among members. Professional organizations tend overtly to be less restrictive than private clubs but have strict criteria based on educational qualifications. However, they can play a significant role in determining entrance to institutions that grant the requisite diplomas, thus determining future membership at the source. Professional associations also limit the acceptance of immigrants with qualifications from foreign universities. Even though the general membership of these organizations may be pluralistic, their executive bodies are often reflective of old boys' clubs. Ultimately, it is not only the formal, publicly available forms of knowledge (i.e., through educational institutions) that are key to societal power, but the cultural knowledge that comes from membership in particular social groups. C. Wright Mills, in his classic study of *The Power Elite*,[14] showed the linkages between the political, business, and military elites of the United States who moved in overlapping social circles and intermarried among themselves. Such people, having access to the highest echelons of social, economic and political power, appear to come closest to enjoying the status of full citizenship.

Membership in the power elite is effected by a combination of inheritance, the right education/training (more accurately expressed in the French term *formation*), and personal initiative. The possession of forms of cultural competency that enable an individual to navigate through the stormy waters of high level power contests are vital to maintain dominance and further one's aims. But the path to full citizenship is populated with individuals who have differential degrees of entry determined by innate characteristics or abilities. The *nouveau riche* are primary examples of those who have succeeded in joining the upper echelons despite lacking the "proper" pedigree; but even they may have to endure the occasional social snub for lapses in cultural judgement arising from subtle gaps in upbringing. Having the "wrong" gender, race, religion, sexual orientation, or a disability also remain significant (although not always insurmountable) obstacles for them to join the inner circles.

The many rungs on the ladder to full citizenship have their own sets of exclusions based on a variety of social characteristics and cultural competencies. Society's multifarious in-groups have their respective restrictions for entry. Some of these are constituted by minorities who are powerless in the larger society but create their own exclusive circles and hierarchies. They are even able to deny membership to individuals belonging to dominant groups who lack the specific biological characteristics or cultural competencies valued by the group. Nevertheless, even the "big fish" in these "small ponds" are unable to claim full citizenship in the larger society.

Cultural Competencies

The state grants specific cultural rights based on collective history and contemporary policy. Even though limited practice of Aboriginal forms of self-government and justice are permitted and multiculturalism is an official federal policy, mainstream institutions (e.g., those of governance, law, social organization) in Canada are primarily drawn from the history of what until recently were termed "the founding nations."[15] The historical experiences of Britain and France are embedded in numerous ways in state institutions and by extension in non-governmental sectors of Canadian society which have to interact with the state. It is impossible to function in the national public sphere[16] without competencies derived from the cultural heritage of the dominant groups. The freedom to speak in one's own language in a public place is the manifestation of significant cultural power, which is probably best understood by those who feel unable to do this as a result of society's norms.

An essential requirement for the practice of full citizenship in Canada is the ability to speak at least one of the two official languages, English or French—preferably both. A newcomer to any society quickly learns that it is not only the knowledge of grammar and diction but the ability to speak in the right accents which is crucial for social acceptability. The dominant language and respective accent usually vary from place to place in the country, and the effective exercise of citizenship needs local knowledge.

Politicians[17] and broadcasters who operate in national or regional public spheres are usually required to be able to enunciate in ways that are familiar to dominant groups in society. These accents do not necessarily have to be those of the social elites (which are often of greater significance in social circles where class is of primary importance), but forms of speech that are viewed as being "indigenous" to the locale. Some, but not all, non-dominant accents will be permitted here. For example, whereas South Asian or African ways of speaking English will rarely be heard on Canadian airwaves, the English services of the Canadian Broadcasting Corporation regularly run the stories of reporters speaking in Québecois accents (although this does not preclude various forms of cultural exclusion against francophones in various parts of the country).

Success in the multitude of formal and informal in-groups, as quite distinct from that in the dominant public sphere, requires competencies in their respective jargon and slang. Each clique has its own sets of inside knowledge and practices. Some are very restrictive in the ways in which they guard their specialized forms of information. Entry into the particular group may range from intricate initiation rituals to security clearances (in addition to requiring adherence to a particular gender, race, class, religion, political ideology, or sexual orientation, or a combination thereof). Many of these circles may be irrelevant to the attainment of full citizenship in the larger society, but some may hold information that is vital to greater participation in various spheres of life.

In order to interact as a member, one needs to have the appropriate cultural competencies that enable sociability with other members of the respective group. This may include the performance of precise rituals such as certain verbal and bodily salutations or merely the ability to engage in small talk. Office banter can be key to forming alliances and networks essential for the effective performance on the job. They can lead to greater camaraderie and the building of trust. Vital information may also be regularly shared in the course of these informal chats that may afford opportunities for career advancement.

The ability to engage in this seemingly simple human interaction may be enormously difficult for particular individuals for a variety of reasons. Some are unable to participate due to personality traits such as shyness. Others lack the knowledge or social skills for such activity.[18] The entry-point into the casual conversations is often the content of popular culture. Television shows or newspaper headlines can be the common base for engaging in banter (or "water cooler talk") that can lead to talk about matters more pertinent to work, but which the organizational communication channels are not disclosing by commission or omission.

Newcomers to an institution are required to learn the cultural competencies to participate in these seemingly superfluous but vital exchanges. Recent immigrants to a country have even more to absorb. The particular television programs, movies, current affairs, sports, and celebrities that are the fodder of office chit-chat are often missing in their cultural knowledge. First, they have to be able to identify the sources of the most popular sets of information that form the bases of the discussions in the respective workplace. Second, having identified the sources, the interpretive skills of making sense of the information within the cognitive frameworks of workmates have to be acquired. Depending on the individual, this ability may take years to finesse.

For many, these cultural competencies remain unattainable, and the access to various resources which they offer is blocked off for them. This failure is repeated in myriad ways in other spheres of life. Whereas full citizenship is an almost impossible goal for such individuals, opportunities for specific forms of social, economic, or political participation are also severely limited. "In a media-dominated politics and economy of symbolic production, just as cultural capital converts into political capital, lack of cultural capital converts into political exclusion."[19]

Both mainstream media content and its forms of interpretation are drawn from broader societal contexts. Persons belonging to dominant cultures are usually socialized into the historical and cultural memories that underlie contemporary cultural discourses.[20] This is carried out in a variety of ways, which include family upbringing, religious instruction, secular schooling, and the learning of societal lore. Those who do not share in this corpus of information will have interpretations of the contemporary events of society that will be of significant variance from those of dominant groups.[21] As a result, they find themselves often being out of step as they try to march along with the rest of society. This usually leads to social, cultural, economic, and political marginalization.

The following passage from an article in an Ottawa-area community newspaper describes how "Canadians" and "multicultural groups" entertained themselves simultaneously but separately in two sides of the same public building:

> Civic Square was brimming with Canadian and multi-cultural pride last Thursday night. In one end of the building, in Centrepointe Theatre, comedian Lorne Elliot shared humorous anecdotes and songs, which only Canadians could love and understand ... In the other end of the building in the Council Chambers, Nepean Outreach to the World (NOW) presented "Africa—A Celebration" in tribute to this city's multicultural groups especially the African community.[22]

The "multicultural groups," who are distinguished from the (real) "Canadians," are presented implicitly in the newspaper as being unable to understand what those whose families have lived in the country for generations can appreciate in the comedian's performance.

This seems to underline what Sigmund Freud remarked about all jokes being inside jokes—their nuances can be truly appreciated only by the in-group familiar with their cultural context.[23] This involves knowing not only how to tell a joke, but also what to joke about, when to joke, and when to laugh. The lack of this cultural competency in a situation like a job interview can spell disaster. Humour is an essential part of social bonding, and those who are left out of the circle of laughter also find themselves excluded from the vital occasions for societal participation.

Even though contemporary society has become more informal than it used to be even in the mid-twentieth century, there still remains a range of taboos for various social situations. Many of these generally remain unstated, but the knowledge of their existence is shared among in-groups. The knowledge of the kinds of speech and actions that are socially expected, or, on the other hand, prohibited or frowned upon is essential for entry into various circles. Gaffes resulting from the lack of this knowledge severely reduce social mobility.

Although the rules of etiquette have loosened substantially in recent decades, almost all social situations require a certain knowledge of how to comport oneself. The contexts which are controlled institutionally or informally by certain groups often have rituals that are unknown to outsiders. Indeed they are the means by which the exclusivity of the group and the power of its leadership is maintained. Knowledge of appropriate clothing for specific social situations can also determine inclusion or exclusion. Newcomers are often confused by the subtle codes of formality and informality that exist in their new locations of settlement—especially those that change from one social context to another. Cultural capital includes the knowledge of when certain rules can be bent or even broken without incurring social penalties.

However, cultural competencies are continually undergoing changes and even members of in-groups can occasionally fall out of the loop. Dramatic technological developments, economic upheaval, social or political revolutions, war, etc., can change the rules in more sudden manners. For example, the skills required for individuals to be upwardly mobile have undergone drastic shifts with the widespread use of the Internet. Globalization and worldwide migration have significantly changed the topography of social exchanges, and have necessitated the learning of a range of new competencies. Such ongoing changes are usually the cause of what is often referred to as the "generation gap."

Cultural Pluralism and Public Sphericules

Almost every country in the world is seeking to come to terms with the diversity of its respective population. In this, governments find themselves having to overcome a structural contradiction relating to the concept of the nation-state. An underlying premise of the nation-state since its emergence in Europe several hundred years ago has been the existence of a populace within its borders that is culturally, ethnically, and linguistically monolithic. There has historically been a deliberate and consistent attempt to disregard most forms of diversity. A limited recognition of linguistic pluralism was granted in a small number of states, and the operation of democracy allowed for political diversity.

However, it was not until the early 1970s that official multiculturalism appeared, first in Canada and Australia, and later in some other countries. This has allowed for the legitimization of a wider range of cultural competencies and their acceptance in the broader public sphere than had existed previously. However, the cultural hegemony of dominant groups continues to be maintained, despite challenges from alternative discourses.[24] For the most part, cultural minorities do not have easy access to the dominant public sphere. They are limited to operating in what Charles Husband[25] terms "the multi-ethnic public sphere" and Todd Gitlin calls "public sphericules." Such "sphericules" reflect the multiple conversations in society, including those carried out by alternative and ethnic media. They may overlap with each other and with the dominant public sphere, but generally do not reach the broader audiences of the latter.[26]

These sphericules tend in some ways to mirror the pluralism of civil society and are an important aspect of democratic practices. Rather than the notion of the largely monolithic public sphere of Jürgen Habermas,[27] this way of conceptualizing the multiplicity of cultural, social, political, and economic activity enables a much better understanding of the many interlocking streams of discourse that permeate social life. It enables a bottom-up view of how communities are shaped and how public opinion is formed.

The cultural competencies required to operate in the many public sphericules vary between each other. Those whose membership is drawn from elite groups generally have easier access to the larger public sphere since the discourses with which they articulate issues have often become entrenched in society through the ability of these groups to dominate public culture. They usually have substantial roles in the regulation and ownership of the mass media and other institutions that influence the interpretation of societal symbols. Their members are skilled and knowledgeable in discussing and shaping public policy in a wide range of areas.

Non-elite groups tend to lack such cultural capital. They have to work much harder to be able to access public discourses and to participate in broader societal arenas. However, they may gain some influence in liberal democracies that give all the members of the population agency in basic political activities. If they are able to manifest political clout, such as the ability to turn out significant numbers of voters for an election to a public office, prominent leaders will beat a path to their door and even attempt to acquire some of their particular cultural competencies to be able to communicate with the participants in the sphericule. For example, leading federal and provincial politicians regularly visit the offices of ethnic media in Vancouver, a city with significant numbers of voters from ethnic minorities, to give interviews.[28]

Bourdieu's analysis, based on empirical work done in France in the 1960s, does not account for the contemporary ethnic diversity in that and other Western countries. Even the assimilative tendencies of contemporary French governments cannot completely disregard the cultural pluralism of the population. The cultural capital required for success in mainstream public spheres continues to undergo change to account for the increasing diversity, but dominant groups strive to maintain their hegemony by staving off any serious challenges to the *status quo* with respect to the distribution of societal power. They establish and maintain their dominance in society by ensuring that the cultural capital and ideologies that best serve their interests are pre-eminent. This does not uphold the equality of citizenship.

Jude Bloomfield and Franco Bianchini state that "If the existence of multiple cultures is taken seriously, citizenship of a democratic state has to be detached from exclusive cultural belonging."[29] A democratic polity striving to ensure the greater distribution of social power would seek to facilitate more access to public discourses by all groups. To restate the central question for this chapter: how does a liberal democracy strive to broaden the access to social power that some citizens have in possessing specific kinds of cultural capital?

First of all, governments need to be aware of the very important place of cultural competencies is in negotiating social power, and that the large stores of cultural capital that elite groups already possess enable them to maintain their place at the top of the pyramid. Those who do not have the cultural competencies to engage successfully in public are unable to participate optimally in the social, cultural, and economic sectors. If the cultural infrastructure of a society favours particular forms of cultural capital over others, it gives unequal advantages to specific groups who possess those types of cultural capital. Whereas it is impossible administratively to equalize all kinds of cultural capital in society (e.g., the choice of particular languages as official languages), it can seek to account for the barriers to fuller social participation that disadvantaged or marginalized groups face and work to develop policies that enable them to overcome such obstacles.[30] Bloomfield and Bianchini talk about linking "sub-cultural capital"[31] to the economy— capital and potential for creativity that would otherwise remain undervalued and wasted.

They offer a number of policy proposals for strengthening citizenship participation opportunities in pluralist societies. Bloomfield and Bianchini are critical of what they call a "corporate multiculturalism" that suppresses internal differences within communities, which are pluralistic in themselves, to present an essentialized, unified identity to others. They support the acknowledgement of continued social evolution and the exchange of ideas between cultures.

While all cultures which respect the rights of other cultures have a right to recognition, they cannot be shut off and denied the opportunity to interact with, and influence the mainstream, or be influenced in turn by other cultures. Cultural recognition must also offer opportunities to renew a culture as well as to preserve it. Otherwise it condemns minority cultures to the margins, in the defensive quest for purism, while depriving the mainstream culture of both the creative interaction and friction which generate innovation and cross-fertilization.[32]

They propose an "inter-culturalism"[33] which facilitates exchanges between various groups as well as a means of interpreting one's own and others' cultures. This de-centred approach allows for creative dialogue and dialectics in multiple directions and levels. It requires acts of courage from the mainstream as well as minority groups.

The intersecting of spherules in this manner enables the learning of newer cultural competencies and the gathering of cultural capital that would otherwise be closed to particular individuals due to their social backgrounds. It leads to vibrant forms of participation in society and to enhanced creativity and innovation, drawing from various forms of thinking and conceptualizing the world. The non-recognition of the educational qualifications of immigrants is only the overt form of suppressing such potential; people from many backgrounds are not integrated into the public sphere because they are seen as not having a broader range of the "right" competencies.

Homi Bhabha[34] has pointed out that the liminal space that a new immigrant occupies in between the old and the new countries can be an extremely innovative place. Living in this "third space," a number of Canadians of recent immigrant origins have won artistic acclaim; for example, filmmaker Atom Egoyan, designer Tu Ly, and novelists Michael Ondaatje, Moez Vassanji, Rohinton Mistry, and Cyril Dabydeen. Their homelessness seems to produce a highly creative state of mind and production that puts them in the ranks of the avant-garde, indeed at the cutting edge of modernity. They demonstrate the possibility of developing hybrid cultural capital that is cosmopolitan, derived from questions they ask in trying to make sense of struggle at the border between at least two worldviews. The cultural competencies that they offer are seen as rising far beyond the traditional notion of the marginal "ethnic." Bloomfield and Bianchini insist that these competencies exist much more widely than just among the cultural elite because the intensified flow of people, goods, and images encourages the emergence of hybrid forms of perception and expression.[35]

They see certain cities in Europe as having been more successful than national governments in engaging with plurality in cultural competencies and capital. Key to their proposals for revitalizing cultural citizenship is a reconceptualization of cultural policy.

Such as strategy would audit and deploy all the cultural resources of the city, from physical layout and design, its architectural and industrial heritage, local craft traditions, skill pools, arts, to the public spaces, educational and cultural institutions, tourist attractions and images of the city which the interaction of myths, conventional wisdom, cultural and media representations produce. It would cut across the divides between the voluntary, public and private sectors, different institutional concerns, and different professional disciplines.[36]

This form of urban cultural planning would lead to the creation of physical spaces enabling an inter-culturalism that would harness the participation and revitalize the citizenship of youth and other marginalized groups. David Theo Goldberg[37] also suggests the establishment of spaces where institutions may negotiate relationships between dominant and subordinate groups, thereby allowing for the kinds of civic participation that are denied under the concept of a monolithic public sphere.

The notion of "ghetto" is exactly the opposite of what these theorists are suggesting: increasing opportunities in public spaces for individuals from different backgrounds to interact with each other produces the kinds of cultural capital that leads to meaningful citizenship for larger numbers of people. However, they are not promoting the assimilation of cultural minorities into the majority. Bloomfield and Bianchi find cultural identity helps to self-organize and educate for effective citizenship through cultural representation and assertion of cultural rights.[38] The sphericules, therefore, have necessarily to intersect with each other and with the larger public sphere to reduce possibilities for marginalization.

Such intersections can also take place in media spaces. Canadian legislation requires broadcasters to reflect the multicultural nature of the country's population in its programming. Mainstream television and radio producers attempt to fulfill this obligation by ensuring that members of on-air staff are drawn from diverse racial backgrounds. However, the cultural contexts they necessarily operate in are those of dominant groups. The cultural competencies and capital they possess from membership in specific social groups is suppressed; for example, broadcast personalities from minority ethnic backgrounds occasionally do this even to the extent of anglicizing the pronunciation of their own names.

Some ethnic media offer an alternative model in which issues are discussed in an official language of the country but from varying cultural positions; for example, programming in OMNI TV, CITY TV, and CHIN radio in Ontario includes English-language slots that discuss a variety of topics from a diversity of cultural perspectives.[39] Cultural capital of various forms is valorized here and presented to a broad plurality of audiences who choose to tune in, not just the members of a particular linguistic or ethnic community. The cultural citizenship of those who participate in such productions is enhanced through broad-based exposure, as are the cultural competencies of their audiences. This is very different from the bulk of traditional ethnic media content, which is generally unable to speak to anyone beyond the respective sphericules for whom their material is designed.

Conclusion

Bourdieu's work addresses only a small part of the cultural capital that human beings hold. This chapter has sought to inquire into some of the other ways in which individuals are dependent on cultural capital to have a place in society. Cultural capital determines the dynamics of power. It is also key to understanding the exercise of citizenship since it gives the individual the wherewithal to participate effectively in society. A person's cultural capital includes the skill sets that enable her to function effectively in situations which include the most mundane and the most sophisticated interactions with other people. The types of cultural competencies that one has acquired through socialization help determine the access one has to various areas of social life. They necessarily have to be taken into account when developing policies that seek to promote the equality of participation.

Whereas full citizenship remains an elusive ideal, it is necessary for policy-makers to understand the function of cultural competencies in ensuring access to various sectors. Participation in social, cultural, economic, or political activities meant for all citizens often have barriers that are invisible from dominant perspectives. Varying degrees of competency mean more access to public resources for those who have the cultural know-how to take greater advantage of government programs. Cultural policy research needs, therefore, to study the obstacles to citizenship that are the result of differential cultural competencies. Whereas the material aspects of cultural production are more easily analyzed using quantitative methodologies, this intangible (yet real) form of cultural capital can be more readily understood through qualitative approaches. Cultural anthropology, particularly ethnography, offers significant scope in providing the information to comprehend the inequalities caused by certain well-meaning efforts to make accessible social goods to disadvantaged groups. Sociological methodologies such as symbolic interactionism can also be useful in providing clues to grasp better how certain kinds of social exchanges that take place between individuals with differing social backgrounds serve to entrench inequity.

Intercultural policies that enable productive interactions between people differentiated not only by race, ethnicity, or language but also by gender, age, class, physical/mental ability, sexual orientation, etc., would provide for a richer society. One learns cultural competencies through contacts with others. It stands to reason that the cultural capital of individuals and of society grows as various sphericules intersect with each other. The potential for the exercise for citizenship in all sectors grows as citizens become familiar with sociability skills pertaining to an increasing number of situations. This also provides their creativity and innovation more arenas for expression, thus potentially benefiting larger numbers of people.

As globalizing tendencies demand broader ranges of cultural competencies, cultural policies of national governments have to account for transnational contexts. On the one hand, policy-makers have to ensure that the cultural products from abroad do not cause economic and social harm to their country. On the other, governments in liberal democracies, apart from having to adhere to international trade agreements and protocols, do not want their populations to be isolated from the rest of the world. Cultural protectionism has become an increasingly unattractive option for governments seeking to prevent this isolation.

More interesting possibilities, perhaps, are contained in the notion of cosmopolitanism, to which I have briefly referred. It provides an opportunity for innovative engagements with emerging domestic and global situations. Embracing outlooks that incorporate multi-dimensional cultural scenarios that often are the norm under globalization, enables populations to gain wider ranges of cultural competencies that are becoming necessary to operate effectively in the transnational contexts interlaced with human, cultural, and technological flows. The learning of such competencies also enables individuals to engage with the multi-level pluralism of domestic societies described in this chapter. A seamless cosmopolitanism that traverses national and transnational milieus can serve to enhance cultural citizenship and enhance fuller participation in society by those who seek it. Working within such an untraditional approach, however, will require extraordinary vision and courage on the part of twenty-first-century governments and policy-makers.[40]

Notes

[1] M. Sharon Jeannotte, "Just Showing Up: Social and Cultural Capital in Everyday Life," chap. 9 in this volume.

[2] Pierre Bourdieu, *Distinction: A Social Critique of Taste* (Cambridge, MA: Harvard University Press, 1984).

[3] Ibid., 12.

[4] Edward T. Hall's influential work, *The Silent Language* (1973), demonstrated how the unspoken interactions of human relationships serve to construct social structures that shape the life of a society.

[5] Nick Crossley, "Citizenship, Intersubjectivity and Lifeworld," in Nick Stevenson, ed., *Culture and Citizenship* (London: Sage, 2001), 38.

[6] Jim McGuigan, "Three Discourses of Cultural Policy," in Stevenson, *Culture and Citizenship*, 124–37.

[7] Derek Heater, *What is Citizenship?* (Cambridge: Polity Press, 1999), 87.

[8] Karim H. Karim, "Relocating The Nexus Of Citizenship, Heritage and Technology," *Journal of the European Institute for Communication and Culture: Javnost—The Public* 4, no. 4 (1997): 82–83.

[9] Bryan S. Turner, "Outline of a General Theory of Cultural Citizenship," in Stevenson, *Culture and Citizenship*, 12.

[10] Crossley, "Citizenship, Intersubjectivity and Lifeworld."

[11] Bourdieu, *Distinction*, 2.

[12] Erving Goffman, *The Presentation of Self in Everyday Life* (Garden City, NY: Doubleday, 1959).

[13] Whereas the concept of "race" rests on contested ground, it is presented here as it is conceived of in dominant social contexts. See Michael Banton, *Racial Theories* (Cambridge: Cambridge University Press, 1998).

[14] C. Wright Mills, *The Power Elite* (New York: Oxford University Press, 1956).

[15] For discussions of Canadian cultural terminology and their implications for inclusion and exclusion see Karim H. Karim, "Public Sphere and Public Sphericules: Civic Discourse in Ethnic Media," in Sherry Ferguson and Leslie Regan Shade, eds., *Civic Discourse and Cultural Politics in Canada* (Westport, CT: Ablex, 2002), 230–42; Karim H. Karim, "Reconstructing the Multicultural Community: Discursive Strategies of Inclusion and Exclusion," *International Journal of Politics, Culture, and Society* 7, no. 2 (1993): 189–207.

[16] I distinguish the national, dominant, or mainstream public sphere from what Todd Gitlin calls "public sphericules," which are discussed later in the chapter. Todd Gitlin, "Public Sphere or Public Sphericules?," in Tamar Liebes and James Curran, eds., *Media, Ritual and Identity* (London: Routledge, 1993), 173.

[17] A major exception to this appears to be former Canadian Prime Minister Jean Chrétien, who seemed from time to time to have difficulty expressing himself clearly in either French or English; however, his other cultural competencies enabled him to develop compensating strategies of sociability that endeared him to large numbers of Canadians during his tenure.

[18] Many have turned to the works of people like Dale Carnegie and others in the burgeoning self-help industry to learn the social skills that will help them interact more successfully with various situations. However, the courses and materials of this industry cannot possibly cover all of the possible contexts that exist in society.

[19] Jude Bloomfield and Franco Bianchini, "Cultural Citizenship and Urban Governance in Western Europe," in Stevenson, *Culture and Citizenship*, 118.

[20] Maurice Halbwachs, *On Collective Memory*, Lewis A. Coser trans., (Chicago: University of Chicago Press, 1992); Paul Connerton, *How Societies Remember* (Cambridge: Cambridge University Press, 1989).

[21] This is not to imply that the interpretations of all members of dominant groups are uniformly similar.

[22] "Civic Square was Brimming," *The Clarion* (Feb. 9, 1993).

[23] Sigmund Freud, *Jokes and their Relation to the Unconscious*, James Strachey trans. (New York: Penguin, 1976).

[24] Karim, "Public Sphere and Public Sphericules."

[25] Charles Husband, "Differentiated Citizenship and the Multi-Ethnic Public Sphere," *Journal of International Communication* 5, no. 1 (1998): 134–48.

[26] Karim, "Public Sphere and Public Sphericules."

[27] Jürgen Habermas, *The Structural Transformation of the Public Sphere*, Thomas Burger, trans. (Cambridge, MA: MIT Press, 1989).

[28] Karim, "Public Sphere and Public Sphericules."

[29] Bloomfield and Bianchini, "Cultural Citizenship and Urban Governance," 105.

[30] One approach to deal with this problem is through what Nobel Laureate Amartya Sen has termed "the capabilities approach." See Karim H. Karim, "Participatory Citizenship and the Internet: Reframing Access Within the Capabilities Approach," *Journal of International Communication* 6, no. 1 (1999), 57–68.

[31] Bloomfield and Bianchini, "Cultural Citizenship and Urban Governance," 103.

[32] Ibid., 106.

[33] This is not the same form of "interculturalism" as that in Quebec, where the dominant culture positions itself as implicitly hegemonic *vis-à-vis* all others.

[34] Homi K. Bhabha, *The Location of Culture* (London: Routledge, 1994).

[35] Bloomfield and Bianchini, "Cultural Citizenship and Urban Governance," 106–08.

[36] Ibid., 120. The authors indicate that these ideas draw from Colin Mercer, "Brisbane's Cultural Development Strategy: The Process, the Politics and the Products" (prepared for EIT, The Cultural Planning Conference, Mornington, Victoria, Australia, 1991).

[37] David Theo Goldberg, *Multiculturalism: A Critical Reader* (Cambridge, MA: Basil Blackwell, 1994), 1–41.

[38] Bloomfield and Bianchini, "Cultural Citizenship and Urban Governance,"108.

[39] CHIN has expressed an interest in acquiring broadcasting licenses for radio stations for which such programming would be the mainstay.

[40] Other sources of interest include Arjun Appadurai, "Spectral Housing and Urban Cleansing: Notes on Millennial Mumbai," in Carol A. Breckenridge, Sheldon Pollack, Homi K. Bhabha, and Dipesh Chakrabarty, eds., *Cosmopolitanism* (Durham, NC: Duke University Press, 2002), 54–81; Arjun Appadurai, *Modernity at Large: Cultural Dimensions of Globalization* (Minneapolis: University of Minnesota Press, 1996); Engin F. Isin and Patricia K. Wood, *Citizenship and Identity* (London: Sage, 1999); Edward T. Hall, *The Silent Language* (Garden City, NY: Doubleday, 1973); Derek Heater, *World Citizenship* (London: Continuum, 2002); David Held, *Democracy and the Global Order: From the Modern State to Cosmopolitan Governance.* (Stanford, CA: Stanford University Press, 1995); Aihwa Ong, *Flexible Citizenship: The Cultural Logics of Transnationality* (Durham, NC: Duke University Press, 1999); Maurice Roche, "Citizenship, Popular Culture and Europe," in Stevenson, *Culture and Citizenship*, 74–98.

11.

Les pratiques culturelles en mutation à la fin du XXe siècle :
la situation au Québec

Rosaire Garon

Introduction

Le Québec, comme les autres sociétés occidentales modernes, a connu de profonds changements durant la seconde partie du XXe siècle. Les pratiques culturelles, elles aussi, se sont modifiées imperceptiblement au fil des ans, sous l'influence de plusieurs facteurs. Aujourd'hui, un recul de deux décennies fournit une distanciation suffisante pour déceler qu'une mutation profonde et irréversible est survenue dans les loisirs de la population. L'évolution observée vient par ailleurs remettre en question les orientations en vigueur quant au développement culturel. Cette problématique est soulevée non seulement par le niveau de développement culturel atteint avec le temps, mais aussi par l'organisation des pratiques culturelles selon de nouveaux schémas qui subissent l'influence de l'industrie culturelle et des valeurs dont elle fait la promotion. Comme le souligne Bernard Miège dans le *Rapport mondial sur la communication et l'information 1999-2000*, l'extension de l'offre marchande amène quasi mécaniquement sinon une disparition, du moins une diminution de l'importance de l'offre non marchande ou semi-marchande[1]. Ce déplacement provoque une tension entre la culture marchande et la culture non marchande; présente sur le marché, cette tension s'observe dans le comportement des consommateurs.

Les logiques symboliques qui président à la production des institutions artistiques divergent de celles qui animent l'industrie, mais toutes deux s'affrontent sur le même marché : celui du temps libre et du divertissement. C'est le constat auquel nous amène l'examen des pratiques culturelles durant la période allant de 1979 à 1999. Nous montrerons dans le présent chapitre, exemples à l'appui, comment le changement survenu au cours des dernières décennies dans la pratique culturelle de la population est majeur en ce qu'il repose sur un renouvellement et sur une restructuration de pratiques fondées sur des valeurs qui sont essentiellement différentes.

Nous étudierons ci-dessous quatre cas qui illustrent l'évolution des pratiques culturelles pendant la période considérée et qui révèlent un certain remplacement des valeurs sous-jacentes, soit celles qui étaient défendues hier par les institutions culturelles et celles qui sont aujourd'hui vantées par les campagnes publicitaires. Il sera question du vieillissement des publics, du déclin des pratiques du type classique, du poids des *baby-boomers* dans la demande institutionnelle et des types de consommateurs culturels existant en 1999. Au préalable, nous présenterons la source des données sur lesquelles reposent nos analyses, soit les enquêtes du ministère de la Culture et des Communications (MCC) sur les pratiques culturelles des Québécois, et nous rappellerons les principaux facteurs du changement survenu au Québec durant la seconde moitié du siècle dernier, facteurs susceptibles d'avoir joué un rôle important dans la transformation des pratiques culturelles.

Cet exercice de mesure du changement culturel est instructif à plusieurs égards, tant pour le chercheur désireux de repérer les facteurs des mutations sociales en cours que pour les organismes culturels et les compagnies artistiques en quête d'une connaissance de leur public et de ses tendances en matière de consommation culturelle, sans oublier les pouvoirs publics, qui se sont donné des objectifs en ce qui a trait à la participation de la population à la vie culturelle et à la cohésion sociale par la culture. Les différentes composantes de la société québécoise se transforment rapidement, à des vitesses variables, cependant, et selon des modalités différentes. L'analyse permet de révéler l'ampleur des changements survenus dans le tissu social et de désigner les groupes où ils se sont produits plus intensément. De son côté, l'appareil productif, notamment les organismes culturels et les compagnies artistiques, est directement touché par le renouvellement des pratiques culturelles. La modification des habitudes de consommation peut avoir des effets déterminants sur l'offre culturelle. Enfin, même si l'analyse des pratiques culturelles ne permet pas d'évaluer les politiques culturelles des pouvoirs publics, elle les remet en question toutefois en matière de démocratisation culturelle. Comme nous le verrons plus loin lors de la présentation des types de consommateurs culturels, une part appréciable de la population vit en retrait de la culture et, pour une autre aussi importante, la culture se voit réduite à un rôle instrumental de divertissement.

La tradition de recherche sur les pratiques culturelles

Depuis 1979, le MCC mène des enquêtes dans le domaine des pratiques culturelles. Elles ont lieu tous les cinq ans, et la dernière enquête s'est déroulée en 1999 : nous avons donc accès à une série de données s'échelonnant sur une période de vingt ans à la fin du XXe siècle[2]. Conduites auprès de la population québécoise âgée de quinze ans et plus[3], ces enquêtes ont permis de recueillir des données, par entrevues téléphoniques, auprès d'un échantillon représentatif des ménages québécois. Notons que les entrevues téléphoniques ont été effectuées sur l'ensemble du territoire québécois, à l'exception des villages nordiques et des villages cris.

Le contenu des entrevues s'est élargi d'une enquête à l'autre, de manière à circonscrire les pratiques ayant émergé du fait de l'industrialisation de la culture et de l'arrivée des nouvelles technologies de l'information et de la communication (NTIC). Malgré cette ouverture à la nouveauté, plusieurs questions sont heureusement demeurées presque inchangées depuis la première enquête, de sorte qu'il est possible de tracer l'évolution de plusieurs comportements sur deux décennies. Ces séries de données forment dès lors un ensemble suffisamment homogène qui permet de vérifier si la participation culturelle, valorisée à la fin des années 1970 et au début des années 1980 et fortement inspirée des valeurs de la démocratisation culturelle, a gagné du terrain. C'est à cet exercice que nous nous sommes prêtés dans une analyse que le lecteur trouvera dans *Déchiffrer la culture au Québec : vingt ans de pratiques culturelles*[4]. L'évolution des pratiques y est considérée tant sur le plan territorial qu'à l'intérieur du tissu social.

Quelques facteurs influant sur la pratique culturelle

La transformation des pratiques culturelles de la population québécoise ne se comprend bien qu'en ayant en mémoire le contexte dans lequel elles ont évolué. Amorcée dans la foulée de la Révolution tranquille, la modernisation de la société québécoise s'est poursuivie dans les décennies 1970 et 1980. Ces années sont marquées par un mouvement nationaliste qui traverse et inspire la création québécoise. Le climat est alors propice à une affirmation de la culture québécoise qui se manifeste par un développement accéléré de l'offre culturelle, d'abord institutionnelle, puis industrielle. Une aide financière soutenue et des politiques volontaristes auront eu pour résultat de hausser le niveau et la qualité de l'offre culturelle. L'élargissement de l'offre par l'industrie a pour sa part joué un rôle indéniable dans la formation de la demande et dans le développement des pratiques parmi la population.

De plus, conscients des enjeux de la démocratisation de la culture, les pouvoirs publics se sont aussi fixé comme objectifs de diffuser plus largement la culture sur le territoire et de développer les marchés des industries culturelles. La politique culturelle du Québec de 1992 affirme que « de nouveaux moyens devront être [...] mis en œuvre pour que les arts et la culture s'immiscent dans le quotidien des gens[5] », et encore que « l'État doit favoriser à la fois la circulation de produits divers et une plus grande interaction entre les régions[6] ». Les pouvoirs publics ont été des acteurs de premier plan dans la mise en place des infrastructures culturelles et dans la modernisation des appareils institutionnels et industriels. Leur action a été orientée vers la professionnalisation des milieux artistiques, le maintien des standards de qualité dans la production, la diffusion des produits et l'accessibilité des services culturels sur l'ensemble du territoire, de même que vers le soutien à la diversité des formes d'expression et la promotion de la participation des citoyens.

Par ailleurs, les négociations relatives à la signature de l'Accord de libre-échange (ALE) canado-américain, en 1988, puis à celle de l'Accord de libre-échange nord-américain (ALENA) en 1994, ont projeté la question des industries culturelles au premier plan de l'actualité. L'intervention des pouvoirs publics à leur égard s'en est trouvée politiquement et socialement légitimée. La mondialisation des échanges commerciaux a cependant amplifié l'importance de l'industrie dans la production culturelle et dans la circulation de ses produits, renversant ainsi le rapport de production entre institutions et industries.

Un autre fait tout aussi marquant est celui de l'adoption des NTIC par les ménages québécois. Ces technologies, comme le rapporte Miège, interviennent de façon décisive dans la production culturelle et modifient radicalement aussi bien les contenus que la forme sous laquelle se présentent les œuvres et les produits[7]. La progression accélérée des NTIC, le recours à l'intelligence artificielle dans le traitement des flux de données et la suppression des frontières avec la circulation virtuelle des œuvres, favorisent alors une nouvelle approche dans l'acquisition et la diffusion du savoir. Les nouveaux médias et les NTIC induisent dans la population des rapports différents à la culture et engendrent des modalités particulières de participation à la vie culturelle. Ils ont remodelé l'univers des loisirs domestiques. Si les enquêtes sur les pratiques culturelles ne peuvent mesurer directement toute l'ampleur de ces phénomènes, elles permettent tout de même d'en appréhender indirectement les effets en montrant l'affaiblissement des pratiques culturelles plus traditionnelles. Il ne faut cependant pas mettre sur le compte des industries et de la technologie tous les changements ayant eu cours. Si le nouveau contexte de la production et de la diffusion culturelle facilite la participation, il n'est toutefois pas le seul responsable de la transformation profonde des pratiques culturelles durant la période à l'étude; elle s'est aussi accomplie sous l'effet conjugué de plusieurs autres facteurs économiques, sociaux et démographiques, souvent incontrôlables[8].

Les mécanismes de la distinction sociale

L'importance des mécanismes de la distinction sociale qui jouent dans l'adoption ou le rejet de certaines pratiques ne doit pas être minimisée. Même si les valeurs culturelles traditionnelles semblent jouer un rôle moins actif qu'il y a trente ans dans le processus de différenciation sociale, les modalités d'appropriation de la culture se manifestent encore selon une dynamique propre à chaque groupe social. Cela se concrétise par une occupation plus ou moins grande et plus et moins diversifiée de certains champs de la culture. Cette occupation déborde souvent sur des stratégies de stratification et de distinction sociale. Si des parties du champ culturel, notamment celles qui appartiennent à la culture populaire, sont partagées par tous, d'autres sont réservées à des factions qui occupent les positions sociales dominantes. Il en résulte des clivages qui se manifestent par une distance culturelle entre les groupes, laquelle recoupe souvent des disparités économiques et sociales. Toutefois, la culture traditionnelle à dominance artistique et littéraire, qui présidait à la distinction de l'élite québécoise à la fin des années 1970, s'est modernisée en intégrant des éléments de la culture populaire.

Les mutations démographiques

Il est connu que les pratiques culturelles sont conditionnées en bonne partie par des facteurs démographiques. Au Québec, le boom des naissances de l'après-guerre a entraîné un rajeunissement de la population. Cette génération s'est imposée dans toutes les sphères de la société en y induisant une volonté de changement. Elle a imprimé ses goûts et ses préférences sur le marché, y compris celui du divertissement et de la culture. Elle continue d'ailleurs largement à le faire alors qu'elle est vieillissante, sur le point d'atteindre l'âge de la retraite. Pour cette génération, la maîtrise de la fécondité a entraîné une baisse de natalité en deçà du seuil de renouvellement de la population. Les nouvelles générations se sont alors faites de moins en moins nombreuses tandis que l'espérance de vie a augmenté.

Un autre groupe démographiquement important est formé des gens aujourd'hui âgés de quinze à trente-quatre ans, qui sont en bonne partie les enfants des *baby-boomers*. Ce groupe prétend lui aussi s'imposer sur le marché des arts à partir toutefois d'un ensemble de valeurs qui lui est propre et qui modèle singulièrement son comportement de consommateur culturel. Le tableau 1 présente l'évolution démographique au Québec selon les groupes d'âge, de 1986 à 2001. Il donne un aperçu du poids démographique des moins de trente-cinq ans et l'importance grandissante des personnes agés.

La scolarisation

La scolarité est un des facteurs les plus déterminants dans l'acquisition des pratiques culturelles. Comme le signale Gilles Pronovost, le champ culturel demeure profondément stratifié selon les indicateurs classiques de revenu, d'emploi et de scolarité[9]. L'éducation formelle et celle qui est reçue dans le milieu familial contribuent à la formation d'un capital culturel. Au Québec, la transmission des valeurs artistiques et culturelles s'est faite largement par les établissements d'enseignement supérieur, soit le collège classique et l'université. Les produits de l'art savant attirent un public fortement scolarisé, lequel

Tableau 1 - Répartition de la population selon les groupes d'âge, Québec, 1986 - 2001

Groupes d'âge	1986 %	1991 %	1996 %	2001 %
Moins de 15 ans	20,5	19,8	19,0	17,6
15 à 24 ans	16,2	13,7	13,4	13,2
25 à 34 ans	18,3	18,3	15,6	13,4
35 à 44 ans	15,1	16,4	17,4	17,3
45 à 54 ans	10,5	11,6	13,6	15,2
55 ans et plus	19,3	20,2	21,0	23,3
Total	100,0	100,0	100,0	100,0
Population (n)	6 532 450	7 064 735	7 274 019	7 410 504

Sources : Le Québec statistique, 59e édition éd. 1989, Bureau de la statistique du Québec, Québec, Les Publications du Québec, Québec, 1989, p. 303. La situation démographique au Québec, bilan 2003, Les ménages au tournant du XXIe siècle, Québec, Institut de la statistique du Québec, Les Publications du Québec, Québec, 2003, p. 164.

a acquis à leur égard une familiarité, alors que les produits de l'art populaire sont accessibles à la majorité de la population. Par ailleurs, l'accession de la génération des *baby-boomers* aux études supérieures a formé une catégorie sociale sensible aux valeurs de la culture classique qui sont présentes dans leurs pratiques culturelles d'aujourd'hui. En revanche, la partie de la population moins scolarisée se voit largement exclue des pratiques exigeant un capital culturel. Si, dans le passé, la hausse générale de la scolarité a favorisé la demande culturelle, son influence, quoique prépondérante, est moins déterminante de nos jours qu'auparavant. Les établissements d'enseignement postsecondaire ont perdu de leur influence comme agents de sensibilisation aux arts et à la culture, ainsi que comme vecteurs de transmission de ceux-ci, au profit des médias et de l'industrie. Il en résulte que l'élite et les étudiants d'aujourd'hui ont une culture qui se différencie de moins en moins de celle de la population en général.

Le prix des produits et le revenu

Le prix des produits et le revenu disponible sont d'autres éléments importants reconnus pour influer sur l'intensité des pratiques[10]. Même si la demande pour bien des produits culturels demeure inélastique, leur consommation est généralement plus forte parmi les groupes sociaux qui disposent d'un revenu élevé. En outre, la consommation culturelle peut varier selon les cycles économiques. Ainsi, la conjoncture économique défavorable au cours des années 1990 pourrait expliquer la raison pour laquelle plusieurs pratiques culturelles sont apparues à la baisse dans les enquêtes de 1994 et de 1999. Par ailleurs, le produit culturel, ayant une forte connotation symbolique, présente des caractéristiques ou des attributs qui en font un produit pas tout à fait comme les autres. Il est d'abord une affaire de goût. Comme le souligne X. Dupuis, nombre de produits culturels sont ignorés, voire rejetés, parce que souvent méconnus de la majorité des consommateurs[11].

Plusieurs autres facteurs, outre ceux que nous avons mentionnés, ont façonné la consommation culturelle. Par exemple, les technologies informatisées font en sorte que le foyer s'impose de plus en plus comme centre de loisirs[12]. L'occupation du temps libre est conditionnée par les formes atypiques de travail, par la transformation du travail avec la technologie et par les changements survenus dans la structure des professions. De même, l'éclatement de la famille traditionnelle et l'avènement des familles reconstituées créent un contexte particulier pour la transmission des valeurs culturelles familiales[13]. Tous ces changements économiques et sociaux, autant que l'action culturelle proprement dite, ont transformé le rapport au loisir et les comportements culturels. Les exemples qui suivent en sont en quelque sorte l'illustration.

Quatre cas illustrant l'evolution des pratiques culturelles

Le vieillissement des publics

Le vieillissement des publics est le terme normal des tendances démographiques actuelles. En effet, au fur et à mesure que s'accroît l'âge moyen de la population québécoise, celui du public des activités culturelles s'élève également. Par ailleurs, compte tenu du fait que les jeunes sortent davantage que les aînés, l'âge moyen des publics devrait, en principe, augmenter moins rapidement que celui de la population. Cela étant dit, il convient de signaler la grande variabilité de l'âge du public des produits culturels. Certains produits sont destinés à un public d'un âge ciblé, tandis que d'autres s'adressent à tous.

Le tableau 2 montre l'âge moyen du public de différentes activités ainsi que le taux de pratique en 1999. Il apparaît que les pratiques plus traditionnelles telles que la lecture et les sorties au concert classique, au concert western, au théâtre, au spectacle de danse folklorique ou de danse classique, de même que la fréquentation des salons des métiers d'art et des musées, sont le fait d'un public plus vieux que d'autres pratiques telles que le cinéma, les spectacles rock ou de groupes populaires, les concerts de jazz et les matchs sportifs. On voit également que les activités dont le public est âgé sont présentes depuis longtemps sur le marché québécois et ont été valorisées par les pouvoirs publics depuis plusieurs décennies. Les activités dont le public est d'un âge moyen plus bas sont apparues plus récemment sur le marché québécois et sont majoritairement issues de l'industrie culturelle. Les premières sont plus fréquentes chez les aînés et les *baby-boomers* alors que les secondes sont à l'honneur chez les jeunes de quinze à trente-quatre ans.

La question de la relève de certains publics se pose lorsqu'on considère leur âge moyen et le taux de pratique d'une activité. La danse folklorique, le théâtre d'été et le concert classique, par exemple, sont des activités dont le public est âgé et la pratique faible. La relève de leur public n'est pas assurée et elles risquent de tomber en désuétude dans un avenir plus ou moins rapproché. Afin de mieux discerner les différentes facettes du vieillissement des publics, nous en avons calculé l'effet net en neutralisant celui qui est attribuable au vieillissement de la population en général. Cet effet net est l'écart entre le vieillissement d'un public en particulier, de 1989 à 1999, moins les 2,2 ans que représente le vieillissement général de la population au cours de cette période. Il devient alors aisé de distinguer les publics qui rajeunissent de ceux qui vieillissent. Cette mesure, mise en relation avec les taux de pratique, permet de vérifier s'il y a renouvellement ou non des publics et, dans l'affirmative, d'indiquer par quel groupe d'âge il s'effectue. Quatre possibilités se présentent à cet égard :

1. La participation s'intensifie et l'âge moyen du public s'accroît : la croissance du public provient d'un intérêt plus grand manifesté par la population plus âgée. Un nombre

Tableau 2 - Âge moyen et taux de pratique d'activités culturelles, 1999

Activité pratiquée	Âge moyen (ans)	Taux de pratique %
Lecture (régulière)		
Quotidiens	44,5	70,9
Magazines	42,5	55,6
Livres	43,3	52,0
Achat de livres	42,0	54,8
Écoute musicale (régulière)	41,6	81,9
Achat d'œuvres d'art ou des métiers d'art	45,6	11,0
Sorties		
Cinéma	39,3	72,0
Théâtre d'été	47,2	15,7
Théâtre en saison	42,2	28,8
Concert classique	48,3	13,0
Concert rock	32,3	12,4
Concert hard rock, metal	26,4	2,4
Jazz	37,9	6,6
Western	42,4	2,0
Chansonnier	38,9	8,2
Groupe ou artiste populaire	37,6	7,7
Danse classique	43,0	5,0
Danse moderne	38,2	5,5
Danse folklorique	45,6	2,3
Match sportif	37,8	31,6
Établissements culturels		
Salon du livre	44,4	14,8
Salon des métiers d'art	46,4	20,8
Librairie	41,0	61,5
Galerie d'art	44,4	21,0
Site ou monument historique	41,5	38,9
Centre d'archives	41,9	9,3
Musée d'art	42,8	30,6
Autre musée	41,2	22,8

Source: *Ministère de la Culture et des Communications, Enquête sur les pratiques culturelles au Québec, 1999.*

limité de pratiques sont dans cette situation. Il s'agit des sorties au cinéma et au théâtre en saison, de la fréquentation des centres d'archives et de la visite des salons du livre. Le vieillissement du public n'est pas problématique dans ce cas-ci puisqu'il provient d'un investissement accru des personnes plus âgées;

2. La participation s'intensifie et l'âge moyen du public rajeunit : la croissance du public vient d'un apport des jeunes. On assiste ainsi à une véritable relève du public. Deux pratiques seulement se présentent de cette façon : la visite des musées d'art de même que celle des sites et monuments historiques;

3. La participation diminue alors que l'âge moyen du public baisse: le rajeunissement se fait en raison du désengagement des personnes plus âgées, alors que les plus jeunes n'ont pas modifié leur comportement. Certaines pratiques dont le public est déjà âgé sont dans cette situation : l'achat d'œuvres d'art ou de produits des métiers d'art, les sorties au concert western et au spectacle de danse folklorique et la visite des salons des métiers d'art. C'est le cas également d'autres pratiques qui ont un public moins âgé que les précédentes, comme la sortie au match sportif ou encore au concert d'artistes ou de groupes populaires et l'écoute musicale. À plus ou moins long terme, ces activités risquent d'être marginalisées, surtout celles qui obtiennent de faibles taux de participation;

4. Un dernier cas se présente lorsque le public régresse alors que son âge moyen augmente : ce sont dans ce cas les jeunes qui délaissent une activité pendant que les personnes plus âgées continuent de s'y livrer. On note ici les sorties aux concerts de chansonniers, de jazz, de rock et de musique classique, ainsi que celles au théâtre d'été et au ballet. La visite des galeries d'art et celle des musées autres que d'art accusent également une perte de leur jeune public. Enfin, le lectorat des quotidiens, des magazines et des livres présente lui aussi les mêmes symptômes. Un problème de relève du public se pose pour ces activités. Leur situation risque même d'être alarmante dans quelques années lorsque les *baby-boomers*, vieillissants, ne pourront plus s'y adonner.

Le déclin des pratiques du type classique

Le vieillissement des publics a été observé sur une période de dix ans, soit de 1989 à 1999[14]. Pour le déclin des activités du type classique, la période d'observation est allongée, s'étendant de 1979 à 1999. Nous entendons ici par « activités du type classique », les pratiques autrefois valorisées par la culture classique telles que la lecture, les sorties aux spectacles des arts d'interprétation, la visite des institutions muséales, des galeries d'art et des lieux historiques et patrimoniaux, la fréquentation des événements liés aux arts et à la littérature ainsi que l'achat d'œuvres d'art ou des métiers d'art. Ces pratiques étaient valorisées par les institutions culturelles. C'est pourquoi nous parlerons de culture institutionnelle pour renvoyer à ces mêmes pratiques. Nous pouvons observer vingt pratiques différentes réparties sur deux décennies. Comme il serait trop laborieux de suivre l'évolution détaillée de ces activités sur une période aussi longue, nous avons construit un indicateur synthétique qui rend compte du phénomène global[15].

Voici ce que révèle cet indicateur : la culture valorisée par les institutions culturelles a connu une progression au cours de la première décennie à l'étude. L'année 1989 marque un sommet dans la participation aux activités du type classique. Une baisse d'intérêt pour ce genre d'activités s'amorce par la suite, comme on le voit nettement sur le graphique 1. Au plan statistique, la croissance de l'activité culturelle au cours de la décennie de 1979 à 1989 est significative ($p < 0,05$), tout comme la baisse qui suit au cours de la décennie suivante, de 1989 à 1999.

Faut-il poser un constat d'échec de la démocratisation culturelle? Dans l'affirmative, à qui et à quoi doit-on l'attribuer? Convient-il de mettre en cause les politiques culturelles publiques? Quelles sont les raisons du déclin de la culture valorisée politiquement et socialement? Nous devons admettre, à la suite d'autres chercheurs tel Olivier Donnat[16], que la culture savante ne s'est pas propagée à l'intérieur des factions sociales moins instruites et que la segmentation demeure toujours persistante, les mêmes groupes sociaux continuant de participer à cette culture et les exclus demeurant toujours des laissés-pour-compte.

Il est impossible de ne pas associer la perte d'influence des institutions culturelles au phénomène de la montée des industries culturelles. Ces dernières, comme nous l'avons signalé, ont acquis avec le temps une légitimité et une reconnaissance sociales et ont connu un essor important depuis les années 1980. La place dominante qu'ont prise les médias, les industries culturelles et les NTIC dans la production et la commercialisation de la culture a eu pour effet de minorer la culture savante. La commercialisation de la culture a également donné lieu à une culture du marketing, pour reprendre l'expression de Firat et de Dholakia: « *Marketing, thus, is indeed the culture of our time [...] As marketing becomes the culture, culture becomes the most successful marketable*[17] ». En outre, la mécanisation des ménages par les appareils audiovisuels a restructuré les loisirs domestiques en associant de plus en plus l'expérience culturelle au divertissement et à un geste de consommation de programmes. Comme nous le verrons plus loin dans la présentation des types de consommateurs, la culture se réduit pour une partie de la population à une affaire de divertissement, le plus souvent commercialisé.

Le changement de comportement à l'égard de la culture classique est toutefois plus important dans certains groupes sociaux. Plusieurs travaux ont déjà révélé que les pratiques culturelles liées à la « haute culture » se répartissent inégalement à l'intérieur des catégories sociales et professionnelles[18]. C'est un domaine marqué par des écarts importants entre les individus. Les professionnels de la culture, comme les enseignants et les artistes, arrivent en tête dans les taux de pratique, devançant nettement toutes les autres catégories. Les ouvriers, de même que les personnes inactives et faiblement scolarisées, accordent une place très limitée aux activités artistiques et fréquentent peu les établissements culturels. La transformation des pratiques gagne toutefois même les catégories socioprofessionnelles les plus élevées, c'est-à-dire celles que la scolarisation et le milieu social ont familiarisées avec la culture classique. Bien que ces catégories aient

Graphique 1 - Indice de diversité des pratiques culturelles du type classique

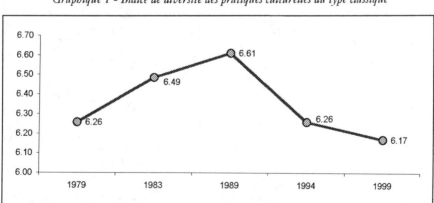

les taux les plus élevés de lecture, de fréquentation des établissements culturels et de sorties, elles ont depuis longtemps commencé à prendre une distance par rapport à la culture classique. Les étudiants et l'élite québécoise[19] en fournissent un bon exemple. Le graphique 2 montre l'évolution des pratiques du type classique dans ces groupes.

On distingue nettement chez eux une antériorité du mouvement par rapport au reste de la population. Dès le début des années 1980, ils montrent les signes d'une mutation caractérisée par l'affaiblissement des valeurs culturelles institutionnelles et par le renouvellement de leurs pratiques avec les produits diffusés par les médias et l'industrie. Le changement est nettement visible parmi les étudiants d'aujourd'hui, dont le comportement est beaucoup moins distinctif que celui de leurs prédécesseurs. La culture étudiante est ainsi de moins en moins d'inspiration humaniste et s'alimente de plus en plus à la culture commercialisée. Les tests statistiques viennent confirmer ces affirmations. Les différences de taux entre l'élite et les étudiants d'une part, de même que celles entre ces deux groupes et la population en général sont significatives en début et en fin de période ($p < 0,05$). En outre, les variations enregistrées chez l'élite et les étudiants entre le début et la fin de la période sont significatives alors que celle de la population en général ne l'est pas. On doit donc en tirer la conclusion que la culture de l'élite et celle des étudiants demeurent toujours distinctes l'une de l'autre, tout comme elles le sont par rapport à la population en général, mais que, au cours de ces vingt années, il y a eu une baisse significative des valeurs classiques tant parmi l'élite que parmi la population étudiante.

Les tableaux 3 et 4 présentent l'évolution, de 1979 à 1999, de quelques taux de pratiques, valorisées par les institutions culturelles, chez les étudiants et l'élite. Les changements les plus perceptibles apparaissent dans la lecture des imprimés et les sorties au spectacle. Ainsi, la lecture de revues et de livres n'est plus aussi intense qu'auparavant. Avec l'apparition des NTIC (notamment le multimédia et Internet), le livre a perdu de son influence comme moyen d'accès au savoir et comme moyen de distinction. La

Graphique 2 - Évolution de l'indice de diversité des pratiques culturelles du type classique chez les étudiants et l'élite et dans la population en général

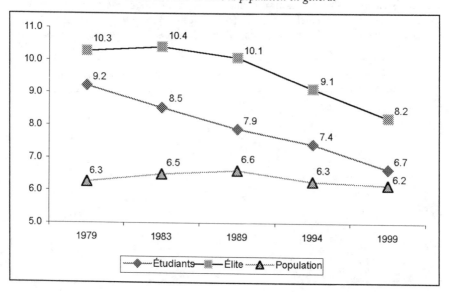

Tableau 3 - *Évolution des taux d'activités culturelles parmi la population étudiante, 1979-1999*

ACTIVITÉ CULTURELLE	ANNÉES					RATIO
	1979	1983	1989	1994	1999	1999/1979
LECTURE						
Revues	70,6	74,5	71,0	77,6	61,1	86,5
Livres	79,0	71,0	59,9	72,7	58,8	74,4
SORTIES						
Théâtre	59,7	50,6	43,3	34,4	41,7	69,8
Concert classique	23,9	19,1	11,4	10,4	10,4	43,5
Concert populaire	56,2	55,9	61,5	60,5	42,9	76,3
Danse classique	11,8	14,0	17,8	6,4	5,6	47,5
Danse moderne	15,7	19,9	15,3	5,1	8,5	54,1
Danse folklorique	8,7	3,1	3,2	2,1	2,0	23,0
Match sportif	61,2	54,0	60,0	47,1	44,9	73,4
Cinéma	–	–	85,2	86,8	91,9	–
Humour	–	–	–	33,8	28,1	–

Source: *Ministère de la Culture et des Communications, Enquêtes sur les pratiques culturelles au Québec.*

Tableau 4 - *Évolution des taux d'activités culturelles parmi l'élite québécoise, 1979-1999*

ACTIVITÉ CULTURELLE	ANNÉES					RATIO
	1979	1983	1989	1994	1999	1999/1979
LECTURE						
Revues	80,2	79,4	85,6	78,5	65,6	81,8
Livres	76,8	70,6	73,4	71,3	63,9	83,2
SORTIES						
Théâtre	59,2	53,7	62,8	51,9	46,9	79,2
Concert classique	31,6	38,1	35,3	26,8	23,8	75,3
Concert populaire	55,7	50,7	57,6	56,7	40,6	72,9
Danse classique	15,0	13,7	18,3	12,2	7,9	52,7
Danse moderne	16,8	6,7	15,7	9,6	9,8	58,3
Danse folklorique	6,0	10,3	14,8	4,8	3,8	63,3
Match sportif	54,0	51,7	48,7	51,3	36,8	68,1
Cinéma	–	–	77,7	80,7	86,3	–
Humour	–	–	–	35,0	28,0	–

Source: *Ministère de la Culture et des Communications, Enquêtes sur les pratiques culturelles au Québec.*

multiplication des titres, la publication d'ouvrages de tous genres et la vente de livres dans des lieux non spécialisés ont contribué à la démocratisation du livre. La lecture de livres ne constitue plus de nos jours une pratique distinctive de l'élite. Il en est de même des sorties au spèctacle. Au fur et à mesure que l'offre de spectacles s'est faite plus abondante et plus variée par l'arrivée sur le marché de nouveaux produits tels que les variétés musicales et l'humour, ceux-ci ont gagné en popularité en supplantant les formes plus anciennes. Les sorties au théâtre, au concert classique et populaire ainsi qu'aux spectacles de danse sont moins répandues et régressent plus rapidement chez les étudiants et l'élite que dans l'ensemble de la société. La popularité du concert classique, par exemple, a diminué au fil des ans. Celui-ci n'attire plus, en 1999, que 10 p.cent des étudiants. La sortie aux matchs sportifs, quoiqu'elle soit moins distinctive que celles qui viennent d'être énumérées, n'y échappe pas non plus. Par ailleurs, le cinéma a gagné en popularité auprès des étudiants et de l'élite de 1989 à 1999. De même, ils se sont laissés entraîner par les humoristes, à un niveau qui dépasse même celui de la population en général. Un changement s'est donc produit dans ce qui constituait autrefois le noyau dur des pratiques culturelles identitaires de l'élite et des étudiants. Le centre de gravité se déplace des formes traditionnelles vers d'autres formes plus modernes associées aux véhicules commerciaux. Une raison de ce phénomène pourrait bien être l'effet de ce que P. Coulangeon appelle la « massification scolaire » et la « massification de la culture[20] », avec comme conséquence l'affaiblissement des frontières entre la culture savante et la culture populaire, entre la culture de l'élite et la culture de masse.

Le poids des baby-boomers dans la demande institutionnelle

Les conséquences de l'affaiblissement de la culture classique chez les jeunes et les étudiants font en sorte que celle-ci est soutenue principalement par la population plus âgée qui correspond, *grosso modo*, à celle des *baby-boomers*. Ces derniers, alors qu'ils étaient jeunes durant les années 1980, s'impliquaient dans une culture en effervescence et en changement. Il était alors davantage question de diffusion culturelle que de marketing. Cette génération est donc demeurée fidèle à la culture offerte par les institutions, bien qu'elle ne dédaigne pas non plus les produits industriels. Les marchands de culture ont ainsi remplacé graduellement les diffuseurs culturels, et leur influence s'est plus largement fait sentir auprès des générations montantes. Aussi la production institutionnelle recrute-t-elle davantage son public auprès des *baby-boomers*, alors que la production industrielle le trouve chez les plus jeunes, soit les enfants des *baby-boomers*. Le marché de la culture est donc polarisé en deux blocs importants : le premier, émanant surtout de l'institution culturelle; le second, émanant surtout de l'industrie.

Rappelons que les *baby-boomers* ont grandi avec la conscience de la valeur de la culture québécoise comme lieu d'affirmation nationale. Le Québec culturel des années de leur jeunesse s'est construit en mettant en place un ensemble de structures publiques et privées à partir desquelles s'est édifiée la culture québécoise. Celles-ci ont marqué la création, la production et la diffusion culturelle de l'époque. Avides de cultures, ces générations, qui avaient à l'époque de quinze à trente-quatre ans, ont envahi tous les nouveaux lieux de culture qui surgissaient : les établissements du patrimoine, les établissements du livre, les lieux de spectacle et les boîtes à chanson. En 1979, les préférences se démarquaient toutefois selon les groupes d'âge : les moins de vingt-cinq ans manifestaient alors un intérêt particulier pour les bibliothèques, les sites et monuments historiques, le théâtre en saison, les spectacles de danse classique et moderne, les concerts de musique populaire ainsi que les matchs sportifs. Les vingt-cinq à trente-

quatre ans se caractérisaient alors par la diversité de leurs champs d'intérêt culturels :
ils fréquentaient les librairies et les bibliothèques, les établissements du patrimoine tels
que les musées, les sites et les monuments historiques, les galeries d'art; ils achetaient des
œuvres d'art et des produits des métiers d'art; ils assistaient à des spectacles, notamment
de théâtre et de danse classique. Ces activités étaient le signe d'une culture jeune. Le
graphique 3 montre comment les pratiques du type classique étaient segmentées selon
les groupes d'âge en 1979, alors que les différences intergénérationnelles ont presque
disparu en 1999[21]. On voit également la persistance des comportements: les jeunes de
quinze à trente-quatre ans de 1979 n'ont pas perdu leurs habitudes culturelles, vingt ans
après, maintenant qu'ils sont âgés de trente-cinq à cinquante-quatre ans. Le changement
de comportement à l'égard de la culture classique, entre 1979 et 1999, est significatif (p
< 0,05) dans tous les groupes d'âge à l'exception des trente-cinq à quarante-quatre ans.
Il se traduit par une baisse d'intérêt pour cette culture, en 1999, parmi les groupes plus
jeunes alors c'est l'inverse parmi les quarante-cinq ans et plus.

Le public des activités culturelles du type industriel est différent. Il se trouve
principalement parmi les jeunes générations, qui signifient ainsi leur ouverture à la
nouveauté. Elles sont les premières à adopter les nouveaux produits mis sur le marché.
Le graphique 4 permet de visualiser la diversité de pratiques culturelles de type classique
et de type industriel en 1999 selon les groupes d'âge. Signalons sa similitude avec le
graphique 3, comme si le phénomène qui se présentait en 1979 à l'égard de la culture
classique se reproduisait en 1999 dans le cas de la culture industrielle.

Les jeunes qui sont aujourd'hui âgés de quinze à trente-quatre ans sont les
plus grands consommateurs de culture. Leurs champs d'intérêt sont très diversifiés,
notamment ceux des jeunes de quinze à vingt-quatre ans. Bien qu'ils soient nés avec
les médias de masse et les industries culturelles, ils se déplacent vers les institutions
artistiques et culturelles d'une manière presque aussi intensive que leurs aînés. Ils
aiment explorer les différentes facettes de la culture. Ils ne sont pas seulement des
consommateurs de culture : ils expérimentent la pratique de l'art en amateur, se
perfectionnent en suivant des cours d'art et s'engagent dans le bénévolat et l'organisation
d'activités culturelles dans leur milieu. La diversité de leurs formes d'expérimentation
culturelle laisse croire que ces jeunes sont encore dans un processus de formation

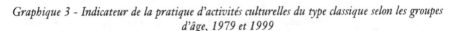

*Graphique 3 - Indicateur de la pratique d'activités culturelles du type classique selon les groupes
d'âge, 1979 et 1999*

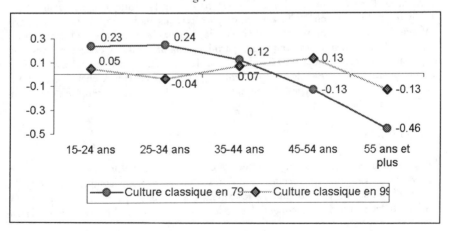

identitaire. Les pratiques des trente-cinq à cinquante-quatre ans présentent également un panorama diversifié, mais, à la différence de la situation chez les plus jeunes, celles qui sont liées à l'industrie y ont moins d'importance. La plus grande fréquence des pratiques de type classique chez ces personnes s'explique par le fait qu'elles ont été marquées par les institutions culturelles qui ont connu un essor important au temps de leur jeunesse. Quant aux personnes plus âgées, soit les cinquante-cinq ans et plus, l'éventail des activités qu'elles pratiquent, notamment celles qui sont associées à la culture industrielle, est plus réduit. Les tests statistiques confirment ces affirmations. Il y a une différence d'attitude ($p < 0{,}05$) à l'égard de la culture classique et de la culturelle industrielle dans tous les groupes d'âge. La culture industrielle l'emporte avant quarante ans environ, mais un retournement s'opère par la suite au profit de la culture classique. Le graphique 5 illustre l'importance que prennent les cultures classique et industrielle selon les groupes d'âge.

Le marché de la culture, comme l'illustre le graphique 5, se découpe donc en deux composantes principales : l'une est liée aux activités institutionnelles et d'inspiration classique, tandis que l'autre est développée par l'industrie selon les lois du marché. La première est surtout accueillie par la population plus âgée, la seconde, par les plus jeunes. Le poids démographique des groupes d'âge amplifie les tendances de la consommation culturelle. Ainsi, le groupe des trente-cinq à cinquante-quatre ans, dans lequel sont inclus en 1999 les *baby-boomers*, est celui qui comporte le plus grand nombre d'individus, et il impose ses valeurs non seulement en matière de culture institutionnelle, mais aussi sur le marché de l'industrie, comme en témoignent la spécialisation de certaines stations radiophoniques dans la musique des années 1960 (*sixties*) et 1970 (*seventies*) ainsi que le repiquage de la musique de ces années-là. Par ailleurs, le poids des quinze à vingt-quatre ans sur le même marché n'est pas négligeable. Très grands consommateurs de produits culturels, les jeunes sont convoités par l'industrie qui en fait la population cible de son marketing. Pour sa part, la population plus âgée est une moins grande consommatrice de culture, surtout des produits de l'industrie. Elle se distingue également par ses valeurs plus conservatrices en matière de culture. Son poids démographique est plus faible que celui des deux autres groupes d'âge mentionnés. La présentation des types de consommateurs qui suit mettra mieux en évidence les modalités d'appropriation culturelle au sein de la population.

Les types de consommateurs culturels[22]

La typologie des consommateurs exposée ici a été élaborée à partir de différentes techniques d'analyse multivariée[23]. Elle est basée sur la pratique d'une quarantaine d'activités différentes en 1999. Les cinq types retenus montrent autant de rapports différents en fait d'intensité et de diversité dans la pratique culturelle. Le graphique 6 illustre la répartition des cinq types parmi la population. Les deux types les plus importants numériquement sont l'« absent » et le « fêtard », chacun englobant le tiers de la population. L'« humaniste », qui vient par la suite, se rencontre chez une personne sur cinq. Les deux autres types, l'« inconditionnel » et l'« engagé », représentent moins de 10 p.cent de la population.

L'inconditionnel

Le consommateur culturel du premier type, que nous appelons l'« inconditionnel », assiste à beaucoup de spectacles, qu'ils soient de forme classique ou moderne. L'inconditionnel apprécie notamment les concerts de toutes sortes et il ne manque aucun festival. Il fréquente les bars-spectacles et le cinéma. C'est de loin celui qui a la vie

Graphique 4 - Indicateur de la pratique d'activités culturelles du type classique et du type industriel selon les groupes d'âge, 1999

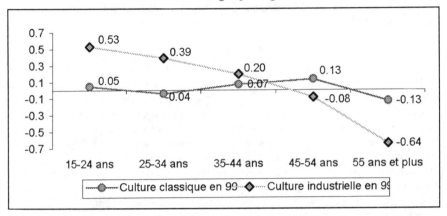

Graphique 5 - Répartition des composantes du marché de la culture en fonction de l'âge

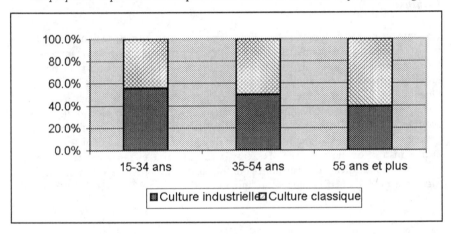

Graphique 6 - Typologie des consommateurs culturels québécois, 1999

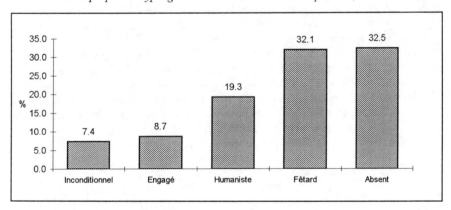

culturelle la plus intense. Ce type est peu important du point de vue du nombre, soit 7,4 p.cent de la population québécoise. L'inconditionnel est relativement jeune et plus scolarisé que la moyenne. Les hommes se retrouvent un peu plus souvent dans cette catégorie que les femmes, de même que les personnes qui sont sur le marché du travail ou qui poursuivent des études.

L'engagé

Le deuxième type de consommateur, l'« engagé », se caractérise par son engagement culturel et social. C'est un organisateur d'activités culturelles dans son milieu, il s'adonne à la pratique d'activités en amateur, il suit des cours d'art, il fait partie d'associations culturelles et il donne de son temps comme bénévole à des organismes culturels. L'engagé est une personne-ressource précieuse en milieu municipal en raison de son dynamisme et de sa capacité mobilisatrice. Ce type a un niveau d'activité culturelle de beaucoup supérieur à la moyenne, sans égaler toutefois celui de l'inconditionnel. Environ 9 p.cent de la population est de ce type, qui compte plus de femmes que d'hommes. L'engagé est jeune et scolarisé. La majorité des personnes relevant de ce type sont sur le marché du travail, mais un bon nombre sont aux études.

L'humaniste

L'« humaniste » est ainsi nommé en raison de son penchant prononcé pour des pratiques plutôt classiques. Il fréquente les établissements du patrimoine comme les musées d'art, les autres musées, ainsi que les sites et monuments historiques. Son goût pour l'art le porte à l'achat d'œuvres d'art. L'humaniste ne court pas les spectacles autant que l'inconditionnel et il demeure conservateur en cette matière : théâtre, concert classique, opéra, opérette et comédie musicale. Il aime également la lecture et il fréquente assidûment les établissements du livre, la librairie en particulier. On trouve une plus grande proportion de femmes parmi ce type de consommateur. L'humaniste est plus âgé et plus instruit que la moyenne: il atteint la cinquantaine et a souvent fait des études universitaires. Plusieurs des personnes qui font partie de cette catégorie sont retraitées. Signalons qu'il y a peu de jeunes et d'étudiants. On peut ranger près de 20 p.cent des Québécois sous ce type.

Le fêtard

D'autres personnes ont une approche de la culture différente des trois types que nous venons de voir. Elle est, pour ces personnes, une occasion de divertissement. Celui que nous qualifions de « fêtard » préfère les activités culturelles qui vont le divertir ou qui présentent des occasions de fréquenter des gens et de s'amuser. Il aime sortir au cinéma et visionner des vidéocassettes. Il fréquente les bars-spectacles et les discothèques. Le fêtard est amateur de musique et il court les festivals. Son niveau d'activités culturelles n'excède cependant pas la moyenne. Il se recrute surtout chez les hommes et il est le plus jeune de tous les types de consommateurs. Le fêtard est le plus souvent actif sur le marché du travail lorsqu'il n'est pas encore aux études. On note une proportion élevée de fêtards, soit près du tiers de la population québécoise.

L'absent

Le dernier type de consommateur se caractérise par son faible niveau d'intérêt pour la culture. C'est pour cette raison que nous l'avons appelé l'« absent ». Son niveau d'activités se situe à l'opposé de l'inconditionnel. L'absent sort peu et lit peu. Son univers culturel est limité. C'est toutefois un auditeur plus assidu de la télévision et de la radio que les autres. Il est le plus âgé de tous les types de consommateurs : il dépasse en effet de quelques années la cinquantaine. On y dénombre autant d'hommes que de femmes. L'absent a rarement fait des études postsecondaires. Une bonne proportion des personnes de ce type ont quitté le marché du travail et sont à la retraite. L'effectif de ce type est aussi nombreux que celui du fêtard, un Québécois sur trois pouvant être qualifié d'absent de la vie culturelle.

Cette typologie rend compte de la variété des motivations sous-jacentes à la pratique culturelle et de la place variable que les citoyens accordent à la culture. Elle témoigne également des principales phases du développement culturel qui ont marqué les générations vivantes. Ainsi, les personnes plus âgées, qui ont peu fréquenté les établissements scolaires et qui ont vécu à une époque où la production culturelle professionnelle était embryonnaire, se retrouvent souvent parmi les absents. La génération qui a suivi, celle des *baby-boomers*, a un niveau de scolarité plus élevé et elle a connu l'effervescence culturelle des années 1970 et 1980, période pendant laquelle les institutions artistiques et culturelles ont surgi et se sont développées. Plusieurs personnes de cette génération se trouvent dans le type humaniste ou dans le type engagé. Par ailleurs, on perçoit chez les plus jeunes l'emprise des industries culturelles et des NTIC.

Ces dernières ont transformé les modes de production et de consommation culturelles. À la profusion des produits mis sur le marché par l'industrie, les consommateurs (les jeunes consommateurs, principalement) ont répondu par une diversification de leurs pratiques. L'inconditionnel en est le type le plus manifeste.

Tableau 5 - Taux de pratiques de certaines activités culturelles chez les types engagé et absent, Québec, 1999

Pratiques culturelles	L'engagé %	L'absent %
Fréquentation de la bibliothèque publique	56,7	10,2
Fréquentation des musées	58,4	8,6
Lecture régulière des quotidiens	68,8	60,9
Lecture régulière des revues et des magazines	70,2	34,4
Lecture régulière de livres	69,0	29,0
Perfectionnement en art	41,1	3,0
Pratique artistique en amateur	87,8	33,4
Pratique scientifique en amateur	48,7	16,4
Bénévolat	64,9	20,4
Philanthropie culturelle	23,0	12,9
Organisation d'activités culturelles dans son milieu	69,2	2,3

Source : Ministère de la Culture et des Communications, Enquête sur les pratiques culturelles au Québec, 1999.

D'autres, et ils sont nombreux, ont privilégié surtout la dimension du plaisir et du divertissement que procure la pratique culturelle : on les trouve principalement sous le type des fêtards.

Pratique culturelle et citoyenneté culturelle

Des engagés et des absents

La typologie des consommateurs culturels qui vient d'être présentée n'est pas sans questionner le statut de certains citoyens en regard de leur vie culturelle. Deux aspects particuliers de la relation entre la pratique culturelle et la citoyenneté culturelle seront abordés : tout d'abord celui du citoyen engagé et du citoyen en situation d'exclusion culturelle, puis celui de l'intégration culturelle des immigrants et des minorités linguistiques.

La typologie que nous avons présentée fait état d'une partie de la population fortement engagée dans sa construction identitaire par la pratique d'activités culturelles. L'engagé, tel que nous l'avons nommé, représente moins de 10 p.cent de la population, mais c'est un individu qui s'implique fortement dans la formation d'une culture citoyenne. Non seulement est-il bien informé par ses lectures, mais en outre il maîtrise la formation de sa personnalité culturelle et concourt à l'enrichissement de celle de la collectivité à laquelle il appartient. Il édifie son propre corpus culturel en étant un citoyen actif et participatif en matière de la culture – contrant ainsi les effets de la massification culturelle engendrée par l'industrie et les mass médias – et, en plus, il assure un leadership au sein de la collectivité en participant à la vie associative et en devenant producteur culturel. Il devient alors un créateur de liens et d'espaces culturels nécessaires à la cohésion sociale. L'absent se situe pour sa part à l'opposé. Sa vie culturelle se déroule peu dans l'espace public, étant plutôt confinée au domaine privé et aux loisirs domestiques. À son désengagement face à la culture se juxtapose souvent une exclusion économique et sociale. Le fort contingent d'absents, une personne sur trois, montre qu'il existe un fort décalage entre la reconnaissance des droits culturels du citoyen et leur exercice réel. Le tableau 5 montre par quelques exemples comment l'engagé et l'absent ont des pratiques culturelles différentes.

De la population immigrante et des minorités linguistiques

Une part appréciable de la population est issue d'une immigration récente au Québec. Le renouvellement de la population québécoise se fait désormais, pour une large part, par l'arrivée d'immigrants qui choisissent de s'installer dans la région de Montréal. En 2001, 1,3 p.cent seulement de la population québécoise était issue d'une immigration antérieure à 1961, alors que 8,5 p.cent avait immigré entre 1961 et 2001[24]. La composition ethnique de l'immigration au Québec a changé. Alors que la population immigrante d'avant 1961 provenait principalement de pays européens, celle d'après vient plutôt de l'Asie et de pays francophones tels que Haïti, la France et le Liban. La composition linguistique de la population s'est également modifiée, surtout sur l'île de Montréal. Selon le recensement de 2001, la proportion des personnes qui parlent le français le plus souvent à la maison a crû, passant de 55,6 p.cent en 1996 à 56,4 p.cent en 2001. Par ailleurs, la proportion des personnes qui utilisent l'anglais le plus souvent à la maison a diminué, passant de 25,6 p.cent à 25,0 p.cent, tandis que celle qui utilise une autre langue a légèrement fléchi, passant de 18,8 p.cent à 18,6 p.cent[25].

La participation aux activités culturelles varie en diversité et en intensité selon que la population est de souche québécoise ou qu'elle provient de l'immigration. On observe également des fluctuations importantes selon la langue parlée à la maison. Nous vérifions ces phénomènes à partir d'un indice global de participation aux activités culturelles établi à partir des données du sondage de 1999. Les activités entrant dans la formation de cet indice sont les mêmes que celles qui ont servi à l'élaboration de la typologie dont nous avons fait mention[26]. Il apparaît que, selon que l'on provient ou non de l'immigration ou selon la langue parlée à la maison, le niveau de participation à la vie culturelle diffère.

Les personnes dont les deux parents sont nés à l'étranger présentent un taux d'activité culturelle supérieur à celles dont un seul parent est né à l'étranger ou dont les deux parents sont nés au Canada, comme l'illustre le graphique 7 ($p < 0,05$). C'est là une révélation importante démontrant que la culture peut être un vecteur efficace d'intégration des immigrants de date récente – nés à l'étranger ou dont les parents sont nés à l'étranger – à leur communauté d'adoption. Selon la typologie évoquée antérieurement, les Québécois dont les deux parents sont nés à l'étranger présentent une probabilité plus forte que les autres de faire partie du type humaniste (23,2 p.cent comparativement à 18,8 p.cent chez les Québécois dont les deux parents sont nés au Canada et à 18,4 p.cent chez ceux dont un parent seulement est né au Canada); en contrepartie, les Québécois dont les deux parents sont nés à l'étranger se retrouvent moins fréquemment parmi le type absent (25,8 p.cent comparativement à 33,4 p.cent chez les Québécois dont les deux parents sont nés au Canada et à 36,1 p.cent chez ceux dont un parent seulement est né au Canada).

Une autre relation fort intéressante est présentée au graphique 8 entre le niveau d'activité culturelle et la langue parlée le plus souvent à la maison. Les anglophones ont une vie culturelle plus diversifiée que les francophones et les allophones ($p < 0,05$), alors que ces deux derniers groupes ne se distinguent pas vraiment l'un de l'autre à cet égard. Les anglophones du Québec ont d'ailleurs joué un rôle important dans la création

---

Tableau 6 - Indice global standardisé de participation aux activités culturelles selon le pays de provenance du père des immigrants, Québec, 1999

PAYS D'ORIGINE DU PÈRE DES IMMIGRANTS	SCORE STANDARDISÉ
France	0,53
Angleterre	0,33
Europe occidentale (sauf Italie)	0,33
Europe orientale	0,30
Afrique	0,27
Asie	0,03
Québécois de souche	-0,02
Italie	-0,08
États-Unis	-0,08
Amérique du Sud	-0,20
Haïti	-0,33

Source : Ministère de la Culture et des Communications, Enquête sur les pratiques culturelles au Québec, 1999.

---

et le développement des institutions culturelles québécoises. Ils sont davantage orientés vers la culture du type humaniste. On retrouve d'ailleurs une proportion plus forte de consommateurs du type humaniste chez eux (28,9 p.cent comparativement à 18,4 p.cent chez les francophones et à 14,8 p.cent chez les allophones) alors que, à l'inverse, ces deux derniers groupes renferment une plus grande proportion de fêtards et d'absents que les anglophones.

Nous pouvons préciser davantage le degré d'intégration culturelle des immigrants de date récente selon la langue parlée à la maison. Les immigrants anglophones, les immigrants francophones, de même que les anglophones et les allophones implantés au Québec depuis plusieurs générations, ont un niveau d'activité culturelle plus élevé que les immigrants allophones et les Québécois francophones de souche, comme le montre le graphique 9 ($p < 0,05$).

Les immigrants anglophones et francophones s'adaptent rapidement à la vie culturelle québécoise, alors que les immigrants allophones rencontrent plus de difficultés.

C'est ainsi que certains immigrants[27] obtiennent un score variable selon le pays de provenance de leur père, comme le montre le tableau 6. Les immigrants en provenance de la France, de l'Angleterre, des autres pays d'Europe occidentale (à l'exception de l'Italie), de l'Europe orientale et de l'Afrique offrent une palette plus large d'activités culturelles que les immigrants en provenance d'Haïti, de l'Amérique du Sud, des États-Unis, de l'Italie et des Québécois de souche.

Cela fait donc la démonstration que la culture peut être un puissant vecteur d'intégration de la population immigrante. Cette intégration est plus facile lorsqu'il n'y a pas de barrière linguistique et lorsque la culture du pays d'origine est proche de celle du Québec. On voit qu'il existe une plus grande proximité culturelle entre les Québécois et les immigrants européens qu'avec ceux en provenance d'Asie, d'Amérique centrale ou d'Amérique du Sud.

Conclusion

Notre analyse a montré comment des changements majeurs sont survenus dans la pratique culturelle des Québécois au cours de la période 1979-1999. Cette transformation s'explique en bonne partie par la modification de la société québécoise dans sa composition socioéconomique et sa structure démographique, par les changements dans les modes de vie, de même que par la transformation profonde de l'offre culturelle sous l'effet de facteurs industriels et technologiques. Ainsi, la massification de l'offre culturelle et l'élévation du niveau de vie, jointes à une scolarisation plus grande, ont eu pour effet d'atténuer les écarts culturels entre les groupes sociaux, entre les jeunes et les aînés, entre les étudiants et l'élite, d'une part, et le reste de la population, d'autre part. Bien que les *baby-boomers* demeurent toujours attachés à une culture de type plus classique, ils entretiennent aussi des rapports avec la culture populaire. Les marqueurs, qui servaient notamment à délimiter les territoires culturels de l'élite, ont perdu peu à peu de leur force. Ce que les pratiques culturelles de cette dernière ont gagné en éclectisme, elles l'ont perdu en spécificité. Si un déclin des pratiques du type classique a eu lieu, c'est que ces dernières ont laissé place à d'autres divertissements qui ont surgi avec l'entrée dans les ménages des équipements audiovisuels et des NTIC, de même qu'à ceux qui sont liés au sport, au conditionnement physique et au tourisme.

Les jeunes, en particulier, apparaissent comme les partisans d'un modèle de pratiques qui prend de plus en plus ses distances par rapport à la culture consacrée et à la

Graphique 7 - Indice global standardisé de participation aux activités culturelles selon l'origine géographique des parents

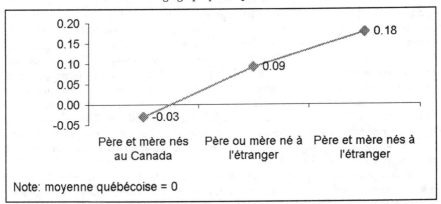

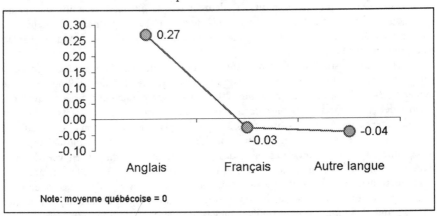

Graphique 8 - Indice global standardisé de participation aux activités culturelles selon la langue parlée à la maison

Graphique 9 - Indice global standardisé de participation aux activités culturelles des Québécois de souche et des immigrants selon la langue parlée à la maison

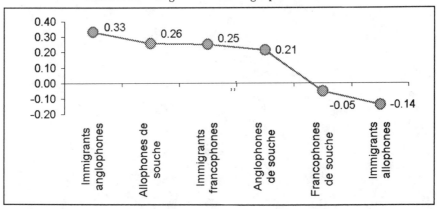

culture humaniste. Leurs sorties culturelles se font sous le signe du divertissement et de la sociabilité. Ils ont grandi dans un contexte où l'audiovisuel a connu d'importants bouleversements, et ils vivent dans un environnement où le son et les images animées occupent une place considérable. Ces supports en viennent à former leurs schèmes de pensée et à imposer leur rythme. Nous avons vu, en présentant la typologie des consommateurs culturels, qu'une bonne partie des jeunes ont un univers de pratiques structuré autour du divertissement, du plaisir et de la sociabilité. Si l'on s'appuie sur l'expérience de la génération des jeunes des années 1960 et 1970, ces nouvelles pratiques ne disparaîtront pas avec le vieillissement de ces générations. Nous croyons plutôt qu'elles vont sanctionner à terme la fin de la dominance de la culture classique dans la définition de la culture « consacré e». Il demeurera toujours des « absents de la culture » en raison des inégalités sociales, mais leur nombre est appelé à diminuer avec le remplacement des générations plus vieilles par les générations montantes, qui sont dorénavant plus scolarisées.

Enfin, nous avons montré que les nouveaux arrivants peuvent s'intégrer facilement à la culture québécoise et y participer de façon encore plus grande que la population de souche lorsqu'il existe déjà des affinités linguistiques ou des parentés culturelles entre le Québec et le pays d'origine. Les anglophones, qu'ils soient arrivés au pays récemment ou depuis longtemps, ont une vie culturelle intense, tournée principalement vers la culture humaniste. Les données ont montré également que la citoyenneté culturelle n'était pas acquise automatiquement aux Québécois de souche francophone, ni d'ailleurs aux immigrants de certaines régions du globe, et qu'elle demandait à être conquise par un engagement plus ferme.

Les données sur lesquelles nous nous sommes appuyés dans le cadre de cette analyse sont celles provenant des sondages effectués par le MCC de 1979 à 1999. Une nouvelle enquête a eu lieu au printemps 2004, mais l'analyse de ses données n'avait pas encore débuté au moment de la rédaction du présent texte. Il sera toutefois intéressant de constater si les tendances observées à l'égard de la culture classique, de la culture industrielle et de la culture citoyenne se maintiennent, si la polarisation des marchés s'accentue selon les générations et si des gains ont été enregistrés en vue de faire reculer les frontières de l'exclusion culturelle. Les données de 2004 permettront, nous le souhaitons, de vérifier à nouveau l'importance des changements structurels sur les pratiques, comme le déclin des institutions (notamment de l'école), l'influence grandissante de l'industrie culturelle et la mécanisation des loisirs domestiques.

Notes

1 B. Miège, « La production culturelle et
le maintien du pluralisme », dans UNESCO,
Rapport mondial sur la communication et l'information 1999-2000, chap. 3III, disponible au
http://www.unesco.org.webworld/wcir/fr/
report.html]] (12 novembre 2003.

2 Cette enquête a été renouvelée au printemps
2004 et les premières données sont attendues à
l'automne 2004.

3 La population à l'étude, lors de l'enquête de
1979, était celle de dix-huit ans et plus.

4 R. Garon et L. Santerre, *Déchiffrer la culture
au Québec : vingt ans de pratiques culturelles*,
Québec, Les Publications du Québec, 2004.

5 Ministère des Affaires culturelles, *La politique
culturelle du Québec : notre culture, notre avenir*,
Québec,: Ministère des Affaires culturelles,
Québec, 1992, p. 104.

6 *Ibid.*, p. 109.

7 B. Miège, *op. cit.*, note 1.

8 Voir à ce sujet la première partie du document
de R. Garon et L. Santerre, *op. cit.*, note 3.

9 G. Pronovost, « Les transformations des pratiques culturelles : une perspective intergénérationnelle », dans F. Colbert (dir.), *Les organisations culturelles de l'avenir : actes du colloque,
Montréal, 7-8 novembre 1997*, Montréal, Chaire
de gestion des arts, École des hautes études
commerciales, p. 105.

10 J. Heilbrun et C.M. Gray, *The Economics
of Art and Culture, An American Perspective*,
Cambridge, New York, Cambridge University
Press, 1993, p. 67-68.

11 F. Rouet, *Les tarifs de la culture*, Paris, La
Documentation française, 2002, p. 93.

12 J. Jouët, « Pratiques de communication et
figures de la médiation », *Réseaux*, no 60, (1993,
): p. 112.

13 Voir à ce sujet J. Jutras, « Les pratiques de
lecture des Québécoises et des Québécois de
1989 à 1999 », *Survol*, n° 11 (février 2004), p.
7.

14 Il aurait été plus difficile d'établir le vieillissement réel des publics à partir de 1979 puisque, lors des premières enquêtes, nous n'avions
pas l'âge exact des répondants mais plutôt une
catégorie d'âge.

15 Les vingt activités entrant dans la formation
de l'indicateur du type classique ont été distinguées selon que le répondant pratiquait ou non
ces activités. L'indicateur exprime la somme des
scores de ces activités. En voici le détail : la
lecture des quotidiens, des revues ou des magazines et des livres, la fréquentation des bibliothèques publiques, des librairies, des musées
d'art, des autres musées, des sites et monuments historiques, des galeries d'art, des salons
du livre et des métiers d'art, l'écoute musicale
sur une base régulière, l'achat d'œuvres d'art ou
des métiers d'art, la fréquentation du théâtre
d'été, du théâtre en saison, du concert classique, du concert populaire et des spectacles de
danse classique, moderne et folklorique.

16 O. Donnat, *Les Français face à la culture: de
l'exclusion à l'éclectisme*, Paris, La Découverte,
1994, p. 163-169.

17 A.F. Firat et D. Nikhilesh, « People.
From Political Economy to Theaters of Consumption », dans P.G. Foxall (dir.), *Consumer
Research and Policies Series*, Londres, New York:
Routledge, 1998, p. 195.

18 Citons les travaux de P. Bourdieu, de O.
Donnat et de G. Pronovost, pour ne mentionner que quelques-uns des chercheurs qui ont
fait état de ce phénomène.

19 L'élite est définie de façon opératoire comme
les personnes qui ont fait des études universitaires, qui sont actives sur le marché du travail
et qui sont des cadres, des dirigeants d'entreprise ou des professionnels.

20 P. Coulangeon, « Le rôle de l'école dans la
démocratisation de l'accès aux arts », *Revue de
l'OFCE*, no 86, (2003), p. 155-169.

21 Le graphique 3 présente un indicateur standardisé de la pratique d'activités culturelles
du type classique en 1979 et en 1999, où la
moyenne est zéro.

22 Cette description des types est tirée de R.
Garon, « Vingt ans de pratiques culturelles au
Québec », *Survol*, no 12, mars (2004), p. 14-15.

23 Une analyse factorielle a d'abord permis
d'établir cinq dimensions à la consommation
culturelle. Ensuite, une analyse typologique
effectuée à partir des poids factoriels a mis en
évidence cinq types mutuellement exclusifs de
consommateurs.

24 Statistique Canada, *Profil des langues au Canada: l'anglais, le français et bien d'autres langues*, Recensement de 2001 : série « analyses », Ottawa, Statistique Canada, 2002, no 96F0030XlF2001005 au catalogue).

25 *Ibid.*

26 Les éléments entrant dans la mesure sont, pour les établissements culturels, la fréquence des visites des bibliothèques, des salons du livre, des salons des métiers d'art, des librairies, des sites et monuments du patrimoine, des musées et des centres d'archives; pour les sorties, il s'agit de la fréquence de celles qui ont lieu dans les bars-spectacles, les discothèques, au cinéma et aux autres spectacles; quant aux pratiques engagées, l'intensité est mesurée à partir du nombre de pratiques en amateur, de cours suivis dans le domaine des arts, du temps accordé au bénévolat et à l'organisation d'activités et par le montant des dons faits à des organismes artistiques ou culturels.

27 Ici, l'origine des immigrants est établie à partir de celle du père seulement.

12.

Pathways of Cultural Movement

Will Straw

In 1997, the Swedish ethnologist Orvar Lofgren invited scholars to study the ways in which cultural artefacts move through the spaces of national cultures.[1] Research on culture, he argued, should direct its attention to "the ways in which national differences become embedded in the materialities of everyday life, found not only in the rhetoric of flag-waving and public rituals, but also in the national trajectories of commodities."[2] What is novel here is not the challenge to scholars and policy-makers to study everyday life—this has been a well-meaning commonplace in academic discussions of culture for the last two or three decades. More suggestive, I would argue, is Lofgren's invitation to study the life of cultural artefacts as "trajectories," pathways of movement through national life. This chapter attempts to gather and develop some of the resources we might use in charting these pathways.

The place of these pathways within notions of cultural citizenship is not immediately apparent, but it merits consideration. In an influential definition of cultural citizenship, Aihwa Ong suggests it is shaped by "negotiating the often ambivalent and contested relations with the state and its hegemonic forms that establish the criteria of belonging within a national population and territory."[3] The examples of negotiation which follow will seem trivial alongside the dramas of displacement and struggle which fill Ong's ethnographic work. Let us see the realm of culture, nevertheless, as one in which each gesture (each new film or act of artistic activism, for example) presumes an implicit negotiation with the context in which it seeks to emerge. That context includes other people, artefacts, and the structures of power or institution. Each such negotiation, in turn, functions as an act of transformation, if only by once more marshalling resources for an oft-repeated confrontation. Cultural citizenship is less about residing within culture than about the necessity of moving within it, and the negotiations and transformations which that movement entails.

The trajectories of movement which interest me here are those by which creators and cultural intermediaries act so as to join together places, people, activities, technologies, and clusters of cultural meaning. This involves an emphasis on production rather than consumption, but both must be seen as transformative gestures within a field of artefacts and social relations. In the sorts of joining I will discuss, cultural artefacts (books, films, nightclub events, art exhibitions, and so on) will be produced, but these artefacts are arguably less important than the patterns of interaction which are forged, reinforced, or broken in the process. Vibrant networks of cultural activity may leave behind few visibly successful works or cultural milestones. It is in the movement of social energies along such networks, nevertheless, that we might usefully seek indications of cultural achievement or vitality. Analysts of Canadian culture have become skilled at pausing the movement of our cultural artefacts in order to examine them for the traces of a national sensibility. This has produced an abundance of claims about the character or function of Canadian films, books, and music. These include, for example, the argument that Canadian literature best fulfills its national mission when it adopts "allegorical, and mythopoeic or romance forms,"[4] or that much of "Canadian art and Canadian thought … is devoted to a last-ditch effort to establish a satisfactory relationship with nature."[5] These definitions bolster that longstanding sense of cultural citizenship as founded upon what Toby Miller calls the "moment of automimesis," when a national imaginary finds substance in a frozen image of its collective self.[6] Cultural criticism has identified piles of works which meet these (and many other) criteria, but these works are left to stand as milestones, static embodiments of national sentiment. Time and movement become little more than the empty substance which lies between such milestones, taking us from one to the other.

Orvar Lofgren's ideas on the trajectories of cultural life might be fleshed out with notions developed within another recent intervention in cultural analysis. In his book *Metaculture*, anthropologist Greg Urban instructs us to see culture, less as a series of artefacts to be consumed than as the movement which produces that series. "Culture is not in fact prior to movement," Urban writes, "but is, rather, a derivative of movement. It is not that structure does not exist, it is rather that structure is a consequence of the way in which cultural elements move through space and time."[7] It is the movement of culture, he writes elsewhere, that "makes possible the recognition of a system or structure."[8] I would quickly add that Urban does not see culture as structure in any static or strictly formalist sense of the latter term. Structure is a particular balance between what Urban calls the "inertial" and "accelerative" aspects of cultural movement.

All cultural products are "inertial" to the extent that they inevitably repeat elements from earlier products or works. This is one of their features which makes them intelligible; the inertia within cultural artefacts ensures degrees of continuity, from one artefact to another. At the same time, of course, very few cultural products simply repeat the already-known. The familiar is constantly reiterated in new works, which displace those which came before them and move the cultural field along through their novelty. Recent successful Quebec films, like *Les Boys III*, *Elvis Gratton III*, or *Séraphin*, draw explicitly on older prototypes and thus serve as inertial forces, restating older preoccupations and thus slowing the disappearance of these preoccupations from culture life. At the same time, by pushing these prototypes into an engagement with more contemporary themes (the globalized world into which Elvis Gratton is pulled, for example) these films fulfill an accelerative function. They renew the familiar by bringing it into an engagement with the new and the unfamiliar. For Urban, it is the distribution of inertial and accelerative forces across the field of cultural products which gives cultural life its character—rendering it stable or fragile, static or turbulent. The weak hold of English-Canadian cinema on its audiences, arguably, stems from a consistent imbalance of these forces. Outside of the *œuvres* of individual directors, few themes or styles are passed along, from one film to another. The result, perhaps, is an excessively accelerative cinema, one marked by constant novelty but by little of the inertial force which would ensure an ongoing engagement with its audiences.

I want to pursue some of these ideas further, drawing on three examples from research in which I am involved in an ongoing fashion (either on my own or with students and colleagues.) Two of these examples (those of 1930s magazines and 1970s disco records) may appear trivial, but that triviality grounds the point I wish to make. Cultural activity which is highly productive and effervescent may, nevertheless, leave behind no canonical, notable works. In the production of "minor" cultural artefacts, nevertheless, we see producers initiating movement across space and through time. This movement shapes and reshapes the cultural domain, pulling people and professions into new relationships with each other, building audiences or publics out of clusters of people, tastes, and habits. Citizenship, arguably, takes much of its character from one's place within these processes and is expressed in the commitments that place presumes.

These processes are described more formally in the work of Henry Lefebvre. In his book *The Production of Space*, Lefebvre claims that

> *[S]ocial space contains a great diversity of objects, both natural and social, including the networks and pathways which facilitate the exchange of material things and information. Such "objects" are thus not only things but also relations. As objects, they possess discernible peculiarities, contour and form. Social labour transforms them, rearranging their positions within spatio-temporal configurations....*[9]

This social labour works to give culture its shape, but the nature of that labour or its effects are not easily grasped by existing methods for measuring culture or judging its vitality. Recent work on the production of Canadian television, by such scholars as Kotsopoulos[10] and Tinic,[11] has usefully examined cultural creativity in terms of the "social space" in which it unfolds, tracing the links between geographical location, structures of collaboration, and a national imaginary. It is, perhaps, from detailed case studies such as these that new tools for analyzing culture and tracing the pathways of its movement will emerge.

Toronto, 1937

In Toronto, in 1937, a man named Morris Rubin began publishing a series of risqué fiction, scandal, and humor magazines aimed at the Canadian market. These periodicals bore such titles as *Broadway Brevities*, *Garter Girls*, and the *Canadian Tattler*. They fell loosely within the category of the "spicy" magazine: each title combined saucy short stories, pin-up photography, and collections of jokes and ribald poetry.[12] Magazines of this sort have a long history, but their popularity and visibility had exploded in the United States in the late 1920s. In launching his Canadian titles, Rubin was motivated by the recognition of a two-fold opportunity. On the one hand, few entrepreneurs in Canada were exploiting the potential market for this sort of publication, in part for fear of censorship. At the same time, the growth of the market for "spicy" publications in the United States had produced an abundance of materials which might be repackaged for Canadian readers. In a move which has been much repeated in the history of the Canadian cultural industries, Rubin exploited gaps between Canada and the United States in the availability of certain classes of cultural material.

In Lofgren's terms, Rubin was engaged in the "nationalization of trivialities," devising means by which an ephemeral kind of cultural commodity might be introduced and adapted to a Canadian market. In his first years of operation, Rubin purloined most of the content of his magazines from U.S. sources, notably from titles whose importation into Canada had been banned through a series of rulings by the Commissioner of Customs. At the same time, Rubin functioned quite literally as a cultural broker, dealing with editors and publishers from the more disreputable rungs of the New York publishing industry. His Toronto-based magazines were full of advertisements for sex manuals, hypnosis guides, and other forms of exploitational literature described as coming "from leading New York publishers." Indeed, the magazines which Rubin published in Canada often seemed little more than vehicles for advertising imported goods which Rubin sold through his various mail-order businesses. Like many Canadian sound recording companies, private broadcasters, and book publishers Rubin used the importation of US-based cultural goods to partially finance the production of indigenous materials for the Canadian markets.

Rubin's pursuit of profit and livelihood led him through the publication of various sorts of magazines and books. Most of the magazines launched in his first years of operation survived only for a few issues. We might ask, though, what else was produced as these activities unfolded. Like most forms of cultural entrepreneurship, Rubin's career traced and solidified patterns of exchange between places and people. His various activities unfolded at the intersection of the newsstand distribution, job printing, graphic design, and mail-order industries. Links between such industries, which he regularly retraced, served to solidify pathways along which cultural forms which had originated elsewhere might circulate through the spaces of Canadian culture. Rubin's status as broker was most pronounced in the early years of his various enterprises, as he assembled Canadian magazines from materials (illustrations, jokes, concepts) transported into Canada by himself or his collaborators. These materials were transformed through processes of adaptation and disguise. Pages of ribald stories stolen from U.S. magazines were reprinted under headings like "Gossip of Canada" or "More Dominion News."[13]

With time, Rubin's mediating function was expressed in the attempt to build more explicitly Canadian versions of cultural forms from the United States. Most notably, he launched tabloid newspapers (among them, *The National Tattler* and the *Tattler Review*) which combined topical exposés of Toronto life with images and fictional features reprinted from "spicy" U.S. magazines from several years earlier. In the late 1930s, Morris Rubin changed his last name to Ruby and, in 1940, launched Duchess Printing and Publishing, which went on to become one of Canada's most successful popular publishers of the 1940s. War-time measures introduced by the Federal Minister of Finance in December of 1940, intended to preserve sterling currency within Canada, resulted in a ban on the importation into Canada of various categories of U.S. periodicals. Ruby's company took advantage of this ban, offering a full line of magazines, comic books, and paperback fiction produced for the Canadian market under the "Superior" imprint. These publications were only slightly less lurid than his magazines of the 1930s, but their content was now acquired legally. As World War II unfolded, the magazines began to boast, proudly, that they were "edited, illustrated, and produced in Canada by Canadian workmen, on Canadian paper."

The clusters of collaboration within which Rubin operated brought together creative personnel of widely varying career trajectories and stages. Rubin's first magazines were launched with the help of Stephen G. Clow, a Canadian with literary ambitions who had found disgrace in New York City and returned briefly to Canada, near the end of his life, to wring additional value from previously published materials in his possession. Harold Bennett, who illustrated many of Rubin's early magazines, went on to a well-respected career as a comic book and paperback cover artist in the post-war years. Milton Cronenberg, a mainstream journalist and father of filmmaker David Cronenberg, wrote true crime stories for Rubin's magazines during the 1940s. Montreal's leading post-war anglophone chronicler of night-life, the journalist Al Palmer, began his career covering the city in columns for Toronto-based tabloids such as *The Week-Ender* and Rubin's short-lived *National Tattler*. In the production of Rubin's magazines, distinct creative worlds came into contact and found new sorts of proximity. Some of the dynamism of these creative worlds stems from the fact that, within them, individual careers live out very different phases of their histories. Creative clusters on the margins of cultural legitimacy, such as that in which Rubin began, condense the dynamism of the cultural field by bringing together those seeking entry to the cultural field with others facing their final exclusion from it.

The role of public policy and regulation in shaping Rubin's activities as a cultural mediator is not obvious. In 1930, the Bennett government had removed tariffs on the importation of U.S. magazines, leading to what many regarded as a "flood" into Canada of publications from the United States.[14] This flood intensified public anxiety over the importation of immoral and obscene popular literature; it resulted in pressures on all levels of government in Canada to keep out "spicy" magazines from the United States. Canadian Customs officials and provincial authorities struggled, throughout the 1930s, to meet public demands for censorship, while working out policies for the control of foreign periodicals in the absence of tariffs. Gaps in public policy and hesitations over its interpretation produced the opportunities which Rubin and others moved to exploit. As "spicy" magazines were stopped at the border, Rubin and others moved to publish Canadian equivalents. It is in the contradictions and hesitations of public policy, rather than any enabling function, that Rubin and others found the conditions of their continued activity.

Historians undertaking research on the CBC or National Film Board may find resources in the comprehensive archives which these institutions have built, or in the volumes of research commissioned by Royal or parliamentary commissions. Those studying Canadian popular entertainments (like magazines, recordings, or magazines) must begin by imagining all the ways in which those producing these artefacts will run into trouble with the law. It is in their infractions of legal authority, rather than their recognition by policy bodies or cultural critics, that the more illicit or illegitimate forms of popular culture enter the public record. Indeed, the information needed to reconstruct the history of Rubin's various corporate entities is rare outside those details collected by police and prosecutors, and contained in the various indictments charging him with publishing pornographic materials. It is to be found, as well, in the archives of moralizing interveners within civil society, such as the Knights of Columbus or National Council of Women, both of whom documented Rubin's activities in an ongoing effort to stop them.

Much of the time, Rubin persevered in his clashes with legal authority; the government's difficulties in convicting him played some role in an easing of the Ontario District Attorney's clampdown on "immoral" publications in the late 1930s.[15] Rubin's testing of the boundaries of acceptability was rarely, if ever, presented as an act of civic engagement, and he has found no place within a history of heroic interventions within Canadian cultural policy. Nevertheless, he was one of many cultural mediators who have contributed to the recalibration of norms of acceptability within Canadian popular culture. We might say, of Rubin's publications, what the sociologist George Simmel once said of sociable conversation: that the "content is merely the indispensable carrier of the stimulation."[16] By this I mean that the substance of Rubin's publications was less significant than the entrepreneurial and creative energies through which places (New York and Toronto) were joined, artefacts were assembled, and readers addressed in a variety of ways. I mean, as well, that any one of Rubin's publications was less important than the forms of unacknowledged testing in which he engaged through the ongoing release of such publications over many years. In these releases, the limits of moral and judicial acceptability were challenged time after time. So, too, were the multitude of ways in which the Canadian cultural commodity might be put together, from materials both foreign and domestically produced.

Ira Wagman has noted that the idea of a "Canadian content," long central to discussions of Canadian media policy, appears first in policies for regulating the trade in automobiles.[17] Canadian cultural mediators almost invariably do their work with an explicit understanding that the Canadian cultural artefact is assembled from a particular ratio of domestic to imported materials. That ratio will be shaped by a jumble of overlapping policy conditions: the state of tariffs, currency differentials, customs regulations, postal rates and restrictions, and so on. The ongoing testing of all these conditions—in the production of magazines, recordings, books, and other artefacts—is a form of experimentation unfolding over time. In that experimentation, cultural producers try out almost all conceivable means of interweaving and balancing Canadian and non-Canadian materials. Their labour, typically driven by the quest for profit or legitimacy, might be seen as a form of research which typically produces highly complex kinds of knowledge. Through it, multiple ways of imagining the Canadian cultural artefact and its distinctiveness take shape and are made to circulate.

We should see the activity of Rubin and others as engaged, to varying degrees of explicitness, in working through the dilemmas of national identity and distinctiveness. This *working through* was a collective endeavour; entrepreneurs, police forces, judges, and governments all played their part within it. This process was not deliberative, of course, in the sense of offering a circumscribed space of collective dialogue. Nevertheless, the cultural practices which produced Canadian magazines in the 1930s were also, in a sense, forms of civic argument, gestures which tested the conditions under which artefacts and their creators might participate in a national culture.

Montreal, 1979

In 1979, the US music trade magazine *Billboard* described Montreal as "the second most important disco market on the continent, outside New York."[18] *Billboard* was referring to the enormous popularity within Montreal of disco music, a form which had emerged in the early 1970s and whose international commercial success confirmed the important role of discotheques in popularizing musical recordings. The success of disco music in Montreal was manifest at three levels. It was evident in the observable vitality of Montreal's night clubs in the latter half of the 1970s. This vitality built its foundations upon Montreal's longstanding image as a city of nighttime entertainment but did so, in the mid 1970s, with new levels of investment and entrepreneurial inventiveness. At the same time, the sales of disco records were notably higher in Montreal than in most other North American cities, a fact noted regularly in the music trade press. In the late 1970s, as well, Montreal became an important centre for the production of disco recordings themselves, as local producers released music which found audiences and buyers throughout Europe and the Americas.

Music is one of the most mobile of cultural forms, if only because its transportation requires little investment and may employ multiple forms of storage or transmission. For this and other reasons, music regularly evokes the fear that it is a challenge to the integrity of national cultures. Early-twentieth-century panics over the immoral influence of tango music on European culture, for example, emphasized tango's alien character even as they acknowledged its seductive ubiquitousness.[19] In the 1970s, disco music was seen as a challenge to prevailing definitions of "Quebecness" in popular music, and as an invasive interruption of Quebec popular musical history. Disco was often posited as a corrupting musical movement which had ended the golden age of Quebec rock, luring audiences and musicians alike away from the ongoing development of an indigenous popular musical tradition. For journalists of the time, such as Nathalie Petrowski, disco represented a "démagogie dansante," a totalitarian distraction from the more obviously political project of indigenous popular musical forms.[20] Writer Renée-Berthe Drapeau, while acknowledging that many Québécois musicians involved themselves in the production of disco music, nevertheless saw this involvement retrospectively as new evidence of a cultural dependence on musical styles whose origins were elsewhere.[21] The sense that disco represented an invasion of foreign musical styles was common in music journalism of the late 1970s, and has been repeated in subsequent histories of Quebec popular music.

The diagnosis of discotheque music as "alien" rested on claims about its style and musical form. (This diagnosis generally overlooked the longstanding popularity of Latin-derived dance music forms within the popular culture of Quebec.) To the international music press, however, disco was a significant and seemingly organic component of Montreal's distinctiveness. As noted, the popularity of disco in Montreal was seen to perpetuate that city's long history as a city of nightlife and musical entertainment, to prolong the sense of youthful modernity which had presided over Expo '67, and to reinforce the city's stereotypical image as the "Paris of Canada," a capital of leisure and semi-illicit entertainment. All these comparisons presumed a natural affinity between disco music and Montreal, and worked against the perception of disco as an alien, invasive force.

For my purposes, the extent of disco music's formal or stylistic rootedness within local histories is less important than the cultural textures and pathways within which it was embedded. Like the Francophone yé-yé music of the 1960s (Francophone versions of Anglo-American pop), disco music gave density to a national musical culture, less through the themes which found thematic expression within it than in the new sorts of institutional and economic relationships which took shape around it. Disco came to be deeply rooted in the micro-economies of small record companies, retail shops, nightclubs, and distributors in Montreal. More so than many forms, it was the focus of a sociologically complex "scene," whose participants built effective links between a wide range of institutions and activities.

It is for these reasons that Montreal's disco scene of the 1970s returns us to the ideas of Orvar Lofgren and Greg Urban. The growth of a discotheque scene in Montreal required cultural brokers who could guide the movement of disco recordings into that scene at a time when the music was largely ignored by mainstream media. Those who fulfilled this function moved between a variety of roles and occupations, making money and building careers on the basis of their strategic position within a scene and an industry characterized by multiple trajectories of movement. In 1976, for example, Montreal nightclub disc jockeys formed one of the continent's first disco "pools." Disco pools were associations which acquired promotional copies of new records from international record companies and distributed these to disc jockeys throughout the city. The organization of such pools in Montreal served to integrate disc jockeys within the circuits of information upon which record company promotional strategies depended. Pool members reported to pool managers each week on the success of particular records with dancers in their clubs. This information was transmitted to record companies, who used this information to determine which records were taking off and which were clearly destined to flop.

The culture of disco was marked by velocities of change and rates of commodity obsolescence which were generally much quicker than those common within other genres of music. Disco records might die a commercial death in the first or second week of release, and the buzz which surrounded promising new titles led all disc jockeys to demand copies almost immediately. Disco music required, of those engaged in its production and promotion, high levels of flexibility and an acute attentiveness to the signs of change and innovation. The institutional infrastructure of disco music was thus one marked by a fluidity of professional roles, in which individuals stood at the intersection of multiple flows of information and influence. The owners or managers of disc jockey pools, themselves nightclub disc jockeys, often opened specialty record shops to cater to other DJs, or distribution companies that imported disco recordings for an expanding market of non-professionals. Disco music specialty stores, in turn, became meeting places for disc jockeys and important sites for the exchange of information and the socialization of newcomers within the disco scene.

The cultural brokers at the centre of disco music in Montreal interacted with others operating on the international level, ensuring the flow of information outwards (to record companies and international publications) and the movement of new recordings back into the local scene. One effect of this brokerage was the integration of Montreal's disco scene within the rate of change which characterized disco as a worldwide phenomena. While this integration was never total, the efficient structuring of disco's institutions ensured the availability, within Montreal, of the latest recordings and clues as to the music's direction. As effective mediators between the dance floor and the record company, disc jockeys increasingly took over the production of records, as well. Typically, they began by producing specialty remixes of recordings destined for the Top 40 or Album Charts, using their familiarity with audience tastes to "adapt" records for a dancing public. With time, however, disc jockeys came to produce dance records on their own, setting up small record companies and circuits of distribution for that purpose. By the end of the 1970s, several locally-based record companies were producing and marketing disco records of Montreal origin throughout the world.

One face of Montreal's disco culture was thus turned towards the cosmopolitan, international institutions of disco music. At the same time, the cultural brokers at the heart of Montreal's scene worked to implant disco within the city's broader worlds of media and celebrity. Even before the success of the film *Saturday Night Fever*, in 1977, Montreal television stations broadcast weekly disco-oriented programs (such as "Disco tourne"), and hosted annual disco awards shows. The interaction between discotheques and the mainstream worlds of commercial broadcasting was strengthened by longstanding features of the Quebec media industries, most notably the popularity of the musical variety program on Quebec television. Even as its invisible, subcultural foundations grew ever denser and insular, disco's public appeal spread outwards, into the domains of local social elites and the public theatricality of urban nightlife.

While the records produced and heard in Montreal's disco scene of the 1970s may seem disposable, even trivial, the fabric of connections and careers which took shape around them was substantive. Between the Montreal nightclubs to which a suburban clerk might go on Friday nights and the underground New York discotheques in which records from Montreal might be heard, a finely-layered set of economic and institutional relationships had taken shape. Like local theatre or skateboarding scenes, Montreal's disco scene of the mid-to-late 1970s was the object of no formal cultural policy but was shaped by multiple forms of public regulation and incentive. In the case of disco, these included the following: alcohol licensing laws, municipal zoning regulations, public performance regulations controlling the use of recorded music as entertainment,

Canadian content regulations to encourage the airplay of Canadian music (or French-language music), tariff regulations governing the importing of foreign recordings, agreements between nightclubs and local musicians' unions, and so on. At higher levels of generality, Montreal's disco culture rested on a demographic base which was itself the product of immigration laws and trends, linguistic regulation, and education policies which made Montreal home to four large universities. To these we might add those economic policies and trends which made the decline of downtown nightlife much less precipitous for Montreal in the 1970s than for other North American cities.

All of these factors helped to "produce" the disco scene as one of effervescent, creative movement. Within that movement, the values of cosmopolitanism and localism were regularly renegotiated in creative, novel ways. Montreal's disco culture was, at some levels, a system for adapting international commodities for local usage, and producing local cultural artefacts for a dispersed international musical culture. Within it, the high-velocity development of disco music across time unfolded simultaneously with the expansion of disco culture across cultural and geographical space. Portions of that culture (the nightclubs of suburban shopping malls, for example) came to act as inertial forces, resistant to the forward movement of the music; other components (such as those clubs opening on the Eastern fringes of downtown) articulated themselves to the most rapidly moving parts of that culture, serving as accelerative forces for the scene as a whole.

Multiple trajectories of movement were interwoven in all these processes. The development of individual professional careers was often bound to the fate of disco recordings as commodities and dependent on shifting ratios between their exclusivity and mass popularity. Widely-accepted subcultural lore said that Italians and other "allophone" language groups had found a place within disco culture that was largely denied them in other parts of Montreal's music industries. Neither Anglo-Saxon or French in any obvious ways, disco music moved with relative ease into the spaces of Montreal nightlife, producing mixes of population different from those to be found in the audiences for other musical genres. Each act of building a discothèque or producing records required, nevertheless, calculations about the place of disco music within Montreal's linguistic and demographic divisions. These acts tested tradition and prejudice and transformed the cultural cartography of Montreal. Like Morris Rubin's ongoing launch of magazine titles, they should be seen as acts of civic engagement, expressions of a cultural citizenship which negotiated new relationships between music, place, and people.

Cultural News

The movement of national cultures is most forcefully registered in the coverage of cultural life by the media. Media serve to organize cultural life in terms of their own daily, weekly, or monthly rhythms of publication or programming. Cultural industries and institutions, likewise, have their own rhythms of change and turnover: the theatrical "season," the gallery exhibition's "run," the release date of books or recordings, the single event of the musical concert. The relationship between these two sets of rhythms has been one of ongoing adaptation and negotiation. The Friday release of new films is tied, in part, to the expansion of entertainment coverage in weekend editions of newspapers, in a manner that serves the interests both of newspaper editors and of cinema owners. Musical genres of limited commercial appeal, such as free jazz or klezmer music, now receive more newspaper coverage as part of festivals than as recording styles, if only because newspapers now see music festivals as punctual events of local significance and cover them more exhaustively.

In 2004, a number of faculty and students at McGill University began a three-year research project tracking the manner in which the Canadian media cover certain issues.[22] The contribution of Anna Feigenbaum and myself to this research is in its very early stages, but it involves an analysis of the evolution of cultural coverage within Canadian media over the short and medium terms. We are less interested in the deep substance of this coverage than in its shifting presence within newspapers, and in the extent of its reach outwards from a cultural centre or mainstream. We began this research with the hypothesis that the amount of cultural coverage within Canadian newspapers has increased over the last few decades. Indeed, very preliminary examination of the *Globe and Mail* newspaper suggests that the percentage of newspaper space devoted to cultural coverage grew more rapidly over the last fifty years than did the size of the newspaper itself. The average issue of the *Globe and Mail* in 2004 contained roughly twice as many pages as did a typical issue on the same weekday in 1954. The number of pages devoted to culture and entertainment, defined rather strictly, has tripled on average over the same period. With some variation, this increase in cultural coverage seems to be true of other Canadian daily newspapers as well. Dailies which did not have book review sections in the past (like the *Hamilton Spectator* or *Montreal Gazette*) have added these in recent years. Cultural events such as urban festivals are often covered now by several reporters, in coverage that may extend over several pages.

The significance of these changes is by no means obvious. A study of cultural journalism in the United States noted that this growth in coverage lags behind the social and economic expansion of the arts sector itself.[23] Observers of the changing function of newspapers will observe that, as cultural coverage has grown, so, too, has coverage of business, sports, and a variety of other phenomena (personal finance, for example, scarcely existed as a focus for journalism a half-century ago, but has mushroomed in the last two decades). As newspapers seek to serve a broad, varied readership (rather than partisan minorities, as was the case 150 years ago) they have expanded the range of ways in which they speak to their readers. The newspaper of the present is a compendium of sections directed at specific audience segments, and there is little expectation that any single reader will read the entirety of any issue.

Nevertheless, it is possible to point with some certainty to at least one trend in cultural journalism which has reshaped its purpose over the last two decades. There has been an observable growth in coverage of the entertainment and cultural industries *as industries*. The National Arts Journalism Program study, to which we have already referred, claimed the coverage of commercial entertainment had come to displace coverage of the non-profit cultural sector; other commentaries have echoed this claim. We are not convinced that the same displacement is discernible in Canadian daily newspapers, where coverage of the visual arts and quasi-public cultural festivals seems to have grown considerably in recent years. Still, the commercial character of cultural activity is now openly acknowledged and discussed in newspapers to an extent unknown in the past. The cultural sections of newspapers now include reviews and profiles, as they did in the past, but to these are added a variety of other kinds of coverage: inside information on developments within the cultural industries, or charts ranking the sales of books, recordings, or movie tickets. As Charles Acland has noted, many of these sorts of information were once the preserve of industry insiders; now they are an expected part of each newspaper's coverage of the cultural realm.[24] Cultural works (like plays or books) are discussed in language which elevates their status and offers judgment, but evaluation sits comfortably alongside coverage of corporate manoeuverings or financial scandals within the cultural field. The relationship of the contemporary newspaper reader to culture is one which combines a cynical awareness of backstage machinations with an equally strong acknowledgment of culture's power and appeal.

The movement of cultural coverage to include its industrial foundations is merely one of its extensions outwards, however. Over the last half-century, the definition of the cultural field has changed in a broader sense. First of all, we may note a decline in the coverage of two sorts of activities which were prominent in *The Globe and Mail* of the 1950s: "society" events (debutante and charity balls, for example), on the one hand, and traditional hobbies (like fishing or chess) on the other. Both of these linger in some form, but they have been pulled within new forms of coverage and diluted in the process. Coverage of local social elites has been gradually (if not totally) absorbed within a cultural journalism dominated by the worlds of celebrity and commodified entertainment. Coverage of the worlds of amateur hobbydom (of stamp collecting and Boy Scouts or Girl Guides) has been partially displaced by a lifestyle journalism centred on the individualistic arts of self-fulfillment (like cooking and fitness.)

These changes would appear to confirm widely circulated claims about the decline of civil society's older practices and institutions. More interesting, in our view, are the ways in which newspapers have found themselves compelled to venture further afield in their efforts to report on the cultural realm. Daily newspaper arts coverage in the 1950s rarely moved outside the realm of events (such as plays or symphony concerts) which involved well-established institutions. The "serious" or elite character of these institutions is less significant than the fact that their cultural character was beyond dispute. In the decades since, newspaper arts coverage has more and more come to treat culture as an elusive world which can be captured only through an activity of exploration. As the restless mobility of the cultural field has seemed to increase, so, too, has the degree to which the newspaper's gaze upon that world appears to shift and remain unstable.

Arts coverage in the 1950s appears centrifugal, describing achievements at the centre of the social structure and sending this description outwards to readers, in an act of duty or willful democratization. Increasingly, however, arts coverage functions as a centripetal force, as if it is the responsibility of the newspaper to venture to the margins or obscure corners of our culture and pull back, into the orbit of our attention, practices, and works about which it imagines we should be informed. Thus, tattooing, CD-burning, swing music revivals, fringe theatre festivals, raves, flash mobs, activist documentary films, and innumerable other phenomena have come to find their place within the cultural sections of newspapers. Ongoing uncertainty as to what constitutes the cultural realm has gone hand in hand with the expansion of cultural sections in newspapers and with an intensification of their effort to address multiple audiences. Writing of urban journalism, Peter Fritzsche has suggested that, in the city, "the incompleteness of civic rule is accompanied by the instability of narrative authority."[25] It is certainly the case that, with the slow withering of traditional cultural authority, the newspaper's coverage of the cultural field manifests an unstable sense of its own authority and capacity to "narrate" the city. The cultural realm appears more and more as one of endless, restless movement, over which newspapers no longer seem to exercise a stable and authoritative omniscience.

This expansion of cultural coverage in the daily newspaper has coincided with a decline in the readership of conventional newspapers, particularly among younger people.[26] In Canada, as in other countries, an important part of this shift has been the growth of the so-called "alternative weekly" newspaper since the early 1980s. Alternative weeklies are typically more youthful in their orientation and readership than the traditional daily newspaper. Their most distinctive characteristic, however, is their overwhelming emphasis on cultural life. The central sections of most alternative weeklies are devoted to cultural phenomena and events, typically organized into such sections as "Film," "Dance," "Theatre," "Cinema," and so on. There are practical reasons for this emphasis. Cultural journalism usually anticipates or reviews events which have been publicized in advance, and such coverage is organized more easily and inexpensively than coverage of crimes or political events (which requires full-time reporters assigned to often unpredictable beats). The weeklies' appeal to advertisers has much to do with their publication of entertainment listings, which encourage readers to keep issues lying around for regular consultation.

In their emphasis on culture and entertainment, alternative weeklies have reversed a longstanding hierarchical relationship between day and night. This may seem a trivial feature of the alternative weekly, but, in fact, it stands as highly emblematic of the movement of cultural coverage into social and moral "regions" hitherto left unexplored. One of the lessons of recent cultural policy initiatives is that nighttime is no longer to be seen simply as the time of consumption—as that span of time in which people spend money earned from the labours of the day. Numerous studies and policy interventions over the past decade have repeated the observation that cities contain vital and weighty nighttime economies and nocturnal workforces. Taxis, bars, restaurants, sex, work, and office cleaning are not merely epiphenomena which support, renew, or dissipate the more fundamental energies of daytime work. They are "industries" of autonomous economic weight, and the labour which they involve is increasingly acknowledged as such. At the same time, the practices of the night sustain lifestyle experimentation, cultural innovation, and the building of diverse communities. While this has almost always been true, it is only recently that these practices have been recognized as fundamental to a city's appeal and potential prosperity.[27] Alternative weekly newspapers rarely acknowledge the pervasiveness of their emphasis on urban nightworlds, but that emphasis reveals itself to even the most cursory analysis.

In Greg Urban's terms, we might say that these newspapers have reordered our sense of the cultural field through several sorts of movement. On the one hand, they have followed culture into its ever more elusive locations: into undergrounds and subcultural worlds, into the hidden corners of cultural production. More strikingly, as suggested, they have expanded the scope and substance of the night as a cultural terrain, often in tandem with cities' own acknowledgement of their night-time economies. And, finally, the urban weekly newspaper participates in a broader enterprise through which the limits of culture have expanded to circumscribe multiple spheres of social and political engagement. The alternative weekly is founded on the assumption that the youthful, downtown dweller is connected to urban life principally as a consumer of culture. In their overwhelming emphasis on the cultural realm, alternative weekly newspapers have strengthened culture's role as privileged site for the elaboration of citizenship and civic belonging.

In 1994, in an insightful analysis of Quebec cultural policy, Allor and Gagnon noted that the cultural field had become primary in the process by which governments constructed their legitimacy and fostered a sense of citizenship.[28] The alternative weekly newspaper effects a similar absorption of the civic and the social within the cultural. It is within culture, coverage suggests, that the urban dweller encounters sensation, adventure, and exoticism—dimensions of experience which, in other newspapers or in other times, were more likely to be found in coverage of crime, war, or politics. It is principally within the cultural field, as well, that we negotiate our relationship to the illicit, the scandalous, and other forces which challenge the social order. Civic responsibility and citizenship thus come to be tested and defined through encounters with the cultural field.

It would be wrong, however, to see the alternative newspaper as necessarily more accelerative in its impulses than the daily newspaper. In the uncertainty of its contemporary cultural authority, perhaps, the daily newspaper has come to treat the cultural field as one whose margins are perpetually tested and regularly pushed outwards. There are multiple reasons for this outward movement, but they presume that the reader's regular encounter with the unknown is necessary, in a sense, to an improved and enlightened citizenship. The alternative weekly moves the boundaries of legitimacy even further from a cultural centre, but, at the same time, it works to give order and stability to the peripheries of cultural life, hastening their economic rationalization and public accessibility. In doing so, the alternative weekly produces a stabilized version of civic engagement, one carefully calibrated to the lists of upcoming concerts or other events covered in its regular features. Neither of these media, then, is wholly inertial or accelerative in easily diagnosed ways.

Conclusion

The examples discussed here all return us, however obliquely, to Ong's question of "belonging within a national population and territory." Morris Ruby magazines were meaningful principally as a sequence of experimental gestures; through them, multiple ways of producing Canadian versions of the American "spicy" magazine were tested in both a commercial and a legal sense. The absence of explicit civic purpose in Ruby's activities should not prevent us from seeing, in the movement of his magazines through a national culture and its institutions, a sustained negotiation over the meaning of "Canadianness." The example of Montreal's disco scene raises, quite strikingly, the conflict between texts as bearers of national identity and cultural processes as ways of re-ordering social and cultural relations. The extent to which disco music should be considered an alien form within Quebec musical history may be set aside. More interesting, for my purposes, are the ways in which tensions over its cosmopolitan and local meanings served to generate the myriad of institutions and career trajectories which gave the local scene its complexity. Some of the latter were devoted to the adaptation of international recordings to the local market, others formed around the production of local equivalents. In the tension between them, the question of Montreal's place within international circuits of influence and commodity circulation was posed.

The newspaper's role in sustaining citizenship is more widely acknowledged, of course, and it is around the newspaper that influential notions of civic engagement and collective deliberation have developed.[29] Changes in the content and organization of the newspaper, over the last half-century, reveal important shifts, both in the importance accorded the cultural realm and in its delimitation. As I have suggested, it is in the alternative weekly newspaper, perhaps, that one finds the most stable image of cultural citizenship, one frozen in the categories of coverage and maps of lifestyle options which characterize these papers. Daily newspapers—marked as they are by ongoing anxiety over the fate of a cultural centre whose contours they can hardly see—have become more genuinely experimental in the constant revamping and awkward openings-up of their cultural coverage. As symptoms of uncertainty over the borders of culture and its place in readers' lives, daily newspapers unwittingly manifest that accelerative nervousness which is one part of the condition of culture.

Notes

1 Orvar Lofgren, "Scenes from a Troubled Marriage: Swedish Ethnology and Material Culture Studies," *Journal of Material Culture* 2, no. 1 (1997): 95–113, 106.

2 Ibid.

3 Aihwa Ong, "Cultural Citizenship as Subject-Making: Immigrants Negotiate Racial and Cultural Boundaries in the United States," *Current Anthropology* 37, no. 5 (1996): 737–762, 738.

4 Leon Surette, "Creating The Canadian Canon," in Robert Lecker, ed., *Canadian Canons: Essays in Literary Value* (Toronto: University of Toronto Press, 1991), 24.

5 Bruce R. Elder, *Image and Identity: Reflections on Canadian Film and Culture* (Waterloo: Wilfred Laurier University Press, 1989), 34. See also Michael Dorland, *So Close to the States: The Emergence of Canadian Feature Film Policy* (Toronto: University of Toronto Press, 1998).

6 Toby Miller, *The Well-Tempered Self: Citizenship, Culture, and the Postmodern Subject* (Baltimore and London: The Johns Hopkins University Press, 1993).

7 Greg Urban, *Metaculture: How Culture Moves through the World* (Minneapolis: University of Minnesota Press, 2001), 32.

8 Ibid., 6.

9 Henry Lefebvre, *The Production of Space*, Donald Nicholson-Smith, trans. (Oxford: Blackwell, 1991), 77.

10 Patsy Kotsopoulos, "L.M. Montgomery on Television: The Romance and the Industry of Adaptation," in Sheila Petty et al., eds., *Canadian Cultural Poesis* (Waterloo: Wilfrid Laurier University Press, 2004).

11 Serra Tinic, "Global Vistas and Local Reflections," *Television & New Media* 5, no. 3 (August 2004): 1–30.

12 For a much fuller account of Rubin and his publishing ventures, see Will Straw, "Traffic in Scandal: The Case of Broadway Brevities," *University of Toronto Quarterly* 73, no. 4 (Fall 2004): 947–71.

13 Both these features appeared in Broadway Brevities, no. 8, November 1937.

14 "Competition Continues," *Canadian Printer and Publisher* 48, no. 1 (January 1939): 33.

15 Straw, "Traffic in Scandal."

16 George Simmel, "Sociability," in George Simmel, *On Individuality and Social Forms* (Chicago and London: The University of Chicago Press, 1971), 127–40, 136 (edited and with an introduction by Donald N. Levine).

17 Ira Wagman, "Statistics and Narratives of Canadian Cultural Weakness" (paper presented at the annual conference of the Canadian Communications Association, Halifax, Nova Scotia, June 1, 2003).

18 "Montreal May be Continent's 2nd Best City," *Billboard*, March 17, 1979, 84. See also "Gold Mine Market For Labels," *Billboard*, January 29, 1977, Q-10.

19 Marta E. Savigliano, *Tango and the Political Economy of Passion* (Boulder: Westview Press, 1995).

20 Nathalie Petrowski, "La démagogie dansante du disco," *Le Devoir*, March 3, 1979, 19.

21 Renée-Berthe Drapeau, "Le yé-yé dans la marge du nationalisme québécois," in Robert Giroux, ed., *la Chanson prend ses airs* (Montreal: Tryptique, 1993), 131–57.

22 This project is funded by the Max Bell Foundation, and has its administrative home within the McGill Institute for the Study of Canada. I am indebted to my research assistant on the project, Ph.D. student Anna Feigenbaum, for her contributions to this work, which had just begun at the time of writing.

23 National Arts Journalism Program, *Reporting the Arts* (New York: National Arts Journalism Program, 1999).

24 Charles Acland, *Screen Traffic: Movies, Multiplexes, and Global Culture* (Durham, NC: Duke University Press, 2003), 4–5.

25 Peter Fritzsche, *Reading Berlin 1900* (Cambridge, MA: Harvard University Press, 1996), 3.

26 For a multinational overview, Le Monde, *Les comptes du groupe* (Paris: La Société Éditrice du Monde, 2004) (annual report).

[27] See, among many other sources, Andrew Lovatt, Justin O'Connor, John Montgomery, and Paul Owens, eds., *The 24-Hour City: Selected Papers from the First National Conference on the Night-time Economy* (Manchester: Manchester Metropolitan University, 1994).

[28] Martin Allor and Michelle Gagnon, *L'État de culture–Généalogie discursive des politiques culturelles québécoises* (Montreal: Concordia University, Groupe de recherche sur la citoyenneté culturelle, 1994).

[29] For example, Jurgen Habermas, *The Structural Transformation of the Public Sphere* (Cambridge, MA: MIT Press, 1991).

Part
IV

Governance, Indicators, and Engagement in the Cultural Sector

13.

Creative Pique:
On Governance and Engagement in the Cultural Sector

MONICA GATTINGER

The study of governance has been defined as "the search for the means of ensuring effective coordination when resources, power and information are highly distributed, and when no single actor could possibly go it alone."[1] Through the lens of governance, the state is not viewed as the central and utmost player in policy-making and program delivery, but rather as one of a number of players, including private and civic actors, who engage with one another in non-hierarchical relationships.[2] If we adopt a governance approach to conceptualizing relations in the cultural milieu, it becomes imperative that we examine more closely the nature and functioning of these relationships and the means of working towards effective co-ordination when power, resources, and information are highly distributed across the public, private, and civic sectors.

This chapter aims to contribute in a modest way to this broader research agenda. Drawing on literature in the areas of public administration and public policy, it seeks to investigate three interrelated subjects: the pivotal role of engagement to governance, the individual competencies and capabilities that emerge as crucial for those involved in alternative governance arrangements, and the organizational/structural considerations in managing non-hierarchical governance processes. The title of the chapter, "creative pique," highlights the proposition that governance, understood as less state-centric, hierarchical and centralized forms of co-ordination and policy-making, rests fundamentally on being able to engage—and sustain the engagement of—public, private and civic players. Further, horizontal forms of policy-making and program delivery require particular professional capacities and the ability to generate trust, leverage dissent, and promote collaboration within policy networks. In this light, engagement and the capacity to build and sustain engagement emerge as crucial elements underpinning discussions of and experiments with alternative governance arrangements. The title "creative pique," refers to "pique" as in "to pique interest" (i.e., to catalyse and maintain engagement) but also "pique" as in "irritation" (i.e., the capacity to leverage and manage dissent within policy networks and horizontal initiatives).

Understanding governance processes and the role of engagement in these processes contributes to the development and strengthening of cultural citizenship, the concern of the present volume. Cultural citizenship involves rethinking and renewing policy rationales underpinning cultural policy and objectives pursued through cultural policy. The process of developing rationales and objectives is not unimportant. Engaging non-government actors—be they private or civic—in the policy development process will materially contribute to the procedural and substantive legitimacy of any resulting cultural citizenship policy frameworks. Moreover, participation in policy development for cultural citizenship will strengthen cultural citizenship itself. As Wolfe and Creutzberg point out in their examination of economic development policy, the process of engaging non-government actors in defining economic development policy is a capacity building exercise in itself that develops and strengthens the networks that will ultimately contribute to policy success at the implementation stage.[3] Further, to the extent that cultural citizenship emphasizes the role of participation (see Murray in this volume), understanding how to stimulate individuals', groups', and organizations' participation in policy and program initiatives contributes to the broader cultural citizenship agenda.

This chapter proceeds in five sections. The first explores engagement in governance processes. In particular, it makes the claim that the capacity to engage—and to sustain the engagement of—public, private, and civic actors, is pivotal to effective co-ordination. The second section explores horizontally-managed policy and program initiatives and brings to light that these processes possess a dynamic that differentiates them from vertical, centralized arrangements. In a horizontal milieu, personal competencies, such as the capacity to build and maintain trust among horizontal partners, emerge as critical elements in generating and sustaining engagement.

The third section examines the range of organizational structures underpinning alternative governance arrangements. Horizontal initiatives call for differing levels of formalization in their organizational arrangements. The requisite degree of formalization depends primarily on the function of the project in question, e.g., information sharing versus resource pooling versus authority sharing. The fourth section explores ways in which the concepts and themes investigated in the first three sections play out in practice. I examine two federal policy and program initiatives: the Cultural Industries Sectoral Advisory Group on International Trade (hereafter the Cultural Industries SAGIT) and the Stabilization Component of the Canadian Arts and Heritage Sustainability Program. Concluding remarks follow in the final section.

Engagement: A Core Element of Governance

Governance scholars examining public policy issues often conceptualize the pattern of relations between actors as *policy networks*: "more or less stable patterns of social relations between interdependent actors, which take shape around policy problems and/or policy programmes."[4] This conceptualization of public-private-civic relations presupposes that actors who possess resources, expertise, and/or authority in a particular policy milieu are in fact *engaged* in the community of actors that coalesce around policy and program issues. Is this a reasonable assumption from which to depart?

A glance at academic research in the area of globalization and public consultation suggests that it is not. Indeed, this research often takes as its point of departure the claim that governments are not doing *enough* to consult private and civic actors, or, when they are, they are *doing it inadequately*. In keeping with the insights of governance studies—that information, resources, and authority are vastly distributed—this research emphasizes that non-state actors possess crucial expertise, critical resources, and bases of authority that could be brought meaningfully to bear on policy challenges facing governments.

Studies of globalization and domestic policy-making note the growing importance of close, continuous, and collaborative consultation between the state and domestic interests.[5] Researchers maintain that consultation constitutes a central means for governments to respond to the challenges and adjust to the changes globalization brings about. In his introductory remarks to the findings and recommendations of a major national policy study examining the most significant trends affecting policy making in Canada, William Coleman contends that a crucial factor influencing how well countries respond to globalizing processes is the nature of government relations with civil society actors. He warns governments that foregoing consultative relationships with domestic interests may imperil state capacity to facilitate national adjustment to the new global environment: "If governments eschew the cultivation of regularized, meaningful, consultation with representative and relatively democratic interest groups and social movements, they may also be reducing the likelihood of the country adjusting well to the changed global environment in which it is presently operating."[6]

Globalization scholars call not only for meaningful consultation with civil society actors, but for ongoing exchange with private sector interests as well. Weiss argues that linkages between governments and economic sectors are fundamental to states' capacity to respond to domestic industrial change resulting from transformations in the international economy. She posits, "Of central importance is the state's ability to use its autonomy to consult and to elicit consensus and cooperation from the private sector ... through its linkages with key economic groupings, the state can extract and exchange vital information with producers, stimulate private-sector participation in key policy areas, and mobilize a greater level of industry collaboration in advancing national strategy."[7]

The federal government's establishment of the Cultural Industries SAGIT, examined below, offers a rich illustration of non-government actors' capacity to contribute to Canada's adjustment to its changing global circumstances—in this case, to confronting the challenges trade liberalization poses for domestic cultural industries policy-making capacity. The expertise of cultural industries representatives was brought to the SAGIT table and assisted the government in confronting the culture-trade quandary. Moreover, not only did the government consult and exchange information with key representatives of the cultural industries sector through the SAGIT, this forum also catalyzed information exchange and collaboration *across* a wide variety of industry subsectors.

Coleman's insistence on the importance of regularized and meaningful consultation with non-state actors and Weiss's vision of a "catalytic" state, consulting the private sector to seek consensus, co-operation, and collaboration make good theoretical sense. In a globalized policy-making milieu rife with uncertainty and rapid economic and social change,[8] policy-makers face considerable informational requirements and the need for assistance in issue conceptualization and the development of policy alternatives: "Any actors holding technical knowledge—whether these be expert committees of trade associations, large corporations, universities, private research institutes, or even trade unions—have become potentially crucial participants in the policy process of any advanced capitalist economy."[9] The Cultural Industries SAGIT offers a persuasive case in point in the cultural milieu.

These calls for more meaningful and regularized exchanges with domestic interests find good company in the work of public consultation scholars. Consultation has acquired an increasingly important role in the policy process in recent years, spurred on by a range of factors. These include growing public expectations for involvement in the policy process, the increasing complexity of policy problems, trends toward more horizontal governance models, a more empowered civil society, as well as developments in communications technologies that have created new means for non-state actors to become involved in policy-making.[10]

While a range of rationales for consultation can be identified, the primary objective of the practice is to improve both policy design and implementation.[11] Design and implementation improvements come about through such activities and outcomes as information-sharing and exchanges of views between the government and consultation participants, greater public support for policy initiatives, and improvements at the implementation stage because non-state actors have been involved in policy development.[12] More general benefits resulting from consultation include improved mutual understanding between government and its various publics, opportunities for active citizenship, community capacity building, and greater openness, transparency and democratic legitimacy of the policy process.[13]

In a recent review of citizen involvement in policy processes, Phillips (with Orsini) identifies the problems associated with conventional methods of public consultation— "government controls the agenda and who is invited; information flows in one direction; and the process is episodic and *ad hoc*."[14] Like Coleman and Weiss, these researchers encourage more regularized, deliberative, and collaborative forms of consultation.

In sum, these various appeals argue that sustained, deliberative interactions between the state and non-state actors constitute a crucial activity in contemporary policy-making. Governments are not capitalizing to the extent that they could on the opportunity to exchange information with those external to government, they tend to exert too much control over the process, and they tend not to maintain ongoing dialogue and exchange with policy stakeholders. In short, there is an element of relationship-building that seems to be missing from current efforts to consult and involve non-state actors in policy-making. Returning to our initial definition of governance—effective co-ordination in a world where power, knowledge, and resources are distributed between the public, private, and civic sectors—there is a need to engage actors across these three sectors and to work across organizational and sectoral boundaries. The main challenge (and role) for the state in these associative governance arrangements is to create conditions for learning.[15] The state can play a role of strategic facilitator, working to engage key actors and catalyzing the development and strengthening of policy networks.

Despite the growing role for governments as catalysts for engagement, there is scant theoretical or empirical research on engagement processes. Elsewhere, the author has elaborated a simple model of engagement in consultation initiatives.[16] This chapter will draw on (and lightly modify) a number of elements of this model to establish a vocabulary and conceptual framework with which to discuss engagement in broader governance arrangements. As Figure 1 shows, actors may adopt different *levels* of engagement in governance processes: they can be actively engaged, passively engaged, or disengaged.

Starting at the left-hand side of the spectrum, "active engagement" refers to the highest level of involvement in a policy network or governance process. Here, people actively partake in a policy network, representing their interests, and lending their expertise, resources, and power to horizontal programs and initiatives.

At the opposite end of the spectrum is "disengagement," where actors who could potentially engage in a policy network are not engaged, or those who have previously been engaged exit the network. With respect to the former, some actors may not be engaged in governance arrangements to begin with if they are not "on the radar screen"

Figure 1: Level of Engagement in Governance Processes

Active Engagement —— Passive Engagement —— Disengagement

of existing policy frameworks. The question, then, becomes how to creatively "pique" their engagement. With respect to the latter, as Bradford notes in a study of associative governance in the province of Ontario, in liberal polities, private sector interests can always exercise their option to "exit" partnership regimes.[17] Bradford confines his remarks to the private sector, but participants representing other sectors (e.g., the voluntary sector or labour groups) also possess the option of exiting deliberative forums. Simply put, participation in collaborative governance processes is voluntary, and actors can withdraw their participation if they choose. The challenge then, becomes one of maintaining engagement in the face of these circumstances.

Returning to Figure 1, "exit" can refer not only to a physical withdrawal from a network or initiative (i.e., walking away from the table) but can also mean an implicit withdrawal, for example, by partaking in governance processes or projects, but choosing not to actively participate in the deliberations (e.g., choosing to withhold information, resources, or authority that could usefully be employed in the network). The middle of the spectrum captures this sedentary form of involvement, "passive engagement." Actors might choose an implicit rather than an explicit exit because they stand to benefit from engagement in a policy network or project even though they do not actively participate. These benefits could include information acquisition, networking with other actors in the network, or the use of continued participation as a delay tactic. With respect to the first, information acquisition, actors may be involved in a policy network or project for the strategic purpose of acquiring information. Participants in a deliberative consultation, for example, may be somewhat mute in their advisory function to the government, but attend consultation meetings in order to acquire government information that they can then individually put to strategic use to press for their preferred policy alternatives in encounters with government in other policy arenas.[18]

The second rationale, intra-sectoral networking, derives from an indirect benefit actors may gain by participating in governance processes or projects. In a survey of industry participants in a 1978 federal consultation seeking industry input into Canada's industrial policy, respondents cited "making new useful contacts" as one of the most productive outcomes of the process.[19]

The third potential rationale for passive engagement, continuing participation as a delay tactic, underpinned private sector actions in the Ontario government's Workplace Health and Safety Agency (WHSA), a collaborative agency involving private sector and labour representation. Bradford notes the "strategic disengagement" of business from the WHSA in the lead-up to the 1995 provincial election. Even though business representatives opposed the WHSA process, they continued to passively participate in the agency because both opposition parties were committed to reforms that would ultimately abolish the Agency.

To sum up, actors may adopt a number of engagement stances in governance processes, ranging from active engagement to passive engagement to disengagement. To the extent that active engagement underpins effective governance arrangements, it becomes crucial to understand the drivers of active engagement, as well as those of passive engagement and disengagement. The chapter discusses these drivers below and explores them empirically in the forthcoming examination of the Cultural Industries SAGIT.

In addition to speaking of actors' level of engagement in policy networks or governance arrangements, a second attribute of engagement may be distinguished: the *nature* of engagement. The nature of engagement pertains to the quality, character, or dynamic of relations between public, private, and civic actors. Unlike "level," which examines individuals' or organizations' engagement, the nature of engagement speaks to the quality of interactions among individuals, organizations, and sectors. It seeks to capture the group dynamics animating policy network relations, governance arrangements, or collaborative program initiatives. Do participants co-operate with one another, collaborating to identify common policy preferences and negotiating or co-ordinating their differences? Or do they choose to compete, each advancing their own individual or sub-sectoral interests? Are relations characterized by continual conflict? Or do private, public, and civic actors collaborate and seek consensus?[20]

Although collaborative engagement stimulates healthy governance arrangements, we know little of the drivers of collaboration. Which factors promote collaborative dynamics? Which promote conflict? What underpins collaboration amid conflict, i.e., when there is conflict between policy network or project participants, what factors encourage collaboration and the continued active engagement of the parties—as opposed to passive engagement or disengagement? And returning to the preceding discussion of the level of engagement, what promotes active engagement? How does one go about creatively "piquing" the interest and engagement of—and maintaining the interest and engagement of—individuals and organizations?

The paragraphs that follow propose that three key considerations underpin the level and nature of engagement. The first pertains to the structure of governance arrangements. Decisions and behaviour—usually those of government—regarding such factors as membership in a collaborative project, resource allocation, and, most importantly, the degree of influence non-government actors perceive they possess in a collaborative arrangement, significantly influence participant engagement. Where these arrangements are favourable to participant interests, they are more likely to actively engage in the process, and the group is more likely to display collaborative dynamics. Where these arrangements are inimical to participant interests, the opposite result is likely to occur: non-government players will tend to disengage from the process and the group dynamics will tend toward conflict.

The second consideration shaping engagement is the existence of common threats or opportunities for policy actors. Globalization, for example, may prompt or require domestic actors to reframe their traditional conceptions of policy problems and thereby alter the patterns of conflict and collaboration within a policy network. Common threats or opportunities can serve to align—or uncouple—the interests of government and non-government actors. Indeed, in the cultural industries sector, as discussed below, the process of trade liberalization represented a common threat for many actors in the cultural industries, promoting both collaboration and the shared pursuit of means to address the challenges of trade liberalization for the cultural industries. In the domain of cultural citizenship, the prospect of reframing cultural policy via the concept of cultural citizenship is likely to influence engagement in the cultural sector—engaging those who see opportunity in this policy trajectory, prompting disengagement for those who do not, and generating collaboration or conflict depending on the pattern of interests of affected individuals and organizations.

Third, the personal competencies of individuals involved in alternative governance arrangements—particularly government participants—can play a strong role in piquing participant interest and sustaining participant engagement, and can promote collaboration, particularly collaboration amid conflict. On this last point, Horibe has examined the importance for managers in the knowledge-based innovation economy of "leveraging dissent" within their organizations.[21] She identifies the capacity to surface —rather than suppress—dissent, as a core competency that will not only sustain the engagement of those holding contrary views, but that can also catalyse innovation. Dissenting viewpoints may carry the seeds of innovation, enabling the development of creative alternatives to established ways of thinking or doing. In this light, the choice of who "takes the lead" on a collaborative governance project matters, indeed is critical, to engagement in the process. The following section explores this third element in the context of managing horizontal projects—initiatives involving public, private, and/or civic actors.

Engagement in a Horizontal Milieu: Managing Across Boundaries

The policy network literature's emphasis on non-hierarchical relationships finds company with public administration scholarship examining new public management and horizontal management. One of the thrusts of new public management is to decentralize public decision-making processes and program and service delivery, particularly moving from hierarchical management practices to participatory management and teamwork and to greater involvement of non-state actors in policy-making and service delivery.[22] While some scholars maintain that the federal government's policy-making processes remain— indeed are becoming increasingly—centralized,[23] the principles of decentralization and collaboration espoused by the new public management are often manifest at the operational level, i.e., at the level of program and service delivery.[24]

The literature on horizontal management is among the most advanced areas of research examining these forms of decentralization and collaboration. Horizontal management "is about working collaboratively across organizational boundaries,"[25] including departmental boundaries, intergovernmental boundaries, and boundaries between the public, private, and civic sectors at the national, subnational, and international levels.[26]

Studies of horizontal management echo the departing postulate of governance studies: no one can go it alone. Under these operational circumstances, collaboration emerges as an indispensable practice of co-ordination. Indeed, one of the major findings to emerge is the fundamental importance of developing attitudes and competencies in the public service to manage initiatives that are horizontal and collaborative—as opposed to vertical and hierarchical.[27] These attitudes and competencies—which arguably must also be developed among private and civic actors—pertain to consultation, influence and persuasion, trust, and timing.[28]

Consultation of other horizontal actors acquires an importance unrivalled in a vertical management environment. Working collaboratively in a non-hierarchical setting where authority, resources, and knowledge are highly distributed requires constant and ongoing consultation. Moreover, in the absence of traditional vertical authority, the capacity to influence and persuade through deliberation and sustained dialogue is of utmost importance in collaboratively defining group objectives, roles, and responsibilities. This applies not only to consultation on relatively uncontroversial matters, but also consultation and deliberation around matters of conflict and dissent. Ensuring that horizontal partners have the opportunity to "have their say," and that dissenting viewpoints are surfaced—and leveraged if possible—contributes materially to the success of a horizontal project. In this light, trust and the ability to develop and maintain trust among the actors in a network is also of critical import when working horizontally. Finally, timing is a crucial consideration: participants must continually monitor their operational and political milieu for windows of opportunity to press forward on horizontal programs. The fourth section of this chapter will return to these competencies in its examination of the Cultural Industries SAGIT and the Canadian Arts and Heritage Sustainability Program.

Organizing in a Horizontal Milieu: Structuring Governance Arrangements

A second strong current running through horizontal management literature is that of selecting and developing the most appropriate "supportive structures" for horizontal initiatives.[29] These structures are the organizational forms that support a horizontal project, and include informal contacts, verbal agreements, memoranda of understanding, and the creation of formal organizations and institutions. The selection of appropriate governance arrangements is informed primarily by the function or objective of the horizontal activity. As shown in Table 1, there are at least four different functions of a horizontal project: advisory, contributory, coordination and collaboration. Harkening back to the definition of governance studies at the outset of this chapter, there is a clear relationship between the functions in the table and the insights of governance regarding the distribution of knowledge, resources and power between public, private, and civic players.

Table 1: Functional and Structural Considerations for Horizontal Projects

FUNCTION OF THE HORIZONTAL PROJECT	ORGANIZATIONAL ARRANGEMENTS
Advisory – sharing expertise and information	Can be formal or informal
Contributory – resource pooling between parties	Tend towards formality
Co-ordination – sharing work or administration	Tend towards formality
Collaboration – sharing authority	Tend towards formality

Source: Adapted from Andrea D. Rounce and Norman Beaudry, Using Horizontal Tools to Work Across Boundaries: Lessons Learned and Signposts for Success. CCMD *Roundtable on Horizontal Mechanisms (Ottawa: Canadian Centre for Management Development, 2002), Table 1, 13.*

The advisory function relates to knowledge and the sharing of information and expertise between horizontal actors. Under these circumstances, there is great flexibility in the variety of organizational arrangements that may be utilized. When the focus of parties' interactions is on information—as opposed to sharing authority or resources—informal arrangements such as verbal agreements based on trust can represent strong supportive structures.

As the table shows, however, the more projects move toward the pooling of resources and authority, the more organizational arrangements require formality. Formal agreements and the creation of new organizations or institutions are often necessary when horizontal projects involve resource pooling (the contributory function), sharing work or administration (the co-ordination function), and sharing authority and decision-making power (collaboration). In sum, more formal supportive structures (formal agreements, shared institutions, etc.) tend to be required as the degree of horizontal activity intensifies.[30] As discussed in the following section, the organizational arrangements for the Cultural Industries SAGIT and the Stabilization Component of the Canadian Arts and Heritage Sustainability Program illustrate this tendency.

Putting These Concepts to Work: An Examination of Two Initiatives in the Cultural Sector

The preceding discussion proposes a framework for exploring engagement and organizational considerations in associative governance processes. This section applies the framework to two cultural policy and program initiatives: the Cultural Industries SAGIT and the Stabilization Component of the Canadian Arts and Heritage Sustainability Program (CAHSP). The Cultural Industries SAGIT represents an instance of consultation, where the federal government sought ongoing and meaningful input into trade policy in the cultural industries sector. This deliberative consultation illustrates the facilitative role the state can play in governance processes: the SAGIT brought into contact representatives of the various cultural industries subsectors and catalyzed an unprecedented process of intrasectoral dialogue. The CAHSP provides a fruitful example of the catalytic role of the state when resources, power, and information are highly dispersed. CAHSP's Stabilization Component offers an intriguing illustration of decentralized governance arrangements, where the state contributes resources to community actors, implicitly recognizing that local players are in a better position in terms of their knowledge and expertise to make funding decisions at the community level.

The Cultural Industries Sectoral Advisory Group on International Trade[31]

In 1986, the federal government created the Sectoral Advisory Groups on International Trade to provide trade policy advice from the private sector to the Minister for International Trade. These advisory bodies continue to exist largely in the same format as they did at their inception.[32] Senior business executives, with some representation from industry associations, labour, non-government organizations, and academe are appointed on a non-remunerated basis for two-year renewable terms. They meet several times per year with bureaucratic and sometimes ministerial attendance from International

Trade Canada (ITC) for "an open exchange of ideas and information between the SAGIT members and government."[33]

The SAGITS have been recognized as an important development in Canada's international public policy process.[34] The government's establishment of the groups marked an important turning point in business-government relations in the field of trade policy. Prior to their creation, the private sector had mostly informal involvement in trade negotiations and in the development of trade policy. Industry involvement, such as it was, was unstructured, minimal, episodic, and ad hoc. The SAGITS heralded a fundamental change in Canada's trade policy-making process, by institutionalizing business-government consultation in trade policy matters, by developing a deliberative consultation process between the government and industry sector representatives, and by creating an ongoing forum for business-government consultation. The groups are especially unique in their capacity to serve as forums for domestic non-government actors to reconcile divergent intrasectoral interests.

The Cultural Industries SAGIT has long been an active group, with the vast majority of members highly engaged and committed to participation in the consultation. While a full review of the SAGIT's activity since its inception is beyond the scope of this chapter, this discussion focuses on the group's deliberations in the latter half of the 1990s. During this period, which culminated with the 1999 World Trade Organization (WTO) Ministerial Conference in Seattle, the SAGIT collaboratively developed and recommended a new approach to the federal government for the cultural industries in trade. As the paragraphs below describe, state behaviour—particularly with respect to membership selection and participant perceptions of the policy influence of the group—played a vital role in the level and nature of participant engagement in the process. Common threats posed by globalization also exerted an important influence on SAGIT members' involvement, generating active and collaborative engagement in the shared pursuit of means to address Canada's culture-trade quandary. Further, the SAGIT process illustrates some of the competencies that emerge as essential in a horizontal governance milieu.

From the mid-1980s to the present, the relationship between Canada's cultural industries policies and its obligations in trade agreements has been an ongoing source of consternation for the Canadian government, those in the cultural community, and the Canadian public. Since the creation of the General Agreement on Tariffs and Trade (GATT) in 1947, the objectives of the international trading system have been two-fold: to reduce, and over time, eliminate trade barriers to permit open and secure market access, and to ensure that market access is non-discriminatory.[35] At the source of the friction between cultural industries policy and trade policy is the fundamental incompatibility between a number of cultural industries policy measures and two of the cardinal principles of the international trade regime: national treatment and most favoured nation (MFN) treatment. The first, national treatment, maintains that government measures affecting market access must not have the effect of discriminating between domestic and foreign producers of similar goods and services. The second principle, most-favoured nation, holds that a country's market access commitments must not discriminate between foreign countries. That is, nations are not to discriminate between foreign countries by according more favourable market access to one country over another. According to the MFN principle, the most favourable trade arrangements a nation maintains with one country, it must also extend to all others.

Cultural industries policies can run afoul of these two principles where governments enact measures that discriminate between domestic and foreign firms or that discriminate between different foreign nations. Because many of Canada's cultural industries policies *by design* discriminate in favour of Canadian producers, they collide head-on with the principle of national treatment. For example, Canadian content regulations, if they were subject to the disciplines of the international trading regime, would not comply with the requirements of national treatment because they favour the cultural output of Canadian nationals over foreign firms (thereby discriminating against the latter).[36]

These underlying tensions between cultural industries policy and the international trading regime—the "culture-trade quandary"—can place seemingly irreconcilable pressures on the Canadian government.[37] On the one hand, the government is under pressure at the domestic level to retain its cultural policy-making capacity, and on the other, it faces demands at the international level, notably from the United States, to eliminate cultural trade barriers.

Until the mid-1990s, the primary means of shielding the cultural industries from trade liberalizing obligations was to negotiate a cultural industries exemption (CIE) in trade agreements. Canada sought and obtained such an exemption in both the Canada-United States Free Trade Agreement (CUSFTA) and the North American Free Trade Agreement (NAFTA). The CIE provides a broad-based exemption for the cultural industries from the agreements' provisions. It is subject to a right of retaliation for the United States, however. Where Canada enacts or maintains cultural industries policy measures that would be inconsistent with the CUSFTA or NAFTA in the absence of the exemption, the US can retaliate with measures of equivalent commercial effect. Many in the cultural policy community believe that this retaliatory clause significantly weakens the protection the exemption affords. Moreover, as the *Sports Illustrated* dispute demonstrated, the United States can bypass regional trade agreements and resolve cultural trade disputes through the WTO, where Canada possesses no such exemption.

For critics of the exemption, Canada-US cultural trade disputes, particularly the dispute over the Canadian edition of *Sports Illustrated*, demonstrated the weakness of a cultural exemption approach and evidenced the need to rethink Canada's stance on the cultural industries in trade.[38] The Cultural Industries SAGIT, long a supporter of—indeed the principal force behind—Canada's cultural industries exemption, decided that the group needed to rethink Canada's approach to the cultural industries in trade. Following a 1997 Ministerial request for advice from the SAGIT as to how Canada should address the cultural industries in a global trading environment, the SAGIT worked for over two years on a report to the government on the matter. In early 1999, the government publicly released a summary version of the SAGIT's report, the main recommendations of which fed into government preparations for the 1999 WTO Ministerial Conference in Seattle.

The SAGIT's deliberations gave rise to a new policy approach to address the culture-trade quandary: the development of a "new international instrument on cultural diversity" (NIICD). The SAGIT recommended the Canadian government initiate this instrument, which "would lay out the ground rules for cultural policies and trade, and allow Canada and other countries to maintain policies that promote their cultural industries. ... The new instrument would identify the measures that would be covered and those that would not, and indicate clearly where trade disciplines would or would not apply."[39] In the months following the February 1999 release of the SAGIT's report, the government adopted this new negotiating position for the cultural industries.[40]

The government began to seek the long-term objective of negotiating an international instrument that would ultimately affirm the right of signatory countries "to maintain policies that promote their culture, while respecting the rules governing the international trading system and ensuring markets for cultural exports."[41] The government has been pursuing the negotiation of such an instrument through its work with the International Network on Cultural Policy (INCP). The INCP, created in 1998 by then Minister of Canadian Heritage Sheila Copps, is a global network of national culture ministers that serves as a forum for discussion of issues of common interest. The INCP has been working towards the development of an international instrument.[42] In addition, the Canadian government stated that it would not make any new commitments in the cultural sector in trade negotiations until such time as an instrument could be negotiated.[43]

The Cultural Industries SAGIT illustrates the importance of, mechanisms for, and competencies essential to governance and engagement. It also highlights the catalytic role of the state in contemporary governance arrangements. First, the SAGIT case vividly demonstrates the capacity for non-government actors to make meaningful contributions to the processes of national adjustment to globalization. The CUSFTA negotiations were the first set of international trade negotiations to raise the possibility that Canada's cultural policies could become subject to international trade obligations.[44] Since this time, cultural industries policy-making has become increasingly intertwined with global concerns. The SAGIT has played a strong role in developing policy alternatives and recommending policy approaches to the federal government. The group, by first advocating the cultural industries exemption and then proposing the negotiation of the NIICD, has provided meaningful policy alternatives to the government as it seeks to adjust to ever more palpable global pressures. The SAGIT process demonstrates the potential to leverage non-state actors' expertise in conceptualizing issues and developing policy approaches in a global milieu. The establishment of this consultation mechanism and the outcomes of the group's deliberations strengthened the co-ordination of information, resources, and authority between the public, private, and civic sectors.

Second, the SAGIT sheds empirical light on the drivers of engagement in governance processes. Throughout the latter 1990s, the vast majority of SAGIT members displayed very active levels of engagement, and the group exhibited collaborative dynamics in intrasectoral and sector-governmental relations. Virtually all SAGIT members held a favourable impression of the role of the government in the consultations and believed that the group possessed a high degree of policy influence. SAGIT members actively engaged in the consultation process based on these positive perceptions. Further, the body was composed of representatives of some of Canada's largest cultural industries firms and of noted legal and scholarly cultural industries experts. The expertise and relative homogeneity of the membership (in terms of the members represented and their interests) contributed to members' high levels of engagement and facilitated collaborative relations between group members and the government. In addition, a number of high profile cultural trade disputes, notably the dispute over the Canadian edition of *Sports Illustrated*, stimulated collaboration among SAGIT members. The *Sports Illustrated* case was seminal for many members of the cultural community. In their eyes, it demonstrated the limitations of the cultural industries exemption and the need to develop a new approach. Thus, while intrasectoral conflict may have animated some of the group's deliberations, the shared interest in developing new strategies for culture and trade promoted collaboration amid conflict.

Third, the SAGIT illustrates the importance of competencies pertaining to consultation, influence, persuasion, trust, and timing in a horizontal milieu. The process surrounding the SAGIT's report to the government is instructive in this regard. SAGIT members indicated that then Minister for International Trade Pierre Pettigrew and officials at the Department of Foreign Affairs and International Trade were not initially supportive of the group's recommendations. The group undertook to consult, influence, and persuade the Minister and key officials on the merits of their recommended approach, and believed they were successful in this regard.

The public release of the SAGIT's report also evidences the importance of the competencies noted above to horizontal governance arrangements. SAGIT members felt that the public should get a crystallized view of the more elaborate and confidential report submitted to the government, but because members serve at the pleasure of the Minister for International Trade and provide confidential advice in this capacity, the group could not release its report without prior approval from the Minister. The SAGIT sought this authorization and the government agreed—provided it could revise the report to ensure its suitability for public release. From the perspective of the government, this meant attending to the overall Canada-United States relationship and reviewing the report with an eye to Canada's broader diplomatic relations with the US. This process was undertaken in a collaborative and consultative fashion, with SAGIT members understanding the need for the government to revise the report before its public release and with a good deal of trust underpinning the revision process.

Timing was also crucial to the public release of the report. In 1999, the Standing Committee on Foreign Affairs and International Trade was undertaking trade consultations in the lead-up to the Seattle WTO Ministerial at the end of that year. SAGIT members were eager to have the report in the public domain so as to bring additional pressure to bear on the government to adopt the NIICD stance the report recommended. The government, too, was interested in releasing the report as a "trial balloon" and took advantage of the ongoing Standing Committee hearings to seek feedback and comment on the report. It referred the document to the Standing Committee (some of the SAGIT members appeared before the Committee in these hearings).

A fourth way in which the SAGIT illuminates governance and engagement pertains to the role of the state: this case reveals the catalytic role states can play in governance processes. Through the SAGIT, the government brought together representatives from across the subsectors of the cultural industries (audiovisual, books, sound recording, etc.), many of whom would not otherwise have come into contact. The consultation offered an opportunity for members to gain an appreciation of the extent to which the various cultural industries subsectors shared similar concerns and interests, and provided a forum within which to develop common approaches to shared problems.

The Cultural Industries SAGIT offers a fifth illustration of governance and engagement: it is an instance where the government sought to meaningfully consult on an ongoing basis with non-government actors. In contrast to the critique scholars frequently level at governments for inadequately consulting private and civic interests, the present case is an example of a consultation process meeting many of the conditions identified as necessary for contemporary consultation initiatives. The cultural SAGIT, as a regularized, collaborative process, allowed for the ongoing exchange of information, participation in policy-making, and collaboration with industry. Moreover, it illustrates the value of dissent—and leveraging dissent—in policy networks. The majority viewpoint coming forth from the SAGIT was one of dissent. The group was dissatisfied with the government's approach for the cultural industries in trade. Rather than dismiss or suppress this opposition, the government capitalized on the opportunity for the SAGIT to develop a new trade approach for the sector, in the process generating active levels of engagement and stimulating innovative thinking and the development of new alternatives.

Finally, the SAGIT process illustrates the tendency for organizational arrangements to lean toward informality when the function of horizontal activity is advisory (the sharing of expertise and information). The relationship between the government and SAGIT members was largely informal, and for the most part not structured with institutional, legal, or other formal arrangements.[45]

Overall, the Cultural Industries SAGIT illustrates the drivers and mechanisms of governance and engagement in policy development. It reveals the important role of non-government actors in contemporary policy-making, the strong influence of perceptions on engagement, the potential for catalytic state intervention in contemporary policy-making, and the adequacy of informal arrangements to support consultation initiatives. The Canadian Arts and Heritage Sustainability Program, examined below, complements the policy focus of the SAGIT case by shedding light on governance and engagement at the level of program and service delivery.

The Canadian Arts and Heritage Sustainability Program

The Canadian Arts and Heritage Sustainability Program (CAHSP) seeks to "strengthen organizational effectiveness and build capacity of arts and heritage organizations."[46] Established as part of the May 2001 Tomorrow Starts Today federal funding package, the CAHSP consists of four components: Stabilization Projects, Capacity Building, Endowment Incentives, and Networking Initiatives.[47] Through Stabilization Projects, the government funds non-profit organizations at the community level that in turn use these funds to assist local arts and heritage organizations. The funding emphasis is on furnishing technical expertise. CAHSP's Capacity Building component provides direct funding to arts and heritage organizations that do not have access to support through Stabilization Projects. Capacity Building funds are used to improve organizational effectiveness. Through Endowment Incentives, the government provides matching funding to arts organizations that raise private donations to build endowment funds. The Networking Initiatives component funds national networking projects that seek to strengthen policy, planning and management capacity, and initiatives that involve partnerships with business organizations.

CAHSP's four program elements seek to strengthen arts and heritage organizations by building capacity at the organizational level. Rather than focusing on providing operational or project funding to individual arts and heritage organizations, CAHSP aims to help organizations build a sustainable future. It does so primarily by providing incentives for organizations to acquire technical expertise and to put in place solid management practices. The program reflects the concept of arts stabilization, which encompasses "a host of creative responses that funders have developed to address the long-term health and sustainability of arts organizations."[48] Based on pioneering work in the 1960s by the Ford Foundation in the United States, arts stabilization aims to address the challenges of reductions in public and private funding, the lack of growth or decline in audience numbers and earned income, and weakening public acceptance of the arts.[49] Arts stabilization takes a long-term view, moving from discrete project and operational grants to support that aims to build long-term organizational capacity, stability, and sustainability. Stabilization programs can involve technical assistance, financial assistance, or both.[50]

The arts stabilization concept has taken root in the Canadian context relatively recently. In 1995, the first stabilization programs were established in British Columbia and Alberta. The Vancouver Arts Stabilization Team (VAST) and the Alberta Performing Arts Stabilization Fund (APASF) were created through collaboration between key public, private, and civic players in local/provincial arts communities (including the federal government, the Vancouver Foundation, the Kahanoff Foundation, and the Alberta Foundation for the Arts). In the last number of years, stabilization programs have been established in Saskatchewan, Manitoba, Ontario, Quebec, and Atlantic Canada.

Stabilization funds involve contributions from public and private sources, undertake targeted stabilization programs, and are generally set to operate for a fixed period of time. The APASF, for example, was established with five million dollars of public funding and six million dollars of private donations.[51] The Fund has primarily supported Alberta's largest arts groups, including the Alberta Ballet, the Edmonton Symphony, Decidedly Jazz Danceworks, and Theatre Calgary. Its stabilization program requires organizations to prepare a business plan, to grow a capital reserve through surpluses, and to operate at a scale commensurate with the size of the community they serve. Beneficiary organizations receive up to one million dollars of funding over the life of the Fund (planned for ten years) if they meet their annual management requirements. This concept of "rewarding" high performing organizations is central to the Fund's operations.[52] Since its inception, the APASF was intended as a temporary fund, and its funding activities have now sunset. The APASF currently provides mentoring to new stabilization initiatives in the planning and implementation stages.

The concept of arts stabilization is very intriguing from a governance perspective. First, it involves working across boundaries between the public, private, and civic sectors. Stabilization projects are collaborative ventures involving various levels of government, corporate and individual donors, foundations, and community arts and heritage leaders. This diverse group of policy network actors collaboratively works toward the common goal of building capacity in local arts and heritage organizations.

Second, arts stabilization aspires toward effective co-ordination where information, resources, and power are highly distributed. CAHSP's Stabilization Projects component makes grants to projects "administered by an independent nonprofit group that represents the interests of the larger community through the make-up of its Board and through the diversity of its revenue base."[53] Federal funding supports access to technical expertise, trimming down deficits, and building up working capital reserves—but federal funding decisions are made at the macro level of full stabilization projects, not at the micro level of individual arts and heritage organizations.

The choice of which individual arts and heritage organizations are supported is made at the local level. With a board of directors representing various community interests, a stabilization fund is in a far better position than the federal government to make funding decisions that reflect individual community needs and circumstances. This division of resource provision and decision-making authority between the state and local actors is in keeping with governance principles: given that greater information and expertise regarding local circumstances reside at the community level, so to, should the authority to make funding decisions to local groups. These governance arrangements are a far cry from state-led and state-centric policy and program initiatives that carry the implicit assumption that the only information, resources, and power that count are those in the public sector.

The third characteristic of arts stabilization that resonates with governance pertains to engagement. Arts stabilization seeks to engage—creatively pique—public, private and civic actors through a variety of means and mechanisms. The shared funding approach enables arts stabilization projects to be established in circumstances where no single actor could possibly go it alone. Public, private, and individual donors may become actively engaged where they see solid potential for the creation of a stabilization fund through multi-stakeholder collaboration. It is here that strategic government intervention—in this case through CAHSP—can have a facilitative or catalytic effect, piquing engagement and implication of private, civic, and other public actors. As Lussier notes of federal involvement in arts stabilization in the latter half of the 1990s, "the interdependence [between public, private, and civic partners] which perhaps always existed, has been operationalized, forcing implication, or disengagement, as the case may be, in the recognition and adoption of new roles and responsibilities."[54]

This creative trigger for engagement strengthens program delivery in the short run, but also leverages knowledge, resources, and authority to improve policy design and program effectiveness in the long run. The engagement process itself contributes to improved policy and decision-making—in short, to better governance. On this point, Lussier states of the Department of Canadian Heritage's work with non-government actors in the arts stabilization domain: "… long term solutions require a collective commitment by all the partners. Arts stabilization has allowed for a more open communication about issues which in the long run affect the Canadian public at large."[55]

Fourth, arts stabilization aims to put in place highly decentralized arrangements. Local communities take the lead in developing and administering stabilization programs: "While there are common operating principles [for arts stabilization programs], each initiative has its own dynamics and develops a momentum of its own based on the local or regional community served and on the collaborators."[56] This move to decentralization—a shift from state-centric policy-making and program planning to collaborative governance arrangements—brings with it a concomitant evolution in public-private-civic relations: "… the former relationships among stakeholders must break down to create a level playing field where co-operation and collective action take priority."[57]

Finally, arts stabilization emphasizes the importance of identifying the organizational and structural arrangements that best support the horizontal nature of the activity. One of the defining characteristics of arts stabilization programs is their tendency to operate for a fixed term, usually less than a decade. The explicit objective is to provide the resources and expertise to enable local arts and heritage organizations to build the technical capacity that will better position them to sustain operations in the long term. It is a strategic short term intervention that aims for sustainability and seeks to strengthen arts and heritage organizations' capacity for self-governance.

As would be suggested by Table 1 earlier on in this chapter, arts stabilization's organizational arrangements tend toward formality given the contributory (resource pooling) and collaboration (shared authority) functions inherent in the concept. Federal stabilization funding takes the form of grants that require stabilization funds to provide for control and reporting mechanisms. At the local level, as noted above, stabilization funds require that recipient arts and heritage organizations submit annual reports on their financial, operational, and management situation in order to qualify for funding.

Overall, the Stabilization Component of CAHSP illustrates the potential for public, private, and civic actors to collaborate and seek the most effective means of co-ordination where information, resources, and authority are dispersed. The program demonstrates the potential for strategic state intervention to build and sustain engagement where no single actor could feasibly go it alone, and illuminates the positive influence of engagement at both the policy and program levels. Moreover, it reveals the shift from hierarchical state-centric to horizontal relationship-based management that the move to governance brings about. Individual competencies for collaboration, persuasion, consultation, and shared problem solving are critical to the success of arts stabilization programs.

Closing Words:
Governance, Engagement, and the Cultural Sector

This chapter offers a modest contribution to the study of governance in the cultural milieu, chiefly by proposing a vocabulary and conceptual starting point for examining alternative governance mechanisms. It has argued that engagement of the multiplicity of actors possessing the knowledge, resources, and power that could usefully be brought to bear on problems, issues, or opportunities facing the cultural sector, constitutes a crucial precondition when working towards effective co-ordination across organizational and sectoral boundaries.

The title of the chapter, "creative pique," aims to sound a clarion call for those in the cultural sector—be they individuals seeking to press forward with cultural citizenship or with other horizontal forms of governance. The cultural policy community must achieve a "creative peak" in its approaches to policy and programming. The shift from "government" to "governance" positions engagement—the capacity to build and sustain implication of public, private, and civic players—as fundamental to contemporary state intervention. Governance requires "creative pique"—the ability to pique interest (i.e., catalyze and maintain engagement) and also the ability to address irritation (i.e., the capacity to face, manage—even leverage—dissent within policy networks and horizontal initiatives).

The cases examined in this chapter offer much room for optimism in the cultural sector's capacity to respond—and capitalize on—the governance challenges and opportunities it faces. The Cultural Industries SAGIT illustrates the importance of tapping into the expertise of non-state actors in the development of policy alternatives, demonstrates the potential for government to facilitate the development of intrasectoral networks, and sheds light on the importance of key competencies in a horizontal milieu (i.e., consultation, influence, persuasion, trust, and timing). Future consultative initiatives across the range of policy issues confronting the cultural sector must engage the diversity of interests with power, information, and resources germane to whatever the issue at hand. The capacity building resulting from these efforts will contribute to policy success at the implementation stage. Horizontal arrangements at the program level, such as those prevailing in the Stabilization Component of the Canadian Arts and Heritage Sustainability Program, are a further contributor to sound implementation. Not only do they improve program delivery, they may even be necessary to get a program off the ground to begin with.

In the realm of cultural citizenship, the focus of this volume, the development of policy and programming will require the active engagement of a host of governmental and non-governmental interests at the national, provincial, and local levels. Recognizing that actors may engage to varying degrees in this process and that a range of reasons will underpin this diversity of engagement stances is a necessary starting point for those pressing forward on cultural citizenship. Identifying the appropriate organizational structures to support cultural citizenship initiatives will also be crucial. These will be significantly informed by the function of individual initiatives. And last—but certainly not least—given the central role of engagement, competencies, and consultation to horizontal initiatives' success, relationship-based approaches will be crucial for those charting a future for cultural citizenship.

Notes

[1] Translated from Gilles Paquet, *Gouvernance: une invitation à la subversion* (Centre d'études en gouvernance, Université d'Ottawa, été 2003), 11.

[2] Tanjia Borzel, "What's so Special about Policy Networks? An Exploration of the Concept and its Usefulness in Studying European Governance," *European Integration Online Papers* 1, no. 16 (1997), available at http://www.eiop.or.at/eiop/texte/1997-016a.htm.

[3] David A. Wolfe and Tijs Creutzberg, *Community Participation and Multilevel Governance in Economic Development Policy* (paper prepared for the Ontario Government Panel on the Role of Government, August 2003), 38–44.

[4] Eric-Hans Klijn, "Policy Networks: An Overview," in Walter J.M. Kickert, Eric-Hans Klijn and Joop F.M. Koppenjan, eds., *Managing Complex Networks: Strategies for the Public Sector* (London: Sage, 1997), 14.

[5] The following discussion of consultation draws from the first two chapters of my doctoral dissertation. Monica Gattinger, "Trading Interests: Trade Policy Consultations with the Cultural Industries Sector," (Ph.D. dissertation, Carleton University, Ottawa, 2003).

[6] William D. Coleman, "The Project on Trends: An Introduction," *Canadian Public Policy* 26, Special Supplement on The Trends Project (2000), S6.

[7] Linda Weiss, *The Myth of the Powerless State: Governing the Economy in a Global Era* (London: Policy Press, 1998), 39.

[8] Coleman, "The Project on Trends," S4.

[9] Michael M. Atkinson and William D. Coleman, "Policy Networks, Policy Communities and the Problems of Governance," *Governance* 5, no. 2 (1992), 162.

[10] Susan D. Phillips and Michael Orsini, "Mapping the Links: Citizen Involvement in Policy Processes," (discussion paper no. F|21 prepared for the Canadian Policy Research Networks, Ottawa, April 2002), 4–8; and Peter Sterne and Sandra Zagon, "Public Consultation Guide: Changing the Relationship Between Government and Canadians," *Management Practices*, no. 19 (Ottawa: Canadian Centre for Management Development, May 1997), 1.

[11] Leslie A. Pal, *Beyond Policy Analysis: Public Issue Management in Turbulent Times*, 2nd ed. (Toronto: Nelson, 2001), 259.

[12] Ibid.; Phillips and Orsini, *Mapping the Links*, 8–9.

[13] Pal, *Beyond Policy Analysis*; Phillips and Orsini, *Mapping the Links*.

[14] Phillips and Orsini, *Mapping the Links*, iii.

[15] David A. Wolfe and Tijs Creutzberg, *Community Participation and Multilevel Governance*.

[16] Gattinger, "Trading Interests."

[17] Neil Bradford, "Prospects for Associative Governance: Lessons from Ontario, Canada," *Politics and Society* 26, no. 4 (1998): 539–73.

[18] For an example of this, see my discussion of the Sectoral Advisory Group on International Trade on Agriculture in "Trading Interests," 9.

[19] Mark C. Baetz, "Business-Government Consultation at the Industry Sector Level: To What Extent is it Productive?," in Victor V. Murray, ed., *The Consultative Process in Business-Government Relations* (Ontario: York University, 1986), 68–89 (edited proceedings of the annual conference on business-government relations in the Max Bell Programme for Business-Government Studies).

[20] The word "collaboration" as I use it does not signify the absence of conflict. Rather, it means that parties work together to overcome differences and conflict where they exist.

[21] Francis Horibe, *Creating the Innovation Culture: Leveraging Visionaries, Dissenters and Other Useful Troublemakers in Your Organization* (Toronto: John Wiley & Sons, 2001).

[22] The work of David Osborne and Ted Gaebler typifies this perspective. David Osborne and Ted Gaebler, *Reinventing Government: How the Entrepreneurial Spirit is Transforming the Public Sector* (New York: Plume Books, 1993).

[23] One of the most prominent exponents of this perspective is Donald Savoie. See Donald J. Savoie, *Governing from the Centre: The Concentration of Power in Canadian Politics*. (Toronto: University of Toronto Press, 2000).

[24] David Johnson, "Contemporary Issues in Management Reform," in *Thinking Government: Public-Sector Management in Canada* (Peterborough: Broadview, 2002), 533–88.

[25] Mark Hopkins, Chantal Couture, and Elizabeth Moore, "Moving From the Heroic to the Everyday: Lessons Learned from Leading Horizontal Projects" (Ottawa: Canadian Centre for Management Development Roundtable on the Management of Horizontal Initiatives, 2001), 2.

[26] Ibid.

[27] Mark Sproule-Jones, "Horizontal Management: Implementing Programs across Interdependent Organizations," *Canadian Public Administration* 43, 1 (2000), 93–109.

[28] Hopkins, Couture, and Moore, "Moving From the Heroic to the Everyday," and Sproule-Jones, "Horizontal Management."

[29] Hopkins, Couture, and Moore, "Moving From the Heroic to the Everyday."

[30] Andrea D. Rounce and Norman Beaudry, "Using Horizontal Tools to Work Across Boundaries: Lessons Learned and Signposts for Success" (Ottawa: prepared for the Canadian Centre for Management Development's Roundtable on Horizontal Mechanisms, 2002).

[31] This section draws on Chapters 4 and 7 of the author's doctoral dissertation, "Trading Interests," 2003.

[32] It bears mentioning that SAGIT activity levels have declined substantially since the inception of the groups, with the Cultural Industries SAGIT recognized as one of the most active SAGIT s over the past decade.

[33] International Trade Canada Web site: http://www.dfait-maeci.gc.ca/tna-nac/sagit-en.asp.

[34] Tim Draiman and Betty Plewes, "Civil Society and the Democratization of Foreign Policy," in Maxwell A. Cameron and Maureen Appel Molot, eds., *Canada Among Nations 1995: Democracy and Foreign Policy* (Ottawa: Carleton University Press, 1995).

[35] Anne McCaskill, "La culture et les règles commerciales internationales: enjeux et perspectives" (working document prepared for the First International Meeting of Professional Associations in the Cultural Milieu, a conference presented by the Coalition for Cultural Diversity, Montreal, Quebec, September 10-13, 2001), 5.

[36] Canadian content regulations meet Canada's international trade obligations because they apply to cultural services, and therefore are not subject to the provisions of GATT 1994. Nor are they subject to Canada's obligations under the General Agreement on Trade in Services (GATS) because Canada has as yet made no market access or national treatment commitments in the cultural sector in GATS negotiations. See Ivan Bernier, "Mondialisation de l'économie et diversité culturelle: les enjeux pour le Québec," Working paper prepared for la Commission de la culture de l'Assemblée nationale du Québec (March 2000), 16–17.

[37] See, for example, Dennis Browne, ed., *The Culture/Trade Quandary: Canada's Policy Options* (Ottawa: Centre for Trade Policy and Law, 1998).

[38] Other notable culture-trade frictions include the disputes over Country Music Television and over direct-to-home (DTH) satellite broadcasting. For a review of these and other trade disputes, see Keith Acheson and Christopher Maule, *Much Ado about Culture: North American Trade Disputes* (Ann Arbor: University of Michigan Press, 1999).

[39] Cultural Industries Sectoral Advisory Group on International Trade, *Canadian Culture in a Global World: New Strategies for Culture and Trade* (Ottawa: Department of Foreign Affairs and International Trade, February 1999), 31.

[40] Department of Foreign Affairs and International Trade, *Initial Canadian Negotiating Proposal, Negotiations on Trade in Services (GATS 2000)*, (March 14, 2001), 2.

[41] International Network on Cultural Policy, "Recent International Initiatives on Cultural Diversity" (document prepared by the Liaison Bureau following the Contact Group Meeting in Lisbon, April 2000), 3, available at http://www.64.26.177.19/w-group/wg-cdg/init e.pdf.

[42] Progress continues apace both at the federal level and via non-government organizations to develop what is now referred to as the International Convention on Cultural Diversity. The convention process is proceeding through the United Nations Educational, Scientific, and Cultural Organization (UNESCO), with the intergovernmental negotiation process expected to begin in late 2004.

[43] Department of Foreign Affairs and International Trade, *Initial Canadian Negotiating Proposal*, 2.

[44] William A. Dymond and Michael M. Hart, "Abundant Paradox: the Trade and Culture Debate" (paper prepared for the Centre for Trade Policy and Law's Conference on Trade and Culture, Ottawa, November 28, 2001), 4.

45 One notable element of formality in the SAGIT process pertained to confidentiality. Given the confidentiality that traditionally surrounds trade negotiations, SAGIT members were required to sign a security declaration affirming they would respect the confidentiality of any sensitive information or material presented or discussed.

46 Department of Canadian Heritage Web site, http://www.pch.gc.ca/progs/pcapc-cahsp/index_e.cfm.

47 The CAHSP replaces the Strategic Development Assistance component of the former Cultural Initiatives Program (CIP). Established in 1985, CIP funded Canada's first arts stabilization projects in British Columbia and Alberta discussed further on in this section.

48 Thomas Wolf and William Keens, "Arts Stabilization: A New Frontier for Local Arts Agencies?," *Monographs* 4, no. 9 (Washington: National Assembly of Local Arts Agencies, November 1995), 1.

49 Ibid, 4.

50 Ibid.

51 "The Alberta Performing Arts Stabilization Fund," *AlbertaViews* (January-February, 2004), 47.

52 The APASF has also provided financial support to smaller arts groups, with funding of close to one million dollars between 1995 and 2000 to almost forty arts groups with annual budgets under one million dollars.

53 "Joint Formative Evaluation of Arts Presentation Canada, Cultural Spaces Canada, and the Canadian Arts and Heritage Sustainability Program: Final Report" (report prepared by the Department of Canadian Heritage, Ottawa, October 22, 2003), available at http://www.canadianheritage.gc.ca/progs/em-cr/eval/2004/2004 07/index e.cfm.

54 Hubert Lussier, "Stabilization of Arts Organizations–Lessons from Practical Experience," *Management Matters* (September, 1997).

55 Ibid.

56 Ibid.

57 Ibid.

14.

Governance of Culture:
Words of Caution

GILLES PAQUET

The slenderest knowledge that may be obtained of the highest things
is more desirable than the most certain knowledge obtained of lesser things.
– Thomas Aquinas

There is a high degree of fuzziness surrounding the word "culture." The use of the word "cultural" is even more licentious. If one adds that the notion of governance is itself less than limpid, one is led to conclude that, of necessity, the very notion of "governance of culture" is bound to be somewhat opaque. Yet there are many reasons to believe that unless one is able to elicit what one means by culture and by governance, there is a great danger that spurious indicators are going to blossom, and perverse policies are going to prevail.

So some ground clearing is in order.

Yet this *débroussaillage* needs to proceed with great care. This is due not only to the foundational nature of culture (as beliefs, values, mores, skills, practices) but also to the fact that extraordinary caution is required when it comes to intervening in the affairs of the mind. The forum (where these beliefs, practices, etc., are forged) needs governing as much as the market, and there is most certainly a role for government in "providing and protecting the forum, and intervening within it."[1] Indeed, there is nothing necessarily totalitarian implied by such a stance. But extreme prudence is required, because any such framework imposed on or intervention in the forum may readily be perceived as manipulative and in the nature of brain-washing, and indeed may easily degenerate into being so.

It has been argued that culture is a form of social capital, an enabling resource helping all members of a group to proceed with effective cognition and learning and to act well in concert—an empowering sociality; and that it is unlikely to emerge organically in its optimal form both because of its degree of publicness (and the consequent shirking it entails) and of its diffracted and distributed nature (and the consequent co-ordination problems it generates). On that basis, it has been further argued that a case can be made that "some governing" is required.[2] In such governing, some role exists for government as a provider of varieties of infrastructure capital. But governance of culture cannot be reduced to government of culture: the latter is only a small segment of the former.

In this chapter, I 1) provide a quick sketch of the complexity of the cultural world; 2) define governance both as a *manière de voir* and as effective co-ordination through social learning when power, resources, and information are widely distributed; 3) suggest that only a chaordic arrangement can provide the mix of regimes and modes of governance that is likely to provide effective cognition/coordination in the cultural world; and 4) identify subtle and delicate ways in which, on the basis of a few principles, one may ensure an effective polycentric governance in this game without a master by focusing on removing unfreedoms and taking advantage of tipping points.

The Cultural World

The world of culture, like the world of medicine or business or carpentry, is extraordinarily variegated. It is a totality of pieces of *equipment* (for example, nails) to carry out tasks. These tasks (hammering a nail) are undertaken to achieve some *purposes* (building a house), and performing such tasks leads one to develop *identities* (such as being a carpenter). Disclosing such a world means revealing how it deploys into *practices*, and is organized in *styles*, i.e., the ways that co-ordinate actions and underpin the manner in which practices are transferred from situation to situation.[3]

Equipment, purposes, identities, practices, and styles (EPIPS) are components of a socio-technical system that support a sort of *culture première*—an anthropological ensemble of *manières de voir, manières de faire, et manières d'être* (we may refer to these three *manières* as M3) that have evolved as a set of workable and useful social armistices between the geo-technical constraints imposed by the environment, and the values and plans of the meaningful actors.

This *culture première* constitutes both an instrument for the agents, a decoder of the environment, and a constraining mindset that selects what is important and what is not, and shapes the agents' actions. It is often taken as a somewhat subconscious but given reality—but one need not presume that culture is necessarily subconscious or fully given.

Culture as Discriminating and Evolving

Any culturally-inspired act is based on a capacity to perceive differences, to gauge degrees of relevance and quality. But it also requires that diversity be apprehended as a coherent whole, and that this whole integrates hierarchies or scales of valuation.[4] These capacities to differentiate, to integrate, and to provide an evaluative order, evolve. Environment and equipment change; more knowledge accrues, and tasks change; purposes evolve, identities sharpen, practices and styles crystallize differently. Different habituated choices translate into new beliefs, values, etc.—i.e., into a new culture.[5]

These self-reinforcing mechanisms generate two forms of learning: *behavioural learning*, that builds on past experience to respond to new situations, and *epistemic learning*, through which environmental representations are reframed, and strategies consequently modified. This evolution is always unfinished: a culture as an ensemble of social armistices is always imperfectly adjusted to its context because actors have imperfect and incomplete information and limited rationality, and because adjustments take time.

One must distinguish sharply this variegated *culture première* from *cultures secondes* that stand vis-à-vis *culture première* very much like theology vis-à-vis religion.[6] They correspond to "representations" of culture as seen and stylized by key opinion-molders, and the like. These *cultures secondes* are the result of ratiocinations and reconstructions by elites of what the *culture première* is, of what is important and significant in it, and of what needs to be done to nudge it in the "right direction."

These "constructions" are shaped by ideology and false consciousness and trigger cultural interventions designed to bring culture in line with some "desired" or "preferred" form.

Culture as Diffracted Relational/Cognitive Capital

In a world where a large variety of geo-technical circumstances interact with a wide variety of values and plans, Canada's *cultures premières* are variegated and plural. It takes a quite different shape in Alberta and in Quebec for instance. To put it maybe a bit starkly, in the former case, the importance of negative freedom is such that the State as monopolist of public coercion is regarded as a potential threat; in the latter case, the priority to positive freedom calls for a strong State presence as a lever of empowerment. Culture has "no common unit of account."[7] The ensemble of EPIPS *en acte*, underpinning the array of "Canadian cultures," varies considerably from place to place in Canada.

This ensemble of social armistices may cohere in some manner or be made to appear coherent by all sorts of ratiocinations. These are, however, quite different forms of coalescence. In the first case, an *air de famille* may evolve, or a match may be noted or may evolve among the diverse *cultures premières*, and reveal that relatively similar values and environments have generated similar cognitive and relational guideposts. In the second case, a *culture seconde* may be stylized, and represented by some observers as the only meaningful order, and be used to interpret, assess, or even orthopedically constrain the *cultures premières*. In the first case, there is true convergence. In this second case, one representation is used to impose order on the hurly-burly of real-life cultures.

The coinage of "cultural citizenship" connotes the obsessive search for one such "representation" that would bind all this ebullience together. It is, like all representations, a sort of stylization that is theater-inspired: theory and theater have the same Greek root.[8] This is why "cultural citizenship" generates much malaise. It suggests that a basic genotype must exist, that indeed this *être de raison* should be regarded as more important than the "real thing." In such a scheme, *la culture seconde* takes over, and ideology looms large. This fixation on such a "monoculture" is often state-centred and elite-inspired, and underpins ominous cultural policies tainted by a tinge of brain-washing: when Goddess Reason appears on the scene to impose her dominium, Terror is often not far behind—as citizens were reminded during the French Revolution. Whether any officialized "*culture seconde*" can ever avoid smothering the "*cultures premières*" is a moot question. How could it!

But can there be some core ensemble of values or M3 that might be regarded as infrastructure to *culture première* that could be regarded as the common denominator on which the sociality of a group is built? "Cultural citizenship" might connote such a common denominator, shared by all Canadians, for instance. Our view is that this is most unlikely because of the very variegated nature of this relational/cognitive capital, and the extraordinary importance of the local milieu in the way it crystallizes.

What then of the idea of a "multicultural citizenship" that would focus on second-order phenomena (i.e., a common tool box with which the various relational/cognitive capitals might be constructed and loosely cobbled together)? This would appear to be a rather futile effort to fabricate some elusive commonality. Why not go to third-order phenomena (the arsenal of tools used to modify the tool box)? First-order reality is not so reducible, and is more in the nature of an ecology of cultural arrangements that would seem to reek of incommensurability.

Governance: The Central Challenge

Since there is no *culture première unique* (unless an artificial one is fabricated), and since these diffracted cultures translate into different instruments, different purposes, different identities, different practices, and different styles, is a coherent and yet loosely coupled set of governance arrangements possible? The answer is yes, but such a scheme cannot be imposed top-down.

Yet, the danger of some overarching theology being imposed on this effervescent reality is at all times immense. The only way to avoid such a mutilation is to recognize explicitly *ex ante* that *cultures premières* are bottom-up crowd phenomena, and that there is a need to invent a *modus vivendi* that would allow the *cultures premières* to thrive, without chaos ensuing—i.e., while providing a modicum of relational/cognitive common currency that would prevent the country or the broader set of communities from falling apart. This is the challenge of creating some coherence in the face of deep diversity.

The Ground is in Motion

Technological change, economic growth, and socio-cultural effervescence have generated a genuine dispersive revolution. The need for a heightened capacity for speed, flexibility, and innovation, has led to the development of not only new structures and tools but to a whole new way of thinking. Private, public, and social concerns are no longer drivers of people, but have become "drivers of learning."[9]

Learning organizations are the new forms of alliances and partnerships, rooted in more horizontal relationships and moral contracts, that are now necessary to succeed. So this dispersive revolution has crystallized into new network business organizations, into more subsidiary-focused governments, and into increasingly virtual, elective, and malleable communities. The major governance challenge is how to acquire speed, flexibility, and innovativeness in learning while maintaining a modicum of co-ordination and coherence.

Inter-networked technologies have made new linkages possible; but businesses, governments, and communities have concomitantly been confronted with an ever increasing demand for participation by citizens regarding themselves as partners in the governance process. This has redefined the public space, and founded distributed governance regimes based on a wider variety of more fluid and always evolving communities.[10]

Looser Forms of Co-ordination

The old trinity of state-nation-territory has been put in question. The space does not correspond to homogeneous national territories, nor to their topographical sum, but with communities that have articulated a series of "reciprocal extraterritorialities in which the guiding concept would no longer be the *ius* (right) of the citizen, but the *refugium* (refuge) of the singular."[11]

The new "lightness and fluidity of the increasingly mobile, slippery, shifty, evasive and fugitive power"[12] is not completely a-territorial: it is characterized, however, by new forms of belonging that escape the control and regulation of the nation-state to a much higher degree than before, by virtual agoras, liquid networks, variegated and overlapping terrains where citizens may "land" temporarily.

The fabric of these new "worlds" welds together assets, skills, and capabilities into complex temporary communities that are as much *territories of the mind* as anything that can be represented by a grid map, and it does so on the basis of a bottom-up logic that assigns to higher order institutions only what cannot be accomplished effectively at the local level.

Bottom-up Dynamics

In earlier times, when the context was placid, it may have been possible for leaders to govern the cultural game top-down by simply electing to hypostasize some version of *culture seconde*, and ignore *culture première* altogether. Such cultural imperialism may even succeed temporarily in contexts where governments or potentates are regarded as the only legitimate source of authority, as the only legitimate master of the game. But as the context becomes more turbulent, and deference to authority disappears, one is faced with a game without a master. Governance in such a context has to emerge bottom-up.

But there is no assurance that "wise" or "smart" results will ensue unless certain conditions are met: diversity of inputs, independence from coercion, decentralization of decision-making, and some adequate way of aggregating the diverse opinions of the different groups in the crowd. This last requirement explains the popularity of market-based methods in recent years.[13]

There may be differences of opinion about the necessary conditions for this new philosophy of governing to succeed or about the basic forces on which one has to rely as a matter of priority. Some have underlined the centrality of dissent[14] while others have been celebrating the powers of self-organization and emergence, and the capacity of these forces to generate bottom-up co-ordination that works.[15] The core message of the literature on emergence has been that there is much more to self-organization than is usually believed, and that much of it is observed in nature that is based on simple local rules and effective feedback. But the possibility exists of system failures, and consequently that there is a need to have fail-safe mechanisms in place that kick in when the system is in danger.[16]

Co-ordination Failures

There is no assurance of perfect co-ordination, perfect marksmanship, and zero learning lags in a complex world. Co-ordination failures abound. Some failures may self-correct, but others may require external corrective interventions to avoid systemic failure.

In the shorter run, co-ordination failures may be eliminated through *process redesign*, i.e., a change in the social technologies to eliminate obstacles to the collaboration of the different stakeholders within the learning cycle and developing the relationships, conventions, or relational transactions required to define mutually coherent expectations and common guideposts. These conventions differ from sector to sector: they provide the requisite coherence for a common context of interpretation, and for some "cognitive routinization of relations between firms, their environments, and employees," for instance.[17]

Such coherence must, however, remain somewhat loose: the ligatures should not be too strong or too routinized. A certain degree of heterogeneity, and therefore social distance, might foster a higher potentiality of innovation, because the different parties bring to the "conversation" a more complementary body of knowledge.[18]

In the intermediate run, co-ordination failures may be eliminated more radically through *organizational architecture work*, i.e., structural repairs, the transformation of the structural capital (networks and regimes) defining the capabilities of the learning socio-economy.

Coherence and pluralism are crucial in the organizational architecture of a learning concern. And such an architecture must be based on principles that allow organizations to have maximum flexibility to fully embrace diversity and change.

This is true in all sectors. Dee Hock has described in great detail the saga that led to the creation of VISA—the credit card empire.[19] VISA is presented as the result of a process through which deliberation about purpose and principles led to the creation of new organizational structure that Hock calls chaord. Chaord is a combination of *cha*os and *ord*er. It is defined by Hock as "any self-organizing, adaptive, non-linear, complex system, whether physical, biological or social, the behavior of which exhibits characteristics of both order and chaos or, loosely translated to business terminology, cooperation and competition."[20]

The same features make federal structures attractive from a learning point of view: they provide co-ordination in a world where the "centre ... is more a network than a place."[21] This is also the reason that federal-type organizational structures have emerged in so many sectors in most continents.

Potentially, federalism represents a sort of fit or effective alignment between the different components of structural capital, in the sense of Saint-Onge—i.e., the systems (processes), structures (accountabilities and responsibilities), strategies, and culture (shared mindset, values and norms).[22] But since there is always a significant probability of misalignment between these components, there is often a need to intervene directly to modify the organizational architecture in order to ensure effective learning.

In the longer run, co-ordination failures may have to be dealt with through some reframing of the purposes pursued by the community. Often, the reconciling of technology, structures, and theory may be achieved by tinkering with the plumbing or the architecture of the system: technology and structures. But often, the theory must be revisited: the assumptions on which the system and actions within the system are based—assumptions that one may or may not be aware one is making—must be questioned and the very enterprise one is involved in (philosophy, broad directions, etc.) refounded.[23]

This entails nothing less than a re-invention of the business the community is in to ensure an effective alignment. Values, norms, objectives, assumptions may have to be recast, and a new game altogether put in place.

The shift in the vision of the State over the last twenty years—from the old Welfare State to the new Welfare State—as described by Julian Le Grand[24] (with its change in the perception of the way the public sector works and its change in the way in which recipients of welfare should be considered) provides an interesting example of such a refoundation process: the move from a world of public sector professionals regarded as knights at work for the benefit of passive citizen-pawns, to a world of self-interested public sector workers (à la public choice) regarded as knaves facing citizens requesting to be treated like queens.

A new public philosophy and *outillage mental* then become necessary to serve as a gyroscope as motivation, agency, and the whole learning process are completely transformed when the worlds change in this way.[25]

Ecologies of Governance

The practical imperative in the world of culture calls for a governance that will succeed in squaring the circle, i.e., in finding effective ways to have most of the advantages of a coherent system while also obtaining all the advantages of a decentralized system.

This entails avoiding two pitfalls: *the illusion of control* (because, in the real world, one is rarely faced with a complex socio-technical system that has a fixed shape and predictable behaviour, and therefore that one can fully control), and *the delusion of Candide* (because it is equally naïve to believe that the appropriate retooling, restructuring, and reframing will always emerge organically in the best way, and in a timely fashion, as Candide optimistically believed that we are always faced with the best of all worlds).

The best one may hope for is a new fluid form of governance—something called "ecology of governance" by Walt Anderson. He describes it as "many different systems and different kinds of systems interacting with one another, like the multiple organisms in an ecosystem."[26] Such arrangements are not necessarily "neat, peaceful, stable or efficient ... but in a continual process of learning and changing and responding to feedback." Their main objective is to ensure resilience, i.e., the capacity for the system to spring back on its feet undamaged.

An ecology of governance amounts to a group of loosely integrated "uncentralized networks," each focused on an issue-domain. Two examples might help flesh out what is meant by such an arrangement—one that yields most of the benefits of centralized and decentralized organizations: VISA and regime-based federalism.[27]

VISA as Chaord

Hock has shown that in attempting to govern something as complex as the financial empire of VISA, for instance, the design problem was so extraordinary that a new form of uncentralized organization had to be created. This was seen as the only way to ensure durability and resilience in such a complex organization, having to adjust constantly to a vast array of turbulent contextual circumstances, but also having to face the immense co-ordination challenge involved in orchestrating the work of over 20,000 financial institutions in more than 200 countries, and trying to serve hundreds of millions of users.

In such circumstances, neither a fully centralized system nor a completely decentralized one would appear to be capable of providing the sort of arrangement likely to ensure the requisite resilience. Consequently, a new form of organization had to be designed that would serve the "main purpose," but would also provide the mix of norms and mechanisms likely to underpin its realization through bottom-up effervescence within the context of some loose framework of guiding principles agreed to by all.

Hock has given some examples of these principles, defining the sort of organization used to cope with these challenges in the construction and design of organizations of this sort:

- The organization must be equitably owned by all participants; no member should have an intrinsic advantage; all advantages should result from ability and initiative;
- Power and function must be distributive to the maximum; no function and no power should be vested with any part that might be reasonably exercised by any lesser part;

- Governance must be distributive; no individual or group of individuals should be able to dominate deliberations or control decisions;
- To the maximum degree possible, everything should be voluntary;
- It must be infinitely malleable, yet extremely durable; it should be capable of constant, self-generated modification without sacrificing its essential nature; and
- It must embrace diversity and change; it must attract people comfortable with such an environment, and provide an environment in which they can thrive.[28]

There is an "essential nature" in VISA as an organization, but there are also many dimensions and categories in the architecture and operations of this socio-technical system that do not necessarily fall into a centralization or decentralization box, because they correspond to both.

Regime-based Federalism

The traditional concept of federalism is territorial. It partitions the responsibilities of the organization (private, public, or civic) among different layers of the organization, more or less firmly based in certain geographical areas. This is the case for American federalism[29] and also for some firms that have adopted a federal structure, such as Shell, Unilever, etc.[30]

But, as Handy puts it, federalism is much more than a territorial management grid: it is "a well-recognized way to deal with paradoxes of power and control: the need to make things big by keeping them small; to encourage autonomy, but within bounds; to combine variety and shared purpose, individuality and partnership, local and global."[31] One can easily see the possibilities of federalism as an agency of reconciliation of various sets of purposes: a social architecture providing for multiple logics to cohabit.

Subsidiarity is one of the key principles underpinning federalism. It establishes that no higher order body should take unto itself responsibilities that can be dispatched properly by a lower order body. In territorial terms, this means that only if the local or state levels cannot effectively shoulder some responsibilities should they be taken over by the federal government. The same logic would lead the head office of a company to provide subsidiaries with as much autonomy as they can properly exercise.

In the cultural world, the subsidiarity principle would lead to the recognition that much more is happening and should be happening at the local level.

In the absence of a higher order authority (as in the case of the trans-national scene, because of the void at the level of world government), networks very often emerge that are focused on issues like weather, environment, racism, etc. Such networks correspond roughly to both issue-domains and "communities of meaning." Such specific forums are created to handle critical issues (management of oceans, for instance), and accords or agreements of all sorts (the Kyoto protocol, for instance) are arrived at in such agoras.

The arrangements that they embody are referred to as "regimes."

Stephen Krasner has defined regimes in the international context as "sets of implicit and explicit principles, norms, rules and decision-making procedures, around which actors' expectations converge in a given area of international relations."[32] This definition has been refined and expanded by Hasenclever, et al., who have made more explicit the different conceptual elements of the definition: "Principles are beliefs of fact, causation and rectitude. Norms are standards of behavior defined in terms of rights and obligation. Rules are specific prescriptions or proscriptions for action. Decision-making procedures are prevailing practices for making and implementing collective choice."[33]

One can argue that any private, public, or civic entity adopting a chaordic or a federal structure (and these are not incompatible) is choosing to match the complexity of the environment with the complexity of the organizational form.

What This Means for the Cultural World

Governance of culture through a chaordic approach is a matter of consequence. It challenges the simplistic association of culture and identity. The world of culture is a world of EPIPS. Overemphasizing the identity dimension opens the door to much ideological framing, and much planning of the cultural field in line with such an ideological frame.

The major flaws of any univocal approach to culture are holism and reification. Instead of appraising culture as an ensemble of social technologies, structures and frames, and recognizing that they play a wide diversity of roles, it is referred to as a totality with a singular mission. This illusion of totality is cleverly hidden behind some lip-service references to sub-cultures, but it generates a global and reified view of culture. Indeed, once the "cultural field" is labeled as such, there is a great temptation to map it and to plan it: i.e., to "flatten" the cultural world onto a two-dimensional managerial surface.

A chaordic approach recognizes that the cultural world cannot be mapped and planned. As an ecology of sub-systems, it does not lend itself to value chain analysis, whatever specialists of national social accounts might suggest.[34] Indeed, there is a danger in allowing a useful statistical metaphor to become a substitute for a complex elusive reality. It is not surprising that such tools are in good currency in Cuba.

A more pragmatic strategy recognizes both 1) the process-oriented and enabling character of cultural capital (which means that it cannot easily be measured through elusive and ill-defined outcomes) and 2) the inherent complexity and non-linearity of the emergent self-reinforcing processes that define the world of culture. As a result, it is even more difficult to define the value of cultural capital than to define the value of physical capital (and yet we know how difficult the problems of measurement and valuation are in the latter case). Consequently, the use of national accounts approaches may not hold as much promise as has been suggested. One should most certainly not use such quantophrenic tactics (however useful they may appear at the rhetorical level, in dealing with competing demands on public sector budgets, by making culture more tangible and more visible) as a guide to broad-brushed interventions.

A more modest and more effective approach would be more in the nature of *bricolage*. The most one can hope for in the world of culture is the highest and best use of certain basic principles *à la* Hock, and of certain tipping points likely to generate discontinuities or at least to make good use of self-reinforcing mechanisms. And this must be regarded as rather fortunate. This is at least the case for those who fear confusion somewhat, but fear totalitarianism more.

Polycentric Governance: Guiding Principles and Tipping Point Leadership

The drift from a monoculture, state-centric, elite-driven "government of culture" to a multicultural, pluralist, private-public-civic sectors shared, and diversity-driven "governance of culture" is less a conjecture than a fact. Consequently, most advanced countries already have a form of polycentric governance of culture. It emerges from an image of governance as a wide array of concurrent games, plagued with multiple authorities and overlapping jurisdictions, and linked into complex networks of interactions. Indeed, the cultural game is structured to avoid anyone being able to become a master of the game, and appropriately so.

Yet this fact is neither fully acknowledged nor fully understood. This is because acknowledging it entails some recognition that culture is a game without a master—a proposition that denies any potentate or "cultural czar," the possibility or even the "right to think" of deliberately shaping culture; and because of the fact that most observers still fail to get a good sense of what complexity entails, and fear immensely any process where there is no master of the game.

As a result, there is a constant effort to "represent" the cultural world as a simple extension of the input-output production process of industrial goods. And a corollary of this stance is that there is still much pretense in government circles that State cultural policy (especially at the federal and provincial levels) is not only entitled to but must, as a matter of duty, "govern" culture. This argument is based on the presumption that through its corrections of market failures, its production of social capital, and its promotion of some aspects of culture as a merit good, the State will be truly "steering the cultural ship."

As any ethnographic probing would indicate, culture (in its various forms) is not a State artefact, but emerges mostly unplanned through the marketplace and civil society. Hundreds of groups and small firms contribute to cultural development in each city in Canada. While this process is messy and often takes forms that the elites would not condone (pace subsidiarity Céline Dion and Shania Twain), it rules the roost.

A more useful approach builds on a better understanding of what polycentric governance means, on a better appreciation of the guiding principles likely to be of use, and on the central focus on the tipping point mechanisms likely to eliminate blockages and unfreedoms.

Polycentric Self-governance

One of the main reasons why cultural indicators are in good currency is that they help to make cultural issues more visible. Yet those indicators tend to focus on averages, and therefore misrepresent greatly the essential diversity of the cultural field. Like the fixation on GDP measurements, the focus on macro cultural indicators lionizes aggregate measures of "output" and correlates them with other aggregate measures of "inputs" without any meaningful appreciation of the complex systems to which those measurements refer. This leaves the whole process of cultural creation in a sort of "black box," and tends to lend credence to the meaningfulness of the correlations among these aggregates, when in fact they are often meaningless.

Unless one has a much better appreciation of what generates creativity, innovation, effective social learning, etc., and how—i.e., of the dynamics of the self-governing nexus of culture—one cannot propose meaningful measurements and argue for meaningful interventions.

A systematic deconstruction of culture suggests that the cultural ecosystem is not governable top-down, that its main features emerge bottom-up and therefore originate in local milieus, and that it is largely self-governed.[35]

Yet this does not mean that everything happens in an indistinct governance soup, or that there is not a certain division of labour among the different families of stakeholders. There is a *prima facie* case for the State's being charged with providing infrastructure, and not intervening in purposes and practices.

The role of the public sector in the cultural world is twofold: first and foremost, to provide the public space and the basic equipment for an effective forum, and then to work at eliminating the blockages constituting unfreedoms that emanate from deprivation of political liberties, economic facilities, social opportunities, transparency guarantees, and protective security.[36]

In the following table, we provide a plausible view of what might be a well-balanced overall picture of the world of culture. In this pattern, the public sector would focus on providing the public equipments and on removing the blockages mentioned above, while allowing the private sector to shape the purposes and practices (the preserve of private citizens and groups) and delegating to the civil society the responsibility for shaping identities and styles (not ever to become shaped by officialdom). This is not the only nor necessarily the most desirable pattern but it might serve as a useful reference.

The politics of cognition and social capitalization should not shy away from the task of raising awareness, and should accept the duty of enlightening, so as to urge citizens to attend to the necessary agenda. But it should be quite focused on extending the realm of choices, on playing a role of facilitator, on helping a robust sociality to emerge, rather than trying to influence choices and shape sociality. This will always be imperfectly done because government cannot be entirely neutral: besides informing, exposing, balancing, developing critical senses, chaperoning, etc., government also often enters the forum as an authoritative voice. This is why government has an important *"devoir de réserve."*

For example, there is nothing contentious in suggesting that the provision of public space or the promotion of literacy constitutes a basic facilitation role that would appear to fall clearly within the bailiwick of the public sector. But through bans on certain use of airwaves and selective granting activities, the State allows vocal minorities to influence dramatically the contours of "official culture," and to inflict their views on the citizenry. This is the world of minority preferences at public expenses. One can only fathom, with much unease, the prospect of such preferences being transmuted into "cultural rights" and becoming the "official culture."

Such concerns underpin our sense that there should be limits to the scope of cultural regulation by the State. It is most certainly difficult to defend the interventions that reek of censorship or that hide massive inter-group redistribution behind the cloak of defending some form of "high culture." In matters of the mind, the provision of the relational/cognitive capital should not in any way limit choices. It should indeed be clear that State actions must ensure that private citizens and groups are enabled to develop "their purposes and practices."

Table 1: A Radiography of the World of Culture

COMPONENTS SECTORS	Equipment	Purposes	Identities	Practices	Styles
Public	X				
Private		X		X	
Civic			X	X	

As for identities and styles, they should be left to the forces of emergence in civil society. Attempting to control them would inevitably lead government to become explicitly manipulative and therefore objectionable.

This is why much attention must be given to scrutinizing the principles that should guide government in intervening beyond the uncontroversial act of providing opportunities through infrastructure, i.e., when it becomes regulator of "time, place and manner."[37]

Guiding Principles

These principles are quite general and must be balanced: efficiency (avoiding waste), legitimacy, transparency, a recognition that some competition helps, that greater participation also helps, that price-cost relations must not be obfuscated, etc.[38]

Identifying these guiding principles and calibrating their valence is probably the most difficult task facing stakeholders. In gauging their guideposts, they must recognize the need to mix these principles in a meaningful way. Any governance entirely dedicated to the maximization of one single particular objective is likely to be unduly reductive.

This is where the reliance on self-governance plays its most important balancing role. It is the dynamics of the forum that should inflect the mix in one direction or another, not the State. The subtle if necessary action of the State should focus on providing the relational/cognitive capital that underpins M3 in ways that promote inclusiveness and transparency as much as possible.

Tipping Point Leadership

The sort of prudence required from the State does not prevent it from intervening lightly but effectively by removing blockages that may prevent mechanisms of self-correction, self-re-enforcing, self-steering, and self-transformation to play themselves out.

Such blockages prevent agents and groups from taking full advantage of all the available opportunities and facilities. They are often detected by economic, social and political entrepreneurs, and taken advantage of. But they may require collective action.

Among the mechanisms to eliminate unfreedoms, one should focus in particular on tipping points where a small action is likely to have a significant effect.[39]

In the language of Kim and Mauborgne,[40] this approach focuses on breaking through awareness, resources, motivation, and political hurdles: 1) by putting the practitioners face-to-face with operational problems (Commissioner William Bratton requesting that all police transit officials in New York ride the subway to work, to meetings, and at night); 2) by focusing on areas most in need where intervention is likely to have maximal impact, instead of indulging in scattered interventions and "*arrosage generalisé*;" 3) by getting through to key influencers and counting on contagion (who would have thought that schoolyard violence might be eradicated by the use of "*vous*"?); and 4) by identifying and confronting naysayers early on.

In all such cases, the State is not entirely neutral: such dealing with bottlenecks is bound to be selective and therefore to have uneven impacts on the different groups. But the requirement for a light-touch-approach at the very least prevents intrusive and destructive interventions of an orthopaedic nature.

Tipping point leadership is what is required in the cultural world.

Conclusion

Culture, cultural value, and heritage are all weasel words and connote multidimensional, shifting, and elusive realities.

The deconstruction of these concepts and of these realities with the scalpel of a national accountant is likely to generate precise but meaningless numbers unless one first clarifies a few notions:

- The complexity of the notion of culture;
- The reductionist nature of the focus on cultural goods and industries;
- The inherent self-governing nature of cultural ecosystems;
- The limited possibility of cultural bricolage;
- The centrality of this modest work for both economic and political development;
- The dynamics of polycentric governance; and
- The meaning of tipping point leadership.

While some arithmetic and some quantitative indicators may be useful for more effectively arguing the case for culture in political fora, they will mostly tend to legitimize additional State interventions that may have important negative impacts on the very health of culture.

The celebration of polycentric self-governance and words of caution about quantophrenia and intrusive government interventions should not be interpreted as a plea for eliminating the government's role in the affairs of the mind and in the cultural world. They should be interpreted as nothing more or less than what they are: words of caution.

The celebration of bricolage and tipping point leadership should not be interpreted either as a form of reprehensible resignation in the face of the many crises that the cultural world is going through. It is only a plea for extraordinary prudence, but also much creativity, imagination, and a reasonable dose of patience—all virtues that are most important when one deals with affairs of the mind.

Notes

1 Joseph Tussman, *Government and the Mind* (New York: Oxford University Press, 1977), vii.

2 David Throsby, *Economics and Culture* (Cambridge: Cambridge University Press, 2001).

3 Charles Spinosa, Fernando Flores and Hubert L. Dreyfus, *Disclosing New Worlds* (Cambridge, MA: Massachussetts Institute of Technology Press, 1997), 17.

4 Bruno Lussato, *Le défi culturel* (Paris: Nathan, 1989).

5 Emmanuel G. Mesthene, *Technological Change* (New York: Mentor Books, 1970).

6 Michael A. Weinstein, *Culture Critique: Fermand Dumont and New Québec Sociology* (Montréal: New World Perspectives, 1985).

7 Throsby, *Economics and Culture*, 159.

8 Robert Nisbet, *Sociology as an Art Form* (New York: Oxford University Press, 1976).

9 Walter B. Wriston, *The Twilight of Sovereignty* (New York: Scribner's, 1992), 119.

10 Don Tapscott and David Agnew, "Governance in the Digital Economy," *Finance & Development* (December 1999): 34–37.

11 George Agamben, *Means Without End: Notes on Politics* (Minneapolis: University of Minnesota Press, 2000), 24.

12 Zygmunt Bauman, *Liquid Modernity* (Cambridge: Polity Press, 2000), 14.

13 James Surowiecki, *The Wisdom of Crowds* (New York: Doubleday, 2004).

[14] Cass R. Sunstein, *Why Societies Need Dissent* (Cambridge, MA: Harvard University Press, 2003).

[15] Steven Johnson, *Emergence* (New York: Scribner, 2001).

[16] Ruth Hubbard and Gilles Paquet, "Ecologies of Governance and Institutional Métissage," *optimumonline* 32, no. 4 (2002): 25–34.

[17] Michael Storper, "Institutions of the Knowledge-Based Economy," *Employment and Growth in the Knowledge-Based Economy* (Paris: Organization for Economic and Cultural Development, 1996), 259.

[18] Mark Granovetter, "The Strength of Weak Ties," *American Journal of Sociology* 78, no. 6 (1973): 1360–80.

[19] Dee Hock, *The Birth of the Chaordic Age* (San Francisco: Berrett-Koehler Publishers, 1999), 137–39; Dee Hock, "The Chaordic Organization: Out of Control and Into Order," *World Business Academy Perspectives* 9, no. 1 (1995), 4.

[20] Hock, "The Chaordic Organization," 4.

[21] Charles Handy, *Beyond Certainty* (London: Hutchinson, 1995).

[22] Hubert Saint Onge, "Tacit Knowledge: The Key to the Strategic Alignment of Intellectual Capital," *Strategy and Leadership* (March-April 1996): 10–14.

[23] Donald Schon and M. Rein, *Frame Analysis* (New York: Basic Books, 1994); D. Schon, *Beyond the Stable State* (New York: Norton, 1971).

[24] Julian Le Grand, *Motivation, Agency and Public Policy* (Oxford: Oxford University Press, (2003).

[25] Gilles Paquet, "The Strategic State," part 1, *Ciencia Ergo Sum* 3, no. 3 (1996): 257–61; "The Strategic State," part 2, *Ciencia Ergo Sum* 4, no. 1 (1997): 28–34; "The Strategic State," part 3, *Ciencia Ergo Sum* 4, no. 2 (1997): 148–54.

[26] Walter T. Anderson, *All Connected Now* (Cambridge, MA: Westview Press, 2001), 252.

[27] Hubbard and Paquet, "Ecologies of Governance."

[28] Hock, *The Birth of the Chaordic Age*; Hock, "The Chaordic Organization."

[29] Stephen L. Carter, *The Dissent of the Governed* (Cambridge, MA: Harvard University Press, 1998).

[30] Charles Handy, "Balancing Corporate Power: a New Federalist Paper," *Harvard Business Review* 70, no. 6 (1992): 59–72.

[31] Ibid.

[32] Stephen D. Krasner, *International Regimes* (Ithaca, NY: Cornell University Press, 1983), 2.

[33] Andreas Hasenclever, Peter Mayer, and Volker Rittberger, *Theories of International Regimes* (New York: Cambridge Press, 1997), 9.

[34] Colin Mercer, *Towards Cultural Citizenship: Tools for Cultural Policy and Development* (Hedemora, Sweden: Bank of Sweden Tercentary Foundation and Gidlunds Forlag, 2002).

[35] Michael Dean McGinnis, ed., *Polycentric Games and Institutions: Readings from the Workshop in Political Theory and Policy Analysis* (Ann Arbor: University of Michigan Press, 2000); Howard Rheingold, *Smart Mobs* (Cambridge, MA: Perseus Publishing, 2002).

[36] Amartya Sen, *Development as Freedom* (New York: Knopf, 1999).

[37] Tussman, *Government and the Mind*, 110.

[38] Pierre Jacquet, Jean Pisani-Ferry and Laurence Tubiana, "De quelques principes pour une gouvernance hybride," *Problèmes économiques*, no. 2755 (3 avril, 1–6, no. 2767 (26 June 2002), 1–4; Gerhard Banner, "La gouvernance communautaire au cœur du processus de décentralisation," *Problèmes économiques*, no. 2783 (6 November 2002), 14–21.

[39] Joseph L. Badaracco, *Leading Quietly: An Unorthodox Guide to Doing the Right Thing* (Boston: Harvard Business School Press, 2002); Harvey Seifter and Peter Economy, *Leadership Ensemble: Lessons in Collaborative Management from the World's Only Conductorless Orchestra* (New York: Henry Holt, 2001); Malcolm Gladwell, *The Tipping Point: How Little Things Can Make a Big Difference* (Boston: Little, Brown, 2000).

[40] W. Chan Kim and Renée A. Mauborgne, "Tipping Point Leadership," *Harvard Business Review* 81, no. 2 (2003), 60–69.

15.

Vers des indicateurs culturels élargis?
Justificatifs des politiques culturelles et indicateurs de performance au Québec et en Europe

CHRISTIAN POIRIER

Résumé

Cette étude examine la nature des relations qui s'établissent entre justificatifs des politiques culturelles et indicateurs de performance au Québec, au sein de l'Union européenne et au Royaume-Uni. Si ces trois zones géographiques adoptent de plus en plus une définition élargie de la participation culturelle et mettent l'accent sur les partenariats avec les villes, le secteur privé et la société civile, des différences sensibles existent entre les cas québécois et européens. L'Union européenne et le Royaume-Uni adoptent une définition de plus en plus élargie des indicateurs culturels, tentant de mesurer les impacts sociaux des arts sur les individus et sur les communautés. Cela est en adéquation avec les finalités récentes de leurs politiques culturelles, qui visent tant le développement économique que celui des individus et des communautés. Le Québec adopte quant à lui une définition majoritairement économique et traditionnelle des indicateurs (production, consommation, fréquentation, etc.). Il y a donc inadéquation entre les objectifs de la politique, qui combinent les impératifs de développement économique, d'affirmation identitaire collective et de développement personnel, et les principaux indicateurs élaborés. L'étude en profite pour dégager quelques pistes de réflexion entourant la portée et les limites de l'utilisation d'indicateurs culturels élargis, notamment dans un contexte de gouvernance urbaine et de développement d'une citoyenneté culturelle.

Introduction

Ce texte a pour principal objectif de rendre compte d'une recherche préliminaire, effectuée à la demande de Patrimoine Canadien, concernant le développement d'indicateurs de performance au Québec et en Europe, plus spécifiquement au Royaume-

Uni. Ces indicateurs ont pour but d'évaluer l'impact des politiques culturelles. Le but de cette étude est d'effectuer un tour d'horizon ainsi qu'une analyse des principaux indicateurs développés par les gouvernements de ces régions. Les indicateurs sont des mesures récurrentes et actualisées permettant à un individu ou à une organisation de décrire des conditions, de relever des tendances et de cerner des résultats. Ils s'inscrivent dans le cadre de processus évaluant si les objectifs fixés ont été atteints. L'élaboration d'indicateurs de performance est donc une étape cruciale au sein de ces processus, comme en témoigne la multiplication récente des écrits (voir la bibliographie) et des colloques sur la question.

Il n'y a pas lieu ici d'analyser de façon détaillée les raisons de cette évolution du secteur des politiques de l'évaluation. Soulignons cependant que, dans un contexte de choix difficiles concernant les priorités des investissements publics et d'impératifs d'efficacité pour les organisations et les pouvoirs publics, artistes, gestionnaires d'organismes culturels et représentants des gouvernements expriment le besoin d'outils pratiques susceptibles de les aider à évaluer, à mesurer et à légitimer l'impact de leurs pratiques et de leurs politiques. Il existe aussi une volonté plus grande de la population d'insister sur la transparence et sur l'imputabilité des politiques publiques. On peut également noter que la dimension culturelle a pris, depuis quelques années, une importance grandissante dans nos sociétés, notamment en raison de l'élargissement du temps de loisirs et de la part grandissante prise par les valeurs postmatérialistes dont la génération des *baby-boomers* et celles qui la suivent sont porteuses.

Afin de mener à bien notre recherche, nous développons l'hypothèse selon laquelle l'élaboration d'indicateurs est en relation étroite avec les principaux justificatifs des politiques culturelles. Autrement dit, les principes d'évaluation des politiques et les indicateurs élaborés par les gouvernements sont en relation avec les principaux paramètres justifiant la politique culturelle et ses différents programmes. Il est à noter qu'un tel couplage n'est pas nouveau. Luis Bonet et Emmanuel Négrier ont bien montré l'évolution globale impliquant logiques, finalités, secteurs d'intervention et indicateurs en Occident (Bonet et Négrier, 2002). Ainsi, du XIXe siècle à 1945, prévalait une logique patrimoniale, élitiste et nationaliste dont les finalités étaient la conservation, la construction identitaire nationale, l'instruction publique et la formation artistique d'élite, les secteurs d'intervention le patrimoine, les bibliothèques et les beaux-arts, et les indicateurs les monuments, livres scolaires produits, écoles d'art, etc. La période s'échelonnant de 1945 à 1960 témoigne globalement d'une logique artistique dont les finalités sont la diffusion de la haute culture et la créativité, les secteurs d'intervention les beaux-arts et les arts contemporains, et les indicateurs les institutions et festivals de qualité.

Une logique socioculturelle succède de 1960 à 1980; ses finalités sont la démocratisation culturelle et la participation, ses secteurs d'intervention privilégient les équipements multifonctionnels, la culture populaire et les moyens de communication, et ses indicateurs mesurent la participation de diverses classes sociales, les pratiques amateur, la décentralisation de l'offre culturelle, etc. Une logique de développement économique et culturel domine ensuite de 1980 à 2000; ses finalités sont la production, la diffusion, le développement économique, la compétitivité, la croissance et la diversité culturelle, ses secteurs d'intervention sont liés à l'audiovisuel, aux nouvelles technologies de l'information et de la communication (NTIC) et au multimédia, et ses indicateurs sont associés à la production, à la consommation et à l'exportation de produits culturels.

Nous proposons cependant de complexifier quelque peu ce schéma et de concevoir deux types de relation entre justificatifs et indicateurs : celui où il y a adéquation entre les fondements des politiques et les indicateurs, et celui où il y a inadéquation ou manque de cohérence entre justificatifs et indicateurs. Cela nous permettra d'examiner de façon plus précise le déploiement historique et récent du rapport entre élaboration et évaluation des politiques culturelles.

Trois zones géographiques retiendront particulièrement notre attention : le Québec, l'Union européenne et le Royaume-Uni. Les institutions et gouvernements de ces trois aires ont développé au fil des ans des politiques culturelles ambitieuses et ont exprimé la nécessité d'élaborer des indicateurs afin d'en mesurer les effets. L'analyse démontrera deux éléments principaux. D'abord, la tendance vers l'élaboration d'indicateurs statistiques de base et vers une définition strictement économique de la performance est repérable au sein des trois cas étudiés. Toutefois, les indicateurs statistiques tiennent de plus en plus compte d'une définition englobante de la participation culturelle, incluant les pratiques amateur, les nouveaux médias, les pratiques audiovisuelles, la culture populaire, la participation culturelle par médias interposés (admirer un tableau dans Internet, par exemple), etc. Des enquêtes de plus en plus ciblées auprès de certains publics sont également effectuées.

Ensuite, il existe des différences sensibles entre les trois zones étudiées. Ainsi, l'Union européenne et le Royaume-Uni adoptent une définition de plus en plus élargie des indicateurs culturels, tentant de mesurer les impacts sociaux des arts sur les individus et sur les communautés. Cela est en adéquation avec les finalités récentes de leurs politiques culturelles, qui visent tant le développement économique que celui des individus et des communautés. Le Québec adopte quant à lui une définition majoritairement économique et traditionnelle des indicateurs (production, consommation, fréquentation, etc.). Il y a donc inadéquation entre les objectifs de la politique, qui combinent les impératifs de développement économique, d'affirmation identitaire collective et de développement personnel, et les principaux indicateurs élaborés.

La présentation de l'analyse se fera en quatre temps. Les trois premières parties seront consacrées à l'examen des cas du Québec, de l'Union européenne et du Royaume-Uni. Chaque partie est divisée en deux sections, présentant d'abord des éléments historiques de contextualisation ainsi que les objectifs des politiques récentes, puis les principaux indicateurs élaborés. Enfin, la quatrième partie propose quelques pistes de réflexion entourant la portée et les limites de l'utilisation d'indicateurs culturels élargis.

Le Québec

Contexte et justifications de la politique culturelle

Malgré la présence d'une panoplie d'institutions et d'organismes mis sur pied par le gouvernement québécois – souvent en partenariat avec l'Église – à la fin du XIXe siècle et au début du XXe siècle (qui ont toutefois joué un rôle majeur dans la sauvegarde et le développement culturels des Canadiens français), le gouvernement n'entame son implication véritable qu'au début des années 1960 (Poirier, 2004). La priorité de l'État est d'abord de mettre en place un ministère des Affaires culturelles (1er avril 1961), qui constituait le premier article du programme du Parti libéral de Jean Lesage, porté au pouvoir en juin 1960. Le mandat du ministère des Affaires culturelles (MAC) est de favoriser l'épanouissement des arts et des lettres au Québec et leur rayonnement extérieur. Il s'agit (malgré les ambitions du ministre Georges-Émile Lapalme, qui souhaitait adopter une définition large de la culture) d'une conception traditionnelle, élitiste, de la culture, axée sur les subventions aux créateurs.

Sous la direction de Pierre Laporte, le ministère rédige un *Livre blanc* qui ne sera jamais déposé en Chambre ni publié, le conseil des ministres le jugeant trop «

nationaliste » et, de façon incidente, les libéraux subissant une défaite aux élections de juin 1966 (son successeur n'y donnera aucune suite). Ce document anticipe toutefois sur les années 1970 en opérant un lien entre culture, identité nationale et intervention étatique. Signe d'une ouverture de l'identité québécoise en émergence vers la pluralité, P. Laporte accorde une attention soutenue à l'immigration, qu'il intègre alors dans les fonctions du MAC. Très rapidement émerge alors une définition plus anthropologique et englobante de la culture (voir les recommandations de la Commission d'enquête sur l'enseignement des arts au Québec, sous la direction de Marcel Rioux, en 1968).

L'approche du Ministère au tournant des années 1970 s'oriente davantage vers la diffusion et l'accessibilité aux œuvres. Puis, la culture déborde progressivement le cadre de l'individu pour rejoindre la conception proposée par Laporte en 1965 : une politique culturelle doit être une politique de la personne et de la communauté dans un but de définition de l'identité, l'État servant de point d'appui à la communauté. Cette nouvelle orientation repose également sur la volonté manifestée par Robert Bourassa de mettre l'accent sur la souveraineté culturelle du Québec dans le cadre canadien. En 1975, le ministre des Affaires culturelles, Denis Hardy, opère la jonction entre diffusion, démocratisation de la culture et mise en valeur de la spécificité québécoise par le contrôle des moyens de production et de mise en marché des biens et services culturels.

Un *Livre vert*, proposé par Jean-Paul L'Allier en 1976, suggère d'accentuer l'orientation du Ministère vers la déconcentration administrative et la décentralisation par le biais d'une collaboration accrue avec les organismes d'intervention culturelle, les municipalités et les régions. Le document propose également de transférer des responsabilités à des organismes parapublics (Conseil de la culture, Régie du patrimoine, Commissions régionales, Commission des musées, etc.) et d'accroître le rôle des organismes artistiques. Ces orientations préfigurent le rôle d'animateur et de coordonnateur (plutôt que celui, interventionniste, de gestionnaire et de planificateur), qui sera bientôt la marque principale du MAC.

Le gouvernement de René Lévesque, qui prend le pouvoir en 1976, place la culture au centre de son projet collectif, et ce, tant sur le plan des référents de l'action publique que sur celui des gestes politiques. Une des premières initiatives du nouveau gouvernement est la création de quatre comités ministériels permanents rattachés au Conseil exécutif. Il s'agit d'accentuer la cohésion interministérielle en regroupant plusieurs ministères autour d'un grand thème commun. Sont ainsi visés l'aménagement du territoire, le développement économique, le développement social et le développement culturel. Un ministre d'État au Développement culturel est nommé (Camille Laurin), à côté du ministère des Affaires culturelles et du ministère des Communications. Cela donne une portée sociale et politique inédite à la culture.

La politique culturelle du gouvernement est présentée dans un *Livre blanc* deux ans plus tard (Ministre d'État au Développement culturel, 1978a; 1978b). La culture ne se réduisant pas à des œuvres de création individuelle ou à des objets de musée, elle est conçue comme un milieu de vie et devient rattachée à l'identité de la collectivité en s'inscrivant dans tous les lieux : langue, éducation, travail, économie, habitat, environnement, loisir, tourisme, communications. L'identité culturelle donne cohérence, selon Camille Laurin, au projet collectif d'appropriation de sa destinée. Le levier majeur de cette politique sera constitué par un glissement sémantique important, de la culture aux industries culturelles. Les industries culturelles sont caractérisées par une symbiose – et par un équilibre à atteindre – entre la reproductibilité industrielle (production sur une grande échelle afin de minimiser les coûts et de maximiser les profits, extension sans limites du nombre d'usages du service), et le contenu correspondant à un mode d'expression personnelle ou collective (identité). Politique, économie et culture ne forment alors qu'une seule et même réalité dans le discours gouvernemental. Une conférence sur les industries culturelles, tenue du 3 au 5 décembre 1978, confirme cette orientation (Secrétariat permanent des conférences socio-économiques, 1979). Le chercheur français François Rouet affirme d'ailleurs que le Québec a été le précurseur de la généralisation d'un soutien public aux industries culturelles (Rouet, 1991).

Autre étape importante, le gouvernement fait adopter, le 22 décembre 1978, la loi constituant la Société de développement des industries de la culture et des communications (SODICC). Il s'agit d'une société d'État qui, par l'octroi de prêts et de garanties de prêt, par une participation au capital-action, se veut une société financière de développement de la culture, des communications et du patrimoine immobilier. Les objectifs poursuivis sont de maximiser la création d'emplois, de hausser les exportations, d'impliquer les institutions financières traditionnelles et d'appliquer à la culture des approches de développement économique habituellement réservées au secteur manufacturier. On souhaite ainsi concentrer l'action du Ministère sur la définition des grandes orientations, régionaliser certaines fonctions et déléguer des fonctions de gestion à des organismes autonomes à caractère représentatif. À partir du début des années 1980, le MAC intervient de moins en moins directement dans les institutions nationales dotées de leur propre loi ou d'un statut de corporation publique avec conseil d'administration (Bibliothèque nationale, musées nationaux, etc.). Il s'agit d'une importante déconcentration administrative.

Ainsi, d'année en année, les organismes d'État ou les sociétés autonomes voient leur nombre augmenter considérablement (Société générale du cinéma, Institut québécois du cinéma, Régie du cinéma, Commission des biens culturels, Société de développement de l'industrie de la culture et des communications, Institut québécois de recherche sur la culture, Musée du Québec, Musée de la civilisation, Musée d'art contemporain, Régie du Grand Théâtre de Québec, Régie de la Place des Arts, Commission de reconnaissance des associations d'artistes, Bibliothèque nationale, Office de radio-diffusion du Québec [Radio-Québec, qui deviendra la Société de télédiffusion du Québec, ou Télé-Québec], etc.). Cette orientation vers la coordination passe par un accroissement des responsabilités horizontales plutôt que verticales.

En 1987, le gouvernement de Robert Bourassa (réélu en 1985) décide, dans un souci de rationalisation et de regroupement des structures gouvernementales, de fusionner la SODICC et la Société générale du cinéma en une seule société d'État, la Société générale des industries culturelles (SOGIC), regroupant ainsi l'ensemble de l'action gouvernementale dans le secteur des industries culturelles. De plus, dans un contexte intense de négociations constitutionnelles (entourant l'accord Meech) et de tentative de redéfinition des rapports politiques entre le Québec et le Canada, le Ministère met l'accent sur les aspects identitaires de sa politique culturelle, dont les objectifs sont de favoriser le développement et le rayonnement de l'identité ainsi que le dynamisme culturel du Québec en arts, lettres, industries culturelles et patrimoine.

Cette combinaison des objectifs économiques (création d'emplois et compétitivité à l'échelle internationale) et identitaires, est particulièrement évidente dans le rapport du Groupe-conseil sur la politique culturelle du Québec, présidé par Roland Arpin (Groupe-conseil sur la politique culturelle du Québec, 1991). Afin de donner suite au Rapport Arpin, le gouvernement Bourassa publie *La politique culturelle du Québec. Notre culture. Notre avenir* (1992), dans lequel il développe trois axes d'une nouvelle politique culturelle : l'affirmation de l'identité culturelle (langue française, héritage culturel et dialogue des cultures); le soutien aux créateurs et aux arts (incluant les industries culturelles); l'accès et la participation des citoyens à la vie culturelle. L'action du Ministère est axée sur les orientations, sur le suivi de la politique et, de plus en plus, sur la coordination des actions. Le Ministère est responsable de la gestion déconcentrée des programmes en matière de patrimoine et d'équipements culturels, et de la gestion des ententes de développement culturel avec les municipalités et les instances régionales. Les directions régionales du Ministère, en collaboration avec les conseils régionaux de la culture (il s'agit de structures de concertation régionale), sont d'ailleurs responsables de la planification de ses activités au niveau régional.

Résultat direct des propositions contenues dans *La politique culturelle du Québec*, le ministère des Affaires culturelles devient, le 1er janvier 1993, le ministère de la Culture et des Communications (MCC), se voyant ainsi octroyer, en plus des secteurs déjà sous sa responsabilité (muséologie, patrimoine culturel et scientifique, arts, lettres, bibliothèques, industries culturelles), de nouvelles attributions : médias, télécommunications, télédistribution, NTIC, inforoutes et francophonie. Dans ce contexte de mondialisation, de diffusion massive des produits américains, de conglomérats du multimédia et de développement technologique accéléré, le Ministère se doit de coordonner une action cohérente dans l'ensemble de ces secteurs de la « nouvelle » économie, laissant aux principaux intervenants la détermination des orientations majeures. Le Ministère exerce aussi une fonction d'harmonisation des activités du gouvernement, des ministères et des organismes publics en matière de culture. L'audiovisuel devient le véhicule moderne de l'identité québécoise, et les industries culturelles deviennent prioritaires dans la stratégie de développement économique du Québec. La politique culturelle, dont l'objectif majeur est de mieux positionner les entreprises québécoises sur les marchés domestique et international, rejoint la politique économique dans le cadre de la stratégie gouvernementale des grappes industrielles.

Le gouvernement du Parti québécois, élu à l'automne 1994, accentue cette fonction ministérielle de coordination de même que l'ancrage de l'identité au sein des industries culturelles. Une école nationale de formation aux métiers du cinéma et de l'audiovisuel est créée (l'Institut national de l'image et du son), et le gouvernement entreprend un vaste programme de développement de l'autoroute de l'information. Il fusionne également la SOGIC, l'Institut québécois du cinéma et certains mandats du MCC en créant la Société de développement des entreprises culturelles (SODEC) le 1er avril 1995 (notons que cette fusion avait été décidée par le précédent gouvernement lors de l'adoption du projet de loi 14, le 17 juin 1994). Elle s'inscrit dans un contexte où le vaste secteur des industries culturelles prend une part grandissante dans l'économie québécoise.

La SODEC est, comme ses prédécesseurs, une société d'État relevant du MCC. Son mandat est de promouvoir et de soutenir, dans toutes les régions du Québec, l'implantation et le développement des entreprises culturelles, y compris les médias. Comme la SOGIC ou la SGC, les choix concernant l'octroi de l'aide financière (en somme les indicateurs de performance) sont basés sur le plan d'affaires, la production, la diffusion et l'exportation des produits culturels ainsi que la compétitivité des produits. Les principes d'intervention auprès des entreprises culturelles sont les suivants : des produits et des services de qualité par des entreprises stables, des actions structurantes, des interventions ciblées en complémentarité avec le Conseil des arts et des lettres du Québec, une gestion simplifiée et l'évaluation constante des retombées économiques. L'approche financière, industrielle et économique est ainsi totalement appliquée à la culture.

Avec ce rôle majeur donné à la SODEC, le MCC concentre véritablement ses énergies sur la coordination des différents organismes et sociétés d'aide implantés. La création du Conseil des arts et des lettres du Québec (CALQ), en 1994, accentue cette tendance. Le CALQ est un organisme relevant du MCC, mais indépendant en ce qui a trait au choix des artistes et des projets financés (en arts visuels, lettres, danse, théâtre, etc.). Le Sommet socioéconomique, convoqué par le premier ministre Lucien Bouchard à l'automne 1996, a confirmé cette orientation de la société québécoise, avec l'appui du gouvernement, vers l'économie de la culture, de l'audiovisuel et du multimédia. Le MCC a ainsi créé, en plus des outils déjà existants, un Fonds d'investissement de la culture et des communications, dans le but d'investir du capital de risque dans les entreprises ayant des projets structurants. L'objectif est bien une production de services et de contenus de qualité en langue française, le développement de l'emploi et la compétitivité des entreprises culturelles. Toutefois, on parle très peu d'identité nationale ou collective dans les documents du MCC publiés après 1995 (si on les compare, notamment, avec ceux des années 1990-1993). Les regards se portent vers l'identité culturelle, le plus souvent appréhendée selon la perspective du développement de l'individu. Ainsi, si la mise en chantier de la Bibliothèque nationale du Québec témoigne d'une volonté d'affirmation de l'identité collective québécoise, les actions du MCC en matière culturelle se portent davantage sur la contribution des arts au développement individuel, comme en témoigne le programme annuel des Journées de la culture.

On peut également noter, parmi l'ensemble des crédits du MCC, une augmentation importante des dépenses de transfert vers les sociétés d'État et autres organismes déconcentrés. La décentralisation vers les instances régionales et les municipalités est également au programme, de même que l'accentuation de partenariats avec le secteur privé, les milieux professionnels et les citoyens (Ministère de la Culture et des Communications, 1999). Sous la direction de Louise Beaudoin puis d'Agnès Maltais, le MCC s'oriente vers la démocratisation de la culture et l'accès aux savoirs, la production de services et de contenus en langue française (industries culturelles et multimédia) et l'adaptation des entreprises aux réalités économiques des années 2000. Le MCC met également l'accent sur l'élaboration de politiques sectorielles (politique du livre, politique des musées).

Indicateurs

Comme nous l'avons vu, la SODEC est un acteur clé de l'environnement culturel québécois. Ses principes d'évaluation des projets, organismes et entreprises financés sont donc d'une importance capitale. Or, l'action de la SODEC vise essentiellement à consolider les entreprises existantes (capitalisation accrue, augmentation des aides automatiques) et à favoriser celles qui sont très performantes sur les marchés intérieurs et internationaux, tout en soutenant les étapes les plus fragiles du processus créatif (en multimédia, notamment) et en encourageant le développement des projets. Les indicateurs de performance retenus par la société d'État sont donc essentiellement économiques, voire même financiers. Par exemple, l'aide apportée à la production d'un film sera essentiellement basée sur une estimation du potentiel commercial de son scénario et sur les recettes aux guichets que son producteur aura accumulées dans le passé. Aucune évaluation n'est effectuée de l'impact du film sur l'identité personnelle, sur la communauté ou sur l'identité québécoise.

En ce qui concerne les statistiques, l'Observatoire de la culture et des communications du Québec (OCCQ, affilié à l'Institut de la statistique du Québec) est l'organisme chargé de la collecte des données et des indicateurs. Le mandat de cet observatoire, créé à la fin des années 1990, est de développer un système intégré de statistiques en ce qui a trait au champ de la culture et des communications, de développer des partenariats avec les milieux artistiques, gouvernementaux et universitaires, et de documenter l'importance de ce secteur au sein de la société québécoise. Adoptant une définition large de ce qui constitue un indicateur (définition inspirée du Conseil des affaires sociales et de la famille), à savoir « des statistiques particulièrement significatives, aptes à résumer l'information, à instruire rapidement de l'état d'un phénomène ou à rendre intelligibles les processus et les changements qui ont cours dans une société donnée » (Observatoire de la culture et des communications du Québec, 2002a: 2), l'Observatoire restreint toutefois de façon importante cette approche, ne retenant que les indicateurs quantitatifs et économiques usuels (effectifs, caractéristiques de la population des artistes, revenus, établissements et infrastructures, consommation, fréquentation, pratiques culturelles, préférences, emploi du temps, dépenses gouvernementales, etc.)[1]. Ces données sont compilées et mises à jour de façon régulière (occq 2003).

L'occq mentionne bien que sa mission est de produire des indicateurs dérivés de l'analyse de statistiques existantes. Il n'y a donc pas d'enquête articulée à une problématique ni d'analyse de contenu des messages et des symboles. Il s'agit d'une mesure de l'offre et de la demande, de la création jusqu'à la consommation des produits et services culturels (voir par exemple occq 2002b).

Une des principales qualités de ces statistiques est leur régularité (et ce, depuis la fin des années 1970) ainsi que leur étendue, tous les domaines étant aujourd'hui concernés: arts visuels, arts médiatiques et métiers d'art, arts de la scène, patrimoine, institutions muséales et archives, livre, périodique, bibliothèques, cinéma et audiovisuel, enregistrement sonore, radio et télévision, multimédia et nouveaux médias, architecture et design, publicité et relations publiques, enseignement des arts, relations interculturelles, langue, organismes de représentation, activités multidisciplinaires et établissements multisectoriels. Les enquêtes sur les pratiques culturelles incluent également l'artisanat pour soi, ce qui témoigne d'un élargissement des indicateurs (Institut de la statistique du Québec, et Observatoire de la culture et des communications du Québec, 2003). Par ailleurs, l'occq développe actuellement, en partenariat avec plusieurs villes québécoises, des indicateurs d'activité et de participation culturelles dans un cadre urbain. Pour l'instant, l'accent est placé sur la consolidation des données de base. Le regroupement Les Arts et la Ville, qui se veut un point de rencontre et une ressource pour les actions des municipalités québécoises en matière culturelle (et qui milite pour une implication active du palier local au sein des politiques culturelles) n'a développé que des indicateurs de base. Ces développements sont toutefois susceptibles d'ouvrir la voie à une prise en compte d'indicateurs autres que strictement économiques. Quant au calq, il diffuse un bulletin électronique (*Constats du CALQ*) ne contenant que des données de base.

Les travaux de Gilles Pronovost confirment cette tendance à mettre l'accent sur les enquêtes descriptives. Le chercheur souligne notamment qu'il n'y pas de mise en relation de la participation culturelle avec d'autres facteurs (famille, école, travail, communauté). Bref, on connaît très peu de choses sur le contexte des pratiques culturelles ainsi que sur leurs impacts sociaux plus larges (Pronovost, 2002).

Les justificatifs économiques de la politique culturelle québécoise sont donc en adéquation avec les indicateurs élaborés tandis que les autres finalités identifiées (identité collective, développement personnel) n'ont pas d'équivalent au niveau des indicateurs, à l'exception peut-être des nouveaux indicateurs élaborés en collaboration avec les municipalités. Comme il y a peu de finalités concernant la contribution des arts à la société en général (revitalisation urbaine, lutte contre l'exclusion, enrichissement des communautés, santé, etc.), il est logique qu'on ne retrouve pas d'indicateurs tentant de mesurer ces effets s'inscrivant dans une conception élargie des impacts culturels.

L'Union européenne

Contexte et justifications de la politique culturelle

Le développement et la consolidation de l'Union européenne et de ses diverses institutions furent historiquement dominés par les questions économiques, juridiques et politiques. Si le Conseil de l'Europe débute la collecte de données statistiques sur les politiques culturelles dès 1985, ce n'est qu'en 1992-1993 que le traité instituant l'Union européenne (Traité de Maastricht) octroie à celle-ci le pouvoir d'intervenir en matière de culture et d'audiovisuel parmi les États membres. On souhaite ainsi, après avoir mis en place les structures appropriées, établir une zone de libre-échange et une union monétaire, et développer une véritable citoyenneté européenne. La culture et les nouveaux moyens de communication seront les principaux animateurs de ce développement et de cette création d'un espace social et culturel commun européen. L'article 128 du Traité (devenu l'article 151 dans le Traité d'Amsterdam de 1997) définit quatre principaux objectifs :

1. Contribuer à l'épanouissement des cultures des États membres dans le respect de leur diversité nationale et régionale tout en soulignant l'héritage commun (notamment l'accès du public au patrimoine européen);
2. Promouvoir la création artistique;
3. Articuler une meilleure prise en compte de la dimension culturelle au sein des autres politiques européennes;
4. Encourager la coopération culturelle entre États membres ainsi qu'entre l'Union européenne et les pays tiers (par exemple, coopération artistique entre professionnels).

Plusieurs programmes ont été créés durant les années 1990 (notamment le programme Capitales et Villes européennes de la Culture, toujours en opération), mais ce n'est véritablement qu'avec le programme *Culture 2000* que la Commission européenne, par le biais de sa Direction générale Éducation et Culture, met en place un dispositif souhaitant répondre aux objectifs visés. Ce programme, en vigueur de 2000 à 2004 (il sera vraisemblablement reconduit pour les années 2005 et 2006), s'est ensuite élargi aux pays candidats à l'adhésion. Trente pays sont ainsi touchés par le programme (les 15 États membres, les 3 pays de l'Espace économique européen et les 12 pays candidats). Le programme a précisé les principaux objectifs préalablement définis en mettant l'accent sur le développement et la mise en valeur d'un espace culturel commun. La culture y est perçue comme un facteur d'intégration sociale et politique (mise en place d'actions emblématiques effectuant la promotion d'un sentiment d'appartenance à une même communauté et à un même espace social européen), et comme un levier de développement socio-économique (emplois, industries culturelles, compétitivité internationale). On recherche donc un bon équilibre entre les aspects économiques (emplois, compétition) et identitaires (culture, développement des communautés) (Reding, 2003b). Il s'agit également d'un équilibre entre mondialisation et diversité culturelle (Reding, 2003a).

Les projets artistiques ayant une dimension européenne sont donc valorisés, et tous les domaines sont concernés. Une attention particulière est portée aux jeunes et aux populations économiquement défavorisées. On met également en avant la mobilité des artistes, la circulation des œuvres, les échanges interculturels, le multilinguisme et le multiculturalisme. Les niveaux régionaux et locaux sont aussi favorisés, notamment par le biais des sommes allouées à la culture dans les Fonds structurels pour le développement régional.

Un autre postulat général sous-tend toute la politique culturelle européenne au début du XXIe siècle : la responsabilité des enjeux culturels est et doit être de plus en plus partagée entre les secteurs public, privé et de la société civile fonctionnant en réseaux. On propose ainsi le concept de *creative governance* (European Institute for Comparative Cultural Research, 2003). La philosophie préconisée n'exige pas l'abandon de l'intervention étatique traditionnelle, mais son redéploiement en partenariat avec d'autres acteurs régionaux et locaux. Dans une étude portant sur neuf États européens, Dorota Ilcuzk (2001) conclut que la politique culturelle est de plus en plus marquée par la participation des citoyens. Les États délaissent la gestion directe de la culture sans toutefois diminuer les fonds publics alloués. Elle observe une affirmation croissante du tiers secteur (ensemble d'associations, de fondations, d'églises, de syndicats, à but non lucratif), un desserrement des relations traditionnelles entre les institutions publiques et l'État, l'importance croissante des niveaux régional et local et une mise à distance de l'approche élitiste, ce qui signifie pour les citoyens une habilitation (*empowerment*) et une démocratisation des modes de gestion.

Indicateurs

Les évaluations effectuées jusqu'à maintenant ont principalement porté sur les indicateurs de base. L'European Institute for Comparative Cultural Research (ERICarts) a ainsi réalisé une vaste enquête empirique et conceptuelle à l'échelle européenne (European Institute for Comparative Cultural Research, 2003). ERICarts a de plus développé et met à jour régulièrement un vaste index statistique et qualitatif qui examine l'historique, les politiques, les institutions, les compétences, l'administration, le financement, les objectifs, les enjeux récents et l'environnement légal des politiques culturelles au sein des pays européens (*Cultural Policies in Europe: A Compendium of Basic Facts and Trends*). Une évaluation de l'impact de *Culture 2000* est en cours de réalisation, et les résultats seront diffusés en 2004. En août 2003, la Commission européenne a annoncé qu'elle réalisera dans le courant de l'année 2004, une vaste étude dressant l'inventaire des meilleures pratiques liant la culture et l'éducation formelle, non-formelle et informelle en Europe. La Commission européenne envisage également la création d'un Observatoire européen de la coopération culturelle.

Il ne fait aucun doute que les indicateurs qui seront privilégiés seront non seulement d'ordre économique, mais intégreront aussi des aspects plus larges liés à l'impact de la culture sur les sociétés et sur les communautés. La Commission européenne souligne ainsi que la régulation étatique, les politiques et les programmes soutenant la créativité artistique seront considérés comme des succès s'ils garantissent que des idées et produits innovants sont produits et diffusés (aspect économique) et contribuent aux cultures locales et régionales (impacts sociaux). Pour ce faire, de nouveaux critères (indicateurs) et un nouveau système d'information seront bientôt élaborés, le défi étant d'établir des indicateurs relativement standardisés concernant la qualité de vie des individus et des communautés. Le European Task Force on Culture and Development (1997) mentionne l'importance d'une prise en compte des impacts sociaux de la culture, tels que le développement individuel, le développement communautaire, la capacité d'innovation, etc.

Une résolution sur la coopération culturelle en Europe, adoptée en septembre 2001 (appelée « Rapport Ruffolo »), prévoit un renforcement de l'espace culturel européen par un rôle accru joué par la culture dans la diversité et la cohésion sociales. Il s'agit de faire de la culture une des clés de voûte de la construction et de l'élargissement de l'Europe politique et économique. Cette résolution demande à la Commission de présenter annuellement un rapport sur la politique culturelle européenne et sur les politiques des États au Parlement, et recommande la création d'un Observatoire européen des politiques culturelles afin de standardiser les statistiques et développer des indicateurs.

Le Royaume-Uni

Contexte et justifications de la politique culturelle

L'implication britannique dans le domaine culturel débute dans les années 1940, alors que les arts commencent à être perçus, dans le contexte de la Deuxième Guerre mondiale, comme des instruments favorisant l'épanouissement d'une société libre et démocratique. Le gouvernement crée alors le Council for the Encouragement of Music and the Arts (CEMA), sous le leadership de John Meynard Keynes. Ce conseil est renommé Arts Council of Great Britain (ACGB) en 1946, devenant l'une des premières agences étatiques du monde à distribuer des fonds aux artistes « à distance » des pressions politiques (le célèbre principe du *arm's-length*). En 1948, le gouvernement donne aux villes le droit légal de s'impliquer dans les arts. La responsabilité du Arts Council passe, en 1965, du Treasury au Department for Education and Science, et un ministre responsable des arts est nommé. Une première politique culturelle est adoptée qui hausse de façon significative les fonds alloués au Arts Council. Comme dans plusieurs pays occidentaux, les années 1970 sont marquées par un débat concernant la définition de la culture; on reproche de plus en plus au Arts Council de ne financer que les artistes et institutions correspondant à une approche « élitiste » de la culture. Le Arts Council ferme également ses bureaux régionaux, et des associations régionales se développent.

Durant les années 1980, dans le contexte des vastes compressions budgétaires découlant des politiques néolibérales du gouvernement Thatcher, on reconnaît la nécessité de trouver de nouvelles sources de financement. On met l'accent sur le « marketing » des œuvres et des artistes et on souligne les impacts économiques de la culture. Un Department of National Heritage est créé en 1992; une loterie nationale est mise en place dans les années 1990 qui finance d'abord des projets liés aux infrastructures et aux équipements (par exemple les musées), puis, de plus en plus, des projets plus locaux et communautaires. Le nouveau gouvernement travailliste de Tony Blair crée en 1997 le Department for Culture, Media and Sport (DCMS) avec une augmentation du financement. Le principe du *arm's-length* est toujours respecté, le DCMS fournissant le financement à une panoplie de *Non-Departmental Public Bodies* (organismes publics non ministériels, l'équivalent de nos sociétés d'État et diverses commissions) qui répartissent les fonds et sont responsables de la sélection des projets. En 2002, le Arts Council se réunit de nouveau avec les associations régionales, formant ainsi une structure unique, mais fortement décentralisée. Notons que les autorités municipales ont également l'obligation de développer des politiques culturelles.

Aujourd'hui, la politique culturelle a deux objectifs globaux (DCMS, 2001a) : contribuer au développement économique et améliorer la qualité de vie des individus et des communautés. Le gouvernement britannique met ainsi l'accent sur les impacts économiques (création d'un marché culturel efficient et compétitif, développement des industries culturelles, promotion de la culture britannique à l'étranger, tourisme culturel), sociaux (contribution de la culture à la revitalisation urbaine et rurale ainsi qu'à la lutte contre l'exclusion) et éducatifs (amélioration de l'accès aux arts pour tous, développement de la formation et de l'éducation aux arts afin d'avoir une main-d'œuvre compétente au sein des industries culturelles et du tourisme). Le gouvernement reconnaît ainsi que la culture joue un rôle important dans les objectifs plus globaux de promotion de l'inclusion sociale et de revitalisation urbaine. Selon le plan pour les années 2003-2006 du Arts Council, la culture a une influence majeure sur l'identité des communautés, sur l'amélioration de la santé et sur la lutte contre le crime. Le gouvernement entend de la sorte faire de la publicité sur le pouvoir transformateur des arts dans la vie des individus et des communautés.

Les autres justifications sociales apportées au financement des programmes culturels publics (financement qui a constamment augmenté sous le gouvernement travailliste depuis 1997) sont les suivantes : promotion de l'égalité raciale et préoccupation envers les minorités culturelles (programme *Decibel – Raising the Voice of Culturally Diverse Arts in Britain* du Arts Council England, création du National Cultural Diversity Network pour les musées, librairies et archives, accent sur les festivals et sur les pièces de théâtre luttant contre le racisme), promotion de l'égalité des sexes et préoccupation envers les représentations de la femme, promotion de la diversité linguistique (le Royaume-Uni a signé le *Charter for Regional or Minority Languages* du Conseil de l'Europe), promotion de l'implication des jeunes (National Advisory Committee on Creative and Cultural Education, 2000), contribution du patrimoine à la qualité de vie, à l'emploi, à la régénération des villes et des campagnes et à la communauté (DCMS, 2001b). Les nouvelles technologies sont également mises en avant (programme Culture Online) dans un souci tant économique que social et éducatif.

Tout cela se fait dans le contexte d'un meilleur dialogue entre Londres et les autorités régionales et locales (prenant la forme de partenariats) et dans le cadre d'une décentralisation des arts vers l'Écosse, le Pays de Galles et l'Irlande du Nord. Les partenariats public-privé sont également encouragés. Le gouvernement reconnaît le rôle joué par le bénévolat et par les arts amateurs dans le développement des communautés locales (création d'un Voluntary Arts Network qui soutient différents projets). On met donc de plus en plus l'accent sur des projets se situant au niveau local et qui impliquent la société civile, le secteur privé, la ville, les structures régionales et le gouvernement britannique (Landry *et al.*, 1996).

Indicateurs

En accord avec les justifications de la politique culturelle, les indicateurs de performance élaborés par le gouvernement britannique (en l'occurrence le DCMS assisté du Quality, Efficiency and Standards Team [QUEST] ainsi que du Arts Council England) sont de deux types : économiques et sociaux. L'évaluation de l'impact économique est présentée régulièrement dans *Creative Industries Mapping Document* (2001c) ainsi que dans *Arts in England* (2002). On y retrouve des données de base traditionnelles (production, consommation, fréquentation, etc.) de même qu'un ensemble d'indicateurs traduisant une conception élargie de la culture (participation aux carnavals, festivals culturels, arts de la rue, cirque, pantomime, tous types de performance de danse, performances vidéo et arts électroniques). On évalue également, dans un souci de préoccupation à propos des impacts sociaux, la façon dont les gens perçoivent le rôle des arts dans leur vie (leurs attitudes et opinions), de même que l'implication d'individus appartenant aux communautés ethniques et de jeunes à partir de six ans. Les autorités locales sont impliquées (voir l'évaluation de la National Policy for Theatre in England en 2002) et une aide est apportée aux organismes culturels pour développer l'autoévaluation. Le gouvernement évalue, au moyen d'analyses ciblées et selon des méthodes tant qualitatives que quantitatives, l'apport des arts dans la lutte contre l'exclusion sociale (Carpenter, 1999; Jermyn, 2001). On examine de la sorte comment la culture développe chez les individus la confiance en soi ainsi que le potentiel, encourage les efforts collectifs et le renforcement de l'identité locale, construit des liens interpersonnels positifs et fournit des atouts pour se trouver un emploi. Le DCMS entend à l'avenir mettre l'accent sur ces indicateurs sociaux (DCMS, 2003).

Le Arts Council effectue également beaucoup de recherche concernant le développement d'indicateurs sociaux (2000, 2003). Dès 1993, il finançait Comedia (une organisation britannique spécialisée dans la recherche sur les politiques culturelles) afin d'évaluer, à partir d'une série d'études de cas, l'impact social des arts. Les résultats furent présentés en 1997 dans *Use or Ornament?* (Matarasso 1997). Ce document établit un cadre méthodologique pour l'examen des impacts sociaux et fournit des instruments d'évaluation précis. La publication de ce document a coïncidé avec l'élection du gouvernement travailliste qui avait pour volonté, d'une part, d'inclure la culture dans sa stratégie de revitalisation des villes et de lutte contre l'exclusion et, d'autre part, de rendre la fonction publique et les structures gouvernementales plus efficientes et imputables. De plus, comme nous l'avons souligné plus haut, des changements sont survenus dans le financement provenant de la loterie nationale, les subventions s'éloignant des vastes projets liés aux équipements culturels pour s'orienter vers de petits projets animés par des associations et organismes locaux. Afin d'attirer le plus de financement possible, ces organismes ont ainsi reçu un incitatif puissant pour développer des indicateurs soulignant les différents impacts sociaux de leurs projets.

De nombreuses autres recherches se sont également intéressées à l'impact social de la culture. Selon Landry *et al.* (1993) et Lingayah *et al.* (1997), s'intéresser à l'impact social implique d'examiner l'ensemble des effets (ou résultats) qui vont au-delà de la production de produits ou d'événements culturels et qui ont une influence sur les individus et la communauté en général. On distingue de la sorte les *outputs* (le produit ou l'événement) des *outcomes* (les conséquences sociales de la production du produit ou de l'événement). Landry *et al.* (1996), Matarasso (1996, 1997), Moriarty (1998), Shaw (2000), Kelly et Kelly (2000), Blake Stevenson Limited (2000) et Jermyn (2001) se sont tous penchés sur le développement d'indicateurs sociaux. Par exemple, Landry *et al.*, (1996), ont examiné quinze études de cas portant sur les liens entre les arts et les programmes de régénération urbaine, la cohésion sociale et l'identité locale.

Matarasso (1997) a analysé les impacts sociaux de plusieurs projets culturels au sein de nombreuses villes britanniques en se basant sur six thèmes généraux : développement personnel, cohésion sociale, développement et habilitation (*empowerment*) communautaire, identité et image locale, imagination et vision, santé et bien-être. Il a ainsi élaboré une liste de cinquante impacts sociaux, présentés dans le tableau 1. Cette liste peut ainsi constituer une base pour le développement d'indicateurs.

Matarasso soutient que la culture peut être évaluée selon de nombreux indicateurs: développement de la confiance en soi et de diverses compétences personnelles (planification, accomplissement d'un projet, etc.), amélioration de la communication d'idées et d'information, développement du potentiel éducatif, création de capital social (réciprocité, coopération civique, confiance mutuelle au sein de réseaux, développement des capacités d'action collective [Putnam 2000], renforcement des communautés, développement d'une identité collective, locale et nationale), diminution de l'exclusion sociale, amélioration de la compréhension de cultures différentes, amélioration de la

Tableau 1 - Indicateurs selon Matarasso (1997)

- Increase people's confidence and sense of self-worth
- Extend involvement in social activity
- Give people influence over how they are seen by others
- Stimulate interest and confidence in the arts
- Provide a forum to explore personal rights and responsibilities
- Contribute to the educational development of children
- Encourage adults to take up education and training opportunities
- Help build new skills and work experience
- Contribute to people's employability
- Help people take up or develop careers in the arts
- Reduce isolation by helping people to make friends
- Develop community networks and sociability
- Promote tolerance and contribute to conflict resolution
- Provide a forum for intercultural understanding and friendship
- Help validate the contribution of a whole community
- Promote intercultural contact and cooperation
- Develop contact between the generations
- Help offenders and victims address issues of crime
- Provide a route to rehabilitation and integration for offenders
- Build community organizational capacity
- Encourage local self-reliance and project management
- Help people extend control over their lives
- Be a means of gaining insight into political and social ideas
- Facilitate effective public consultation and participation
- Help involve local people in the regeneration process

- Facilitate the development of partnership
- Build support for community projects
- Strengthen community cooperation and networking
- Develop pride in local traditions and cultures
- Help people feel a sense of belonging and involvement
- Create community traditions in new towns or neighbourhoods
- Involve residents in environmental improvements
- Provide reasons for people to develop community activities
- Improve perceptions of marginalised groups
- Help transform the image of public bodies
- Make people feel better about where they live
- Help people develop their creativity
- Erode the distinction between consumer and creator
- Allow people to explore their values, meanings and dreams
- Enrich the practice of professionals in the public and voluntary sectors
- Transform the responsiveness of public service organizations
- Encourage people to accept risk positively
- Help community groups raise their vision beyond the immediate
- Challenge conventional service delivery
- Raise expectations about what is possible and desirable
- Have a positive impact on how people feel
- Be an effective means of health education
- Contribute to a more relaxed atmosphere in health centres
- Help improve the quality of life of people with poor health
- Provide a unique and deep source of enjoyment

cohésion sociale et réduction des tensions et crimes, activation du changement social, augmentation de l'attention du public à certains enjeux socio-politiques, amélioration de la santé mentale et physique ainsi que du bien-être, contribution à la revitalisation urbaine.

François Matarasso a également développé, dans l'optique d'évaluer les impacts de la culture au niveau local, trois grands types d'impacts avec les indicateurs correspondants (1999). Il présente d'abord les indicateurs liés aux *inputs* avec des données de base (nombre d'établissements culturels, d'organisations et d'artistes, dépenses pour la culture des différents paliers de gouvernement, politiques culturelles nationales, régionales et locales). Il développe ensuite des indicateurs liés aux *outputs* comme les impacts d'activité, d'accès et de participation (nombre de performances et d'événements, fréquentation, étendue de la participation), la diversité de l'offre culturelle et l'implication des minorités ethniques, l'éducation et la formation, l'impact économique (emplois, multiplicateur, etc.). Il présente enfin des indicateurs plus larges d'*outcomes* comme le développement personnel (confiance en soi, vie sociale plus active, identité personnelle, capacité de gérer des projets, meilleure santé physique et mentale) et le développement communautaire (contacts intergénérationnels et interculturels, coopération, réduction du crime, capacité de changement, identité collective, amélioration de l'environnement urbain, volontariat et bénévolat).

Kelly et Kelly (2000) ont développé un questionnaire dont l'information recueillie est liée à treize secteurs. Le tableau 2 montre les indicateurs retenus. On y retrouve des indicateurs économiques traditionnels (indicateurs 1 à 7) et d'autres mesurant les impacts sociaux (indicateurs 8 à 12).

Une autre recherche évaluant les actions du Belgrade Theatre fut effectuée par le Arts Council en collaboration avec le West Midlands Arts, Comedia et la New Economics Foundation. Les relations entre le théâtre et les arts, la communauté, la ville et d'autres types d'organisation furent examinées à l'aide d'indicateurs combinant les aspects économiques, sociaux et culturels (Matarasso et Pilling, 1999).

La New Economics Foundation a également développé des indicateurs sociaux liés au capital humain (confiance en soi, estime de soi, attitudes face au milieu de vie, acquisition d'habilités et de connaissances, implication) et au capital social (réciprocité, participation au sein d'organismes communautaires, réseaux, projets élaborés et réalisés en commun, partenariats) (Walker *et al.*, 2000). Ce que Putnam (2000) appelle le capital social, c'est-à-dire les composantes de la vie sociale qui permettent à des citoyens d'agir ensemble plus efficacement dans la poursuite d'objectifs collectifs, constitue un élément particulièrement important de ces indicateurs sociaux.

La firme Annabel Jackson Associates a quant à elle procédé à une évaluation de l'impact social des Millennium Awards (2000). Quatre zones d'impact furent identifiées et des indicateurs appropriés furent développés. Le tableau 3 présente le schéma d'évaluation.

Pour sa part, Jermyn (2001) a développé un cadre d'évaluation afin d'analyser dix-huit projets culturels. Elle a identifié quatre grandes catégories et des indicateurs correspondants, présentés dans le tableau 4.

Notons enfin que la plupart des méthodes adoptent une approche composite combinant des données quantitatives et qualitatives recueillies dans le cadre de sondages, d'entretiens, d'études de cas, de *focus groups*, d'observation participante et d'autoévaluation. Le développement d'indicateurs visant à aller au-delà des aspects économiques et le respect des principes fondamentaux de la gouvernance nécessitent l'association d'approches quantitatives et qualitatives et, à partir d'un schéma d'entretien élaboré avec les citoyens, de laisser émerger le point de vue des intervenants.

Tableau 2 - Indicateurs selon Kelly et Kelly (2000)

Impact	Indicateurs
1. Organization	Art form and activities, amenities provision and opening hours.
2. Income	Contributed income – grants, lottery awards, donations, sponsorship, earned income admissions, sales, fees, membership, room hire, café/bar, bookshop, interest.
3. Outgoing	Staff costs – wages, travel, training, running costs, marketing, fund-raising, VAT, National Insurance and PAYE, local trade as percentage of turnover.
4. Capital Improvements	Income and expenditure.
5. Attendances and performances	Total number of audience opportunities (for example, performances, cinema screenings) in city/town, region, nationally and internationally, number of admissions/attendees (paid full, concessions, free, Web site and hits).
6. Staffing	Paid, full- and part-time staff and volunteers, mix of artistic, marketing and technical staff, board.
7. Current and Future Plans and Challenges	Facilities development
8. Cultural Benefits and Impact	Work which took place which otherwise wouldn't have reached the area, new work created, role of organization in promotion of a positive image for city/town, contribution to tourism.
9. Social Capital	Contribution to the communication of ideas, information and values, helping improve participant's skills in planning and organising, improving understanding of different cultures and lifestyles, improving the understanding of the role of arts and culture in the community, partnership building, active membership of staff/board in other organizations and artistic collaboration with others.
10. Building and developing Communities	Contribution to developing sense of community identity, social cohesion, recreational opportunities, development of local enterprise, improvement of public facilities and amenities, and help to convey history and heritage of an area.
11. Social Change and Public Awareness	Contribution made to stimulating and developing public awareness of important issues and changing people's attitudes on political, ethnical, religious or moral issues.
12. Human Capital	Contribution to improving participant's human and communication skills, analytical and problem-solving skills, creative talents, and social awareness.

Discussion : portée et limites de l'élargissement des indicateurs de performance

Tentons maintenant de prendre un certain recul en identifiant de façon plus générale la portée et les limites d'une conception élargie des indicateurs culturels. Il s'agit de considérer les principaux défis qui se posent au développement et à la collecte de ces indicateurs.

Le premier défi consiste à atteindre un juste équilibre dans la combinaison d'approches quantitatives et qualitatives. S'il est important d'élaborer des indicateurs plus qualitatifs, il ne faut pas évacuer pour autant la production d'indicateurs quantitatifs.

Ensuite, il est peut être particulièrement difficile de quantifier des impacts sociaux qui ne manifestent souvent leurs effets que sur le long terme (Galloway, 1995). D'ailleurs, comment peut-on bien identifier et différencier les impacts sociaux à court, moyen et

Tableau 3 - Indicateurs selon Annabel Jackson Associates (2000)

IMPACTS	INDICATEURS
Develop Personal Skills	• Confidence • Motivation • Team working • Leadership • Communication and public speaking • Negotiation skills • Literacy/numeracy • Other skills
Develop Personal Knowledge	• Environment • Health • Social issues • Community
Develop Personal Practical Experience	• Making something • How to engage the community • Research • Arts and sport • Teaching or training others • Caring, therapy • Computing • Managing projects • Business planning • Fund raising • Media and publicity
Community Impacts	• Raised awareness of an issue • Provided new service or facility • Improved the quality of life • Improved the environment • Reduced isolation/enabled networking • Increased local pride • Strengthened links within the community • Increased understanding of local history

Tableau 4 - Indicateurs selon Jermyn (2001)

IMPACTS	INDICATEURS
Impacts directs	• Amélioration de la santé et de l'éducation • Réduction du crime • Meilleurs taux d'emplois
Capital humain	• Confiance en soi et estime de soi • Acquisition de compétences • Perspectives d'avenir
Impacts collectifs	• Contacts sociaux • Tolérance • Travail d'équipe • Liens interpersonnels
Impacts civiques	• Implication communautaire • Identité communautaire • Démocratie locale • Communauté active

long terme? Il n'est pas non plus aisé d'élaborer des indicateurs pour des concepts aussi larges et complexes que l'identité, la communauté, le capital social, etc. À cet égard, il manque encore de données solides et il est impératif de multiplier les études de cas afin de dégager des indicateurs pertinents (Arts Council of England, 2003).

Il est aussi très important de distinguer spécifiquement les impacts qui relèvent de l'action culturelle. Autrement dit, l'impact social qui est identifié est-il seulement lié aux arts ou bien à d'autres facteurs jouant également? Il existe à cet égard un risque de simplification consistant à établir un lien de cause à effet entre une activité culturelle et un impact social plus large.

De plus, malgré les progrès importants enregistrés en Angleterre, il n'existe toujours pas de consensus dans le secteur culturel concernant le développement d'indicateurs communs élargis de performance, compte tenu de la diversité des programmes, du financement et des projets soutenus. Il semble particulièrement difficile d'effectuer des généralisations à partir d'études de cas parfois difficilement comparables. Il importe à cet égard d'élaborer des questions standardisées afin d'obtenir des comparaisons systématiques tout en respectant les spécificités et les variations locales.

Du côté des organisations et des artistes, Matarasso (1996), Moriarty (1998), Shaw (2000) et Jermyn (2001) ont tous souligné que les artistes et les gestionnaires de la culture ne considèrent que rarement l'évaluation et le *monitoring* comme des éléments à part entière de leur travail créatif. L'évaluation des impacts économiques, sociaux et culturels est ainsi perçue comme une tâche supplémentaire et secondaire. De plus, la réalisation d'une bonne évaluation nécessite du temps et des ressources que ne possèdent pas les artistes et les organismes. La mesure de la performance s'effectue également selon des critères définis par les gouvernements (donc financiers), n'incitant pas les organismes à évaluer l'impact de leurs activités sur la communauté. Les gouvernements doivent reconnaître que les citoyens, les gestionnaires de programmes et les artistes ne sont pas seulement des sujets des enquêtes mais des partenaires dans la création et dans l'implantation d'études d'évaluation. Ces individus doivent toutefois développer le réflexe et les outils nécessaires à la collecte des données sur leurs connaissances et sur leurs expériences de façon systématique. Pour ce faire, les gouvernements doivent fournir les ressources et l'expertise nécessaires à l'articulation cohérente et systématique de la collecte de données liées à des indicateurs précis.[2]

On constate aussi la peur que l'évaluation réduise abusivement la complexité de l'acte artistique. Certains artistes sont inquiets de ce qu'une évaluation des impacts économiques et sociaux des arts ne ramène la culture à un moyen utilisé à d'autres fins et ne constitue pas une fin en soi. Il y a alors un risque de dévaluation globale de la culture. Bref, les mesures ne doivent pas remplacer la foi que l'on peut avoir dans l'importance de la culture.

Conclusion

Cette étude a examiné les relations qui s'établissent entre les justificatifs des politiques culturelles et les indicateurs de performance utilisés dans l'évaluation de ces mêmes politiques. On a vu que le Québec est marqué par une dichotomie importante entre ces deux éléments, les finalités de l'action publique en matière culturelle étant légitimées par les impératifs économiques, identitaires et de développement personnel, tandis que les indicateurs relèvent des catégories économiques de base. Il y a toutefois un mouvement allant vers une reconnaissance accrue de l'importance de la culture (notamment en dehors des équipements culturels), comme en témoignent les tentatives d'élaboration de partenariats culturels entre le gouvernement et les villes. L'implication grandissante des municipalités québécoises au sein du secteur culturel ne peut que favoriser l'émergence d'une conception élargie des impacts de la culture sur la société. Toutefois, on ne perçoit pas encore la culture comme un outil pouvant contribuer à l'amélioration de la communauté, de l'éducation, de la santé et des services sociaux. En conséquence, aucun indicateur n'aborde ces aspects pourtant de plus en plus importants.

L'Union européenne et surtout le Royaume-Uni présentent une meilleure adéquation entre justificatifs et indicateurs. Les finalités sont nombreuses, abordant les logiques de développement économique, de développement social, de développement personnel, d'identité communautaire, de revitalisation des villes, etc. Les indicateurs élaborés, combinant des approches quantitatives et qualitatives (études de cas, entretiens semi-dirigés, etc.) tentent également de mesurer l'impact de la culture dans ces secteurs. Il faut toutefois préciser que de nombreuses recherches sont effectuées au sein du secteur non gouvernemental ou d'organismes tels que les conseils des arts, liés aux gouvernements, mais agissant de façon indépendante. Il est alors important d'examiner jusqu'à quel point les gouvernements eux-mêmes se servent d'indicateurs élargis dans l'évaluation de leurs politiques. Des recherches plus approfondies devraient être effectuées dans ce sens.

Toutefois, la documentation et nos connaissances sur l'impact social des arts sont très récentes et n'ont commencé à émerger que durant les dernières années. Il est à cet égard primordial de réaliser des études de cas, notamment au Québec et au Canada, où il existe une lacune certaine à ce sujet. Il faudrait également examiner les études provenant d'autres pays, notamment des États-Unis (voir les travaux de Jackson et Herranz Jr., du Urban Institute, 2002) et d'Australie (Williams 1996, 1997), qui semblent particulièrement actifs dans ce domaine.

La France pourrait également constituer un terrain d'investigation privilégié car, malgré le fait qu'au niveau national les indicateurs soient principalement liés à des caractéristiques traditionnelles de base (Donnat, 2003), il existe de plus en plus d'études ciblées ayant tendance à concevoir de façon élargie les impacts de la culture sur les communautés. De plus, le processus de décentralisation entamé en France au début des années 1980 a placé le niveau local dans une position de force et a légitimé son intervention dans les secteurs traditionnellement réservés au palier national, notamment la culture. Les études sur les politiques culturelles locales sont d'ailleurs foisonnantes en France (voir, entre autres : Dubois, 1996; Saez, 1985; David et Dubois, 1996; Poirrier, 1996, 1997; Taliano-des Garets, 1996; Urfalino, 1996; Pourcher, 1995). Ces développements ouvrent la voie à une conception élargie de l'impact de la culture sur les communautés.

Ainsi, après avoir adopté une conception plus large de la participation culturelle, les gouvernements doivent maintenant se tourner vers une approche élargie de l'impact de la culture dans la société. Les indicateurs de performance traditionnels doivent coexister avec des indicateurs culturels d'un genre nouveau. Cela permettrait non seulement aux gouvernements de légitimer davantage des investissements importants dans le secteur culturel, dorénavant conçu à la fois comme fin en soi et comme outil de réalisation d'autres politiques publiques (politiques sociales, identitaires, de santé, etc.), mais aussi de montrer, dans un contexte idéal de gouvernance partagée, la contribution des arts à la création d'une citoyenneté culturelle (par l'engagement civique et communautaire et le capital social qu'ils impliquent) et au renforcement des communautés (par la création d'un espace social et identitaire commun dans le respect de la diversité).

Notes

[1] Un entretien effectué avec M. Bernier, directeur de l'occq (4 novembre 2003), a confirmé ces orientations.

[2] Pour plus de renseignements sur l'évaluation participative, on consultera Whyte (1991) et Fetterman (2000).

Bibliographie

Arts Council of England (1993), *The Social Impact of the Arts.*

Arts Council of England (2000), *Addressing Social Exclusion : A Framework for Action.*

Arts Council of England (2003), *Measuring the Economic and Social Impact of the Arts : A Review.*

Blake Stevenson Limited (2000), *The Role of the Arts in Regeneration*, Edinburgh, Scottish Executive Central Research Unit.

Bonet, L., et E. Négrier (2002), « L'observation culturelle face à la globalisation, Quelles sources d'information pour évaluer quels objectifs de politique culturelle? » *Actes du colloque international sur les statistiques culturelles*, Montréal, unesco et Institut de la statistique du Québec, 21-23 octobre.

Carpenter, E. (1999), *The Arts and Inclusion, Evaluation of London Arts Board's 1998/1999 Regional Challenge Programme.*

Comedia (2000), *Cultural Indicators, A Preliminary Review of Issues Raised by Current Approaches.*

David, M. et V. Dubois (1996), *Les collectivités territoriales vers une politique de relations culturelles internationales*, Grenoble, Observatoire des politiques culturelles.

Department of Culture, Media and Sport (dcms) (2001), *Culture and Creativity — the next ten years.*

dcms (2001), *The Historic Environment : A Force for our Future.*

DCMS (2001), *Creative Industries Mapping Document*.

DCMS (2002a), *Arts in England*.

DCMS et English Regional Cultural Consortia (2002b), *Regional Cultural Data Framework : A User's Guide for Researchers and Policymakers*.

DCMS (2003), A *Research Strategy for DCMS 2003-2005/06*.

Donnat, O. (2003), *Regards croisés sur les pratiques culturelles*. Paris, La Documentation française.

Dubois, V. (1996), *Institutions et politiques culturelles locales : éléments pour une recherche socio-historique*, Paris, Comité d'histoire du ministère de la Culture et La Documentation française.

European Institute for Comparative Cultural Research (2003), *Creative Europe Report on Governance and Management of Artistic Creativity in Europe*.

European Task Force on Culture and Development (1997), *In From The Margins : A Contribution to the Debate on Culture and Development in Europe*. (Groupe de travail européen sur la culture et le développement. 1998. La culture au cœur. Contribution au débat sur la culture et le développement en Europe). Strasbourg, Conseil de l'Europe.

Fetterman, D.M. (2000), *Foundations of Empowerment Evaluation*, Thousand Oaks, Sage Publications.

Galloway, S. (1995), *Changing Lives : The Social Impact of the Arts*, Edinburgh, The Scottish Arts Council.

Gouvernement du Québec (1992), *La politique culturelle du Québec. Notre culture. Notre avenir*.

Groupe-conseil sur la politique culturelle du Québec (1991), *Une politique de la culture et des arts*.

Ilcuzk, D. (2001), *Cultural Citizenship. Civil Society and Cultural Policy in Europe*. Amsterdam, Boekmanstudies.

Institut de la statistique du Québec et Observatoire de la culture et des communications du Québec (2003), *Enquête sur les dépenses de l'Administration publique québécoise au titre de la culture*.

Jermyn, H. (2001), *The Arts and Social Exclusion : A Review for the Arts Council of England*.

Jackson, M.-R. et J. Herranz Jr. (2002), *Culture Counts in Communities. A Framework for Measurement*, The Urban Institute.

Kelly, A. et M. Kelly (2000), *Impact and Values. Assessing the Arts and Creative Industries in the South West*, Bristol, Bristol Cultural Development Partnership.

Landry, C. et F. Bianchini, M. Maguire, et K. Worpole (1993), *The Social Impact of the Arts. A Discussion Document*. Stroud, Comedia.

Landry, L. et L. Greene, F. Matarasso, et F. Bianchini (1996), *The Art of Regeneration, Urban renewal Through Cultural Activity*. Stroud, Comedia.

Lingayah, S., A. McGillivray, et P. Raynard (1997), *Creative Accounting : Beyond the Bottom Line. The Social Impact of the Arts*. Working Paper 2, New Economics Foundation. Stroud, Comedia.

Matarasso, F. (1996), *Defining Values. Evaluating Arts Programmes. The Social Impact of the Arts*. Working Paper 1. Stroud, Comedia.

Matarasso, F. (1997), *Use or Ornament? The Social Impact of Participation in the Arts*. Stroud, Comedia.

Matarasso, F. (1999), *Towards a Local Culture Index. Measuring the Cultural Vitality of Communities*. Stroud, Comedia.

Matarasso, F. et A. Pilling (1999), *The Belgrade Theatre, A first Social Audit 1998–99*, Study supported by The Arts Council of England. Stroud, Comedia.

Ministère de la Culture et des Communications (Québec) (1999), *De la démocratisation de la culture à la démocratie culturelle. Rapport d'étude*. Direction de l'action stratégique, de la recherche et de la statistique.

Ministre d'État au Développement culturel (Québec) (1978), *La politique québécoise du développement culturel. Volume 1. Perspectives d'ensemble : de quelle culture s'agit-il?*, Québec, Éditeur officiel.

Ministre d'État au Développement culturel (Québec) (1978), *La politique québécoise du développement culturel. Volume 2. Les trois dimensions d'une politique : genres de vie, création, éducation*, Québec, Éditeur officiel.

Moriarty, G. (1998), *Social Impact Monitoring Study. Final Report*. Bolton City Challenge and the Arts Unit, Education and Culture Department, Bolton, Bolton Metropolitan Borough Council.

National Advisory Committee on Creative and Cultural Education (2000), *All Our Futures : Creativity, Culture and Education*.

Observatoire de la culture et des communications du Québec (occq) (2002), *Modèle de construction d'indicateurs d'activités culturelles*, Sherbrooke, Colloque « Les arts et la ville », 10 octobre 2002.

occq (2002), *Rapport d'enquête sur 32 festivals et événements culturels du Québec, 2000-2001.*

occq (2003), *Statistiques principales de la culture et des communications au Québec. Édition 2003.*

Poirier, C. (2004), *Le cinéma québécois. À la recherche d'une identité? Tome 2. Les politiques cinématographiques*, Québec, Presses de l'Université du Québec, à paraître.

Poirrier, P. (1996), « Changements de paradigmes dans les politiques culturelles des villes : de la démocratisation culturelle à l'image des villes », Hermès, 20.

Poirrier, P. (1997), « L'histoire des politiques culturelles des villes ». *Vingtième siècle. Revue d'histoire.* 53, 129-146.

Pourcher, Y. (1995), « La culture peut-elle former un territoire? L'exemple du Languedoc-Roussillon », *Pouvoirs locaux*, 24.

Pronovost, G. (2002), *Les enquêtes de participation culturelle. Une comparaison France-Québec-Etats-Unis.* Rapport remis à l'occq et au mccq.

Putnam, R.D. (2000), *Bowling Alone. The Collapse and Revival of American Community.* New York, Simon and Schuster, 2000.

Reding, V. (2003), *La diversité culturelle.* Strasbourg, Parlement européen.

Reding, V. (2003), EU *Media Policy : Culture and Competition.* Madrid, 5th Conference on Competition Law of the Institute for European Studies of San Pablo-ceu University.

Rouet, F. (1991), « Le soutien aux industries culturelles : analyser, comparer, évaluer ». dans François Rouet et Xavier Dupin (dir.), *Le soutien aux industries culturelles en Europe et au Canada*, Paris, La Documentation française.

Saez, G. (1985), « Les politiques de la culture », dans M. Grawitz et J. Leca (dir.), *Traité de science politique. 4. Les politiques publiques.* Paris, PUF, 387-422.

Secrétariat permanent des conférences socio-économiques (1979), *Les industries culturelles. Rapport.*

Shaw, P. (2000), *Measuring the Impact of Culture? Seminar Report, Arts Research Digest*, 20.

Taliano-des Garets, F. (1996), « Politiques culturelles municipales et image de la ville depuis 1945, à travers les cas de Bordeaux, Marseille, Montpellier et Toulouse », In *Villes en projet(s)*, Bordeaux, Maison des sciences de l'homme d'Aquitaine.

Urfalino, P. (1996), *L'invention de la politique culturelle*, Paris, Comité d'histoire du ministère de la Culture et La Documentation française.

Walker, P., J. Lewis, S. Lingayah, et F. Sommer (2000), *Prove It! Measuring the Effect of Neighbourhood Renewal on Local People.* London, New Economics Foundation, 2000.

Whyte, W. F. (1991), *Participatory Action Research*, Newbury Park, Sage Publications.

Williams, D. (1996), *Creating Social Capital. A Study of the Long-term Benefits From Community Based Arts Funding.* Adelaide, Community Arts Network of South Australia for the Australian Council of the Arts.

Williams, D. (1997), *How the Arts Measure Up : Australian Research Into the Social Impact of the Arts*, Working Paper 8, Comedia.

16.

Cultural Indicators and Benchmarks in Community Indicator Projects

NANCY DUXBURY

Over the past decade, there has been an explosion of interest and activity around quality of life and sustainability indicator projects in communities across Canada and the United States. However, the inclusion of arts and cultural themes, issues, and indicators in the initial wave of quality of life and sustainability projects was rare.[1] In more recent years, the presence of cultural indicators in these community indicator projects has evolved from isolated scenes characterized by fledgling, pioneering attempts to that of an emerging field and more widespread phenomenon.[2] Nonetheless, contributions to this field are dispersed, diverse, and still generally disconnected. It is still relatively undeveloped as an indicator area and in only a few instances have improvements in the quality of the indicators been pursued with productive results.

In these early years, we can observe three interrelated dimensions influencing the development of cultural indicators relating to quality of life and the general evolution of this work: 1) the indicators themselves, i.e., what is being chosen, developed, used, and referenced as indicators, legacies, and reference points; 2) conceptual influences, i.e., the conceptual and theoretical grounding of concepts and frameworks guiding the selection of indicators; and 3) contextual influences, i.e., the use-contexts and pressures of practice that are influencing the choice and development of the indicators.

Using these three dimensions as guides, this chapter aims to highlight and draw linkages among some current projects and initiatives in Canada and the United States that are contributing to the advancement of cultural indicators within the context of community indicator projects. To contextualize this discussion, the chapter begins with a short overview of key developments in the recent evolution of community indicator projects and the emergence of arts and culture indicators within this environment. It then examines the conceptual and contextual influences in the development of these indicators. It concludes by pointing to key gaps that need to be addressed.

The sweeping collection of community indicator projects underway is generally driven by activity in two areas. On one hand, it is a movement driven by "grassroots leaders seeking better ways to measure progress, to engage community members in a dialogue about the future, and to change community outcomes."[3] On the other hand, it is also informed or influenced by efforts to improve "social" indicators generally, which have developed in response to "a widespread aspiration among governments and social scientists to develop better measures of progress and to meet the demands for greater accountability in government policies and programs."[4]

In general, indicators are defined as "bits of information that summarize the characteristics of systems or highlight what is happening in a system," which can "simplify complex phenomena" and enable a community to "gauge the general status of a system to inform action."[5] The choice and development of indicators in each project is informed by a wide range of factors, including: the overarching goals and guiding framework of the project, the values and aspirations of the project participants in the community, and developments in the larger field(s) of indicators and related research areas.

Merging Frameworks, Broadening Scope

Since the mid-1990s, community indicator projects and analyses have been increasingly framed within a quality of life movement, an integrative model which is closely linked to sustainability and healthy communities models, two other integrative models that arrived in the 1980s.[6] Most recent projects follow one of these integrative models, including measures and indicators addressing social, economic, and environmental issues discretely and in an integrative sense which "identifies links and analyzes cross- and cumulative impacts among indicators."[7]

The terrain incorporated into these models has been broadening, with recent interpretations including measures of governance, the physical environment, and the ecological footprint. Furthermore, while quality of life and sustainability labels are still evident, increasingly these projects are being subsumed into multidimensional, comprehensive community indicator programs:

Although initially there were significant differences among ... types of indicators and reporting, over time it has become evident that community reporting needs to cover economic, social and environmental aspects in a balanced and integrated fashion. In recent years the differences among these types of reporting are diminishing.[8]

The broadening scope of indicators is also reflected in a conceptual shift underway "to complement quantitative, objective measure with subjective, opinion-based measures and indicators" within projects. There is also evidence of "greater balance between quantitative and qualitative research methods in newer generation measures and indicators,"[9] an especially important development for culture, where quantitative data is usually economic.

The Emergence of Arts and Culture as an Indicator Area

Within this broader world of community indicators, the cultural and arts environment has gained increasing prominence, especially in neighbourhood-based models, with significant credit due to the inclusion of arts and culture indicators in the community building project within the Urban Institute's National Neighbourhood Indicators Partnership (NNIP). With partners in twelve cities across the United States, the NNIP sought to improve methods for developing new indicators, examining neighbourhood dynamics, and facilitating the advancement and establishment of neighbourhood indicator systems.[10] The arts and culture indicators project brought research on cultural indicators into this broader discussion of "neighbourhood indicators" that the NNIP promoted.

The inclusion of arts and culture in individual projects is now generally widespread, although it varies from very prominent[11] to slight or not at all. Organizations specializing in community indicators generally include at least a few culture-related indicators in their lists. Projects entirely focused on cultural indicators also exist but are rare.[12]

Developments in cultural indicators in the United States are linked, in large part, to the involvement of foundations as sources of funding. For instance, the Rockefeller Foundation funded the Urban Institute's multi-year project and the Knight Foundation has supported initiatives in developing and analyzing community indicators as well as experimental work to improve the development of indicators for arts and culture.[13] In Canada, efforts to include cultural indicators in community indicator projects to date are generally less developed and have emerged out of various community and cultural planning situations. They are informed by organizations and companies specializing in community indicators, and informal communications among municipal colleagues in other communities, but these efforts are not supported by an equivalent financial support infrastructure.

In general, the cultural indicators in the community indicator projects fall into two categories: *what we do* (actions, investments) and *outside conditions* (progress toward our goals). The linking (and evaluative) question of "What impact have we made?" lies between these two measurement areas, but many projects do not adequately address this question. As well, what is also typically missing is "how arts and culture contribute to social health."[14]

Cultural Indicators in Use: Legacies and Influences of Practice

In the development of indicators, the standard practice (or the "leading edge" practice) has a significant influence on new and emerging projects and initiatives. Indicators act as legacies of (sometimes undocumented) thought and decisions, as landmarks and reference points, and inform other projects. As particular indicators are chosen, developed, and used, they become examples or even models for other projects. Similarly, the omission of particular types of indicators in projects also sends a signal, and lays down a pattern others may adopt.[15]

In general, "comprehensive indicators of the cultural vitality of a community" have been difficult to find.[16] The "thinness" of cultural indicators within community indicator projects has meant that the instances of cultural indicators that do exist have played important roles in providing both knowledge and assurance to others. It could be argued that the types of indicators chosen, and their development and interpretation, have been as important for the community's own knowledge as the signals their inclusion and development has sent to others. In part, the level of influence of relatively undeveloped indicators (some without established measurements) has reflected the paucity of alternate information available for reference in a context of growing demands for articulating and measuring "results."

Today, a range of pioneering efforts is available to examine and some of the lessons learned from these projects are being assessed, which is furthering and improving this knowledge base and legacy.[17] The emergence of the newest wave of comprehensive indicator projects that incorporate arts and culture to a significant degree, while of limited numbers, also provide robust examples.[18] However, most of these efforts continue to have a "pioneering air" around them, and a comprehensive, integrating framework has yet to form. Outside of the efforts of the Urban Institute in the United States (and a few consultants working closely with this organization), it appears that the full range of community indicator examples and analysis (and related initiatives) have not yet been brought together in order to inform the creation of an integrative framework based on practice and legacy.

Work just outside of the community indicator context that focuses on governmental accountability and benchmarking performance measurements may also inform evolving community indicators initiatives. For instance, a recent multi-partner project in the United Kingdom put forward a framework and "core set" of indicators for performance measurement that is concerned with the role local authorities play in supporting the arts.[19] The set of indicators focuses on "comparable outcome-related measures of arts provision" as well as flexible standard-based measures to help local authorities to evaluate service quality and improvement over time.[20] While the "outcome" measures resemble those found in community indicator projects[21] and the (generally qualitative) rationales and measures related to "strategic objectives" could help inform conceptual research linking arts and culture to broader policy and community objectives, the project itself does not position itself as potentially linked to broader applications such as community quality of life indicator projects.

Conceptual Influences:
Grounding Concepts and Determining Frameworks

One of the key deficiencies limiting the advancement of cultural indicators has been the lack of a conceptual research base underlying the choice of art and culture indicators.[22] This conceptual deficiency has two components: the need to develop indicators meaningful to understanding and guiding cultural development, and the need to relate cultural indicators to concepts of quality of life and/or sustainability.

Indicators of Cultural Development

As Christopher Madden reveals, there is an abundance of literature on cultural indicators found globally, and much recent activity and discussion.[23] The literature on cultural indicators can be traced at least as far back as the early 1970s,[24] and indicator development has been an active part of cultural policy research since that time. Madden argues that although indicators are not in widespread use in cultural policy, thinking on cultural indicators is now well developed. Even so, a review of the cultural indicator literature reveals a number of common analytical and co-ordination issues: confusion about what indicators are and how they should be used, a lack of quality data, unwieldy frameworks (consisting in many cases of "large matrices of indicator 'wish lists'"), and vague policy objectives.[25] Madden also notes that "analysts rarely devote sufficient time to exploring indicator theory or articulating clearly the interrelationships between indicators, data, and statistics, and between indicators, policy evaluation and cultural analysis."[26] Further research attention to these matters is needed to inform and guide the development and implementation of meaningful cultural indicators in practice.

In relation to community-level cultural indicators, considerations of community goals for cultural development and cultural planning objectives also come into play. In addition to grounding the development of selected indicators, conceptual research also informs the development of conceptual frameworks to *guide and frame* an entire project, and the choice of related indicators within these frames. The best example of this is articulated in Cultural Initiatives Silicon Valley's *Creative Community Index* (2003), which was funded by the Knight Foundation as part of a unique demonstration project. The project features an engaging and cohesive conceptual framework that organizes and ties the indicators to rationales and educative information, which, in turn, is rooted in literature. Significant analysis and careful explanation frame and ground the presentation of the indicators.

Through these framing conceptual rationales and frameworks, distinctive community values and approaches are articulated. For instance, in the United States, the Silicon Valley project focused on building a creative community, rooted in interactions among cultural activity, business innovation, and civic vitality. In contrast, the Urban Institute's cultural indicator efforts are focused on community building in neighbourhoods. Can such diverse efforts be rationalized and drawn together, or would the particular purposes of each project be undermined in the process?

Two Canadian examples are also instructive here. The City of Ottawa and the City of Toronto each proposed a set of cultural indicators to measure progress on the cities' recent cultural plans.[27] The differing priorities, contexts, and approaches to municipal cultural development of these municipalities are evident in their choices of cultural indicators: Toronto's indicators largely relate to economic development and activity levels while Ottawa's suggested measures[28] generally focus on opportunity levels and citizen participation, activities, and partnerships. These examples illustrate the tension between the importance of community relevance and the challenges of consistency and comparability across communities.

Indicators of Culture as a Component of Quality of Life and Sustainability

In addition to improving the development of cultural indicators that meaningfully reflect and inform cultural development, more comprehensive research about the roles, benefits, and impacts of culture in a community or society is also needed. Field research and literature reviews conducted by the Arts and Culture Indicators Project suggest that participation in arts, culture, and creativity at the neighbourhood level[29] may contribute, directly or indirectly, to a list of important positive impacts:

- Supporting civic participation and social capital;
- Catalyzing economic development;
- Improving the built environment;
- Promoting stewardship of place;
- Augmenting public safety;
- Preserving cultural heritage;
- Bridging cultural/ethnic/racial boundaries;
- Transmitting cultural values and history; and
- Creating group memory and group identity.[30]

However, research efforts in these areas are generally pursued in isolation, and rarely linked with one another to form a more comprehensive understanding of "culture in context."

As Jackson and Herranz point out, a rise in research and practice examining the contribution of arts and culture to community building (and other social issues) provides a base for theoretically grounding the arts and cultural indicators used in community indicator programs.[31] They outline results of literature reviews which point to a number of promising avenues, including recently launched projects studying social impacts of the arts,[32] promising areas of research literature,[33] and the knowledge resources residing within practitioners in the community arts field.

From an economic perspective, Richard Florida's work has drawn renewed attention to the economic dimensions of cultural resources and investments, especially in terms of economic competitiveness.[34] His creativity index rankings for cities have sparked action in many communities across the United States (and elsewhere) and now appear as an indicator in many projects. Research to link arts and cultural dimensions and resources into broader concepts of creativity and innovative milieus may be useful here.

Further work in these areas could provide conceptual and empirical roots to underpin arguments for the inclusion of arts and culture in broader frameworks of quality of life or sustainability indicators, and inform the development of selected indicator(s) illustrating particular connections, benefits, or impacts. It would help link *inputs* and *outputs* to *outcomes*. It could also point to how to best integrate, assess, and present these topics and issues within the prevailing quality of life and sustainability analytical and reporting frameworks.

This brings us to another key area to consider: the guiding concepts of quality of life or sustainability that frame and determine the inclusion of categories and measures within the projects. The essential challenge is that while meaningful definitions of quality of life and social sustainability have been articulated through community indicator projects, seldom have they referred to arts and culture. Furthermore, while the inclusion of arts and culture indicators is generally widespread in community indicator projects, this is not yet universal practice nor widely understood and supported. Thus, the beginning point for greater inclusion of arts and culture in quality of life or sustainability projects is to build onto the prevailing frameworks in place.

Quality of Life

For Canadian municipalities, the prevailing way to examine quality of life is that of the Federation of Canadian Municipalities' Quality of Life Reporting System. According to this framework, quality of life is enhanced and reinforced in municipalities that:

1. Develop and maintain a vibrant local economy;
2. Protect and enhance the natural and built environment;
3. Offer opportunities for the attainment of personal goals, hopes, and aspirations;
4. Promote a fair and equitable sharing of common resources;
5. Enable residents to meet their basic needs; and
6. Support rich social interactions and the inclusion of all residents in community life.

Quality of life in any given municipality is influenced by interrelated factors, such as: affordable, appropriate housing; civic engagement; community and social infrastructure; education; employment; the local economy; the natural environment; personal and community health; personal financial security; and personal safety.[35]

This framework was informed but another influential project, the quality of life template developed by Canadian Policy Research Networks.

Sustainability

In prevailing sustainability frameworks, culture is usually included within a concept of social sustainability (if at all). However, culture is also beginning to be explored as a fourth pillar of sustainability, the others being the environmental, economic, and social pillars. In their influential work, Mario Polèse and Richard Stren define social sustainability in the following way:

> Social sustainability for a city is defined as development (and/or growth) that is compatible with the harmonious evolution of civil society, fostering an environment conducive to the compatible cohabitation of culturally and socially diverse groups while at the same time encouraging social integration, with improvements in the quality of life for all segments of the population. ... Social sustainability is strongly reflected in the degree to which inequalities and social discontinuity are reduced. ... To achieve social sustainability, cities must reduce both the level of exclusion of marginal and/or disadvantaged groups, and the degree of social and spatial fragmentation that both encourages and reflects this exclusionary pattern. Social sustainability, in this respect, may be seen as the polar opposite of exclusion, both in territorial and social terms. Urban policies conducive to social sustainability must, among other things, seek to bring people together, to weave the various parts of the city into a cohesive whole, and to increase accessibility (spatial and otherwise) to public services and employment, within the framework, ideally, of a local governance structure which is democratic, efficient, and equitable. This is all about building durable urban "bridges" ... capable of standing the test of time.[36]

In addition to purely theoretical approaches, some existing projects are also defining concepts of social sustainability. For example, the Greater Vancouver Regional District is developing a project on social sustainability within a regional planning framework. For this project, social sustainability was defined using the work of Robert Goodland of the World Bank:

> For a community to function and be sustainable, the basic needs of its residents must be met. A socially sustainable community must have the ability to maintain and build on its own resources and have the resiliency to prevent and/or effectively address problems in the future. Two types or levels of resources in the community are available to build social sustainability (and, indeed, economic and environmental sustainability)—individual or human capacity, and social or community capacity.
>
> Individual or human capacity refers to the attributes and resources that individuals can contribute to their own wellbeing, and to the wellbeing of the community as a whole. Such resources include education, skills, health, values and leadership. Social or community capacity is the basic framework of society, and includes mutual trust, reciprocity, relationships, communications, and interconnectedness between groups. It is these types of attributes that enable individuals to work together to improve their quality of life and to ensure that such improvements are sustainable.
>
> To be effective and sustainable, these individual and community resources need to be developed and used within the context of four guiding principles: equity, social inclusion and interaction, security and adaptability.[37]

Although not explicit in this definition, in the project social sustainability includes components related to arts, culture, and heritage.[38]

Another notable development in this area is found in Ottawa. The newly amalgamated City's first official plans as set out in the *Ottawa 20/20 Arts Plan* were based on a goal of sustainable development, where social, environmental, cultural, and economic issues would be kept in balance. Although this model of sustainability does not explicitly reference arts and culture, one of the overarching 20/20 principles is that Ottawa is a "creative city, rich in heritage, unique in identity." Arts and heritage were positioned as a pillar of the new City of Ottawa, vital to its future development.

Evolving thinking about culture as the fourth pillar of sustainability, which has been most actively discussed in Australia through the activities of the Cultural Development Network, has also recently emerged in Canadian policy circles, and may also be useful in conceptually grounding culture within a broader sustainability context. Rooted in Australia's community cultural development as well as UNESCO's cultural diversity and policy traditions, Jon Hawkes has developed an initial framework on which to explore this concept.[39] Hawkes has further explored this terrain and pointed out the debates embodied in the more well known social, economic and environmental pillars of the sustainability model.[40] Much conceptual work remains to more fully flesh out thinking about culture as a pillar of sustainability so that these ideas are more fully grounded within sustainability theory and are also readily understandable to a general citizenry.

All of these developments—in both official planning and more general community contexts—would be strengthened by further conceptual grounding to link and integrate arts and culture more soundly into the prevailing concepts of quality of life, sustainability, and social sustainability which frame various projects. This need exists in addition to further conceptual thinking to underlie the choice of measures to adopt as cultural indicators.

Improving our understanding of culture in community-building and social and economic contexts entails attention to both conceptual and methodological dimensions. As Chris Dwyer and Susan Frankel have suggested,

> *Instead of indicators emerging from a well-founded theory and research base as may happen in other fields, arts and culture indicators are likely to be designed to link eventually to a developing theory and research base. From the point of view of strengthening the value of indicators, the problem is one of identifying the linkages to the theory and research base with the clearest potential for payoff and then, strengthening the empirical base.*[41]

Cultural indicators can be viewed as tools of research, empirically grounding theory and assisting in its development. The inclusion of arts and culture indicators in larger projects could produce evidence to establish cultural rationales, produce empirical data, and develop theory. The trend towards a more integrative approach to indicator models which identifies links and analyzes cross impacts and cumulative impacts among indicators, combined with the recent emergence of arts and cultural indicators appears to offer an opportunity for the development of greater understanding of the roles of arts and culture within a quality of life/community context. The context of community indicators may provide a research setting to develop "theoretical or empirical research that speaks to how arts and cultural participation contribute to social dynamics."[42] Another outcome could be a richer understanding of cultural contributions to a community's economy.

The complexity of this work should not be understated. As Jackson and Herranz note, "Researchers should not confuse searching for clarity with expecting to find simplicity."[43] They identify two main theoretical and methodological challenges to documenting arts/culture/creativity impacts: "having definitions that are either too narrow to capture what we are looking for or too broad for policy use" and "trying to establish simple causal relationships in an area that is inherently complex—with many interacting forces and about which not enough is yet known to justify efforts to build formal causal models, even complex ones."[44]

Contextual Influences:
Use-contexts and Pressures of Practice

The contextual influences at work in the development and implementation of cultural indicators (and influencing the sustainability of cultural indicator projects) should not be underestimated. The environment in which indicators are developed and used is complex and dynamic. Indicators are used in many processes—co-ordination, planning, evaluation, analysis, education, enlightenment, and decision-making—across contexts such as governance, philanthropy, and advocacy. Ideally, they are used in concert with other sources of knowledge being brought to bear in the situation.

This section briefly outlines some of the multi-dimensional use-contexts in which community-level cultural indicators are applied. Then, it considers the rising pressure to develop indicators that contextualize these uses.

Indicators as a Tool of Governance and Government

Indicators can assist with effective co-ordination of distributed power, information, and resources (i.e., governance). Indicators can serve as a neutral resource shared among participants in a process, which can help level the playing field among various stakeholders.[45] As an analytic tool, indicators can succinctly present a picture of changing conditions and help improve understanding of complex social conditions. Combined with other information tools, indicators can assist with planning and making effective, strategic funding (or other) decisions:

> Indicators projects contribute to—and do not displace—the value of other information tools. In many cases ... they help stakeholders improve and refine their ongoing work. For instance, indicators help Foundation staff prepare for site visits. Indicators help us ask sharper questions in the due diligence phase of grant making. Perhaps most important, indicators force us to question our own biases and conventional wisdom.[46]

Indicators are also incorporated into evaluation frameworks, as tools to evaluate governance/investment success and/or to assess investment impacts. The introduction to one cultural program impact study suggests the broadening scope for program evaluation that may quickly take it into the realm of community indicators:

> Cultural programs serve cultural objectives. Their success is judged by their ability to increase the excellence, diversity and accessibility of cultural activity and to encourage participation in it. However, cultural programs influence the communities in which they operate in other ways. Increasingly, they are seen as having economic and community impacts that increase the vitality of regional communities and contribute to regional development.[47]

Administrative systems and controls may incorporate indicators on internal processes as well as outside community impacts. For instance, an administrative wave currently passing through Canadian municipalities (and other levels of government) is the core services review. The core services review focuses on—it articulates—local expectations, realities, and purposes and aligns civic operations to these expectations.[48] In the case of the City of Ottawa, this process is being used as a means to address a large operating deficit and pressures to cut operations and service levels. This process may link indicators more closely to budgetary processes and funding decisions. In this context, the impact measures should be sensitive enough to illustrate the impact of changes in budget levels in, say, five percent increments.

Indicators are also used to evaluate one's (competitive) position vis-à-vis other jurisdictions. In contrast with the more internal focus of a core services review, there is also a growing desire to be aware of what is being done elsewhere and, most importantly, to know "how we compare." The popularity of Richard Florida's creativity index in indicator projects and the attention it is receiving from politicians in many cities attests to this. The growing need for quickly available comparable information in the area of municipal cultural development was the impetus for the Creative City Network's Inter-municipal Comparative Framework project.[49]

Related to this is the desire to know whether a change in a community is a local issue or more widespread trend, which is in part fueling the desire for consistency in measuring cultural impacts across municipalities.[50]

Indicators as a Tool for Advocacy and Communication

As part of an overall educative process, indicators can play key roles:

> Arts indicators can anchor discussions about arts and culture with objective evidence meaningful to decision-makers outside the sector. They can also track change over time. ... Indicators can also help uncover assets and needs in a community. ... But perhaps most important, the indicators numbers can do the talking in local debates about public funding for the arts.[51]

They can also assist in improving the receptivity of an audience to new ideas: "Numbers give people permission to support something they don't understand" and can increase individuals' "comfort zone."[52]

However, their use must be tempered. Weighing heavily on the use of indicators brings its own dangers. Indicators can produce a "façade of scientific management" which can distort the artistic process and may not add clarity or understanding. And there is the eternal dilemma that "there is no objective way to measure the human spirit in contact with art."[53]

The relationship between creators of indicators and the subject(s) of the indicators is crucial. Acceptance of indicators as meaningful and valid tools that can contribute to shared goals and objectives must be earned through their careful application and use. The allure of quantitative indicators as a basis for action must be accompanied by caution, reflection, and other knowledge:

> Staff and local leaders must not forget what they know when in the presence of data. They must not follow data blindly in setting priorities. Also, indicators data do not dictate what ... stakeholders value. [W]e want to identify grant-making priorities at the intersection of indicators information and local knowledge. ...
>
> One thing we learned from the Community Indicators project is that our ability to make a difference hinges on our understanding of the local context. Taken alone, the customary statistics used to sum up the well-being of the nation are not enough. They mask the remarkable differences. ...
>
> Because each community is its own special case, explanations that fit one community may not fit another.[54]

Mounting Pressures

The level of pressure to develop indicators, while variable from community to community, is generally perceived to be rising. Mounting pressures to develop indicators are originating from multiple sources, and in practice their influences overlap. For municipalities, pressure to develop indicators typically originates from two directions: program review/evaluation/efficiency measures and the growing prevalence of quality of life/community indicator projects:

> Many organizations have embraced the need to monitor and evaluate policy and program effectiveness. While the federal government has the most experience in this area, municipalities across Canada have developed and manage monitoring and evaluation systems. … Many of these efforts address concerns over policy and program efficiency, and they are often oriented towards performance measurement. However, we see a significant and complementary movement towards monitoring and evaluation of sustainability, the healthy community, and finally quality of life.[55]

More specific contextual uses include tying cultural indicators to formally adopted plans with explicit goals and objectives,[56] and in some cases to funding levels as part of *core services review* processes in Canadian municipalities.

In the practice of developing indicators, the various pressures and rationales for indicators cannot always be cleanly separated. Tellingly, the City of Toronto's proposed measurements related to their recently adopted cultural plan are described as benchmarks of the "health of the Creative City," but they are also meant to serve an evaluative function. For example, the city's report states that, "Measuring the success of this Culture Plan is like measuring the efficiency of any other realm of government."[57]

In some situations, cultural development staff can feel trapped by the pressures from the system(s) in which they operate to provide indicators. The potential for misuse of these indicators, and the general fluidity in the use of indicators as measures and as evaluation tools have staff frightened that indicators of the state of their community's cultural sector may reflect negatively on them and their work. This situation underscores the need for both more developed and widely known conceptual and empirical research as well as the development of a support network in this area to which individuals can turn for advice and expertise.

The complexity of context of use must be appreciated. Once developed, the indicators live within a dynamic, changing, and not always predictable environment. Once indicators or benchmarks are developed, their use is uncontrollable and may be inappropriate. Although careful development and framing of indicators can help, the various uses of indicators (e.g., measuring community conditions, measuring success, setting service levels, assessing impacts of funding) can't always be anticipated or neatly unbundled. Misperception of the intent and meaning of an indicator can occur, especially when measures of a complex environment are used to evaluate performance and perhaps set funding levels.

On a more positive note, within the midst of this general obsession with indicators, some individuals feel a more moderate view of indicators may be on the near horizon. This echoes a growing awareness of the need to balance the use of indicators with other types of information and the importance of analysis in the process of producing meaning from them.

Key Gaps to Address

Significant advancements in the development of cultural indicators for community-level quality of life/sustainability indicator projects require attention to all three areas outlined in this chapter.

To begin, greater attention to the indicators in use and in development is needed. A comprehensive review of the full range of community-based cultural indicator examples and analysis, and related initiatives and resources, should be conducted to gain a better understanding of existing practice and trends. This should include both experts in community indicators as well as experts in cultural research, and should be designed, in part, as an educative exercise for both these groups. Such work could also form the basis for the development of a multi-community network to support advancements in the development of cultural indicators in relation to community quality of life and indicator projects as well as (often closely aligned) cultural planning performance measures.

Conceptual and empirical research is needed, both in the development of indicators meaningful to understanding and guiding cultural development, and in relating cultural indicators to quality of life and sustainability contexts. From the perspective of improvements in cultural indicators, Madden proposes that future development of cultural indicators would benefit from focus and clarity in three areas:

- Greater clarity about the nature of artistic activities (why people undertake arts activities and their public and private benefits);
- Greater clarity in the articulation of objectives for cultural policies and in determining the appropriate indicators for measuring performance against objectives; and
- More strategic targeting of development work on cultural indicators, especially the prioritizing of a limited number of indicators.[58]

This work should be underpinned, or accompanied, by conceptual research on the rationales and conceptual groundings for the choice and development of particular indicators, both relating to culture directly and in relating culture to broader concepts of quality of life and/or sustainability. In part, this would help ground and address ongoing disagreements as to "what markers best capture cultural vitality in their communities."[59]

Hand in hand with the development of conceptual rationales is the development of sources of reliable data relevant to this conceptual work. The task of obtaining "evidence," especially causal evidence, currently presents many challenges in this area.[60] Gaps between indicator statements, or topics, and data available to address and measure such indicators, are common, and basic data on community conditions may not be available.[61] And it is more difficult to measure an impact that is more broadly conceived. Indeed, much of the importance of art and culture to individuals, societies, and regions cannot readily be measured at present.

Greater attention to methodologies and practices of interpreting and presenting indicators is also needed. The importance of rigorous analysis of indicator data is often forgotten, and yet it is vital to understanding the significance of changes in the data and interrelationships among data sets.[62]

Finally, co-ordination issues must be addressed. As Madden notes, "there appears to be little contact between agencies that are currently developing cultural indicators."[63] Better sharing and co-ordination would help mitigate two key problems:

1. The multiplicity of work—development work is being replicated worldwide;
2. Differences in approach—despite some broad similarities in much of the cultural indicator work, different indicator developers are adopting different approaches and frameworks, and developing different types of indicators.[64]

This challenge is even more profoundly felt outside the core "cultural indicator" field of study, where diverse contributions and informing contexts are even more difficult to co-ordinate and integrate. Related to this, there is currently limited capacity to comprehensively address multiple dimensions and varied influences. The need to attend to the various dimensions influencing the development and use of cultural indicators—the state of practice and existing examples, the conceptual influences, and the contextual influences—adds complexity to investigations and advancements in the area. With the exception of the ongoing comprehensive efforts of the Urban Institute in the United States, the capacity to adequately consider and advance the area in a comprehensive, multi-dimensional, and inclusive manner is currently difficult to locate.[65]

Notes

[1] Nancy Duxbury, "Exploring the Role of Arts and Culture in Urban Sustainable Development: A Journey in Progress" (paper presented at the Table d'hôte on Building Sustainable Communities: Culture and Social Cohesion, Hull, Quebec, December 5, 2001).

[2] In general, it appears that the earlier work of UNESCO (early 1970s) does not inform the current round of community indicator projects.

[3] John S. and James L. Knight Foundation et al., *Listening and Learning: Community Indicator Profiles of Knight Foundation Communities and the Nation* (Miami: John S. and James L. Knight Foundation et al., 2001), 13, available at http://www.knightfdn.org/publications/listeningandlearning/index.html.

[4] Christopher Madden, *Statistical Indicators for Arts Policy: Discussion Paper* (Sydney: International Federation of Arts Councils and Culture Agencies, 2004), 4, available at http://www.ifacca.org/ifacca2/en/default.asp.

[5] Peter Berry, "Quality of Life Indicators Evaluation Report" (paper prepared for the city of Ottawa's Environmental Advisory Committee, 2002), cited in *Ottawa 20/20 Indicator Workbook*, (Ottawa: City of Ottawa, 2003), 3. See also Madden, Appendix 2, for a review of current literature on cultural indicators, including discussions on what are cultural indicators and relationships between data, indicators, and analysis/evaluation.

[6] The Flett Consulting Group Inc. and FoTenn Consultants Inc., "Quality of Life Reporting System Evaluation: Final Report–Appendices" (paper prepared for the Federation of Canadian Municipalities, 2002). This paper provides a useful and succinct overview of the evolution of indicators through the twentieth century to the current day.

[7] Ibid., A-9.

[8] *Ottawa 20/20 Indicator Workbook*, 3.

[9] Flett and FoTenn, "Quality of Life," A-11.

[10] http://www.urban.org/nnip/acipproject.html.

[11] Boston Foundation, *Creativity and Innovation: A Bridge to the Future–A Summary of the Boston Indicators Report* (Boston: The Boston Foundation, 2002); Boston Foundation, *The Wisdom of Our Choices: Boston's Indicators of Progress, Change and Sustainability* (Boston: The Boston Foundation, 2000), available at http://www.tbf.org/indicators.

[12] Cultural Initiatives Silicon Valley, *Creative Community Index: Measuring Progress Toward a Vibrant Silicon Valley* (Silicon Valley: CISV, 2003), available at http://www.ci-sv.org/cna.shtml; Cultural Initiatives Silicon Valley, "Cultural Initiatives Releases Creative Community Index," news release, July 10, 2002, available at http://www.ci-svorg/whatsnew.shtm.

[13] Ibid. See also Heidi K. Rettig, John S. and James L. Knight Foundation, "Measuring the Impact of the Arts in Communities," news release, Fall 2002; Princeton Survey Research Associates, Inc., *John S. and James L. Knight Foundation Community Indicators Project: A Report on Public Opinion in Philadelphia, Pennsylvania* (Princeton, NJ.: Princeton Survey Research Associates, 1999). The Rettig and Princeton Survey Research Associates documents are available from the John S. and James L. Knight Foundation, at http://www.knightfdn.org.

[14] Chris Dwyer, cited in Alan AtKisson, "Rethinking Cultural Indicators," *Urban Quality Indicators* 12 (Winter 1999): 3–4.

[15] For example, when the team developing the Federation of Canadian Municipalities' (FCM) Quality of Life indicators decided to move from a social indicators model to a comprehensive quality of life model, they decided to use the Canadian Policy Research Networks (CPRN) template as a starting point (Rick Gates, personal correspondence, September 5, 2002). The FCM did not have the resources or time to do a nation-wide survey to determine the main factors people use to define and determine their own quality of life, and the CPRN had recently completed such an exercise. Joseph Michalski, *Asking Citizens What Matters for Quality of Life in Canada—Results of CPRN 's Public Dialogue Process*, (Ottawa: Canadian Policy Research Networks, 2001), available at http://www.cprn.org/en/doc.cfm?doc=90. The exclusion of arts and culture from the FCM's resultant report is in part due to the origins of the new framework to the work conducted by the CPRN . When the CPRN did their survey, this area rated too low in importance to be included. In the process of revising the FCMsystem, team members had to be fairly rigorous about denying various subject requests if they were not backed with "good solid evidence that people really do consider them to be essential to their well-being and happiness." (Rick Gates, personal correspondence, September 5, 2002). Because arts and culture were excluded from the key reference study, and in the absence of this strong supplementary evidence, they were also excluded from the initial release of the FCMreport. See Canadian Policy Research Networks, *Workshop on Quality of Life, February 19, 2003, Ottawa, Ontario: Report* (Ottawa: Canadian Policy Research Networks, 2003).

[16] Rettig, "Measuring the Impact of the Arts."

[17] Maria-Rosario Jackson and Joaquin Herranz Jr., *Culture Counts in Communities: A Framework for Measurement* (Washington, DC: Urban Institute, 2002), available at http://www.urban.org/url.cfm?ID=310834.

[18] See, for instance, Boston Foundation, *Creativity and Innovation*, and Boston Foundation, *The Wisdom of Our Choices*.

[19] Arts Council England, *Local Performance Indicators for the Arts* (2003), available at http://www.local-pi-library.gov.uk/PI_arts.pdf. The indicators were developed as a component of the U.K. Audit Commission and Improvement and Development Agency's Library of Local Performance Indicators.

[20] Ibid., 3.

[21] "Outcome" measures include the level of services offered and capacity of infrastructure available, various attendance/participation measures, the level of usage of local authority funded/managed venues, the number and membership of voluntary arts organizations, and satisfaction ratings of residents and target groups with the arts facilities, events, and services supported.

[22] Duxbury, "Exploring the Role of Arts and Culture."

[23] Madden, *Statistical Indicators*.

[24] Leif H. Gouiedo, "Proposals for a Set of Cultural Indicators," *Statistical Journal of the United Nations*, 10 (2003): 227–89.

[25] Madden, *Statistical Indicators*, 6.

[26] Ibid.

[27] City of Ottawa, *Ottawa 20/20 Arts Plan* (Ottawa: City of Ottawa, 2003), available at http://www.ottawa.ca/2020/arts/toc_en.shtml; City of Toronto, Culture Division, *Culture Plan for the Creative City* (Toronto: City of Toronto, 2003), available at http://www.city.toronto.on.ca/culture/cultureplan.htm. These official plans, and associated indicators, exist alongside of more broadly-based community indicator projects.

[28] The City of Ottawa identified three broad areas of creativity measurement and proposed "suggested measures" which would be developed further in concert with other cities via the Creative City Network.

[29] Issues involved in "scaling up" their neighbourhood-based research framework to encompass a city-wide, region-wide, or even larger areas, have not been investigated.

[30] Jackson and Harranz , *Culture Counts*, 33.

[31] Ibid.

[32] Ibid., 47n46. This footnote lists some promising studies on the social impact of the arts that have been launched in recent years, but many of these studies are still in their early stages.

[33] A valuable outcome of the Arts and Culture Indicator project is the development of a holistic view of the research being conducted which could be applied to better understand the impacts of arts and culture to individuals and communities. Jackson and Herranz note that although "the direct impacts of arts, culture and creative expression on communities—particularly the roles participation plays in communities—are not, for the most part, either well documented or understood in the arts or community-building fields," fields such as education, youth development, and economics have extensive literature on the *direct* impacts of artistic activities on individuals and communities. *Culture Counts*, 31–32. They also identify research with the potential to better describe the *indirect* social effects of arts, culture, and creativity in neighbourhoods: "These include identifying *community assets* and their significant role in community building, *social capital* research suggesting that a broad array of civic activities promotes a stronger civil society and democratic engagement, and research on whether a community's characteristics influence *individual behavior*." Ibid. A literature review indicated that "with a few exceptions, these research approaches have so far overlooked arts and culture as a major influence and neglected the unique and considerable role they can play." Ibid.

[34] Richard Florida, *The Rise of the Creative Class* (New York: Basic Books, 2002); Richard Florida and Meric Gertler, *Competing on Creativity: Placing Ontario's Cities in North American Context* (Toronto: Institute for Competitiveness and Prosperity, 2002), available at www.competeprosper.ca/research/index.php.

[35] Federation of Canadian Municipalities, "The Federation of Canadian Municipalities Quality of Life Reporting System: Highlights Report 2004" (Ottawa: Federation of Canadian Municipalities, 2004), available at http://www.fcm.ca/qol3/archives.html.

[36] Mario Polèse and Richard Stren, *The Social Sustainability of Cities: Diversity and the Management of Change* (Toronto: University of Toronto Press, 2000), 15–16.

[37] Rick Gates, City of Vancouver, memo to Greater Vancouver Regional District Social Indicators Subcommittee, June 12, 2002.

[38] See Duxbury, *Exploring the Role of Arts and Culture*, for an overview of the process up to 2001.

[39] Jon Hawkes, *The Fourth Pillar of Sustainability: Culture's Essential Role in Public Planning* (Melbourne, Australia: Common Ground P/L and Cultural Development Network, 2001).

[40] Jon Hawkes, "Understanding Culture" (address to the Local Government Community Services Association of Australia's national conference, "Just & Vibrant Communities," July 28, 2003), available at http://culturaldevelopment.net/publications.html.

[41] M. Chris Dwyer and Susan L. Frankel, *Reconnaissance Report of Existing and Potential Uses of Arts and Culture Data* (Portsmouth, NH: RMC Research Corporation, 1997) (paper prepared for The Urban Institute's Arts and Culture Indicators in Community Building Project), 32.

[42] Jackson and Herranz, *Culture Counts*, 19.

[43] Ibid., 34.

[44] Ibid., 34–35.

[45] John S. and James L. Knight Foundation, *Listening and Learning*.

[46] Ibid., 16.

[47] Jan Muir, *The Regional Impact of Cultural Programs: Some Case Study Findings* (Canberra: Communications Research Unit, Department of Communications, Information Technology and the Arts, 2003), 1. The study was conducted by the Australia Council and the Australian Department of Communications, Information Technology and the Arts and is available from the author at jan.muir@dcita.gov.au.

[48] Oksana Dexter, personal communication, November 5, 2003.

[49] The Creative City Network's Intermunicipal Comparative Framework Project is a comprehensive, multi-phase information gathering and standardization research initiative. Phase One is a broad qualitative survey of policy, programs, processes, and other infrastructure, and aims to understand the general framework,

scope, and nature of local government involvement in cultural development across Canada. Phase Two is a quantitative survey that will capture the value of local government investment in cultural development across Canada. It will expand the information gathered in Phase One to include the value of direct and indirect support through funding programs, administrative costs, operational costs and other mechanisms. Phase Three will feature further details in selected topic areas, such as heritage support mechanisms and the role of libraries in local cultural development. Results from the pilot Phase One survey will be released in 2004.

[50] See, e.g., the City of Ottawa 20/20 Web site.

[51] Rettig, "Measuring the Impact of the Arts."

[52] Comments made by Anne Russo at the Creative City Network conference, St. John's, Newfoundland, October 2003.

[53] Delegate comments at the Creative City Network annual conference, St. John's, Newfoundland, October 2003.

[54] John S. and James L. Knight Foundation, *Listening and Learning*, 16, 22, 61.

[55] Flett and FoTenn, "Quality of Life," A-3.

[56] See, for example, the City of Toronto Culture Plan, the Ottawa 20/20 Quality of Life Report Card and Arts Plan Progress Indicators.

[57] City of Toronto, 2003, p. 44.

[58] Madden, *Statistical Indicators*, 7.

[59] Rettig, "Measuring the Impact of the Arts."

[60] See, e.g., Muir, 2003.

[61] See, for instance, the variation in data availability for the cultural indicators of the Boston Indicators project, as well as the data problems with cultural indicators encountered by the Vision 2020 Hamilton Sustainability Indicators project, Sustainable Seattle, and others.

[62] Cultural Initiatives Silicon Valley's Creative Community Index (2003) and, more generally, the Knight Foundation's 2001 publication, *Listening and Learning: Community Indicator Profiles of Knight Foundation Communities and the Nation*, are good examples of the benefits realizable through a careful analysis and presentation of indicators.

[63] Madden, *Statistical Indicators*, 7.

[64] Ibid.

[65] Other resources of interest include Nancy Duxbury, *Creative Cities: Principles and Practices* (Ottawa: Canadian Policy Research Networks, 2004); Acacia Consulting and Research, "The Federation of Canadian Municipalities Quality of Life in Canadian Communities 2003 Report: Draft Domain and Indicator Definitions" (paper prepared for the Federation of Canadian Municipalities, May 2003); Harvey Low, *The FCM Quality of Life Reporting System: Methodology Guide* (Ottawa: Federation of Canadian Municipalities, 2002). A significant number and variety of resources on measures and indicators is available on the Internet from various organizations. Recently, Redefining Progress and the International Institute for Sustainable Development have merged their database of indicators projects. Redefining Progress provides an annotated directory of projects around the world and is a very useful hub for indicator projects generally. The organization also operates a listserv on the topic to support inter-project communication. See http:/ /www.rprogress.org. Affiliated with the York Centre for Sustainability at York University in Toronto, http://www.sustreport.org is a useful general reference site on sustainability indicators and projects. Finally, Partners for Livable Communities maintains an extensive compilation of community indicators. The organization surveyed community indicator efforts to track quality of life, selecting ten representative programs for in-depth analysis and creating a database of 2000 indicators, sorted into three broad categories: People, Economy, and Environment.

Conclusion

Reflections on the Cultural and Political Implications of Cultural Citizenship

M. Sharon Jeannotte And Will Straw

Reflections on the Socio-cultural and Socio-political Implications of Cultural Citizenship—Paradoxes and Contradictions

The introduction to this volume outlined the shifting rationales and contexts for public policy in the cultural realm. It did so, in part, by charting the dilemmas facing policy analysts as they grapple with questions of governance, accountability and the indicators on which policy rests. Our concern in this concluding chapter is with the more elusive (and hotly debated) ways in which the cultural realm itself has been transformed in recent years. During this period, we would suggest, longstanding assumptions about the organization of cultural life or the direction of its development have been cast into doubt. This doubt often appears as a set of paradoxes—as puzzles or contradictions whose resolution sometimes seems beyond us. Some of these paradoxes have been raised in the contributions to this volume by Sherman, Murray, and others. Others are developed here in schematic form so as to highlight possible directions for future thinking and research.

In the first of these paradoxes, it seems clear that the steady implantation of global communications networks within the worlds of work and leisure has led to an explosion of cultural activity we might consider "artisanal." This activity includes the writing of blogs, the posting of family genealogies, the setting up of MP3 music exchange sites and innumerable other examples of small-scale, hobby-like activity. Interestingly, such activity runs both behind and ahead of the "innovation" agendas which increasingly underpin government investment in culture (as described by Cunningham in this volume). These communication networks have ensured the survival of traditional forms of expression (such as the diary or family tree) just as forcefully as they have produced new, experimental forms of cultural or entrepreneurial engagement. This new artisanal activity strengthens the lines of interconnection on which social capital depends. It turns longstanding connections (such as family ties) into the pretext for new acts of communication and community-building. At the same time, however, this explosion of micro communities compels people to organize much of their life around the commitment to highly specialized interests. Devotion to such interests, arguably, risks furthering their social disconnection, their retreat from other forms of collective civic engagement.

All definitions of citizenship presume some sort of balance between public engagement and privatized self-fulfillment. New cultural practices—most notably those involving the Internet, but including, as well, text messaging and the making of digital video "films"—will reorder this balance in ways we are not yet able to grasp. When individuals piece together their family histories through the use of a global communications system, are they retreating from collective public life, into traditionally circumscribed forms of belonging, or are they acknowledging that all belonging now takes place on a shared and mediated public stage? When people spend their mornings reading highly personal blogs rather than newspapers, is this a form of cultural participation or a withdrawal from it? It remains unclear whether what Sarah Thornton[1] called "subcultural capital"—the insider's attachment to the codes and habits of particular specialized interest groups—is a building block for social capital in its broader sense or a force which blocks its further development.

At the same time, while some cultural creators (like the makers of low-budget political films) pursue ever greater access to public attention, some avant-gardes (like certain electronic music communities) seek just as forcefully to become invisible. The search for public attention and the quest to be left alone stand as competing claims on governments and public policy; each represents a distinct version of cultural citizenship. To be understood and counted by the state is, for the first set of actors, the sign of successful intervention. For the second, the state's drive to comprehend and count exemplifies a symbolic violence at the heart of governance. The dilemma here, for those working to develop cultural indicators, should be clear. The state's desire to shine an intrusive light upon wilfully marginalized corners of cultural activity risks undermining an avant-garde's efforts to develop new forms of community and belonging. If, however, the state turns away from that activity (or fails to look for it), policy development will be built upon incomplete images of the cultural sphere. As micro-communities of cultural interest proliferate, the state's move to observe and count them risks appearing like an exercise of control. When those communities seek no subsidy or require no regulatory approval, the legitimacy of oversight or measurement by the cultural policy apparatus becomes unclear.

This tension between public and privatized engagements with culture is slowly displacing another opposition which was long at the heart of cultural analysis: that between producers and receivers of cultural artefacts. The academic project of cultural studies built much of its populism on the claim that cultural consumers were active rather than passive. Reception, it was claimed was always an active process of interpreting cultural artefacts and rendering them meaningful. While controversial, these arguments allowed academics (and those policy-makers influenced by similar ideas) to pay closer attention to everyday forms of cultural participation, to seek the kernel of active engagement in the most seemingly passive of behaviours.

Those who make claims about the empowering character of new media have had to surrender much of this argument. Old media, they suggest (at least implicitly) did in fact render audiences or consumers passive. New media, on the other hand, have transformed consumers, making them active users of tools for cultural creation (such as the CD-burner or Web authoring software). The strength of these arguments is that they acknowledge the growing irrelevance of the producer/receiver distinction; notions like "user community" or "creative network" better grasp the multiple forms of cultural involvement now made possible. The risk, however, is that the consumers of mainstream television or blockbuster art gallery exhibits become newly stigmatized as passive, powerless citizens, caught on the wrong side of a digital divide which devalues their less heroic forms of cultural participation.

Understanding these "ordinary" forms of cultural participation has long been the great challenge for those active in the development or analysis of cultural policy. The consumers of network television and other "old" media (who are traditionally more elderly and rural than the population as a whole) might well be overlooked as a result of two significant developments in cultural policy. One, as suggested, comes with the emphasis on new technologies, and with a valorization of the active, even subcultural production of new media forms and content. Another has arrived with the new emphasis on culture's role in urban regeneration and the nurturing of a creative work force. Richard Florida and others have offered influential claims about culture's power to attract talented young professionals to inner city living. These claims usefully locate culture at the very heart of social texture and community values. They are focused, however, on an active and consumption-oriented engagement with small-scale, high-art cultural forms (such as galleries and live performance). From such forms—for reasons of education, location, linguistic ability, or income—most people are excluded. This analysis both opens up definitions of culture—by acknowledging its place within a broader ethos of urban life and citizenship—and closes it down, by expelling from such definitions the consumption of mass entertainment and information media. At the end of the day, the forms of cultural participation which prove most resistant to analysis may still be those old-fashioned activities (like television viewing) whose significance has always confounded analysts.

Cultural policy's recent focus on cities and urban life has transformed the policy debate in important ways. It has allowed analysts to avoid those messy questions of essential definition which long haunted policy-makers concerned with culture as principally a national phenomenon. In the new urban turn, cultural policy-makers are no longer required to judge the content of cultural works or to embrace certain themes, styles, or forms over others. This has enabled policy to focus on dynamism and creativity as social resources, without having to develop criteria for judging the quality or "Canadianness" of individual works. The risk, as Murray has noted in this volume, is that the specifically cultural dimensions of creative activity become forgotten, in approaches which see culture as simply one ingredient within social capital, or as the finery which dresses up new sorts of financial and human investment in urban locales.

Addressing the Paradoxes—The Way Forward

We undertook the colloquium and this book to answer some fundamental questions about the bases for cultural policy and to examine the tools needed to respond to changes in the cultural policy environment. The contributions to this volume have provided a rich and varied set of perspectives on the general subject of cultural citizenship, as indicated above, and they have also highlighted the paradoxes and contradictions that policy-makers face when seeking to understand and address the social effects of culture.

Is it possible to work through the contradictions and to arrive at a place where the needs of creators, citizens, and user communities can be accommodated through public policy?

As Colin Mercer points out in his chapter, all modern governments must know not only *how* to count, but what to count. Most of the contributors to this volume, even those with the most clearly articulated doubts about instrumental justifications for cultural support measures, acknowledged that a new approach to cultural indicators was one of the places where governments must start if they are to address the paradoxes outlined above.

Why the need for better indicators? The contributions in this volume have eloquently presented a variety of reasons, but buried within each of them is one fundamental message: what governments count as "culture" may not necessarily be what cultural producers, user communities, or citizens consider "culture." Some of this activity may have to continue to lie "below the radar" of cultural policy if it is to retain its vitality and integrity. However, other types of cultural activity appear to be so embedded in communities or so new as to be invisible through current policy lenses, even when they clamour for "voice." In the latter two cases, at least, better indicators are a necessary precursor to better policy.

Tom Sherman in his chapter outlines how the cultural landscape is evolving from one of scarcity to one of abundance, even overload, and how the "cultural production chain" is giving way to mutual engagement by creators and citizen/consumers in the construction of what he calls "recombinant aesthetic strategies." Both Christian Poirier and Nancy Duxbury make the case for a more complete and robust set of cultural indicators to reflect the role that culture plays in the quality of life and social sustainability of communities. Will Straw, in tracing the pathways taken by cultural products and practices through societies, suggests that "artefacts are arguably less important than the patterns of interaction which are forged, reinforced, or broken in the process."

All this suggests that cultural indicators should focus on relationships and flows, and not simply on products, if cultural policy is to respond to the way that citizens, creators, and user communities really live their lives. Taking this even further, one might suggest that until indicators can trace the social effects of culture's trajectories through communities, it will be difficult, if not impossible, to judge whether and to what extent public policy interventions are contributing to the well-being of citizens.

The "road ahead" for cultural policy must certainly pass through a territory that is being reshaped by two somewhat contradictory trends—the globalization of producer/consumer networks and the localization of cultural quality of life. Governments, particularly national ones, have spent a great deal of energy since the 1980s on the first of these trends. John Foote's chapter gives us an overview of the global challenges, which are not only economic and technological, but also social and demographic. However, in the end it can be argued, as Sharon Jeannotte does in her chapter, that social spaces are still largely negotiated at the local level through investments in economic, social, and cultural capital.

Even such a seemingly benign policy outcome as cultural participation, as demonstrated by Catherine Murray and Rosaire Garon, may not achieve policy goals, especially as governments seem to be unclear about the conceptual approach that should underpin participatory policies—should they aim to attract new audiences to traditional art forms? Or should they aim to strengthen social capital, or diversity, or cultural rights, even if this means redirecting public support to different types of cultural expression? The pertinence of this difficult question is reinforced by Karim Karim's observation that the effective exercise of citizenship rights and responsibilities depends as much on cultural participation as on economic and political participation. However, as he points out, the "sphericules" inhabited by different sub-cultures do not always intersect in ways that foster inclusion.

Obviously, the way forward is not easy. Stuart Cunningham and his colleagues make a compelling case for integrating the cultural industries more closely with innovation policies, thus addressing at least two of the global challenges highlighted by Foote. But Allan Gregg makes an equally compelling case from the opposite perspective, arguing that it is culture's ability to bring citizens together and create a sense of community that should be the proper focus of governments. Both their perspectives, however, are tempered by the cautionary advice offered by John Meisel and Gilles Paquet, who view with suspicion any attempt to quantify culture or tie it too closely to economic and social outcomes.

All the contributors emphasize the need to come to grips with what Gilles Paquet has termed the new "ecology of governance"—a terrain where many different systems are intersecting and interacting with each other in unpredictable ways. Dick Stanley argues forcefully that culture is a key strategic good in this challenging environment as it provides the symbolic resources that citizens require to develop a consensus on their collective social lives. Viewed from this perspective, if social cohesion is the glue that holds societies together, culture is the tool kit from which that glue is created. Not only that, but a culture composed of many diverse elements makes for a more resilient bond. This perspective is reinforced by Monica Gattinger who suggests that states must shift their emphasis from "government" to "governance" through the engagement of multiple partners with a diversity of viewpoints. Only through this approach, in her view, can societies marshal the knowledge, resources, and power needed to achieve cultural policy objectives within the new "ecology of governance." Echoing the message of contributors such as Paquet and Mercer, she reinforces the value of multiple horizontal connections within and between an array of public, private, and non-governmental players, while reinforcing the need for leadership from public players involved in the governance networks.

The introductory chapter of this volume began by examining the issue of governance, and there is perhaps a certain symmetry in ending on the same note. Our collective examination of the need for better indicators to measure the social effects of culture and of the possible parameters of a new cultural policy paradigm is rooted in the urgent necessity to adjust governance in the cultural field to the complexities of life in the twenty-first century.

Every time the topic of governance was raised, both at the Colloquium and in the chapters of this volume, the idea of "engagement" was consistently invoked. The Deputy Minister of Canadian Heritage, Judith A. LaRocque, in her remarks at the Colloquium summarized the importance of engagement with culture in this way:

> *Engagement with culture is hard to distinguish from community development and the growth of citizenship. When people engage with culture, they necessarily engage with each other, with people like them in some way, and inevitably with people who are different. Cultural policy has the potential therefore to reach out beyond the traditional realm of industry, artist, and museum to influence citizenship, values, tolerance, and the very construction of Canadian society.*

Such engagement can occur only if everyone feels that they have a stake in the cultural life of their community. The major lesson that we have drawn from the contributions to this volume is that in the turbulent field of cultural production and consumption that exists today, policy-makers cannot afford to focus solely on its industrial/economic aspects. The role of cultural policy as an enabler of citizen well-being and quality of life is also important. In this environment of complexity and overload, no one organization is equipped to do it all, and governments are therefore being forced to think and act more creatively in partnerships with others.

We are convinced that cultural production and heritage preservation thrive best in an environment where citizens understand and appreciate their contribution, not only to the economy and to national identity, but also to the quality of their life and the sustainability of their communities. Much of the evidence and analysis presented in this book would seem to suggest that this appreciation must begin at the local level and that, rather than filtering outwards from the centre to the periphery, the seeds of any new cultural policy paradigm must spring from the soil of multiple localities (and multiple players within those localities) into the rarefied atmosphere inhabited by policy-makers. These localities, as we suggested earlier, encompass a wide variety of forms of cultural engagement. The local contexts of culture are not limited to the highly dynamic urban art scenes which have become so central to cultural policy over the last decade. Localities include multiple forms of cultural involvement, from the traditional to the emergent, from those seeking to engage governments to those eager to resist such engagement. They encompass those working to engage a broader public and others whose interests might appear unashamedly narrow or specialized. Policy must ground itself in the recognition of these multiple forms of cultural engagement.

The greatest challenges but also, perhaps, the greatest opportunities for cultural policy in the twenty-first century will lie in mastering what Gilles Paquet so aptly terms "the dynamics of polycentric governance." Whether we consider culture as capital or as diversity or as a right, we share the view, expressed by Colin Mercer, that "citizenship is what cultural policy is—or should be—about."

Note

[1] Sarah Thornton, *Club Cultures: Music, Media and Subcultural Capital* (London: Verso, 1995).

Annex

Back to the Future:
The Colloquium in Context:
The Democratization of Culture and Cultural Democracy

GREG BAEKER

E. M. Forster famously wrote that "unless we remember we cannot understand." There is a worrisome amnesia confronting the cultural sector in Canada today, as though the collective "hard drive" of the sector has been wiped clean of past policy and research experience. Many explanations for this state of affairs are possible. One is the hollowing out of governments' policy capacity after many years of spending cuts. Another is the loss of institutional memory in government agencies, in funding councils, in universities, in cultural organizations of all kinds. This memory loss is the result of ongoing staff turnover, retirements and, more broadly, a general weakening of historical consciousness in contemporary society. This weakened sense of history leads to the delusion that, unless policy or research has been produced or articulated recently, it cannot possibly offer answers to the pressing concerns of public policy or decision-making.

As a result of all these factors, we have forgotten a great deal. "Truths" or core principles from the past are regularly reinvented from scratch, rather than remaining as solid foundations to current research. One small example suggests itself. Beginning in the early 1970s, Yuri Zuzanek, only recently retired from the Faculty of Leisure Studies at the University of Waterloo, undertook and co-ordinated a tremendous body of important cultural research. One of Zuzanek's research interests during the 1970s was the ways in which Canadian cultural policy until that time had embraced and developed a core tenet of cultural policy—the distinction between the *democratization of culture* and *cultural democracy*.[1] Before I summarize Zuzanek's analysis, it might be useful to offer two short definitions of these two principles (a fuller account of the differences between these two perspectives is provided in Figure 1).

The *democratization of culture* involves broadening access to the products of one culture. In Canada, as in most modern Western liberal democracies, this has been interpreted and operationalized (through dominant policy frameworks and funding priorities) as the promotion and diffusion of European (mostly high culture) forms of expression.[2]

Cultural democracy is a more radical vision of cultural development. It not only seeks the broader dissemination of one culture, but acknowledges the *value and legitimacy of many cultural traditions and forms of expression.*

In the decade and a half following the report of the Massey-Lévesque Commission, Zuzanek suggests, the focus in Canadian cultural policy was very much on the democratization of culture and, more specifically, on raising standards of artistic excellence in order to bring Canadian cultural expression "up to" internationally recognized standards.[3] In the late 1960s and early 1970s, however, amidst a more general embracing of democratic ideas, Zuzanek found evidence of a genuine effort on the part of the federal government to acknowledge the distinction between the two concepts, and to press for the more radical goal of cultural democracy.[4]

This turn to a more expanded notion of democracy in the cultural sphere was short-lived, however. By the early 1980s, Zuzanek argues, cultural democracy had largely disappeared from policy discourse. The economic recession was one reason for this disappearance; so, too, was a rise in neo-conservative ideology. Zuzanek's assessment of cultural policy-making in Canada during this and subsequent periods is not a kind one.

The debate over the relative merits of the *democratization of culture* or *cultural democracy*, and over specific cultural programs themselves, was never resolved. Indeed, it might be argued, it was never pursued at a theoretical level. Rather, in typical Canadian fashion, it was abandoned, left forgotten and forlorn. The focus of cultural policy discussions has shifted from "participatory" activity to "managerial" strategies, from calls for the democratization of arts audiences to studies of economic impact; from personal and subcultural expression to "universal" cultural values and cultural heritage. This shift happened without any intellectual reflection. The turn away from issues of democratization stands as proof of the weaknesses of past efforts in this direction but it is a symptom, as well, of the more restricted vision to be found in the pragmatic and utilitarian approaches adopted by many governments today.[5]

One question which needs to be asked, then, is this: how far has Canadian cultural policy come in the thirty years since Zuzanek began his work? To what extent have governments, the research community, cultural managers, and others interested in the health and vitality of cultural development in Canada truly engaged with the core questions of democracy and democratization which lie at the heart of cultural policy in all modern states?

Looking Back: Priorities in 1998

In his report at the conclusion of the 1998 colloquium of the Canadian Cultural Research Network (CCRN), Professor John Meisel identified the following emerging policy and research needs in the cultural sector:[6]

- A new public interest discourse for cultural policy;
- The need to broaden the definition of culture (to address such factors as sustainability, social cohesion, democracy);
- More research at the sub and supra-national levels;
- Better conceptual base for thinking about social cohesion;
- More research on the so-called third sector;
- More research on internet access;
- More research on the role of culture within civic identity;
- More research on concepts of cultural citizenship in a post-modern era;

- Resolution of the data gap in the analysis of cultural consumption and participation;
- The development of quality of life indicators which would include culture; and
- Advanced theoretical work on multiple identities, cultural diversity, and the relationship of both to social cohesion.

Most of these issues continue to resonate within cultural policy and cultural research, in Canada and elsewhere.

A Fractured Discourse

In January 2002 the *Second International Conference on Cultural Policy Research* took place in Wellington, New Zealand. A major conclusion of the event was that a "fracturing" of traditional cultural policy research and policy development frameworks was taking place. In several cases, presenters stated quite bluntly that cultural policy had lost its way and had ceased to be a significant player in either culture or policy, at least at the national level. The following factors were put forward to explain this fracturing of traditional cultural policy narratives and assumptions.

1. Cultural policy, for the most part, is based on a world-view we might label *modern*— one grounded in the nation-state, and fulfilling the nation state's primary goal of creating citizens whose identity is rooted in the territory bounded by the state. This view of things is being challenged by *postmodern* imperatives, those of creating citizens and consumers whose identities are not defined primarily by national boundaries.
2. Cultural policy at the national level (the principal "unit" of analysis) focuses on cultural products as the results and outputs of that policy. However, cultural policy at the global and sub-national (local and regional) levels focuses on processes or *flows*—the continuous exchange of images, sounds, and ideas. At the global level, the computer has become "the new icon" through which virtual cultural flows are channeled. At the sub-national level, the city has become the "iconic space of consumption" for these flows.

Cultural policy must now operate on three levels, further fracturing its discourse. These levels are as follows:

- *Civil society*, which is becoming more diverse;
- *The nation-state*, which is subject to pressures both from above (*globalization*) and below (*localization*); and
- *The global environment*, which is increasingly dominated by multinational media firms.

The fracturing of cultural policy is the result of other factors, as well. Cultural policy has become more fragmented and diverse as it has become a component of other areas of public policy, such as those having to do more broadly with industrial innovation, technological development, urban planning, and economic development. Unfortunately, the linkages of cultural policy "outward" to these other areas are not clearly understood. Several speakers at the Wellington conference feared that the traditional institutional centres of cultural policy (such as research and government institutions) might lose control or influence as better established fields (such as those concerned with economic development) move to apply their own bodies of thought and practice to cultural matters.[7]

International Perspectives

An invaluable reference point for the analysis of cultural policy was provided by the UNESCO World Conference on Cultural Policies for Development in Stockholm in 1998. The resulting Stockholm Action Plan identified *strengthening the knowledge base for cultural development* as one of its central planks. Indeed, the plan states clearly that no progress can be made in cultural policy unless the knowledge base supporting it can first be strengthened.

An influential background paper for the Stockholm Conference was prepared by Colin Mercer and Tony Bennett.[8] This paper offered an invaluable map of issues central to cultural research and knowledge mobilization challenges in the cultural development field. Mercer and Bennett noted that those in the cultural policy field needed to pay much greater attention to networks and to strengthening relationships between researchers and decision-makers. In order to strengthen the role of cultural research within decision-making, they suggest, it is just as important to cultivate and sustain new *research relations* as to develop new research findings or content.

While this and various other reports offered many reasons for optimism, the challenges associated with advancing what might be called a "knowledge management" agenda in the cultural sector remain substantial. In 1998 Carl-Johan Kleberg drew attention to the following obstacles, all of which remain pertinent today:

- The relative immaturity of cultural policy and its lack of conceptual clarity as an interdisciplinary area of study and research;
- The low priority traditionally accorded to research funding by established cultural policy agencies;
- The lack of research on cultural policy and development by local governments, who remain overly influenced by the national focus of cultural policy and policy-related research;
- The lack of resources for systematic research by the agencies of civil society, including non-governmental organizations;
- Weak linkages between universities and the broader cultural sectors in the development and resourcing of research agendas;
- Inequalities in international research capacities;
- A tradition in cultural research to define issues in discipline-specific terms (separating the visual arts, performing arts, heritage and cultural industries from each other). While discipline-based policy and program traditions carry with them certain strengths, they undermine cross-cutting or overarching research and knowledge building needs; and
- The cuts to research and policy capacity in many countries as a result of budget cuts and government downsizing over the past decade.[9]

Reconstructing Policy Rationales and Tools

Toward Cultural Citizenship: Tools for Cultural Policy and Development[10] takes up many of the challenges outlined above. This report is the result of a three-year international research project aimed at "mapping and systematizing the tools needed for analysing, planning, reporting and assessing cultural policies for development." Its genesis was the 1998 UNESCO Conference and Stockholm Action Plan that established, as one of its key priorities, an enhanced knowledge base for culture and human development. The focus of the report was on the empirical tools and instruments needed to support more informed and rigorous planning, assessment, evaluation, etc., in the area of cultural development. Mercer's report had an "applied" focus that could appeal to policy-makers and other decision-makers in the sector. At the same time, it used this more pragmatic focus to "back into" a larger set of issues and questions. These included the following:

1. *The weak conceptual and knowledge base for cultural planning and decision-making.* As they examine tools and instruments (including impact indicators), Mercer maintains, policy makers and stakeholders in the cultural sector are forced to ask themselves fundamental questions about the "what and why" of cultural development. These questions reveal the weak theoretical and normative foundations for most existing policy.
2. *Weak and inadequate governance models.* The rigorous examination of tools and indicators raises questions about how public planning and decision-making in the cultural field are conducted. As the New Zealand conference noted, many are faced with an increasingly irrelevant set of existing cultural policy methods and processes. Mercer draws particular attention to the need for developing new cultural planning systems and methods *at the local level.*[11]
3. *The need for systems to support continuous knowledge building.* There is a widely acknowledged need for better methods of generating and applying research to decision-making on cultural matters.

Accounting for Culture:
Background to the 2003 Colloquium

The interventions described above formed part of the context within which the Canadian Cultural Research Network conceived the 2003 colloquium "Accounting for Culture: Examining the Building Blocks of Cultural Citizenship." In 2002, CCRN undertook a strategic planning exercise so as to develop a renewed and focused vision for the future of the organization. The planning process clarified the network's mission, mandate, and goals. Its mission is to "support better-informed and more insightful decision-making in Canada's cultural sector, thereby enhancing cultural opportunities for all Canadians." More specifically, CCRN's mandate is "to nurture a national, bilingual network devoted to the generation and improved use of cultural research." Its goals are numerous, but include the following:

- Advancing multidisciplinary approaches to cultural policy research;
- Supporting networking among cultural researchers; and
- Strengthening knowledge exchange between researchers and decision-makers in the cultural sector.

One immediate outcome of the planning process was the recommendation that the 2003 colloquium be used to mark the fifth anniversary of CCRN's founding, and that it serve to mobilize energies and resources towards the fulfillment of the strategic plan. Over the course of the year leading up to the colloquium, the board of CCRN explored this idea, in close collaboration with the Strategic Research and Analysis (SRA) Directorate of the Department of Canadian Heritage (PCH).[12] The year 2003 was also the tenth anniversary of the founding of the Department of Canadian Heritage, and the year in which the Canadian Cultural Observatory was launched. As such, 2003 presented an opportunity to "take stock"—to examine progress on priority policy research issues explored at the first colloquium, and to identify, assess, and define future research needs in Canada.

Mapping Colloquium Themes

Out of the initial brainstorming meetings emerged the theme *Accounting for Culture: Examining the Building Blocks of Cultural Citizenship*. "Accounting for Culture" represented an effort to connect the colloquium to the substantial national and international work on more rigorous tools and indicators to support planning and decision-making in the cultural sector. "Examining the Building Blocks of Cultural Citizenship" was an effort to signal clearly that the focus would not be on "accounting" in the narrow sense of economic value, but would embrace a much broader vision of the importance of cultural production and participation.

"Cultural citizenship" was an appropriate central theme of the colloquium for other reasons, as well. The 1998 CCRN proceedings had identified it as a key element in the development of a "new public interest discourse for cultural policy."[13] Traditional public interest arguments for cultural policy, rooted in notions of a homogenous nation state and inviolable national borders, are undermined in an era marked by the transnational movement of people, capital, images, etc. There is a clear need for new formulations of citizenship that take greater account of its cultural dimension. This recognition of the importance of the cultural within discussions of citizenship is evident in the policy and research agendas of many countries today.[14]

At the same time, "cultural citizenship" served to link the "two halves" of PCH's mandate—cultural policy (in all its dimensions) and citizenship (multiculturalism, official languages, human rights, etc.). Ten years after its founding, the extent to which the department has successfully integrated these two policy domains remains unclear.

Out of the initial meetings of CCRN and PCH emerged an initial conceptual map for capturing some of the issues that could be taken up by the colloquium. The five "territories" that comprise the map may be summarized as follows:

1. The new context for cultural policy. The colloquium sought to take stock of the transformed context for cultural policy. Four issues were highlighted as having a potential impact on policy tools and assumptions: demographic change, technological change, the changing (shrinking?) role of the state; and new relations between the local and the global nexus.
2. The system of cultural production, consumption, and participation. There is a need to examine the adequacy of existing tools and indicators for capturing and analyzing the cultural system upon which cultural policy and planning act.
3. Social and cultural capital. Tools and indicators are needed so as to capture the social and civic outcomes or impacts of cultural policy decisions.
4. Innovation and creativity. There is a need for tools and indicators which capture the more economically-focused outcomes or impacts of cultural policy decisions.
5. Cultural citizenship. All of these issues must be evaluated in terms of their usefulness in a reformulation of the idea of cultural citizenship. At the same time, we must develop tools and indicators with usefulness for those looking to apply these new ways of thinking about cultural citizenship.

This "conceptual map" for the colloquium is reflected in the chapters featured in this volume. Hopefully, this book will serve, as well, as a useful vehicle for the transfer of knowledge between cultural policy researchers and decision-makers in the cultural policy field, thus fulfilling another one of the colloquium's priorities.

Figure A: Democratization of Culture versus Cultural Democracy

DEMOCRATIZATION OF CULTURE	CULTURAL DEMOCRACY
The focus is on making the works of one culture more widely available by financing creation, production, access, and infrastructure	Acknowledges a diversity of cultures in the society that must be supported and better known; greater focus on distribution and access
The foundation of culture, heritage, and the arts policies in the post-war years in most Western countries	Little acknowledged in meaningful terms until the early 1990s in most countries
Assumes largely Western-European forms of expression and posits (explicitly or implicitly) the "supremacy of the Western canon"	Embraces a wider range of forms of creative and cultural expression and a larger and more comprehensive definition of culture
Artistic, cultural and heritage value and meaning are prescribed by cultural producers and cultural institutions and/or authorities	Cultural values and cultural meaning are more negotiated between creators, cultural organizations, and audiences or communities
Government support and intervention is largely centralized, relying on linear top-down approaches and strategies	Here more emphasis is placed on integration with local and regional interests and development Cultural development strategies are more decentralized, relying on more organic and community-based approaches
The focus is on building "hard infrastructure" of institutions and facilities	This focus is complemented by greater attention to building "soft infrastructure" of networks, relationships and, more recently, new distribution strategies using new media
Key partners and stakeholders are communities of professional artists, managers of culture, heritage and arts organizations, policy makers and planners	Partners and stakeholders include all those previously mentioned, but are expanded to include citizens and local community organizations

Notes

[1] Augustin Gérard, an official in the French Ministry of Culture, first articulated the principle in the 1960s.

[2] This is the core vision of the 1952 Royal Commission on the Arts, Letters and Sciences (the Massey-Lévesque Commission) that many argue continues to dominate thinking and practice in the cultural sector in Canada. As such Massey-Lévesque denies, distorts, and falsifies an earlier, more inclusive and more community based vision of culture well documented by scholars over many years. In short, there was "life before Massey-Lévesque."

[3] Yuri Zuzanek, *Democratization of Culture and Cultural Democracy in Canada* (unpublished paper prepared for the Faculty of Recreation and Leisure Studies, University of Waterloo, 1987).

[4] Ibid.

[5] Ibid., 13.

[6] Professor Catherine Murray was the second rapporteur and subsequently edited the colloquium proceedings, available at http://arts.uwaterloo.ca/ccm/ccrn/ccrn_colloq98a.html.

[7] Sharon Jeannotte, *Fractured Discourse: A Report from the Second International Conference on Cultural Policy Research: "Cultural Sites, Cultural Theory, Cultural Policy"* (paper presented in Wellington, New Zealand, January 23-26, 2002, SRA Reference Number: SRA-663).

[8] Colin Mercer and Tony Bennett, "Improving Research and International Cooperation for Cultural Policy" (preparatory paper VI, prepared for UNESCO's Intergovernmental Conference on Cultural Policies for Development, Stockholm, 1998).

[9] Carl-Johan Kleberg, ed., *Promoting Cultural Research for Human Development* (Stockholm: The Bank of Sweden Tercentenary Foundation, 1998).

[10] Colin Mercer, *Towards Cultural Citizenship: Tools for Cultural Policy and Development* (Hedemora, Sweden: Bank of Sweden Tercentary Foundation and Gidlunds Forlag, 2002). This report was commissioned by The Bank of Sweden Tercentenary Foundation and the Swedish International Development Co-operation Agency (SIDA) with the participation of the Swedish Ministry of Culture, the Swedish National Commission for UNESCO and the Dag Hammarskjöld Foundation.

[11] Canadian Cultural Research Network, *Cultural Development in Canada's Cities: Linking Research, Planning and Practice* (Ottawa: CCRN, 2002); available at http://www.culturescope.ca/ev_en.php?ID=1988_201&ID2=DO_TOPIC.

[12] SRA has been a generous and consistent supporter of CCRN since its inception.

[13] Catherine Murray, *Cultural Policies and Cultural Practices: Exploring The Links Between Culture and Social Change* (Ottawa: CCRN, 2002); available at http://arts.uwaterloo.ca/ccm/ccrn/ccrn_colloq98a.html.

[14] Will Kymlicka and Wayne Norman, eds., *Citizenship in Diverse Societies* (Oxford: Oxford University Press, 2002); Nick Stevenson, ed., *Culture and Citizenship* (Cambridge: Theory, Culture and Society Centre, 2000). See also Greg Baeker, *Cultural Planning, Cultural Diversity, and Cultural Citizenship: A View from Canada* (Cultural Policy Note No. 8, prepared for the Council of Europe, 2003).